Census Substitutes & State Census Records

Census Substitutes & State Census Records

An Annotated Bibliography of Published Name Lists for all 50 U.S. States and State Censuses for 37 States

by

William Dollarhide

Volume 2 – Western States

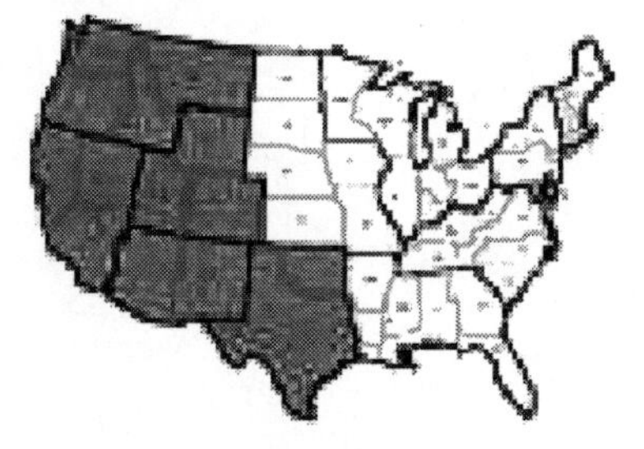

Family Roots Publishing Company

Bountiful, Utah

On the cover: The image on the computer screen comes from Ancestry.com's Washington State Territorial Censuses 1857-1892, and illustrates an 1892 enumeration page of families in the 5th Ward of Seattle, King County, Washington. The various books and documents shown are the property of the publisher.

Published by Family Roots Publishing Co.
PO Box 830
Bountiful, UT 84011
www.familyrootspublishing.com

Library of Congress Control Number 2007939392
ISBN-13: 978-1-933194-38-7
ISBN-10: 1-933194-38-3

Printed in the United States of America

Books by William Dollarhide

Published by Genealogical Publishing Co., Inc., Baltimore, MD:

- *Map Guide to the U.S. Federal Censuses, 1790-1920* (with William Thorndale) (1987)
- *Managing a Genealogical Project* (1988)
- *Genealogy Starter Kit* (1993); also published with the title, *Getting Started in Genealogy* (2001)
- *Getting Started in Genealogy ONLINE* (2006)
- *New York State Censuses & Substitutes* (2006)

Published by Heritage Quest, North Salt Lake, UT:

- *Seven Steps to a Family Tree* (1995)
- *Map Guide to American Migration Routes, 1735-1815* (1997)
- *British Origins of American Colonists, 1629-1775* (1997)
- *America's Best Genealogy Resource Centers* (with Ronald A. Bremer) (1998)
- *The Census Book: A Genealogist's Guide to Federal Census Facts, Schedules, and Indexes* (1999)
- *Grow a Family Tree!* (2001)

Published by Family Roots Publishing Co., Bountiful, UT:

- *Census Substitutes & State Census Records* (2008)

Contents – Volumes 1 & 2

VOLUME 1 – EASTERN STATES

State Finder - viii
Forward - xi
Introduction - 1
Table 1: Non-State Census States - 5
Table 2: State Census States - 6
Table 3: State Censuses in Common Years - 7

Chapter 1 E – The Old Southwest - 9
Timeline – The Old Southwest - 9
Alabama - 13
Arkansas - 19
Florida - 23
Georgia - 28
Louisiana - 33
Mississippi - 40

Chapter 2 E – New England - 47
Timeline – New England - 47
New England Name Indexes - 52
Connecticut - 53
Maine - 58
Massachusetts - 63
New Hampshire - 68
Rhode Island - 70
Vermont - 75

Chapter 3 E – Mid-Atlantic States - 79
Timeline – Mid-Atlantic - 79
Middle Colonies Name Lists - 82
Delaware – 83
District of Columbia - 87
Timeline of DC Jurisdictions - 88
Maryland - 95
New Jersey - 103
New York - 110
Pennsylvania - 117

Chapter 4 E – The Old South - 125
Timeline – The Old South - 125
Kentucky - 127
North Carolina - 131
South Carolina - 135
Tennessee - 139
Virginia - 143
West Virginia - 150

Chapter 5 E – The Old Northwest - 155
Timeline – The Old Northwest - 155
Illinois - 158
Indiana - 164
Michigan - 169
Minnesota - 175
Ohio - 181
Wisconsin - 187

Chapter 6 E – The Central Plains - 195
Historical Timeline for the Central Plains - 195
Iowa - 199
Kansas - 206
Missouri - 217
Nebraska - 229
Dakota Territory - 234
North Dakota - 234
South Dakota – 240

VOLUME 2 – WESTERN STATES

State Finder - viii
Forward - xi
Introduction - 1
Table 1: Non-State Census States - 5
Table 2: State Census States - 6
Table 3: State Censuses in Common Years - 7

Chapter 1 W – Texas, Oklahoma & Indian Territory - 9
Texas Jurisdictions, 1805-1848 - 9
Texas Censuses & Substitutes - 11
Jurisdictional History of the Indian Territory, Oklahoma Territory, and Oklahoma - 28
Censuses & Substitutes for Indian Territory, Oklahoma Territory, and Oklahoma - 31

Chapter 2 W – California & Nevada; Alaska & Hawaii - 47
California to 1850 - 47
California Censuses & Substitutes - 54
Nevada History to Statehood - 75
Nevada Censuses & Substitutes - 77
Alaska Historical Timeline - 84
Alaska Censuses & Substitutes - 85
Hawaii Historical Timeline - 90
Hawaii Censuses & Substitutes - 91

Contents – Continued:

VOLUME 2 – Continued:

Chapter 3 W – Nuevo Mexico - 97
Historical Timeline, AZ & NM - 97
AZ Statewide Censuses & Substitutes -100
AZ Countywide Censuses & Substitutes - 104
NM Spanish-Mexican Censuses, 1681-1846 - 113
NM Statewide Censuses & Substitutes - 116
NM Countywide Censuses & Substitutes - 120

Chapter 4 W – The Mountain West - 139
Colorado Timeline - 139
Colorado Censuses & Substitutes - 143

Chapter 4 W – Continued:
Utah Timeline - 151
Utah Censuses & Substitutes - 153
Wyoming Timeline - 160
Wyoming Censuses & Substitutes - 162

Chapter 5 W – The Oregon Country - 171
Historical Events & Jurisdictions - 171
Oregon Censuses & Substitutes - 179
Washington Censuses & Substitutes - 190
Idaho Censuses & Substitutes - 201
Montana Censuses & Substitutes - 205

State Finder – Volumes 1 & 2:

State	Vol. – Page	State	Vol. – Page
Alabama	1 - 13	Missouri	1 - 217
Alaska	2 - 84	Montana	2 - 205
Arizona	2 - 100	Nebraska	1 - 229
Arkansas	1 - 19	Nevada	2 - 75
California	2 - 47	New Hampshire	1 - 68
Colorado	2 - 139	New Jersey	1 - 103
Connecticut	1 - 53	New Mexico	2 - 113
Delaware	1 - 83	New York	1 - 110
District of Columbia	1 - 87	North Carolina	1 - 131
Florida	1 - 23	North Dakota	1 - 234
Georgia	1 - 28	Ohio	1 - 181
Hawaii	2 - 90	Oklahoma	2 - 28
Idaho	2 - 201	Oregon	2 - 179
Illinois	1 - 158	Pennsylvania	1 - 117
Indiana	1 - 164	Rhode Island	1 - 70
Iowa	1 - 199	South Carolina	1 - 135
Kansas	1 - 206	South Dakota	1 - 240
Kentucky	1 - 127	Tennessee	1 - 139
Louisiana	1 - 33	Texas	2 - 9
Maine	1 - 58	Utah	2 - 151
Maryland	1 - 95	Vermont	1 - 75
Massachusetts	1 - 63	Virginia	1 - 143
Michigan	1 - 169	Washington	2 - 190
Minnesota	1 - 175	West Virginia	1 - 150
Mississippi	1 - 40	Wisconsin	1 - 187
		Wyoming	2 - 160

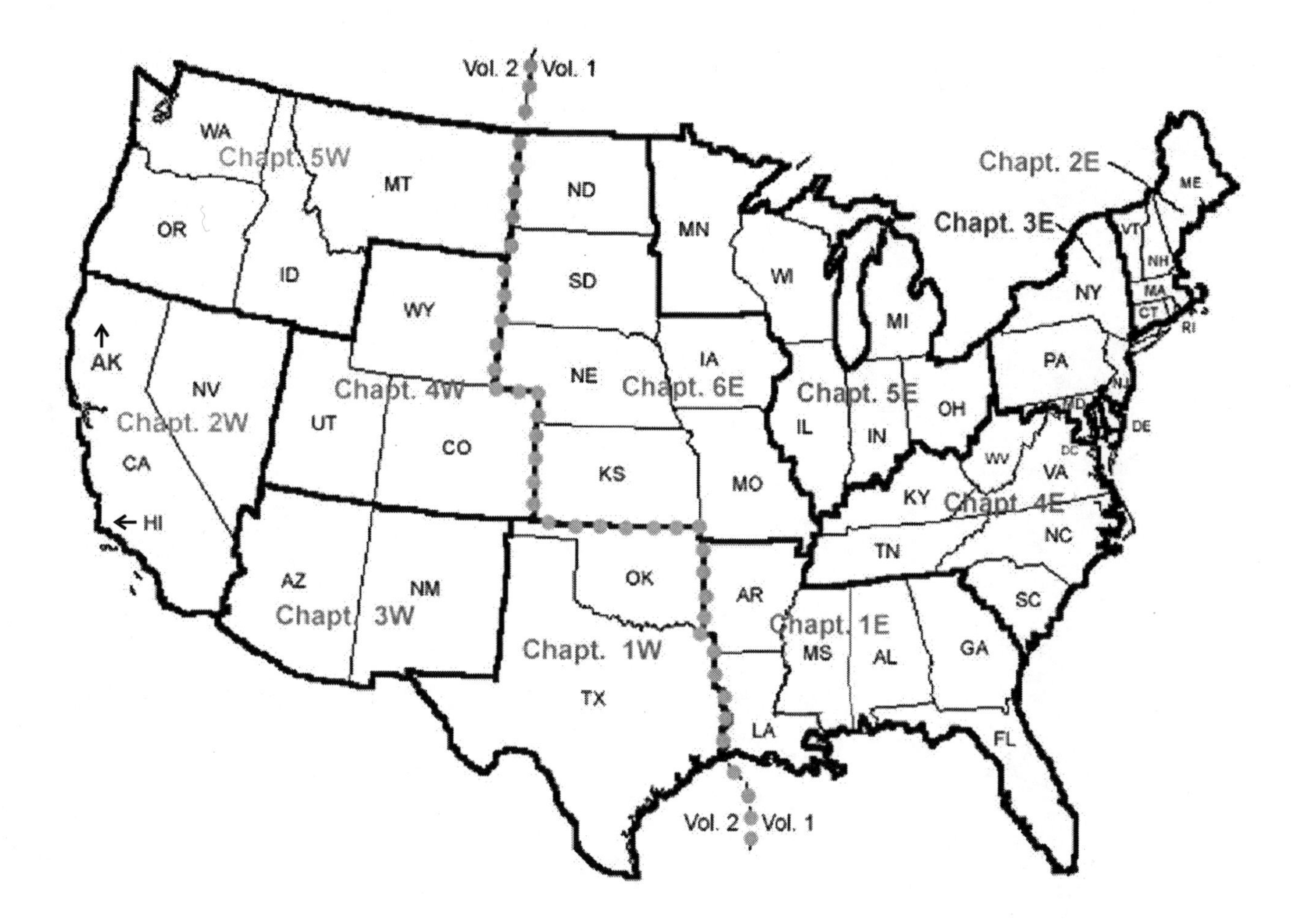

Vol. 2 – Western States
Chapter – Region - Page

1 W - Texas, Oklahoma & Indian Territory - 9

2 W - California & Nevada; Alaska & Hawaii - 47

3 W - Nuevo Mexico - 97

4 W - The Mountain West - 139

5 W - The Oregon Country - 171

Vol. 1 – Eastern States
Chapter – Region - Page

1 E - The Old Southwest - 9

2 E - New England - 47

3 E - Mid-Atlantic States - 79

4 E - The Old South - 125

5 E - The Old Northwest - 155

6 E - The Central Plains - 195

Foreword

by Leland K. Meitzler

In late 2003, Bill Dollarhide came by my office and asked if I had any ideas for *Genealogy Bulletin* articles. As it turned out, I had just finished organizing materials for a lecture on state and territorial census records and had a file folder full of data I had collected over the years on my desk. I suggested he put something together on that subject and gave him the file to review. After looking through my file, Bill decided that we needed to identify the many substitutes to censuses (statewide tax lists, voter registration lists, and such), as he quickly noted that a number of states didn't take any state or territorial censuses at all. Bill began compiling a bibliography of not only extant state and territorial censuses, but substitute lists as well.

Researched and compiled by region, he added timelines of historical references to show the jurisdictions in place at the time of each census. Compiling the material by region was a stroke of genius on Bill's part, as we quickly realized that in most cases, it would have been very difficult to write about one state without writing about those surrounding it.

Much of the data found herein was initially published in serial form in *Genealogy Bulletin.* That said, the Oregon Country, including Washington, Oregon, Idaho, and Montana was never published. However, it is included in this volume. Numerous online sources have been added, reflecting the ongoing efforts of both public and private companies to digitize genealogically relevant records. Name lists have been added. Bill also spent countless hours compiling three charts that may be worth the cost of this book all by themselves. The first, found on page 5, is a chart for the non-state census states. There happens to be 13 of them (plus the District of Columbia, found in Volume 1). This chart lists the states and the years covered by census substitutes recommended in this book, and its companion volume (covering the eastern states). The second chart, found on page 6, lists the 37 states that have extant colonial, pre-statehood, territorial, and state censuses, complete with the census year, as well as an indication if the census is available online as of the date of publication. The third chart, found on page 7, shows in graphic form the states that had censuses taken in common years – "on the fives." Census dates for some states are within a range, e.g., within 3 years of 1825, and indicated in the 1825 column. A state with a number of good examples is Washington, where there was no 1875 census, but there were censuses of 1871 and 1879! And in the 1880s, Washington had an 1881, 1883, 1885, 1887, and an 1889 Census. There was also a census for 1892 and 1894, following statehood.

You might note that the title of this volume is **Census Substitutes & State Census Records, Volume 2 – Western States.** This reflects the fact that the book is really a list of census substitutes, with state censuses turning out to be in the minority. Substitutes outnumber censuses by a factor of ten to one! However, the state censuses identified in this book, and its companion, **Census Substitutes & State Census Records, Volume 1 – Eastern States** are by far the most complete lists of Colonial, Territorial, and State Censuses published to date. The *Eastern States* book includes extensive never-before-published information on the District of Columbia. It might also be noted that Bill did not use the Mississippi

River as the line dividing Eastern and Western states. He decided to include the Central Plains states of Iowa, Kansas, Missouri, Nebraska, and the Dakotas in volume one (*Eastern States*). While it may seem logical to include this area in the *Western States* book, historic ties as well as page count dictated where the line dividing the volumes would be.

State and Territorial Censuses have long fascinated me. Many were taken in order to get congress to allow statehood. Some territories would take censuses on a nearly annual basis, in the attempt to show that they had the population base necessary to justify statehood.

I've waited for two years to see the publication of data on my native Oregon Country. Having grown up in the Puyallup Valley of Washington State, I've always had an active interest in local history and genealogy of the area. Although I no longer have residence in the state, I continue to have many ties. In Washington, the Secretary of State's office oversees the "Digital Archives." Housed in a new facility at the Eastern Washington University campus in Cheney, Washington, this archives is a genealogist's dream. Opening in 2004, the first records brought into the facility's care were marriage records from three pilot counties – Chelan, Snohomish and Spokane – along with the historic Census and Naturalization records from the State Archives & Library in Olympia. Since that time, the Digital Archives has grown tremendously. State and Federal Census records from 1847 through 1910 are indexed and often available in digital format at the Digital Archives website. Although specializing in Marriage, Naturalization, Census, Birth, Death, Military, and Institutional records, the site also contains such widely varying records as Japanese Evacuee Resettlement records and Washington Territory Donation Land Claims. Washington is setting the standard for the digitization of state records. Now – if the other states will just keep up!

As mentioned earlier, census substitutes are a primary part of this volume. Many of the items found in Washington State's Digital Archives can be considered census substitutes also. They are of prime importance, since 13 states, as well as the District of Columbia, took no state censuses at all. And even if your ancestors lived in a state where censuses were taken "on the fives," census substitutes are helpful, especially if the family was on the move.

Although Mr. Dollarhide has used all kinds of substitutes throughout this volume, more attention has been given to tax lists, voter registration rolls, vital records, directories, statewide probate indexes, land records, and even military censuses, than most others. Texas county tax rolls are of prime importance as a census substitute for those researching their Texas heritage. Nearly 10 pages of this book are used in identifying what is currently available. If researching Oklahoma, your search will invariably touch on the many resources for American Indian records. Those with Denver, Colorado ancestry will surely want to check out the 1876 though 1935 Denver City Directories – all available on microfilm through the Family History Library. Those with early Utah pioneers will want to search the 1853 through 1878 Salt Lake County Assessment Rolls. And keep in mind that no matter where your young male relatives lived in the United States during World War One, they may be found quickly on the World War One Selective Service System Draft Registration Cards – all found at Ancestry.com. These records are often easily accessible and using this guide, you will be able to quickly find them for your own use. You are in for a treat, so sit back and look up the states of your ancestors. You will find information on records you never knew existed. Then... go get the records, and happy hunting!

Leland K. Meitzler
Publisher

Introduction

Census Substitutes & State Census Records

Census Substitutes are those name lists derived from tax lists, directories, military lists, land ownership lists, voter registrations, and other compilations of names of residents for an entire state, one or more counties of a state, or one or more towns of a county. A census substitute can be used to determine the names of residents in a given area when a federal or state census is missing. Moreover, a census substitute can be used as an alternative name list; confirming, contradicting, or adding to information found in a federal or state census.

This book identifies at least ten times the number of Census Substitute titles than any previous work ever published. All states are represented with significant alternative name lists – name lists that stop time for a certain year and place, and name the residents of a certain place. Since all of these name lists are specific to a certain year, they are listed for each state in chronological order. Incorporated into the lists are any **State Census** titles – a reference to a state census taken for a specific year.

Federal vs State Censuses

Federal Censuses have their origins in the constitutional provision for apportionment of the U.S. House of Representatives. The first federal census was taken in 1790, and beginning about the same time, state censuses were conducted for the same reason, that is, apportionment of the various state legislatures.

Although the primary purpose of all censuses was to simply count the population, beginning with the first federal census of 1790, more information than a simple tally was added. This included the name and age of a person and progressively more details about a household for each subsequent census year. State censuses followed this same pattern.

State censuses usually add even more information than the federal censuses, and as a result, they are premier genealogical resources. Except in cases where a federal census is lost, state census records are not substitutes for the federal censuses – state censuses were almost always taken between federal census years, and usually add unique information and details about a household not found in a federal census. If a state census exists between federal census years, it may add marginally to the knowledge one gains about a family. But, more often, it will add critical information, such as more exact dates of birth, marriages, deaths; plus additional children, different residences, other relatives living with a family; and more.

Non-State Census States

Fourteen (14) states (including DC) have never conducted a state-sponsored census. For these **Non-State Census States**, this review attempts to identify as many census substitutes as possible. In some cases, the census substitutes are for a single county within a state, and by listing multiple county name lists for about the same time period, regional coverage is achieved.

For an overview of the Non-State Census States, see **Table 1** (page 5) showing the years for which census substitutes exist. More detail for each census substitute year indicated on the table is covered in the bibliographic sections.

State Census States

Thirty-seven (37) states have conducted censuses separate from the federal censuses. The number of censuses taken by each of the **State Census States** ranges from one (1) census year, e.g., the 1852 California; to twenty-four (24) census years, e.g., the 1792-1866 Mississippi territorial/state censuses. For this review, all of the state-sponsored censuses are identified, plus, to a lesser degree than the non-state census states, any census substitutes available. See **Table 2** (page 6) for an overview of the State Census States, the year for each surviving census for a state; and an indication of which specific years are now available online as digitized databases.

Locating the Extant State Census Records

Generally, state censuses were conducted from the time of territorial status or early statehood up until about 1905, but a few continued until 1925, 1935, or 1945. The last state censuses taken by any of the states was in 1945 (Florida and South Dakota). Due to budget restraints, the Depression Era of the 1930s was a contributing factor to states ending their census-taking endeavors. Eventually, all states of the Union stopped using the population figures from state censuses, and began using the federal census figures for apportionment of their state legislatures.

While the surviving federal census manuscripts are all located mostly in one repository (the National Archives), state census manuscripts are spread across the country in the various state archives or local repositories. The accessibility of state censuses may be just as good as federal censuses – but one needs to know where they are located first.

Beginning in 1941, the U.S. Bureau of the Census issued a bibliographic report identifying all known state censuses, those undertaken by the various states separate from the federal censuses since 1790.[1] Prepared by Henry J. Dubester of the Library of Congress, the report was the first known attempt to research all of the state constitutions and subsequent laws related to state censuses for all of the states. The Dubester report sought, first, to identify what state censuses had ever been authorized by a state constitution or legislature; and second, to identify what census manuscripts still survive. The identification of extant state censuses was very incomplete, due to the war and under-funding of the project.

However, Dubester's review of each state's constitutional provisions for taking state censuses still stands as the best overview of what state censuses were ever authorized. The report cites the specific articles of the state constitutions or the actual state laws relating to censuses for all states.

Unfortunately, the fact that a state legislature authorized a state census does not mean one was actually taken. For example, the State Constitution of California of 1849 authorized a census in the years 1852 and 1855 and each ten years thereafter, all for the purpose of apportionment of its state legislature. Yet, only one was ever taken, that for 1852. Later, the California Constitution of 1879 provided that the decennial national census serve as the basis for legislative apportionment.[2]

This was fairly typical of all states. Even in those states for which several decades of state censuses now survive, they eventually got out of the census business, turning to the federal decennial censuses to determine apportionment. For example, New York took state censuses from 1825 and every ten years thereafter until 1925, yet, in 1938, New York decided to use the federal decennial censuses thereafter.[3]

Since the Dubester report, there have been several attempts to list all known state censuses, where they are located, and the contents of the census name lists. All of these attempts differ dramatically, because some of the lists rely on the Dubester report, which may have been accurate in identifying which state censuses were ever authorized, but was not nearly complete in identifying the extant manuscripts of state census records. For example, Table 4-8 of ***The Source,***[4] seems to use the census years cited in the Dubester report for "authorized state censuses" rather than those actually extant. There are lists of state censuses for each state in ***The Red Book,***[5] but are only a slight improvement over those found in *The Source.* And, several Internet sites offer lists of state censuses, all of which seem to take data previously published in the *Source* or *The Red Book,* and similar publications.

Based on survey results from all states, the Family History Library prepared a two-volume publication, ***U.S. State and Special Census Register: A Listing of Family History Library Microfilm Numbers,*** compiled by G. Eileen Buckway and Fred Adams, a revised edition published by the FHL in 1992 (FHL book 973 X2 v. 1 & 2, and fiche #6104851 (vol. 1) and #6104852 (vol. 2). This is a very good guide to military censuses, school censuses, and special censuses of American Indian tribes. As a guide to state censuses, however, the list is incomplete. Since the results of the surveys from each of the states were only partially successful, there are many omissions.

Clearly, the best list of state censuses to date is Ann S. Lainhart, ***State Census Records,*** published by Genealogical Publishing Co., Inc., Baltimore, in 1992. The book identifies state censuses in 43 states, including 6 states without state censuses (but have major state-wide census substitutes available). For the 37 state census states, the lists generally do not include colonial or pre-territorial censuses. With a few exceptions, census substitutes such as those compiled from tax lists, voter registration lists, military lists, or other name sources, are also not included. Still, Lainhart's book stands as the most complete list ever done.

At the time when most of the previous state census lists were put together, there were some research tools unavailable to the authors. Today, the Internet as a resource for finding place-specific records is overwhelming – there are more ways to creatively seek keywords, subjects, places, etc., than most of us have thought of yet. And, special tools such as the Periodical Source Index (PERSI)[6] which indexes articles in over 6,500 different genealogical periodicals (by subject, place, and surname) gives a big boost to the task of finding references to relevant articles using keywords such as "state census," "territorial census," or "tax list." In addition, the State Archives and/or State Libraries where obscure census originals and substitute name lists reside often have a website with an online searchable catalog.

For any genealogical research project, it helps to be close to the Family History Library (FHL) in Salt Lake City. But from any place where a researcher has access to the Internet, the Family Search™ online catalog as a genealogical research tool has no equal. Searching for state censuses and census substitutes in the FHL catalog will not bring up every extant resource, but it is estimated that at least 90% of everything published is there.

Expanding the scope to include census substitutes of tax lists, voter registration lists, military lists, etc., the number of name lists increases by a factor of at least ten.

For this nationwide review, we decided to start with the areas of the United States that had the earliest census/name list records. That meant moving from the East Coast to the West Coast. The first chapter (vol. 1) is for Census Substitutes and State Censuses available for the states of Alabama, Arkansas, Florida, Georgia, Louisiana, and Mississippi. This area could be called "The Old Southwest," and since the settlements beginning in St. Augustine, Mobile, Pensacola, Natchez, and New Orleans were the earliest in North America, this region is where the earliest census/name lists were created. The Old Southwest has gone through several jurisdiction changes under control of the Spanish, French, English, and Americans. To reflect these changes, a timeline for the region was prepared to put the area into historical perspective. This grouping of states and a common timeline for each group was continued for all eleven chapters.

As a bibliography of census substitutes and state censuses, references to the location of schedules and indexes to the federal censuses, 1790-1930, are generally not included. The exceptions are those lists of state and federal censuses using a combined index, such as those found at **www.ancestry.com**, **www.censusfinder.com/** or **www.census-online.com.** Federal censuses may also be mentioned in the chronological timelines or bibliographic lists, to assist in locating census substitutes for a missing federal census year. For several of the western states, federal censuses are included to fill in the lack of state censuses and substitutes. In the case of lost federal censuses which have been reconstructed for a state or part of a state, any book titles or articles that could be found are included.

For those who want to review the federal censuses in more detail along with these substitutes and state census lists, refer to ***The Census Book***[7] to see population figures, maps of the U.S. for each census year, and a review of published federal census indexes.

The maps of the changing county boundaries for all of the states shown in ***Map Guide to the U.S. Federal Census, 1790-1920***[8] should also be helpful for reviewing substitute or state census years between federal census years.

Notes:

1. ***State Censuses: An Annotated Bibliography of Censuses of Population Taken After the Year 1790 by States and Territories of the United States,*** prepared by Henry J. Dubester, Chief, Census Library Project, Library of Congress, published Washington, DC, by United States Department of Commerce, Bureau of the Census, 1941, rev. 1948.

2. Dubester, ***State Censuses,*** p. 3.

3. Dubester, ***State Censuses,*** p. 50.

4. ***The Source: A Guidebook of American Genealogy,*** first edition, edited by Arlene Eakle and Johni Cerny, published by Ancestry, Inc., Salt Lake City, 1984.

5. ***The Red Book: American State, County & Town Sources,*** edited by Alice Eichholz, rev. ed., published by Ancestry, Inc., Salt Lake City, UT, 1992.

6. Allen County Public Library, ***Periodical Source Index.*** Updated semi-annually. [database online] Provo, UT: Ancestry.com, 1998- . Original data: Allen County Public Library. Periodical Source Index, Fort Wayne, IN: Allen County Public Library Foundation, 1985- .

7. ***The Census Book: A Genealogist's Guide to Federal Census Facts, Schedules and Indexes,*** by William Dollarhide, published by Heritage Quest, North Salt Lake, UT, 2000. A PDF file of the entire book is available for downloading at the Heritage Quest website at **www.heritagequestonline.com/prod/genealogy/html/help/census_book.html**

8. ***Map Guide to the U.S Federal Censuses, 1790-1920,*** by William Thorndale and William Dollarhide, published by Genealogical Publishing Co., Inc., Baltimore, 1987-2005.

Table 1 – Non-State Census States. The following 14 states (including DC) have never conducted a state-sponsored census (or no state census survives). Census Substitutes for each state are shown for a range of years. Refer to the bibliographic listings for details about each.

State	Terr.	State	Years for which Census Substitutes are Available
Alaska	1912	1959	1870, 1873, 1878, 1885, 1887, 1890-1895, 1902-1912, 1905, 1908-1914, 1910- 1929, 1913-1916, 1917-1918, 1947, 1950, 1959-1986, and 1960-1985.
Connecticut	—	1788	1636-1670, 1688-1709, 1710-1711, 1756-1774, 1790-1850, 1799- 1838, 1845-1853, 1862-1866, 1883-1886, 1905-1929, 1913-1928, and 1917-1980.
Delaware	—	1787	1609-1888, 1646-1679, 1680-1934, 1682-1759, 1684-1693, 1726, 1755, 1759, 1779, 1782, 1785, 1790, 1800, 1807, 1850-1860, and 1862-1872.
District of Columbia	—	1791	1803, 1807, 1818, 1867, 1878, 1885, 1888, 1894, 1897, 1905-1909, 1912-1913, 1915, 1917, 1919, and 1925.
Idaho	1863	1890	1863, 1865-1874, 1871-1881, 1880, 1890, 1911-1937, 1911-1950, and 1930.
Kentucky	—	1792	1773-1780, 1774-1796, 1780-1909, 1781-1839, 1782-1787, 1782-1875, 1787, 1787-1811, 1787-1875, 1788-1875, 1789-1882, 1792-1830, 1792-1913, 1792-1796, 1793-1836, 1794-1805, 1794-1817, 1795, 1796-1808, 1797-1866, 1800, 1820-1900, 1851-1900, 1859-1860, 1860-1936, 1861-1865, 1862-1866, and 1895- 1896.
Montana	1864	1889	1860, 1856-1993, 1864-1872, 1868-1869, 1868-1929, 1870, 1880, 1870-1957, 1872- 1900, 1879-1880, 1881-1928, 1881-2000, 1891-1929, 1894, 1913, 1906- 1917, 1909- 1910, 1917-1918, 1921, and 1930-1975.
New Hampshire	—	1788	1648, 1709. 1723, 1736, 1740, 1763, 1767, 1775, 1776, 1779, 1789, 1795-1816, 1797, 1802, 1803, 1821, 1826, 1833, 1836, 1838, 1849, 1855 & 1865 MA, 1860, 1862-1866, 1903, and 1902-1921
Ohio	1787	1803	1787-1840, 1787-1871, 1788-1799, 1788-1820, 1790, 1800-1803, 1801-1814, 1801-1824, 1802, 1803-1827, 1804, 1807, 1810, 1812, 1816-1838, 1816-1838, 1825, 1827, 1832-1850, 1833-1994, 1835, 1846-1880, 1851-1900, 1851-1907, and 1907.
Pennsylvania	—	1787	1682-1950, 1759, 1680-1938, 1680s-1900s, 1760s-1790s, 1700s, 1780, 1798, 1740- 1900, 1887-1893, and 1870.
Texas	—	1845	1736-1838, 1700s-1800s, 1756-1830s, 1782-1836, 1809-1836, 1814-1909, 1821-1846, 1826, 1826-1835, 1820s-1846, 1820-1829, 1826-1836, 1829-1836, 1830-1839, 1835, 1835-1846, 1836, 1836-1935, 1837-1859, 1840-1849, 1840, 1846, 1837-1910, 1851-1900, 1858, 1861-1865, 1863, 1865-1866, 1867, 1874, 1882-1895, 1884, 1889-1894, 1890, 1914, 1917-1918, 1896-1948, and 1964-1968.
Vermont	—	1791	1770s-1780s, 1700s-1800s, 1654-1800, 1710-1753, 1721-1800, 1770-1832, 1771, 1782, 1788, 1793, 1796-1959, 1800s-1870, 1807, 1813, 1815, 1816, 1827-1833, 1828, 1832, 1843, 1852-1959, 1855-1860, 1861-1866, 1865, 1869, 1871-1908, 1874, 1880-1881, 1881-1882, 1882-1883, 1883-1884, 1884, 1887-1888, 1888, 1889, and 1895-1924.
Virginia	—	1788	1600s-1700s, 1600s, 1619-1930, 1623-1990, 1623-1800, 1632-1800, 1654-1800, 1704-1705, 1720, 1736-1820, 1740, 1744-1890, 1760, 1769-1800, 1779, 1779-1978, 1779-1860, 1782-1785, 1785, 1787, 1809-1848, 1810, 1815, 1828-1938, 1835, 1835-1941, 1840, 1861, 1861-1865, 1852, 1853-1896, and 1889-1890.
West Virginia	—	1863	1600s-1900s, 1777-1850, 1787, 1782-1907, 1782-1850, 1782-1860, 1782, 1783-1900, 1783-1850, 1785-1850, 1787,1850, 1789-1850, 1792-1850, 1797-1899, 1797-1851, 1799-1850, 1800, 1801-1850, 1810, 1811-1850, 1862-1866, 1863-1900, and 1899-1900.

From *Census Substitutes & State Census Records* by William Dollarhide, published by Family Roots Publishing Co., Bountiful, UT

Table 2 – State Census States. The following 37 states have extant censuses available, including colonial, pre-statehood, territorial, and state censuses.

State	Year a Terr.	Year a State	Years for which State Censuses are available (underlined years, [e.g., 1814] indicates an online database is available)	Notes
Alabama	1817	1819	Colonial: 1706-1796. Terr.: 1816*, 1818; State: 1820**, 1821, 1823, 1832, 1838, 1844, 1850**, 1855, 1866	* as part of MS Terr. ** separate from federal.
Arizona	1863	1912	1864, 1866. County voter registrations are good substitutes.	
Arkansas	1819	1836	French/Spanish Colonial: 1686-1791; Territory: 1814*, 1823, 1827, 1829, 1833, 1835; State: 1838, 1854, 1865	* as part of MO Terr.
California	—	1850	Spanish: 1790. State: 1852 only. Countywide Great Registers are good substitutes.	
Colorado	1861	1876	1861, 1866*, 1885	* 2 counties only
Florida	1822	1845	1825, 1840*, 1855, 1875, 1885, 1895, 1925, 1935, 1945.	* Military census
Georgia	—	1788	1800 federal*, Partial lists for 1827, 1838, 1845, 1852, 1859, 1879, 1890 federal**, 1890 (statewide, reconstructed).	* Oglethorpe Co only ** Washington Co only
Hawaii	1900	1959	Kingdom of Hawaii: 1840-1866, 1878, 1890, 1896	
Illinois	1809	1818	1810, 1818, 1820*, 1825, 1830*, 1835, 1840*, 1845, 1855, 1865.	* separate from federal
Indiana	1800	1816	1807. A few townships only:* 1857, 1871, 1877, 1883, 1889, 1901, 1913, 1919, 1931.	* IN State Library only
Iowa	1838	1846	1836*, 1838, 1847, 1849, 1854, 1856, 1859, 1873, 1875, 1885, 1895, 1905, 1915, 1925	* as part of WI Terr.
Kansas	1854	1861	1855, 1856, 1857, 1858, 1859, 1865, 1875, 1885, 1895, 1905, 1915, 1925	
Louisiana	1809	1812	1804, 1833, 1837, 1890 federal*	* Ascension Parish only
Maine	—	1820	1837 only. Published Town records are good substitutes.	
Maryland	—	1788	1776, 1778, 1783 (tax list)	
Massachusetts	—	1788	1855, 1865	
Michigan	1805	1837	1836, 1837, 1845, 1854, 1864, 1874, 1884, 1894	
Minnesota	1849	1858	1849, 1853, 1855, 1857*, 1865, 1875, 1885, 1895, 1905.	* federal census.
Mississippi	1798	1817	1792, 1801, 1805, 1809, 1810, 1813, 1815-1817, 1816, 1818, 1820*, 1822, 1823, 1824, 1825, 1830*, 1837, 1840*, 1841, 1845, 1850*, 1853, 1857, 1866	* separate from federal
Missouri	1805	1821	1844, 1845, 1846, 1852, 1856, 1864, 1868, 1876	
Nebraska	1854	1867	1854, 1855, 1856, 1865, 1869, 1874, 1875, 1876, 1877, 1878, 1879, 1882, 1883, 1884.	
Nevada	1861	1864	1861, 1862, 1863, 1864, 1875, 1870-1920* (full extraction//index, all federal censuses).	* NV State Archives
New Jersey	—	1787	1855, 1865, 1875*, 1885, 1895, 1905, 1915.	* a few townships only
New Mexico	1850	1912	Spanish: 1600. Terr/State: 1885 only. County voter registrations are good substitutes.	
New York	—	1788	1825, 1835, 1845, 1855, 1865, 1875, 1892, 1905, 1915, 1925.	
North Carolina	—	1789	1784-1787. County tax lists are good substitutes.	
North Dakota	1861*	1889	1885*, 1905 (statistics only), 1915, 1925.	* Dakota Territory
Oklahoma	1890	1907	1890*, 1907 federal (Seminole Co. only)	* separate from federal
Oregon	1848	1859	OR Prov. Terr.: 1842, 1843, 1844, 1846; OR Terr.:1849, 1853, 1854, 1855, 1856, 1857, 1858, 1859. OR State: 1865*, 1875*, 1885*, 1895*, 1905	* indexes for a few counties only
Rhode Island	—	1790	1865, 1875, 1885, 1905, 1915, 1925, 1935.	
South Carolina	—	1788	1829, 1839, 1869, 1875.	
South Dakota	1861*	1889	1885* , 1895, 1905, 1915, 1925, 1935, 1945.	* Dakota Territory
Tennessee	1790	1796	1790 reconstructed, 1891 males over 21 (partial)	
Utah	1850	1896	1856 only. LDS member censuses, 1914-1960, are good substitutes.	
Washington	1853	1889	1851*, 1856, 1857, 1858, 1859, 1861, 1871, 1879, 1881, 1883, 1885, 1887, 1889, 1892, 1894.	* As part of OR Terr.
Wisconsin	1836	1848	1836, 1838, 1842, 1846, 1847, 1855, 1865, 1875, 1885, 1895, 1905	
Wyoming	1868	1890	1869 only. Statewide directories are good substitutes.	

From *Census Substitutes & State Census Records* by William Dollarhide, published by Family Roots Publishing Co., Bountiful, UT

Table 3 – State Censuses Taken in Common Years. As a means of comparing state censuses taken by the 37 state census states, this table shows the common years for which many states conducted a state census. Many were done in years ending in "5." Census dates for some states are within a range, e.g., within 3 years of 1825, are indicated in the 1825 column.

	1815	1825	1835	1845	1855	1865	1875	1885	1895	1905	1915	1925	1935	1945
Alabama	•	•	•	•	•	•								
Arizona						•								
Arkansas	•	•	•		•	•								
California					•									
Colorado						•		•						
Florida		•			•		•	•	•			•	•	•
Georgia		•	•	•	•		•							
Hawaii				•		•	•		•					
Illinois		•	•	•	•									
Indiana														
Iowa			•	•	•		•	•	•	•	•	•		
Kansas					•	•	•	•	•	•	•	•		
Louisiana			•											
Maine			•											
Maryland														
Massachusetts					•	•								
Michigan			•	•	•	•	•	•	•					
Minnesota				•	•	•	•	•	•	•				
Mississippi	•	•	•	•	•	•								
Missouri				•	•	•	•							
Nebraska					•	•	•	•						
Nevada						•	•							
New Jersey					•	•	•	•	•	•	•			
New Mexico								•						
New York		•	•	•	•	•	•		•	•	•	•		
No. Carolina														
No. Dakota								•		•	•	•		
Oklahoma									•	•				
Oregon				•	•	•	•	•	•	•				
Rhode Island						•	•	•	•	•	•	•	•	
So. Carolina		•	•			•	•							
So. Dakota								•	•	•	•	•	•	•
Tennessee									•					
Utah					•									
Washington					•		•	•	•					
Wisconsin			•		•	•	•	•	•	•				
Wyoming						•								
No. of States:	3	8	12	11	20	20	17	15	15	11	7	7	3	2

From ***Census Substitutes & State Census Records*** by William Dollarhide, published by Family Roots Publishing Co., Bountiful, UT

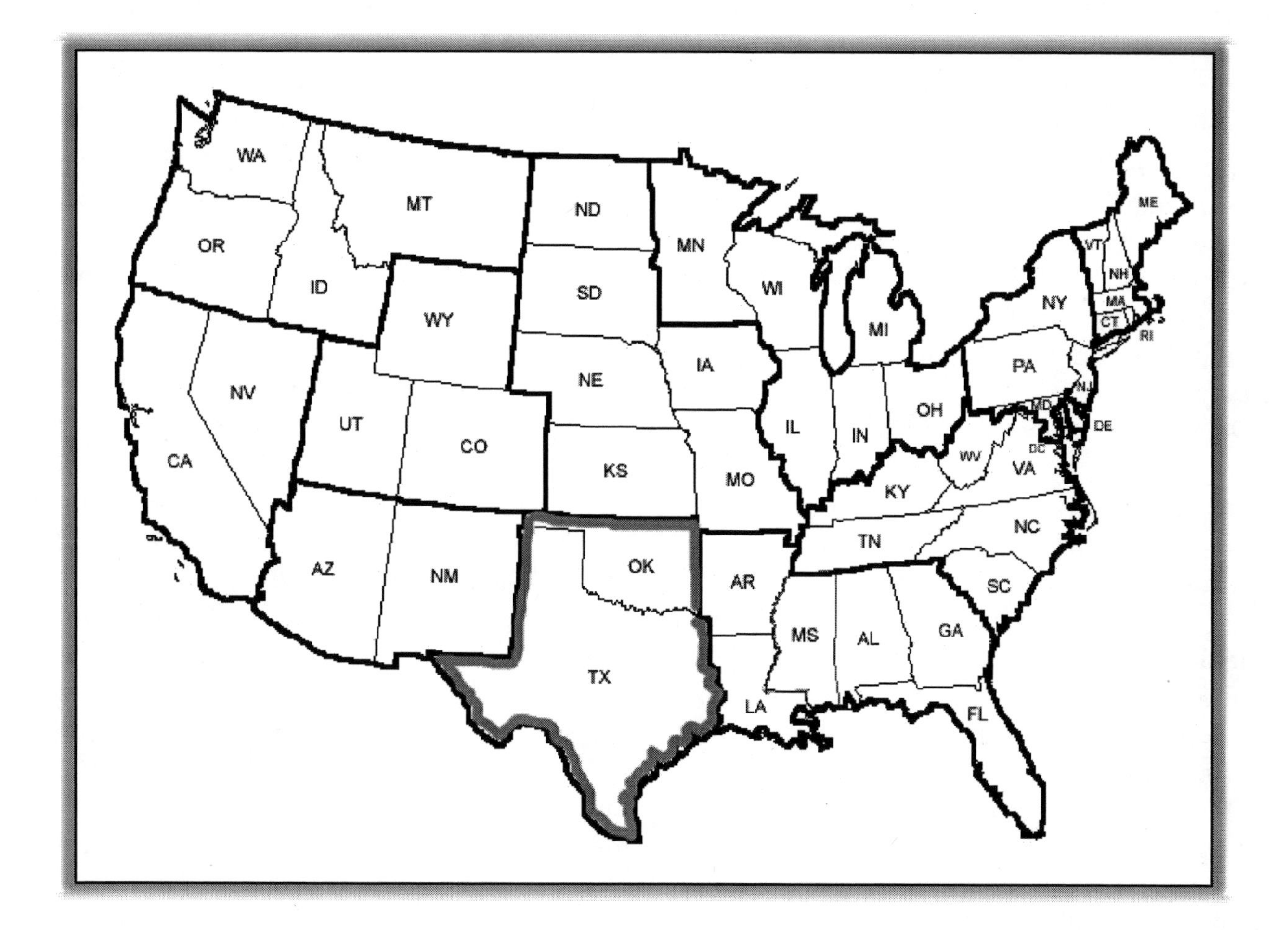

Chapter 1W – Texas & Oklahoma

Spanish & Mexican Texas, Republic & State of Texas; and Indian Territory, Oklahoma Territory, and State of Oklahoma

TEXAS Jurisdictions, 1805-1848

Texas was closely linked with Mexico's Coahuila province for nearly a century and a half – from 1691 to 1835. Troops from Coahuila established Nacogdoches in 1716, San Antonio de Bexar in 1718, and La Bahia del Espiritu Santo in 1722, the last mentioned post being moved in 1749 to what is now Goliad. The Medina River just west of San Antonio became the western boundary of the "Texas" command, while the lower Nueces River marked the boundary with New Santander province. Texas became a separate province about 1726, with San Antonio as its capital from 1773. The Spanish government in Madrid in 1805 formally defined the west boundary (a northwestern trace from the Medina River to the southeastern corner of present-day New Mexico, and from that point to the Red River, at the southwestern corner of present-day Oklahoma). West of that line was the colonial Spanish province of Nuevo Mexico.

At the end of the Spanish era in 1820, Texas was a moribund province, its few thousand Hispanics living mainly in San Antonio, LaBahia (Goliad), and Nacogdoches. The ruins of destroyed and abandoned settlements and missions dotted this Indian besieged province barely maintaining its population in the years 1790-1820. To the east, American frontier families were beginning to cross the Sabine, while in the extreme northeast the Americans along the Red River were a de facto part of Miller County, Arkansas Territory. To the west in 1820, the Rio Grande valley contained a few towns such as Laredo, Presidio del Rio Grande and Paso del Norte, this latter town being on the south bank opposite El Paso. But the valley was not part of Texas until 1848.

The Louisiana Purchase of 1803 by the United States forced a formal clarification of the eastern boundary of Texas. Spain claimed east to the Red River; the U.S., west to the Sabine. They compromised in 1806 with the so-called Neutral Ground, a buffer zone where neither would exercise jurisdiction in what was to be a no-man's land but actually became a haven for pirates, outlaws, fugitives, and others enjoying freedom from government. The Neutral Ground was bounded west by the Sabine and east by Louisiana's Calcasieu River and Bayou Pierre. Finally, the Spanish-American treaty of 1819 (ratified by the parties in 1821 and by Mexico in 1828) set the east Texas border to run up the Sabine to the 32nd parallel and then due north to the Red River. This is the modern Texas line with Louisiana and Arkansas, but it took nearly two decades to clarify just where that due-north line met the Red River. This uncertainty made it possible for Arkansas Territory in April 1820 to create Miller County partly in what is now northeast Texas.

Mexico became independent in 1821. It renamed New Santander province as the state of Tamaulipas and in 1824 joined Texas to Coahuila as the state of Coahuila and Texas.

Mexico in the 1820s tried to build a barrier against on-coming Americans by encouraging "fit" Anglo settlers to take up land.

This began in earnest with an 1823 contract with Stephen Austin to bring in 300 families, giving Austin authority to grant these families land. In 1824 a similar contract was made with Green DeWitt for 400 families. Further such empresario grants were made until by 1830 most of present-day Texas was covered by such grants, although the grants along the Red River and in the Texas panhandle never functioned.

Politically, Texas in 1830 was the department of Bexar within the state of Coahuila and Texas. The western boundary remained unchanged from 1805, though common usage and contemporary maps increasingly marked the whole Nueces River as the boundary. Within the department of Bexar were four jurisdictions called municipalities, these headquartered at San Antonio, LaBahia (Goliad), San Felipe de Austin (Austin's colony), and Nacogdoches.

As American population rapidly increased in east Texas and in the empresario colonies south and southeast of San Antonio, more municipalities were created and some of these were subdivided into districts. By 1828, Austin's colony had seven such districts.

The Mexican congress by act of 6 April 1830 barred further American immigration into Texas. Mexican troops were stationed around east Texas to enforce the ban, though Austin and DeWitt were allowed to bring in a few families in fulfillment of their contracts. Significant legal immigration from the U.S. resumed only in 1834. The last two years of Mexican government in Texas saw a typical American scramble for land.

Local government had to keep pace. By 1834, new departments of Brazos and Nacogdoches were carved from Bexar and four new municipalities were created: Bastrop, Matagorda, San Augustine, and San Patricio. By the end of the Mexican era in 1835, the entity called Texas was composed of three departments, each with representation in the state legislature of Coahuila and Texas. These departments were subdivided into municipalities and some further into districts. Add the empresario grants, new towns, and clusters of farms informally called "settlements" and Texas was a mosaic of jurisdictions, with a population of about 24,000 Americans and 6,000 Hispanics. Maps in William Pool's *Historical Atlas of Texas* (Encino Press, Austin, TX, 1975) may be the best source for locating places in Texas at the time of independence.

The Texas war for independence began in October 1835 at Gonzales and climaxed on 21 April 1836 with the battle of San Jacinto, where the Mexican president-dictator Gen. Antonio Lopez de Santa Ana was captured. He agreed (at least while a prisoner) to Texas independence and to the withdrawal of Mexican forces across the Rio Grande.

The Texas provisional government in December 1835 proceeded to claim the Rio Grande for a western boundary, even up in New Mexico, but the Republic of Texas could never assert its authority west of the Nueces. The Mexican congress refused to confirm the Santa Ana agreement, never recognized the Texas republic, and treated it as a province in rebellion. Mexican forces in 1841 crossed the Nueces and briefly occupied San Antonio, thereby pushing Texas another step toward eventual annexation by the United States in 1845.

With the annexation of Texas came the claim to the Rio Grande and in 1846 U.S. troops crossed the Nueces, bringing war with Mexico and the American capture of the Rio Grande Valley in 1847-1848. Then, having given credence to the Texas claim, the U.S. now bought out that claim to New Mexico, paying ten million dollars to Texas by act of 9 September 1850, ratified by Texas 25 November 1850. This act established the present Texas boundaries. A later claim by Texas in 1860 for the northern branch of the Red River as its boundary, allowed Greer County to be created and settled by Texans – but the U.S. government forced Texas to transfer old Greer County to Oklahoma Territory in 1896.

Texas Censuses & Substitutes, 1782-1935

The elaborate Spanish bureaucracy required detailed reports from its frontier posts. This included population data, especially after a royal order of 1776 from Madrid commanded periodic censuses from its American colonies. A good many Texas censuses survive for towns, missions, and their environs, and some have been published, such as for Nacogdoches 1792 and Salecedo 1805. Others can be found in the microfilmed archives for San Antonio de Bexar, Nacogdoches, and Laredo, now located at the State Archives in Austin.

There are also lists of American settlers, such as the Austin and DeWitt colony lists of 1826-1828 and the published lists for what seems to be the department of Nacogdoches. An inventory of extant Spanish and Mexican censuses for Texas does not at present exist but would be valuable.

The first U.S. federal census in Texas were those for Miller County, Arkansas Territory. The 1820 Miller census (lost) included the parts of present-day Oklahoma, Texas, and Arkansas where those states now corner. In 1828, the Indian boundary was established at the present Oklahoma-Arkansas line and Arkansas Territory adjusted its counties so that the Miller 1830 census (extant) was totally south of the Red River in what is now Texas.

The republic 1836-1845 took no known national census. Publications purporting to be such "censuses" are usually the tax lists required yearly from 1 Jan 1837 as compiled by the county assessors. Such ad valorem tax lists (containing real, personal, and poll/head tax information) were made in two copies, one sent to the Texas capital. The state's thousands of lists have been microfilmed, those from 1837 through the late 1970s.

The U.S. federal censuses, 1850-1930 offer no unusual difficulties and are nearly all extant. The orderly way large areas of north and northwest Texas were sectioned into counties with little or no population does mean that the 1860 and 1870 censuses have many unorganized counties without population.

References were found to possible state censuses in 1847-48, 1851, 1858, and 1887. It seems likely the county assessors doing the enumeration were required only to tally the population by several age/sex/race categories and send the counts to Austin. The state and university libraries and archives in Austin could produce no actual name lists for any of the state censuses, except one county list for 1858 Austin County. Census substitutes for the early eras of Texas follow:

■ ***Residents of Texas, 1782-1836,*** compiled by the Institute of Texan Cultures, University of Texas, published by the Institute, San Antonio, TX, 1984, 3 vols. Each volume includes an index. Consists chiefly of names of residents and information concerning their wives and children. Vol. 3 contains transcriptions of proceedings involving land and property and other matters. Vol. 1 has period dates 1782-1806. FHL book 976.4 D2rte vol. 1-3.

■ **Bexar County Spanish Archives (San Antonio, Texas),** microfilm of original records in the Bexar County courthouse. Includes index compiled by Richard G. Santos. Filmed by the Genealogical Society of Utah, 1977, 13 rolls, beginning with FHL film #1019360 (Index to Bexar County Spanish archives, 1736-1838; wills and estates No. 1-9, 1736-1838).

■ ***Indexes to the Laredo Archives,*** compiled by Robert D. Wood, published by Burke Pub., 1993, 138 pages. Includes a chronological, topical/subject, person name (surname) and place name index. Index to records referred to as the Laredo Archives that document early government in the town of Laredo, Texas. Those records in the archives of interest to genealogists consist mainly of court records, with some references to probate and tax matters. FHL book 976.4462/L1 N22w.

■ ***Index to Spanish and Mexican Land Grants in Texas,*** by Virginia H. Taylor, published by Lone Star Press, Austin, TX, 1995, 258 pages. FHL book 976.4 R22t.

■ ***Citizens & Foreigners of the Nacogdoches District, 1809-1836,*** by Carolyn Reeves Ericson, published by the author, Nacogdoches, TX, 1981, 2 vols., FHL book 976.4 H2e, v.1-2.

■ **1821-1846.** ***Coahuila y Texas: Desde la Consumación de la Independencia Hasta el Tratado de Paz de Guadalupe Hidalgo,*** (A historical unfolding of Coahuila and Texas from Independence to the Treaty of Guadalupe Hidalgo), by Vito Alessio Robles, published in Mexico, D.F., Editorial Porrea, 2 vols., 1,082 pages. Includes indexes and bibliographical references. FHL book 972.14 H2r v.1-2.

■ ***Apellidos de Tamaulipas, Nuevo León, Coahuila y Texas,*** (Surnames of Tamaulipas, Nuevo León, Coahuila and Texas), by Rudolfo Gonzales de la Garza, published by Nuevo Laredo, Mexico, 1980, 351 pages. FHL book 972 D4g.

■ ***Stephen F. Austin's Register of Families,*** edited by Villamae Williams from the originals in the General Land Office, Austin, Texas. Originally published: St. Louis, MO. Reprint by Genealogical Publishing Co., Inc., Baltimore, MD, 1989. Includes index. Includes land records. FHL book 976.4 W2au 1989.

■ ***Early Texas Settlers, 1700s-1800s,*** CD-ROM publication originally published by Broderbund (now Ancestry, Inc.), Family Tree Maker's Family Archives, Genealogical Records No. 514, published 2000, in collaboration with Genealogical Publishing Co., Inc., Baltimore. Contents: *Austin Colony Pioneers: Including History of Bastrop, Fayette, Grimes, Montgomery and Washington Counties, Texas and Their Earliest Settlers,* by Worth S. Ray; *Ancestor Lineages of Members Texas Society, National Society Colonial Dames Seventeenth Century,* compiled by Jeanne Mitchell Jordan Tabb; *Stephen F. Austin's Register of Families,* edited by Villamae Williams from the originals in the General Land Office, Austin, Texas; *Character Certificates in the General Land Office of Texas,* edited by Gifford White from the files of the General Land Office, Austin, Texas; *Kentucky Colonization in Texas: A History of the Peters Colony,* by Seymour V. Connor; *Republic of Texas: Poll Lists for 1846,* by Marion Day Mullins; *A New Land Beckoned: German Immigration to Texas, 1844-1847,* compiled and edited by Chester W. and Ethel H. Geue; and *New Homes in a New land: German Immigration to Texas, 1847-1861,* by Ethel Hander Geue.

▪ ***The Atascosito Census of 1826,*** transcription from a photostatic copy of an original document in the Library of Congress. From introduction: "The Atascosito District is bounded as follows viz. On the west by the Colony of San Felipe de Austin on the north by the District of Nacogdoches, on the east by the reserved lands on the Sabine, on the south by the Gulf of Mexico including all Islands and Bays within three leagues of the Sea Shore." FHL book 976.4 A1 no. 149; also on microfiche, FHL film #6089073.

▪ ***Lost Spanish Towns: Atascosito and Trinidad de Salcedo,*** by Jean L. Epperson, published by Dogwood Press, Woodville, TX, 1996, 118 pages. This book covers a part of the history of Southeast Texas from 1756 to the 1830s. From introduction: "Atascosito, located near the lower Trinity River, was a recognized geographical place in 1756, a small rancho in 1766, a temporary Indian mission in 1785, and a Spanish military post from 1805 through 1812. "The villa and military post of Santisima Trinidad de Salcedo was founded in January 1806 on the east side of the Trinity River...The Spanish Royalist Army destroyed Salcedo in September 1813." FHL book 976.4 H2ej.

▪ ***Colonial Deeds, 1826-1835, San Felipe de Austin (Texas),*** copy of photocopied loose deeds at the Austin County courthouse, Bellville, Texas. Filmed by the Genealogical Society of Utah, 1977, 3 rolls, as follows:

- Index to Colonial Deeds, 1826-1860; Vol.1, A1-C35; Vol. 2, C36-G34, FHL film #1019280.
- Vol. 3, G35 – L12, Vol. 4, L13- P83, FHL film #1019281.
- Vol. 5, P84-T34; Vol. 6, T35-Y7, FHL film #101982.

▪ ***Red River County Deed Abstracts,*** abstracted by Joyce Martin Murray, published by the author, Dallas, TX, 1986, 2 vols. Includes index of names, index of places, and index of slave names. Contents: Vol. 1: Republic of Texas and state of Coahuila and Texas (Mexico); Abstracts of deed record books A-B, A-B-C, D, F, to 19 Feb. 1846, annexation to United States; Vol. 2: Red River County, Texas, abstracts of deed record books F, G, H, I, J, and part of K. FHL book 976.4212 R28m.

▪ ***Texas, 1820-1829,*** index of county tax lists, edited by Ronald Vern Jackson, et al, published by Accelerated Indexing Systems, North Salt Lake, UT, 1981, 55 pages. FHL book 976.4 X2j 1820-1829.

▪ ***1826-1836 Index of Documents, Department of Nacogdoches,*** compiled and published by Carolyn Ericson, Nacogdoches, TX, 39 pages.

▪ ***The First Census of Texas, 1829-1836: To Which Are Added Texas Citizenship Lists, 1821-1845 And Other Early Records of the Republic of Texas,*** by Marion Day Mullins, reprinted from Special Publications of the National Genealogical Society, No. 22, 1962, 61 pages. Includes census, 1820-1836; citizenship lists, 1821-1845; certificates of entrance into Texas in 1835; election in San Augustine in November 1834. FHL film #844966.

■ ***1830 Citizens of Texas*: *A Census of 6,500 Pre-revolutionary Texas,*** by Gifford White, published by Eakin Press, Austin, TX, 1983, 282 pages. Includes index and list of registered voters of 1867. FHL book 976.4 X2wh.

■ ***Texas, 1830-1839,*** index of county tax lists, edited by Ronald Vern Jackson, et al, published by Accelerated Indexing Systems, North Salt Lake, UT, 1982, 39 pages. FHL book 976.4 X2j 1830-1839.

■ ***1835 Entrance Certificates, Nacogdoches District,*** compiled by Betty Fagan Burr, published by Frances Terry Ingmire, St. Louis, MO, 1982, 40 pages. From bibliography: "From the R.B. Blake translation of the original Spanish certificates." Includes index. FHL book 976.4 P4n.

■ ***1835 Sabine District, Texas, Census,*** compiled by Mrs. Helen Gomer Schluter, published by Ericson Books, Nacogdoches, TX, 1983, 56 pages. From Introduction: "This 1835 Sabine District, Texas, census was copied from the original Nacogdoches Archives, Austin, Texas, by Mr. R. B. Blake." Includes additions to the original census records and a comprehensive index by Mrs. Helen Gomer Schluter. FHL book 976.4177 X2sh.

■ ***A Brief Account of the Origin, Progress and Present State of the Colonial Settlements of Texas: Together With an Exposition of the Causes Which Have Induced the Existing War With Mexico,*** by Curtius, extracted from a work entitled *A Geographical, Statistical and Historical Account of Texas,* originally published by S. Nye, Nashville, TN, 1836, 16 pages. Reprint published by Pemberton Press, Austin, TX, 1964. Filmed by the Genealogical Society of Utah, 1972, FHL film #874251.

■ ***Texas, 1840-1849,*** (index of county tax lists), edited by Ronald Vern Jackson, et al, published by Accelerated Indexing Systems, North Salt Lake, UT, 1982, 69 pages. FHL book 976.4 X2j 1840-1849.

■ ***The 1840 Census of the Republic of Texas,*** edited by Gifford White, published by Pemberton Press, Austin, TX, 1966, 236 pages. In spite of the title – there was no census in Texas in 1840 – the names apparently were taken from county tax lists. FHL book 976.4 X2w 1840.

■ ***First Settlers of the Republic of Texas: Headright Land Grants Which Were Reported as Genuine and Legal by the Traveling Commissioners, January, 1840,*** 2 vols., originally published by Cruger & Wing, Austin, Texas, 1841; reproduced and indexed by Carolyn Reeves Ericson and Frances T. Ingmire, Nacogdoches, TX, 1982. Contents: Vol. 1: Counties of Austin, Bastrop, Bexar, Brazoria, Colorado, Fannin, Fayette, Fort Bend, Galveston, Goliad, Gonzales, Harris, Harrison, Houston, Jackson, and Jasper; Vol. 2: Counties of Jefferson, Liberty, Matagorda, Milam, Montgomery, Nacogdoches, Red River, Refugio, Robertson, Sabine, San Augustine, Shelby, Victoria, and Washington. FHL book 976.4 R2er v. 1&2.

■ ***Republic of Texas: Poll Lists For 1846,*** by Marion Day Mullins, published by Genealogical Publishing Co., Inc., Baltimore, 1974, 189 pages. FHL book 976.4 R4m.

■ ***Early Settlers and Indian Fighters of Southwest Texas: Facts Gathered From Survivors of Frontier Days,*** by A. J. Sowell, originally published by B. C. Jones, printers, 1900; facsimile reproduction, including new index, published by State House Press, Austin, TX, 1986, 861 pages. FHL book 976.4 H2saj 1986.

■ ***Taxpayers of the Republic of Texas: Covering 30 counties and the District of Panola,*** compiled by Beth and Emily Dorman. Published by the authors, 1988, Grand Prairie, TX, 275 pages. Includes index. FHL book 976.4 R4d. Also on microfiche, FHL film #6007392.

■ **1837-1959 Texas County Tax Rolls on Microfilm** are available for onsite use at the Texas State Library in Austin. Virtually every county of Texas is represented, from the early years of each county through the late 1970s. Microfilm through 1901 is available to be borrowed through the Interlibrary loan program. **Series 1** (earliest rolls through 1910): Tax rolls are missing for some periods in the following counties: Archer 1870-1873; Armstrong 1870-1882; Baylor 1870-1873; Bowie 1840-1845, 1874, 1880; Encinal (Webb) 1856, 1868, 1870; Loving 1895-1897; Runnels 1842-1872, 1876; Stephens 1858-1860, 1866, 1868, 1871, 1873, 1876; and Ward 1842-1886. **Series 2 (1911-1921):** The following reels are missing: 1911 Reel #19; 1912 Reel #19; 1913 Reel #20; 1914 Reel #13; 1915 Reel #13; 1916 Reel #13, 14; 1917 Reel #14; 1918 Reel #13; 1919 Reel #13; 1920 Reel #13; 1921 Reel #14. **Series 3 (1922-1947):** The tax rolls have not been filmed for Encinal and Wilson. **Series 4 (1948-1959):** The tax rolls have not been filmed for the following counties: Maverick, McCulloch, McLennan, McMullen, Medina, Menard, Midland, Milam, Mills, Mitchell, Montague, Montgomery, Moore, Morris, Nacogdoches, Navarro, Newton, Nolan, Palo Pinto, Panola, Parker, Parmer, Pecos, Polk, Potter, Presidio, Rains, Randall, Reagan, Real, Red River, Reeves, Refugio, Roberts, Robertson, Rockwall, Runnels, Rusk, Sabine, San Augustine, San Jacinto, San Patricio, San Saba, Schleicher, Scurry, Shackelford, Shelby, Sherman, Smith, Somervell, Starr, Stephens, Sterling, Stonewall, Sutton, Swisher, Taylor, Terrell, Terry, Throckmorton, Titus, Wharton, Wheeler, Wichita, Wilbarger, and Willacy.

The 1837-1959 Texas County Tax Rolls are available through Interlibrary loan from the Texas State Library. Go to their Web page for instructions on how to borrow film through Interlibrary loan at **www.tsl.state.tx.us/.**

■ **1837-1910 Texas County Tax Rolls on Microfilm** at the Family History Library in Salt Lake City. The **Series 1** (earliest rolls through 1910) tax rolls filmed by the Texas State Library are available on 424 rolls at the Family History Library in Salt Lake City. Texas may not have state censuses, but there are thousands of name lists available from the tax rolls for virtually every county. The tax rolls are a boon for finding the name of an ancestor living in Texas, because the name of every taxpayer is shown, including real or personal property holders. Therefore, the tax rolls provide a more complete list of the adult residents of a county than any head of households census list. For the period 1837 to 1910, the Texas county tax lists are shown below by county, available tax year(s), and FHL film number:

- **Anderson,** 1846-1880, 1881, A-C; FHL film #2282072.
- **Anderson,** 1881, D-W; 1882-1889; 1890 A-K; FHL film #2282073.
- **Anderson,** 1890, K-Z; 1891-1896, 1897, A-H (I-Z not available at FHL); FHL film #2282074.
- **Andrews** and **Gaines,** 1883-1886; **Andrews,** 1887-1910, FHL film #2282075.
- **Angelina,** 1846-1891; 1892, A-S; FHL film #2282076.
- **Angelina,** 1892, S-Z; 1893-1906; 1907, A-L (M-Z not available FHL); FHL film #2282077.
- **Aransas,** 1872-1899; FHL film #2282078.
- **Archer,** 1869-1899; 1900, A-H (I-Z not available at FHL; 1874-1880 missing); FHL film #2282079.
- **Armstrong,** 1890-1910; FHL film #2282080.
- **Atascosa,** 1856-1883; 1884, C-G; FHL film #2282081.
- **Atascosa,** 1884, G-Y; 1885-1908; FHL film #2282082.
- **Austin County,** 1837-1880; 1881, A-S; FHL film #2282083.
- **Austin County,** 1881, S-Z; 1882-1892; 1893, A-G; FHL film #2282084.
- **Austin County,** 1893, G-Z; 1894-1901; FHL film #2282085.

- **Bandera,** 1856-1900; FHL film #2282086.
- **Bastrop,** 1837-1881; 1882, A; FHL film #2282087.
- **Bastrop,** 1882, B-W; 1883-1892; 1893, A-S; FHL film #2282088.
- **Bastrop,** 1893, S-Z; 1894-1898; FHL film #2282089.
- **Baylor,** 1869-1910; FHL film #2282090.
- **Bee,** 1859-1894; 1895, A-R; FHL film #2282091.
- **Bee,** 1895, S-W; 1896-1910; FHL film #2282092.
- **Bell,** 1852-1881; 1882, A; FHL film #2282093.
- **Bell,** 1882, B-Y; 1883-1888; 1889, A-C; FHL film #2282094.
- **Bell,** 1889, D-Y; 1889-1894; 1894, A-M; FHL film #2282095.
- **Bell,** 1894, N-W; 1895-1899; FHL film #2282096.
- **Bexar,** 1837-1872; 1873, A-L; FHL film #2282097.
- **Bexar,** 1873, L-W; 1874-1881; 1882, A-J; FHL film #2282098.
- **Bexar,** 1882, K-Z; 1883-1887; 1888, A-S; FHL film #2282099.
- **Bexar,** 1888, S-Z; 1889-1891; 1892, A-O; FHL film #2282100.
- **Bexar,** 1892, P-Z; 1893-1896; FHL film #2282101.
- **Blanco,** 1858-1902 (Years 1881-1883 missing); FHL film #2282102.
- **Borden,** 1880-1910 (includes **Bailey**); FHL film #2282103.
- **Bailey,** 1900 – see **Lamb**.
- **Bosque,** 1885, N-Z; 1886-1897; FHL film #2282105.
- **Bowie**, 1846-1885; 1886, A-L; (1840-1845, 1874, & 1880 missing); FHL film #2282106.
- **Bowie,** 1886, M-W; 1887-1894; 1895, A-B; FHL film #2282107.
- **Bowie,** 1895, B-Y; 1896-1903; FHL film #2282108.
- **Brazoria,** 1837-1883; 1884, A-D; FHL film #2282109.
- **Brazoria,** 1884, D-Z; 1885-1897; FHL film #2282
- **Brazos,** 1842-1887; 1888, A-D; FHL film #2282111.
- **Brazos,** 1888, D-Z; 1889-1894; 1895, A-C; FHL film #2282112.
- **Brazos,** 1895, C-Z; 1896-1908; FHL film #2282113.
- **Brewster,** 1887-1910; FHL film #2282114.
- **Briscoe,** 1879-1910; FHL film #2282115.
- **Brown,** 1859-1887; 1888, A; (1860, 1862-1866, 1869-1871 missing); FHL film #2282116.
- **Brown,** 1888, A-Y; 1888-1901; FHL film #2282117.
- **Burleson,** 1846-1887; 1888, A-J; FHL film #2282118.
- **Burleson,** 1888, J-Z; 1889-1901; FHL film #2282119.
- **Burnet,** 1852-1889; 1890, A-C; FHL film #2282120.
- **Burnet,** 1890, C-Z; 1891-1902; FHL film #2282121.
- **Caldwell,** 1848-1888; FHL film #2282122.
- **Caldwell,** 1889-1901, FHL film #2282123.
- **Calhoun,** 1846-1887; 1888, A-S; FHL film #2282124.
- **Calhoun,** 1888, S-W; 1889-1910; FHL film #2282125.
- **Callahan,** 1862-1903; FHL film #2282126.
- **Cameron,** 1848-1885; 1886, A-G; FHL film #2282127.
- **Cameron,** 1886, G-W; 1887-1900; FHL film #2282128.
- **Camp,** 1875-1905; FHL film #2282129.
- **Cass,** 1846-1877; 1878, A-B; FHL film #2282131.
- **Cass,** 1878, B-Z; 1879-1888; 1889, A-H; FHL film #2282132.
- **Cass,** 1889, H-Y; 1890-1899; FHL film #2282133.
- **Castro,** 1883-1910 (1884-1885 missing); FHL film #2282134. Another filming, FHL film #2282130.
- **Chambers,** 1858-1910 (1884-1885 missing); FHL film 2282135.
- **Cherokee,** 1846-1880; 1881, A-F; FHL film #2282136.
- **Cherokee,** 1881, F-Y; 1882-1892; FHL film #2282137.
- **Cherokee,** 1893-1901; FHL film #2282138.
- **Childress,** 1880-1910 (1881 missing); FHL film #2282139.
- **Clay,** 1861-1887; 1888, A-W; FHL film #2282140.
- **Clay,** 1888 misc.; 1889-1902; FHL film #2282141.
- **Cochran,** 1888-1910; **Yoakum,** 1888-1910 (1902, 1904 missing and 1903 filmed out of order); **Terry,** 1887-1910; **Lynn,** 1881-1910 (1882, 1884-1885 missing); FHL film #2282142.
- **Coleman,** 1867-1899 (1868-1872 missing), FHL film #2282143.
- **Collin,** 1846-1876; 1877, A-J; FHL film #2282144.
- **Collin,** 1877, J-Z; 1878-1882; 1883, A-L; FHL film #2282145.
- **Collin,** 1883, M-Y; 1884-1888; 1889, A-D; FHL film #2282146.
- **Collin,** 1889, D-Z; 1890-1891; 1892, A-Z; FHL film #2282147.
- **Collin,** 1892, misc.; 1893-1897; FHL film #2282148.
- **Collingsworth,** 1880-1888; Tax records primarily for **Wheeler**, 1879-1910. Also includes records of the following counties: **1880:** Childress, Hall, Potter, Gray, Briscoe, Armstrong, Hutchinson, Hartley, Hansford, Lipscomb, Oldham, Hemphill, Donley, and Roberts; **1881:** Childress, Hall, Donley, Roberts, Briscoe, Hutchinson, Gray,

Hansford, Lipscomb, Armstrong, Ochiltree, Greer, Hemphill, and Childress; **1882:** Hall, Lipscomb, Greer, Childress, Hutchinson, Hemphill, Armstrong, Gray, Hansford, Roberts, and Ochiltree; **1883:** Childress, Briscoe, Greer, Hall, Armstrong, Hemphill, Hutchinson, Lipscomb, Ochiltree, Hansford, Roberts, and Gray; **1884:** Roberts, Ochiltree, Lipscomb, Hansford, Hutchinson, Gray, Hemphill, and Greer; **1885:** Roberts, Ochiltree, Lipscomb, Hutchinson, Hemphill, Hansford, and Gray; **1886:** Gray, Greer, Hutchinson, Hemphill, Hansford, Lipscomb, Ochiltree, and Roberts; **1887:** Gray, Hutchinson, Hemphill, Hansford, Roberts, Ochiltree, and Lipscomb; **1888:** Gray, Roberts, Hutchinson, Hansford, and Ochiltree; FHL film #2282149.

- **Collingsworth**, 1889-1910; FHL film #2282150.
- **Colorado**, 1838-1878; 1879, A-W; (1839 missing); FHL film #2282151.
- **Colorado,** 1879, W-Z; 1880-1890; 1891, A-D; FHL film #2282152.
- **Colorado,** 1891, D-Z; 1892-1901; FHL film #2282153.
- **Comal,** 1846-1888; 1889, A-T; FHL film #2282154.
- **Comal**, 1889, T-Z; 1890-1909; FHL film #2282155.
- **Comanche,** 1857-1890; 1891, A-R; (1868-1870, 1872 missing); FHL film #2282156.
- **Comanche**, 1891, R-Z; 1892-1901; FHL film #2282157.
- **Concho,** 1865-1910 (1868-1876 missing); FHL film #2282158.
- **Cooke**, 1848-1883; 1884, A-J; FHL film #2282159.
- **Cooke,** 1884, J-Z; 1885-1891; 1892, A- Z; FHL film #2282000.
- **Cooke,** 1892, misc.; 1893-1900; FHL film #2282001.
- **Coryell,** 1855-1887; FHL film #2282002.
- **Coryell,** 1888-1898; FHL film #2282003.
- **Cottle,** 1881-1910; FHL film #2282004.
- **Crane,** 1887-1910 – see **Midland.**
- **Crockett,** 1875-1910 (1876-1881, 1883, 1888 missing); FHL film #2282005.
- **Crosby,** 1879-1910 (1883 missing); FHL film #2282006.
- **Dallam,** 1888-1910; FHL film #2282007.
- **Dallas,** 1846-1876; 1877, A-M; FHL film #2282008.
- **Dallas,**1877, M-Z; 1878-1881; 1882, A-W; FHL film #2282009.
- **Dallas,** 1882, W-Z; 1883-1886; 1887, A-E; FHL film #2282160.
- **Dallas,** 1887, E-Z; 1888-1889; 1890, A-K; FHL film #2282161.
- **Dallas,** 1890, K-Z; 1891-1892; 1893, A-J; FHL film #2282162.
- **Dallas,** 1893, J-Z; 1894-1896; FHL film #2282163.
- **Deaf Smith,** 1887-1910; FHL film #2282164.
- **Delta,** 1871-1885; 1886, A-C; FHL film #2282165.
- **Delta,** 1886, D-W; 1887-1902; FHL film #2282166.
- **Denton,** 1846-1882; 1883, A-S; FHL film #2282167.
- **Denton,** 1883, S-Z; 1884-1892; 1893, A; FHL film #2282168.
- **Denton,** 1893, A-Z; 1894-1900; FHL film #2282169.
- **Dewitt,** 1846-1889; 1890, A-D; FHL film #2282170.
- **Dewitt,** 1890, D-Z; 1891-1902; FHL film #2282171.
- **Dickens**, 1879-1910; FHL film #2282172.
- **Dimmitt,** 1874-1910; FHL film #2282173.
- **Donley,** 1880-1910; FHL film #2282174.
- **Duval,** 1887-1899; FHL film #2282175.
- **Eastland,** 1861-1897 (1862-1866, 1868-1873 missing); FHL film #2282176.
- **Ector,** 1887-1910; FHL film #2282177.
- **Edwards,** 1868-1910 (1869-1877 missing); FHL film #2282178.
- **El Paso,** 1852-1893; 1894, A-S; (1861-1864 missing); FHL film #2282179.
- **El Paso,** 1894, S-Z; 1895-1903; FHL film #2282180.
- **Ellis,** 1850-1879; 1880, A-H; FHL film #2282181.
- **Ellis,** 1880, H-Z; 1881-1885; 1886,. A-Z; FHL film #2282182.
- **Ellis,** 1886, Z; 1887-1891; FHL film #2282183.
- **Ellis,** 1892-1895; 1896, A-F (G-Z not available at FHL); FHL film #2282184.
- **Encinal,** 1856-1899 – see **Webb.**
- **Erath,** 1857-1889; 1890, A; FHL film #2282185.
- **Erath,** 1890, B-Z; 1891-1899; FHL film #2282186.
- **Falls,** 1851-1884; 1885, A-G; FHL film #2282187.
- **Falls,** 1885, G-Z; 1886-1893; 1894, A-T; FHL film #2282188.
- **Falls,** 1894, T-Z; 1895-1901; FHL film #2282189.
- **Fannin,** 1838-1876; 1877, A-L; FHL film #2282190.
- **Fannin,** 1877, L-Z; 1878-1883; 1884, A-C; FHL film #2282191.
- **Fannin**, 1884, C-Y; 1885-1888; 1889, A-G; FHL film #2282192.
- **Fannin,** 1889, G-Z; 1890-1893; 1894, A-J; FHL film #2282193.
- **Fannin,** 1894, J-Z; 1895-1898; FHL film #2282194.
- **Fayette,** 1837-1876; 1877, A-Z; (1844 missing); FHL

film #2282195.

- **Fayette,** 1877, Z; 1878-1885; 1886, A-P; FHL film #2282196.
- **Fayette,** 1886, P-Z; 1887-1892; 1893, A-B; FHL film #2282197.
- **Fayette,** 1893, C-Z; 1894-1899; FHL film #2282198.
- **Fisher,** 1879-1910; FHL film #2282199.
- **Floyd,** 1879-1910; (1880, 1882 missing); FHL film #2282200.
- **Foard,** 1891-1910; FHL film #228220.
- **Fort Bend,** 1838-1888; 1889, A-B; FHL film #2282202.
- **Fort Bend,** 1889, C-Z; 1890-1900; FHL film #2282203.
- **Franklin,** 1875-1896; FHL film #2282204.
- **Freestone,** 1851-1873; 1874, A-Y; FHL film #2282205.
- **Freestone,** 1874 supp.; 1875-1889; 1890, A-P; FHL film #2282206.
- **Freestone,** 1890, P-Y; 1891-1902; FHL film #2282207.
- **Frio,** 1867-1898 (1868, 1870 missing); FHL film #2282208.
- **Gaines,** 1883-1886 – see **Anderson.**
- **Gaines,** 1883-1910; FHL film #2282209.
- **Galveston,** 1838-1870; 1871, A-C; FHL film #2282210.
- **Galveston,** 1871, C-Z; 1872-1877; 1878, A-J; FHL film #2282211.
- **Galveston,** 1878, J-Z; 1879-1883; 1884, A-M; FHL film #2282212.
- **Galveston,** 1884, M-Z; 1885-1888; 1889, A-M; FHL film #2282213.
- **Galveston,** 1889, M-Z; 1890-1892; 1893, A-H; FHL film #2282214.
- **Galveston,** 1893, H-Z; 1894-1897; FHL film #2282215.
- **Garza** – see **Kent.**
- **Gillespie,** 1848-1891; 1892, A-W; FHL film #2282216.
- **Gillespie,** 1892, W-Z; 1893-1901; FHL film #2282217.
- **Glasscock,** 1887-1910; (1892 missing); FHL film #2282218.
- **Goliad,** 1846-1896; FHL film #2282219.
- **Gonzales,** 1837-1879; 1880, A-M; FHL film #2282220.
- **Gonzales,** 1880, M-Z; 1881-1892; 1893, A-K; FHL film #2282221.
- **Gonzales,** 1893, K-Z; 1894-1902; FHL film #2282222.
- **Gray,** 1879-1893; **Wheeler,** 1879-1910; tax records primarily for Wheeler County 1880-1910. Also includes records of the following counties: **1880:** Childress, Hall, Potter, Briscoe, Armstrong, Collingsworth, Hutchinson, Hartley, Hansford, Lipscomb, Oldham, Hemphill, and Donley; **1881:** Hall, Donley, Robert, Briscoe, Hutchinson, Hansford, Lipscomb, Armstrong, Ochiltree, Greer, Hemphill, and Collingsworth; **1882:** Hall, Lipscomb, Greer, Collingsworth, Hutchinson, Hemphill, Armstrong, Hansford, Roberts, Ochiltree, and Childress; **1883:** Briscoe, Greer, Hall, Childress, Armstrong, Hemphill, Hutchinson, Lipscomb, Ochiltree, Hansford, Roberts, and Collingsworth; **1884:** Roberts, Ochiltree, Lipscomb, Hansford, Hutchinson, Hemphill, Greer, and Collingsworth; **1885:** Roberts, Ochiltree, Lipscomb, Hutchinson, Hemphill, Hansford, Greer, and Collingsworth; **1886:** Collingsworth, Greer, Hutchinson, Hemphill, Hansford, Lipscomb, Ochiltree, and Roberts; **1887:** Collingsworth, Hutchinson, Hemphill, Hansford, Roberts, Ochiltree, and Lipscomb; **1888:** Roberts, Hutchinson, Hansford, Ochiltree, and Collingsworth; FHL film #2282223.
- **Gray,** 1898-1899, & 1901 – see **Roberts.**
- **Grayson,** 1846-1871; 1872, A-C; FHL film #2282224.
- **Grayson,** 1872, C-Z; 1873-1871; 1880, A-P; FHL film #2282225.
- **Grayson,** 1880, P-Z; 1881-1884; 1885, A-H; FHL film #2282226.
- **Grayson,** 1885, H-Z; 1886-1888; 1889, A-M; FHL film #2282227.
- **Grayson,** 1889, M-Z; 1890-1892; 1893, A-C; FHL film #2282228.
- **Grayson,** 1893, C-Z; 1894-1896; FHL film #2282229.
- **Greer,** 1881-1895; FHL film #2282230.
- **Gregg,** 1873-1899; FHL film #2282231.
- **Grimes,** 1846-1878; 1879, A-C; FHL film #2282232.
- **Grimes,** 1879, C-Y; 1880-1889; 1890, A-H; FHL film #2282233.
- **Grimes,** 1890, H-W; 1891-1901; FHL film #2282234.
- **Guadalupe,** 1846-1887; 1888, A; FHL film #2282235.

- **Guadalupe,** 1888, A-Z; 1889-1902; FHL film #2282236.
- **Hale,** 1883-1910; FHL film #2282237.
- **Hall,** 1880-1894; **Wheeler**, 1880-1910; Tax records primarily for Wheeler 1880-1894. Also includes the following counties: **1880:** Childress, Hansford, Potter, Gray, Briscoe, Armstrong, Collingsworth, Hutchinson, Hartley, Lipscomb, Oldham, Hemphill, Donley, and Roberts; **1881:** Hansford, Donley, Roberts, Briscoe, Hutchinson, Gray, Lipscomb, Armstrong, Ochiltree, Greer, Hemphill, and Collingsworth; **1882:** Hansford, Lipscomb, Greer, Collingsworth, Hutchinson, Hemphill, Armstrong, Gray, Roberts, Ochiltree, and Childress; **1883:** Briscoe, Greer, Childress, Armstrong, Hemphill, Hutchinson, Lipscomb, Ochiltree, Hansford, Roberts, Collingsworth, and Gray; **1884:** Roberts, Ochiltree, Lipscomb, Hansford, Hutchinson, Gray, Hemphill, Greer, and Collingsworth; **1885:** Roberts, Ochiltree, Lipscomb, Hutchinson, Hemphill, Hansford, Greer, Gray, and Collingsworth; **1886:** Collingsworth, Gray, Greer, Hutchinson, Hemphill, Hansford, Lipscomb, Ochiltree, and Roberts; **1887:** Collingsworth, Gray, Hutchinson, Hemphill, Hansford, Roberts, Ochiltree, and Lipscomb; **1888:** Gray, Roberts, Hutchinson, Hansford, Ochiltree, Collingsworth; **1889-1890**, & **1892-1894**: Gray; FHL film #2282238.
- **Hall,** 1883-1910; FHL film #2282239.
- **Hamilton,** 1858-1896 (1870 missing); FHL film #2282240.
- **Hansford,** 1880-1888; **Wheeler**, 1880-1888; tax records primarily for Wheeler County 1879-1910. Also includes records of the following counties: **1880:** Childress, Hall, Potter, Gray, Briscoe, Armstrong, Collingsworth, Hutchinson, Hartley, Lipscomb, Oldham, Hemphill, Donley, and Roberts; **1881:** Hall, Donley, Roberts, Briscoe, Hutchinson, Gray, Lipscomb, Armstrong, Ochiltree, Greer, Hemphill, Collingsworth; **1882:** Hall, Lipscomb, Greer, Collingsworth, Hutchinson, Hemphill, Armstrong, Gray, Roberts, Ochiltree, and Childress; **1883:** Briscoe, Greer, Hall, Childress, Armstrong, Hemphill, Hutchinson, Lipscomb, Ochiltree, Roberts, Collingsworth, and Gray; **1884-1886:** Roberts, Ochiltree, Lipscomb, Hutchinson, Gray, Hemphill, Greer, and Collingsworth; **1887:** Collingsworth, Gray, Hutchinson, Hemphill, Roberts, Ochiltree, and Lipscomb; **1888:** Gray, Roberts, Hutchinson, Ochiltree, and Collingsworth; **1889-1894:** Gray, FHL film #2282241.
- **Hansford,** 1889-1910; FHL film #2282242.
- **Hardeman,** 1868-1894; 1895, A-R; FHL film #2282243.
- **Hardeman,** 1895, R-Y; 1896-1910; FHL film #2282244.
- **Hardin,** 1859-1893; FHL film #2282245.
- **Hardin,** 1894-1910; FHL film #2282246.
- **Harris,** 1837-1872; FHL film #2282247.
- **Harris,** 1873-1880; 1881, A-B; FHL film #2282248.
- **Harris,** 1881, B-Z; 1882-1887; 1888, A-P; FHL film #2282249.
- **Harris,** 1888, P-Z; 1889-1893; 1894, A-D; FHL film #2282250.
- **Harris,** 1894, D-Z; 1895-1897; FHL film #2282251.
- **Harrison,** 1840-1875; 1876, A-Y; FHL film #2282252.
- **Harrison,** 1876 supp.; 1877-1885; 1886, A-H; FHL film #2282253.
- **Harrison,** 1886, H-Y; 1887-1893; 1894, A-L; FHL film #2282254.
- **Harrison,** 1894, L-Z; 1895-1901; FHL film #2282255.
- **Hartley,** 1880-1910; (1885-1887 missing); FHL film #2282256.
- **Haskell,** 1875-1897; (1881, 1884 missing); FHL film #2282257.
- **Hays,** 1848-1892; 1893, A-M; FHL film #2282258.
- **Hays,** 1893, M-Y; 1894-1910; FHL film #2282259.
- **Hemphill,** 1880-1887; **Wheeler**, 1879-1910: Tax records primarily for Wheeler County 1879-1910. Also includes records of the following counties: **1880:** Childress, Hall, Potter, Gray, Briscoe, Armstrong, Collingsworth, Hutchinson, Hartley, Hansford, Lipscomb, Oldham, Donley, and Roberts; **1881:** Hall, Donley, Roberts, Briscoe, Hutchinson, Gray, Hansford, Lipscomb, Armstrong, Ochiltree, Greer, and Collingsworth; **1882:** Hall, Lipscomb, Greer, Collingsworth, Hutchinson, Armstrong, Gray, Hansford, Roberts, Ochiltree, and Childress; **1883:** Briscoe, Greer, Hall, Childress, Armstrong, Hutchinson, Lipscomb, Ochiltree, Hansford, Roberts, Collingsworth, and Gray; **1884:** Roberts, Ochiltree, Lipscomb, Hansford, Hutchinson, Gray, Greer, and Collingsworth; **1885:** Roberts, Ochiltree, Lipscomb, Hutchinson, Hansford, Greer, Gray,

and Collingsworth; **1886:** Collingsworth, Gray, Greer, Hutchinson, Hansford, Lipscomb, Ochiltree, and Roberts; **1887:** Collingsworth, Gray, Hutchinson, Hansford, Roberts, Ochiltree, and Lipscomb; **1888:** Gray, Roberts, Hutchinson, Hansford, Ochiltree, and Collingsworth; FHL film #2282260.
- **Hemphill,** 1887 supp.; 1888-1910; FHL film #2282261.
- **Henderson**, 1846-1889; 1890, A; FHL film #2282262.
- **Henderson,** 1890, A-Y; 1891-1903; FHL film #2282263.
- **Hidalgo,** 1852-1905; (1856, 1858-1864 missing); FHL film #2282264.
- **Hill,** 1853-1882; 1883, A-Y; FHL film #2282265.
- **Hill,** 1883 supp.; 1884-1890; 1891, A-B; FHL film #2282266.
- **Hill,** 1891, B-Z; 1892-1897; FHL film #2282267.
- **Hockley,** 1887-1910; FHL film # 2282268.
- **Hood,** 1867-1899; FHL film #2282269.
- **Hopkins,** 1846-1881; 1882, A-B; FHL film #2282270.
- **Hopkins,** 1882, B-Z; 1883-1890; 1891, A-P; FHL film #2282271.
- **Hopkins,** 1891, P-Z; 1892-1898; FHL film #2282272.
- **Houston County,** 1838-1880; 1881, A-W; FHL film #2282273.
- **Houston County,** 1881, W-Z; 1882-1892; 1893, A-FHL film #2282274.
- **Houston County,** 1893 C-Z; 1894-1902; FHL film #2282275.
- **Hunt,** 1846-1872; 1873, A-C; FHL film #2282276.
- **Hunt,** 1873, C-Y; 1884; 1885, A; FHL film #2282277.
- **Hunt,** 1885, A-Y; 1886-1890; 1891, A-J; FHL film #2282278.
- **Hunt,** 1891, J-Y; 1892-1896; FHL film #2282279.
- **Hutchinson,** 1880-1888; Tax records primarily for **Wheeler** County, 1879-1910; also includes records of the following counties: **1880:** Childress, Hall, Potter, Gray, Briscoe, Armstrong, Collingsworth, Hartley, Hansford, Lipscomb, Oldham, Hemphill, Donley, and Roberts; **1881:** Hall, Donley, Roberts, Briscoe, Gray, Hansford, Lipscomb, Armstrong, Ochiltree, Greer, Hemphill, and Collingsworth; **1882:** Hall, Lipscomb, Greer, Collingsworth, Hemphill, Armstrong, Gray, Hansford, Roberts, Ochiltree, and Childress; **1883:** Briscoe, Greer, Hall, Childress, Armstrong, Hemphill, Lipscomb, Ochiltree, Hansford, Roberts, Collingsworth, and Gray; **1884-1885:** Roberts, Ochiltree, Lipscomb, Hansford, Gray, Hemphill, Greer, and Collingsworth; **1886:** Collingsworth, Gray, Greer, Hemphill, Hansford, Lipscomb, Ochiltree, and Roberts; **1887:** Collingsworth, Gray, Hemphill, Hansford, Roberts, Ochiltree, and Lipscomb; **1888:** Gray, Roberts, Hansford, Ochiltree, and Collingsworth; FHL film #2282280.
- **Hutchinson,** 1889 – see **Roberts.**
- **Irion,** 1889-1910; FHL film #2282281.
- **Jack,** 1857-1894; 1895, A-W; (1867 missing); FHL film #2282282.
- **Jack,** 1895, W-Z; 1896-1904; FHL film #2282283.
- **Jackson,** 1837-1898; FHL film #2282284.
- **Jasper,** 1837-1897; FHL film #2282285.
- **Jeff Davis,** 1887-1910; FHL film #2282286.
- **Jefferson,** 1846-1900; (1848 missing); FHL film #2282287.
- **Johnson,** 1855-1882; 1883, A-D; FHL film #2282288.
- **Johnson,** 1883, D-Y; 1884-1891; 1892, A-B; FHL film #2282289.
- **Johnson,** 1892, B-Z; 1894-1898; FHL film #2282290.
- **Jones,** 1867-1908 (1868-1873, 1875-1876 missing); FHL film #2282291.
- **Karnes,** 1854-1898; FHL film #2282292.
- **Kaufman,** 1849-1883; 1884, A-C; FHL film #2282293.
- **Kaufman,** 1884, C-Z; 1885-1891; 1892, A-Y; FHL film #2282294.
- **Kaufman,** 1892, Y-Z; 1893-1900; FHL film #2282295.
- **Kendall,** 1862-1910; FHL film #2282296.
- **Kent,** 1879-1910 (1884-1885 missing); **Garza**, 1880-1910; (1884-1885, 1896-1897 missing); FHL film #2282297.
- **Kerr,** 1856-1901; FHL film #2282298.
- **Kimble,** 1876-1910; FHL film #2282299.
- **Kinney,** 1861-1919 (1862-1864, 1867, 1869-1872 missing); FHL film #2282300.
- **Knox,** 1874-1910; (1875-1900 missing); FHL film #2282301.
- **Lamar,** 1842-1877; 1878, A; (1849 filmed out of order); FHL film #2282302.
- **Lamar,** 1878, A-Z; 1879-1883; 1884, A-L; FHL film #2282303.
- **Lamar,** 1884, M-Z; 1885-1888; 1889, A-V; FHL film #2282304.

- **Lamar,** 1889, W-Z; 1890-1892; 1893, A-E; FHL film #2282305.
- **Lamar,** 1893, E-Z; 1894-1897; FHL film # 2282306.
- **Lamb,** 1883-1910 (1886 missing);
- **Bailey**, 1900;
- **King**, 1881-1910; FHL film #2282307.
- **Lampasas,** 1856-1897; FHL film #2282308.
- **LaSalle,** 1871-1910 (1874-1878, 1880 missing); FHL film # 2282309.
- **Lavaca,** 1846-1885; 1886, A-C; FHL film # 2282310.
- **Lavaca,** 1886, C-Z; 1887-1895; 1896, A-M; FHL film #2282311.
- **Lavaca,** 1896, M-Z; 1897-1905; FHL film #2282312.
- **Lee,** 1874-1894; 1895, A-V; FHL film #282313.
- **Lee,** 1895, V-Z; 1896-1910; FHL film #2282314
- **Leon,** 1846-1886; 1887, A-B; FHL film #2282315.
- **Leon,** 1887, B-Z; 1888-1901; FHL film #2282316.
- **Liberty,** 1837-1894; 1895, A-B; (1849 missing); FHL film # 2282317.
- **Liberty,** 1895, B-Y; 1896-1910; FHL film # 2282318.
- **Limestone,** 1846-1882; 1883, A-Z; FHL film #2282319.
- **Limestone,** 1883 supp.; 1884-1892; 1893, A-S; FHL film #2282320.
- **Limestone,** 1893, S-Z; 1894-1901; FHL film #2282321.
- **Lipscombe,** 1880-1887; Tax records primarily for **Wheeler**, 1879-1910; Also includes records of the following counties: **1880:** Childress, Hall, Potter, Gray, Briscoe, Armstrong, Collingsworth, Hutchinson, Hartley, Hansford, Oldham, Hemphill, Donley, and Roberts; **1881:** Hall, Donley, Roberts, Briscoe, Hutchinson, Gray, Hansford, Armstrong, Ochiltree, Greer, Hemphill, and Collingsworth; **1882:** Hall, Greer, Collingsworth, Hutchinson, Hemphill, Armstrong, Gray, Hansford, Roberts, Ochiltree, and Childress; **1883:** Briscoe, Greer, Hall, Childress, Armstrong, Hemphill, Hutchinson, Ochiltree, Hansford, Roberts, Collingsworth, and Gray; **1884-1885:** Roberts, Ochiltree, Hutchinson, Hansford, Gray, Hemphill, Greer, and Collingsworth; **1886:** Collingsworth, Gray, Greer, Hutchinson, Hemphill, Hansford, Ochiltree, and Roberts; **1887:** Collingsworth, Gray, Hutchinson, Hemphill, Hansford, Roberts, and Ochiltree; **1888:** Gray, Roberts, Hutchinson, Hansford, Ochiltree, and Collingsworth; FHL film #2282322.
- **Lipscomb,** 1887-1910; FHL film #2282323.
- **Live Oak,** 1857-1891; 1892, A-G; (1869 missing); FHL film #2282324.
- **Live Oak,** 1892, H-W; FHL film #2282325.
- **Llano,** 1856-1898; FHL film #2282326.
- **Loving**, 1887-1910 – see **Reeves**.
- **Lubbock,** 1879-1910 (1890 missing); FHL film # 2282327.
- **Madison,** 1854-1899; FHL film #2282328.
- **Marion,** 1860-1887; 1888, A-R; FHL film #2282329.
- **Marion,** 1888, R-Z; 1889-1903; FHL film #2282330.
- **Martin,** 1883-1910 (1885 missing); FHL film #2282331.
- **Mason,** 1859-1898; FHL film #2282332.
- **Matagorda,** 1846-1900; FHL film #2282333.
- **Maverick,** 1861-1910 (1862-1864, 1867, 1869-1871 missing); FHL film #2282334.
- **McCulloch,** 1862-1903 (1864, 1868, 1876 missing); FHL film #2282335.
- **McLennan,** 1851-1878; 1879, A-W; FHL film #2282336.
- **McLennan,** 1879, W-Z; 1880-1885; 1886, A-F; FHL film #2282337.
- **McLennan,** 1886, F-Z; 1887-1890; 1891, A-M; FHL film #2282338.
- **McLennan,** 1891, M-Z; 1892-1894; 1895, A-S; FHL film #2282339.
- **McLennan,** 1895, S-Z; 1896-1899; FHL film #2282340.
- **McMullen,** 1839-1910 (1864-1871, 1874-1876 missing); FHL film #2282341.
- **Medina,** 1848-1877; 1878, A-L; FHL film #2282342.
- **Medina,** 1878, L-Y; 1879-1900; FHL film #2282343.
- **Menard,** 1841-1910 (1842-1866, 1869-1871, 1875 missing); FHL film #2282344.
- **Midland,** 1841-1910; **Upton**, 1887-1910; **Crane**, 1887-1910; (1890, 1901 missing for all counties); FHL film #2282345.
- **Milam,** 1846-1882; 1883, A; FHL film #2282346.
- **Milam,** 1883, F-Z; 1884-1890; 1891, A-K; FHL film #2282347.
- **Milam,** 1891, K-Z; 1892-1898; FHL film #2282348.
- **Mills,** 1887-1898; FHL film #2282349.
- **Mitchell,** 1880-1910; FHL film #2282350.
- **Montague,** 1858-1888; 1889, A-M (1860 missing); FHL film #2282351.
- **Montague,** 1889, M-Z; 1890-1897; FHL film #2282352.
- **Montgomery,** 1838-1887; FHL film #2282353.
- **Montgomery,** 1887 supp.; 1888-1902; FHL film #2282354.

- **Moore,** 1884-1910 (1885-1887 missing); FHL film #2282355.
- **Morris,** 1875-1906; FHL film #2282356.
- **Motley,** 1879-1900 (1880 missing); FHL film #2282357.
- **Nacogdoches,** 1837-1879; 1880, A-B; (1843 missing); FHL film #2282358.
- **Nacogdoches,** 1880, B-Z; 1881-1894; 1895, A-C; FHL film #2282359.
- **Nacogdoches,** 1895, C-Z; 1896-1905; FHL film #2282360.
- **Navarro,** 1846-1878; 1879, A-P; FHL film #2282361.
- **Navarro,** 1879, P-Z; 1880-1887; 1888, A-B; FHL film #2282362.
- **Navarro,** 1888, B-Z; 1889-1893; 1894, A-G; FHL film #2282363.
- **Navarro,** 1894, G-Z; 1895-1899; FHL film #2282364.
- **Newton,** 1847-1888 (1849 missing); FHL film #2282365.
- **Newton,** 1888 supp.;1889; FHL film #2282366.
- **Nolan,** 1879-1910; FHL film #2282367.
- **Nueces,** 1846; 1881-1888; FHL film #2282368.
- **Ochiltree,** 1881-1888; **Wheeler**, 1879-1910; tax records primarily for Wheeler County 1880-1910. Also includes records of the following counties: **1880:** Childress, Hall, Potter, Gray, Briscoe, Armstrong, Collingsworth, Hutchinson, Hartley, Hansford, Lipscomb, Oldham, Hemphill, Donley, and Roberts; **1881:** Hall, Donley, Roberts, Briscoe, Hutchinson, Gray, Hansford, Lipscomb, Armstrong, Greer, Hemphill, and Collingsworth; **1882:** Hall, Lipscomb, Greer, Collingsworth, Hutchinson, Hemphill, Armstrong, Gray, Hansford, Roberts, and Childress; **1883:** Briscoe, Greer, Hall, Childress, Armstrong, Hemphill, Hutchinson, Lipscomb, Hansford, Roberts, Collingsworth, and Gray; **1884:** Roberts, Lipscomb, Hansford, Hutchinson, Gray, Hemphill, Greer, and Collingsworth; **1885:** Roberts, Lipscomb, Hutchinson, Hemphill, Hansford, Greer, Gray, and Collingsworth; **1886:** Collingsworth, Gray, Greer, Hutchinson, Hemphill, Hansford, Lipscomb, and Roberts; **1887:** Collingsworth, Gray, Hutchinson, Hemphill, Hansford, Roberts, and Lipscomb; **1888:** Gray, Roberts, Hutchinson, Hansford, and Collingsworth; FHL film #2282369.
- **Oldham,** 1880-1910 (1882 missing); FHL film #2282371.
- **Orange,** 1852-1902 (1865-1866, 1879, missing); FHL film #2282372.
- **Palo Pinto,** 1857-1896 (1869 missing); FHL film #2282373.
- **Panola,** 1841-1884; 1885, A-J; FHL film #2282374.
- **Panola,** 1885, K-W; 1886-1899; FHL film #2282375.
- **Parker,** 1856-1884; 1885, A-B; FHL film #2282376.
- **Parker,** 1885, B-Z; 1886-1892; 1893, A-G; FHL film #2282377.
- **Parker,** 1893, H-W; 1894-1901; FHL film #2282378.
- **Parmer,** 1887-1910 (1891-1893, 1900, 1902-1904 missing); FHL film #2282379.
- **Pecos,** 1873-1910; FHL film #2282380.
- **Polk,** 1846-1890; 1891, A-R; FHL film #2282381.
- **Polk,** 1891, R-Z; 1992-1904; FHL film #2282382.
- **Potter,** 1879-1905 (1882 missing); FHL film #2282383.
- **Presidio,** 1876-1900; FHL film #2282384.
- **Rains,** 1871-1888; 1889, A-B; FHL film #2282385.
- **Rains,** 1889, B-Y; 1890-1910; FHL film #2282386.
- **Randall,** 1881-1910; FHL film #2282387.
- **Red River,** 1838-1880; 1881, A-G; FHL film #2282388.
- **Red River,** 1881, G-Z; 1882-1890; 1891, A-L; FHL film #2282389.
- **Red River,** 1891; 1892-1899; FHL film #2282390.
- **Reeves,** 1885-1910 (1883-1884 missing). Also includes records of the following counties: **Loving**, 1887- 1910 (1895-1897 missing); and **Winkler**, 1887-1910; FHL film #2282391.
- **Refugio,** 1847-1910; FHL film #2282392.
- **Roberts,** 1880-1888; **Wheeler**, 1879-1910; tax records primarily for Wheeler County 1880-1910. Also includes records of the following counties: **1880:** Childress, Hall, Potter, Gray, Briscoe, Armstrong, Collingsworth, Hutchinson, Hartley, Hansford, Lipscomb, Oldham, Hemphill, and Donley; **1881:** Hall, Donley, Briscoe, Hutchinson, Gray, Hansford, Lipscomb, Armstrong, Ochiltree, Greer, Hemphill, and Collingsworth; **1882:** Hall, Lipscomb, Greer, Collingsworth, Hutchinson, Hemphill, Armstrong, Gray, Hansford, Ochiltree, and Childress; **1883:** Briscoe, Greer, Hall, Childress, Armstrong, Hemphill, Hutchinson, Lipscomb, Ochiltree, Hansford, Collingsworth, and Gray; **1884:** Ochiltree, Lipscomb, Hansford, Hutchinson, Gray, Hemphill, Greer, and Collingsworth; **1885:** Ochiltree, Lipscomb, Hutchinson, Hemphill, Hansford, Greer, Gray, and Collingsworth; **1886:** Collingsworth, Gray, Greer, Hutchinson, Hemphill, Hansford, Lipscomb, and

Ochiltree; **1887:** Collingsworth, Gray, Hutchinson, Hemphill, Hansford, Ochiltree, and Lipscomb; **1888:** Gray, Hutchinson, Hansford, Ochiltree, and Collingsworth; FHL film #2282393.

- **Roberts,** 1889-1910; also includes records of the following counties: **Gray**, 1898-1899, & 1901; and **Hutchinson**, 1899; FHL film #2282394.
- **Robertson,** 1838-1881; 1882, A-M; FHL film #2282395.
- **Robertson,** 1882, M-Y; 1883-1890; 1891, A-S; FHL film #2282396.
- **Robertson,** 1891, S-Y; 1892-1899; FHL film #2282397.
- **Rockwall,** 1873-1890; FHL film #2282398.
- **Rockwall,** 1890 supp.; 1891-1910; FHL film #2282399.
- **Runnels,** 1841-1876 (1841-1872 & 1876 missing); FHL film #2282400.
- **Rusk,** 1842-1876; FHL film #2282401.
- **Rusk,** 1877-1887; 1888, A-F; FHL film #2282402.
- **Rusk,** 1888, F-Z; 1889-1898; FHL film #2282403.
- **Sabine,** 1837-1896; FHL film #2282404.
- **San Augustine,** 1837-1893; 1894, A-S; FHL film #2282405.
- **San Augustine,** 1894, S-Z; 1895-1910; FHL film #2282406.
- **San Jacinto,** 1871-1889; 1890, A-S; FHL film #2282407.
- **San Jacinto,** 1890, S-Z; 1891-1910; FHL film #2282408.
- **San Patricio,** 1846-1910; FHL film #2282409.
- **San Saba,** 1856-1896; FHL film #2282410.
- **Schleicher,** 1887-1910; FHL film #2282411.
- **Scurry,** 1880-1910 (1881-1884 missing); FHL film #2282412.
- **Schackelford,** 1867-1900 (1873-1874 missing); FHL film #2282413.
- **Shelby,** 1837-1887; 1888, A-C; FHL film #2282414.
- **Shelby,** 1888, C-W; 1889-1901; FHL film #2282415.
- **Sherman,** 1885-1910; FHL film #2282416.
- **Smith,** 1846-1878; 1879, A-S; FHL film #2282417.
- **Smith,** 1879, S-Z; 1880-1888; FHL film #2282418.
- **Smith,** 1888 supp.; 1889-1893; 1894, A-T; FHL film #2282419.
- **Smith,** 1894, T-Z; 1895-1900; FHL film #2282420.
- **Somerville,** 1876-1910; FHL film #2282421.
- **Starr,** 1849-1886; 1887, A-F; FHL film #2282422.
- **Starr,** 1887, F-Z; 1888-1910; FHL film #2282423.
- **Stephens,** 1861-1885; 1886, A-T (1858-1860, 1866, 1868 missing); FHL film #2282424.
- **Stephens,** (1871, 1873., 1876 missing); 1886, T-Z; 1887-1907; FHL film #2282425.
- **Sterling,** 1891-1910; FHL film #2282426.
- **Stonewall,** 1879-1906 (1884-1885 missing); FHL film #2282427.
- **Sutton,** 1887-1910 (1887-1889 are at the end of film; 1890 missing); FHL film #2282428.
- **Swisher,** 1884-1910; FHL film #2282429.
- **Tarrant,** 1850-1880; 1881, A-B; FHL film #2282430.
- **Tarrant,** 1881, B-Z; 1882-1886; 1887, A-H; FHL film #2282431.
- **Tarrant,** 1887, H-Z; 1888-1891; 1892, A-H; FHL film #2282432.
- **Tarrant,** 1892, H-Z; 1893-1896; FHL film #2282433.
- **Tarrant,** 1908, G-Z; 1909, A-S (T-Z not available at FHL); FHL film #2282434.
- **Taylor,** 1862-1899 (1863-1866, 1868-1877 missing); FHL film #2282435.
- **Throckmorton,** 1869-1910 (1870, 1872-1874, 1877-1878 missing); FHL film #2282436.
- **Titus,** 1846-1887; 1888, A-S; FHL film #2282437.
- **Titus,** 1888, S-Z; 1889-1902; FHL film #228238.
- **Tom Green,** 1875-1895; FHL film #2282439.
- **Tom Green,** 1895 supp.; 1896-1906; 1907, A (B-Z not available at FHL); FHL film #2282440.
- **Travis,** 1840-1871; 1872, A-S; FHL film #2282441.
- **Travis,** 1872, S-Z; 1873-1879; 1880, A-H; FHL film #2282442.
- **Travis,** 1880, H-Z; 1881-1886; 1887, A-C; FHL film #2282443.
- **Travis,** 1887, C-Z; 1888-1892; 1893, A-C; FHL film #2282444.
- **Travis,** 1893, C-Z; 1894-1898; FHL film #2282445.
- **Trinity,** 1850-1897; FHL film #2282446.
- **Tyler,** 1847-1892; 1893, A-K; FHL film #2282447.
- **Tyler,** 1893, K-Z; 1894-1910; FHL film #2282448.
- **Upshur,** 1846-1874; 1875, A-J; FHL film #2282449.
- **Upshur,** 1875 J-Z; 1876-1894; 1895, A-G; FHL film #2282450.
- **Upshur,** 1895, G-Z; 1896-1904; 1905, A-B (C-Z not available at FHL); FHL film #2282451.
- **Uvalde,** 1856-1900; 1901, A-T (U-Z not available at FHL); (1874 missing); FHL film #2282452.
- **Val Verde,** 1885-1900; 1901, A-E (F-Z not available at FHL); FHL film #2282453.
- **Van Zandt,** 1848-1885; 1886, A-G; FHL film #2282454.
- **Van Zandt,** 1886, G-Z; 1887-1896; 1897, A-H (I-Z not available at FHL); FHL film #2282455.
- **Victoria,** 1838-1892; 1893, A-B; FHL film #2282456.

- **Victoria,** 1893, B-Y; 1894-1902; 1903, A-B (C-Z not available at FHL); FHL film #2282457.
- **Walker,** 1846-1873; 1874, A-M; FHL film #2282458.
- **Walker,** 1874, M-W; 1875-1892; 1893, A-O; FHL film #2282459.
- **Walker,** 1893, P-W; 1894-1905; 1906,A-B (C-Z not available at FHL); FHL film #2282460.
- **Waller,** 1874-1893; 1894, A-N; FHL film #2282461.
- **Waller,** 1894, N-Z; 1895-1906; 1907, A (B-Z not available at FHL); FHL film #2282462.
- **Ward,** 1841-1910 (1842-1886, 1888 missing); FHL film #2282463.
- **Washington,** 1837-1877; 1878, A-H; FHL film #2282464.
- **Washington,** 1878, H-Z; 1879-1886; 1887, A-K; FHL film #2282465.
- **Washington,** 1887, K-Z; 1888-1896; 1897, A-F (G-Z not available at FHL); FHL film #2282466.
- **Webb,** 1851-1894; 1896, A-G; also includes records of Encinal, 1856-1899; FHL film #2282467.
- **Webb,** 1895, G-Y; 1896-1910; FHL film #2282468.
- **Wharton,** 1846-1889; 1899, A-R (S-Z not available at FHL); FHL film #2282469.
- **Wheeler,** 1879-1910; Also includes records of the following counties: **1880:** Childress, Hall, Potter, Gray, Briscoe, Armstrong, Collingsworth, Hutchinson, Hartley, Hansford, Lipscomb, Oldham, Hemphill, Donley, and Roberts; **1881:** Hall, Donley, Roberts, Briscoe, Hutchinson, Gray, Hansford, Lipscomb, Armstrong, Ochiltree, Greer, Hemphill, and Collingsworth; **1882:** Hall, Lipscomb, Greer, Collingsworth, Hutchinson, Hemphill, Armstrong, Gray, Hansford, Roberts, Ochiltree, and Childress; **1883:** Briscoe, Greer, Hall, Childress, Armstrong, Hemphill, Hutchinson, Lipscomb, Ochiltree, Hansford, Roberts, Collingsworth, and Gray; **1884:** Roberts, Ochiltree, Lipscomb, Hansford, Hutchinson, Gray, Hemphill, Greer, and Collingsworth; **1885:** Roberts, Ochiltree, Lipscomb, Hutchinson, Hemphill, Hansford, Greer, Gray, and Collingsworth; **1886:** Collingsworth, Gray, Greer, Hutchinson, Hemphill, Hansford, Lipscomb, Ochiltree, and Roberts; **1887:** Collingsworth, Gray, Hutchinson, Hemphill, Hansford, Roberts, Ochiltree, and Lipscomb; **1888:** Gray, Roberts, Hutchinson, Hansford, Ochiltree, and Collingsworth; FHL film #2282470.
- **Wichita,** 1868-1902; (1869-1871, 1873, 1877-1878, 1881, & 1883 missing); FHL film #2282471.
- **Wilbarger,** 1868-1898; 1899, A-B (C-Z not available at FHL); (1869-1873, 1877-1881, 1883 missing); FHL film #2282472.
- **Williamson,** 1848-1881; 1882, A-C; FHL film #2282473.
- **Williamson,** 1882, C-Z; 1886-1890; 1891, A-D; FHL film #2282474.
- **Williamson,** 1891, D-Z; 1892-1897; FHL film #2282475.
- **Wilson,** 1860-1896; 1897, A-B (C-Z not available at FHL); FHL film #2282476.
- **Winkler,** 1887-1910 – see **Reeves**.
- **Wise,** 1856-1885; 1886, A-L; FHL film #2282477.
- **Wise,** 1886, L-Z; 1887-1894; 1895, A-C; FHL film #2282478.
- **Wise,** 1895, C-Z; 1896-1900; 1901, A-M (N-Z not available at FHL); FHL film #2282479.
- **Wood,** 1850-1887; 1888, A-G; FHL film #2282480.
- **Wood,** 1888, G-Z; 1889-1900; 1901, A (B-Z not available at FHL); FHL film #2282481.
- **Young,** 1857-1884; 1885, A-H; (1865-1867, 1870, 1872-1874 missing); FHL film #2282482.
- **Young,** 1885, H-Z; 1886-1900; 1901, A-B (C-Z not available at FHL); FHL film #2282483.
- **Zapata,** 1858-1910 (1862-1864 missing); FHL film #2282484.
- **Zavala,** 1861-1910 (1862-1864, 1869-1873 missing); FHL film #2282485.

■ ***1858 State Census of Austin County, Texas Copied Under the Supervision of the Littlefield Fund and Assisted by Project No. 43 of the Bureau of Research in the Social Sciences at the University of Texas From Original Manuscripts Located in the Courthouse at Bellville, Texas,*** microfilm of originals in the Austin County courthouse in Bellville, Texas. Filmed by the Genealogical Society of Utah, 1992, 1 roll, FHL film #1838537.

■ ***1861-1865 Index to Compiled Service Records of Confederate Soldiers Who Served in Organizations From the State of Texas,*** microfilm of original records in the National Archives, Washington, DC, an alphabetical card index to the compiled service records of

Confederate soldiers belonging to units from the State of Texas, series M323, 41 rolls, beginning with FHL film #880014 (Surnames A – As). See also, ***1861-1865 Index to Compiled Service Records of Union Soldiers Who Served in Organizations From the State of Texas,*** microfilm of original records in the National Archives, Central Plains Region, Kansas City, MO, series M402, 2 rolls, FHL film #881592 (Index, A-Ma, 1861-1865), and #881593 (Index, Mc-Z, 1861-1865). Both publications included in ***Index to Soldiers & Sailors of the Civil War,*** a searchable name index to 6.3 million Union and Confederate Civil War soldiers now available online at the National Park Service Web site. A search can be done by surname, first name, state, or unit. Texas supplied 163,401 men to the war; 159,031 Confederate, and 4,370 Union. To search for one go to the NPS Web site at: **www.civilwar.nps.gov/cwss/.**

■ **1865-1866 Internal Revenue Assessment Lists for Texas**, microfilm of original records at the National Archives in Washington, DC. Contents: **District 2:** Atascosas, Austin, Bee, Calhoun, Cameron, Colorado, De Witt, Duval, Encinal (no longer exists), Fayette, Fort Bend, Frio, Goliad, Gonzales, Hidalgo, Jackson, Karnes, La Salle, Lavaca, Live Oak, McMullin, Matagorda, Maverick, Nueces, Refugio, San Patricio, Starr, Victoria, Washington, Webb, Wharton, Zapata, and Zavala counties. **District 3:** Archer, Bandera, Bastrop, Baylor, Bill, Bexar, Blanco, Bosque, Brown, Buchanan (no longer exists), Burleson, Burnet, Caldwell, Clay, Colahan (Callahan), Comal, Comanche, Concho, Cooke, Coryell, Dawson, Denton, Eastland, Edwards, El Paso, Erath, Falls, Gillespie, Guadalupe, Hamilton, Hardeman, Haskell, Hays, Hill, Jack, Johnson, Jones, Kemble (Kimble), Kerr, Kinney, Knox, Lampasas, Llano, McCulloch, Mason, Medina, Menard, Milam, Montague, Palo Pinto, Parker, Presidio, Runnels, San Saba, Shackelford, Tarrant, Taylor, Throckmorton, Travis, Uvalde, Wichita, Wilbargar (Wilbarger), Williamson, Wise, and Young counties. **District 4 pt 1:** Anderson, Bowie, Cass, Cherokee, Collin, Dallas, Ellis, Fannin, Freestone, Grayson, Harrison, Henderson, Hopkins, Hunt, Kaufman, Lamar, Limestone, Marion, Navarro, Panola, Red River, Rusk, Smith, Titus, Upshur, Van Zandt, and Wood counties. **District 4 pt 2:** Ellis, Freestone, Limestone, and Navarro counties. Names are arranged by collection district and thereunder by division. Filmed by the archives, 1987, 2 rolls, FHL film #1578479 (District 2) and film #1578480 (Districts 3-4).

■ **1867 Voters' Registration,** microfilm of originals at the Texas State Library & Archives Commission, Austin, Texas. Available through Interlibrary loan from the TX archives. (FHL has microfilm, but not for circulation). FHL title: *Texas 1867 Special Voter's Registration: Includes Information for 1867-1869.* The Reconstruction Act of March 13, 1867 required the commanding officer in each military district to have, before September 1, a registration of all qualified voters in each county. These lists would be used to determine all who would be eligible to vote for any proposed Constitutional Convention in the state. Forms include the following information: date of registration; county and precinct of residence; years resided in state; years resided in county; years resided in precinct; native of what state or county; how, when and where naturalized; signature; general remarks. Not all forms are completely filled out. Filmed by the Texas State Library, 1984, FHL has 7 rolls, as follows:

- **Anderson - Caldwell** counties, 1867, FHL film #1929135.
- **Calhoun - Falls** counties, 1869, FHL film #1929136.
- **Erath - Hamilton** counties, FHL film #1929137.
- **Hardin - Kinney** counties, FHL film #1929138.
- **Lamar - Orange** counties, FHL film #1929139.
- **Navarro - Tyler** counties, FHL film #1929140.
- **Tarrant - Zapata** counties, FHL film #1929141.

■ ***An index to the 1867 Voters Registration of Texas***, CD-ROM publication, compiled by

Donaly E. Brice & John C. Barron, published by Heritage Books, Bowie, MD, 2000. Lists voters arranged by county including name, date of registration, voting precinct, years of residence, state or country of birth. This is the first statewide listing of freed slaves in Texas. FHL CD-ROM No. 898.

■ **1874 History.** See ***A Texas Scrap-Book: Made up of the History, Biography, and Miscellany of Texas and its People,*** compiled by D. W. C. Baker, original published by A.S. Barnes and Co., New York, 1874, 657 pages. Filmed by W. C. Cox, Tucson, AZ, 1974, FHL film #1000596. Indexed in ***Index to D. W. C. Baker's A Texas Scrapbook,*** by Richard Morrison, published by the author, Austin, Texas, 1984, 153 pages. Includes name index, and index to sources and authors. FHL book 976.4 H2mr index.

■ **1884 History**. See ***Rangers and Pioneers of Texas: With a Concise Account of the Early Settlements, Hardships, Massacres, Battles, and Wars, by Which Texas Was Rescued From the Rule of the Savage and Consecrated to the Empire of Civilization,*** by A.J. Sowell, originally published by Shepard Bros. & Co., San Antonio, TX, 1884, 411 pages. Filmed for the FHL by the Library of Congress, 1991, 1 roll, FHL film #1730711.

■ **1890 Reconstructed Census**, name lists compiled from local tax and other records, by Mary C. Moody and others, published for the following Texas counties:

- **Bexar County,** (tax rolls of 1890), FHL book 976.435 R4a.
- **Caldwell County**, FHL book 976.433 X2m.
- **Limestone County**, FHL book 976.4285 X2m.
- **Montgomery County**, FHL book 976.4153 X2m.
- **Nacogdoches County** (index to 1890 tax list), FHL book 976.4182 R42e.
- **Smith County** (index to 1890 tax book), FHL book 976.4225 R48e.
- **Travis County**, FHL book 976.431 X2m, pt. 1 & pt 2 (index).
- **Walker County**, FHL book 976.4169 X2m.
- **Cass County**, FHL book 976.4195 X28m.
- **Hamilton County**, FHL book 976.4549 X2m.
- **Kerr County**, FHL book 976.4884 X2d.
- **Leon County**, FHL book 976.4233 X28m.

■ **1914 History**. See ***History of the Cattlemen of Texas: A Brief Résumé of the Live Stock Industry of the Southwest and a Biographical Sketch of Many of the Important Characters Whose Lives are Interwoven Therein,*** with an introduction by Harwood P. Hinton; series editor, David Farmer, originally published by Johnston Printing & Advertising Co., 1914, 350 pages. Reprint by Texas State Historical Association in cooperation with the Center for Studies in Texas History at the University of Texas at Austin. Includes index and bibliographical references. FHL book 976.4 U2h. See also ***The Trail Drivers of Texas: Interesting Sketches of Early Cowboys and Their Experiences on the Range and on the Trail During the Days That Tried Men's Souls, True Narratives Related by Real Cow-punchers and Men Who Fathered the Cattle Industry in Texas,*** originally compiled and edited by J. Marvin Hunter; introduction by B. Byron Price, published by the University of Texas Press, Austin, TX, 1985, 1,085 pages. Includes index. FHL book 976.4 H2hj.

■ **1917-1918 World War I Selective Service System Draft Registration Cards,** microfilm of original records in the National Archives in East Point, Georgia. The draft cards are arranged alphabetically by state, then alphabetically by county or city, and then alphabetically by surname of registrants. Cards are arranged in a rough alphabetical order by surname. Filmed by the National Archives, 1987-1988, 183 rolls, beginning with FHL film #1927189 (Texas, Anderson County, A-I).

ONSITE Genealogy Resources at the Texas State Library

■ *Texas Convict Record Ledgers and Indexes.* The record ledgers are excellent sources of individual convict descriptions and information regarding their incarceration. This series, available for use only on microfilm, may be viewed on-site in the Genealogy Reading Room, Tuesday - Saturday, 8 a.m. - 4:45 p.m. or borrowed through the Interlibrary loan program.

■ **Selected Texas City Directories** from the past are available for onsite use in the Genealogy Reading Room, Texas State Library, Austin, TX, Tuesday through Saturday, 8 a.m. - 5 p.m.

■ **Newspapers Available on Microfilm.** These are available for onsite viewing in the Reference/Documents Collection, Monday - Friday, 8 a.m. - 5 p.m. or to be borrowed through Interlibrary loan.

ONLINE Genealogy Resources at the Texas State Library Website

■ **Index (Inventory) of County Records on Microfilm** is available online, along with instructions for borrowing rolls through Interlibrary loan. County records include vital records, court records, and tax rolls. Most of the microfilm is housed in depository libraries throughout Texas. The State Library's Genealogy Collection houses the film for a number of counties. A county list can be found at **www.tsl.state.tx.us/arc/local/index.html**. Select a county and see a list of records and years available, e.g., Titus County Index to Deeds, 1846-1901; or Titus County Tax Rolls, 1846-1910; and more.

■ **Index to Confederate Pension Applications** provides the names, county of residence, and pension number for some 54,634 approved, rejected, and home pensions issued by the Texas government between 1899 and 1975. Searchable index is at **www.tsl.state.tx.us/arc/pensions/index.html.**

■ **Index to Texas Adjutant General Service Records, 1836-1935.** The Service Records Series combines both official service record files from the Adjutant General's Office and alphabetical files created by other agencies which contain records related to an individual's service in a military unit. Searchable index located at: **www2.tsl.state.tx.us/trail/ServiceSearch.jsp.**

■ **Index to Republic Claims.** This series is now available in digital form as well as microfilm. It includes claims for payment, reimbursement, or restitution submitted by citizens to the Republic of Texas government from 1835 through 1846. It also includes records relating to Republic pensions and claims against the Republic submitted as public debt claims after 1846. Go to **www2.tsl.state.tx.us/trail/ServiceSearch.jsp.**

■ **Confederate Indigent Families Lists.** View the names of families that received aid through the 1863 "Act to Support the Families and Dependents of Texas Soldiers." Go to: **www.tsl.state.tx.us/arc/cif/index.html.**

Other ONLINE Databases, Texas Censuses and Substitutes

www.ancestry.com

- 1820-1890 Federal Census Indexes (AIS)
- 1850-1930 United States Federal Census
- Social Security Death Index
- Obituary Collection
- Texas Deaths, 1964-98
- Texas Marriages, 1814-1909
- Texas Marriages, 1851-1900
- Passenger and Immigration Lists Index, 1500s-1900s
- American Emigrant Ministers, 1690-1811
- Galveston Passenger Lists, 1896-1948
- World War I Draft Registration Cards, 1917-1918
- American Soldiers of World War I, Original Documents
- American Civil War Regiments

- U.S. Army Historical Register, 1789-1903, Vol. 2
- War of the Rebellion - Original Documents
- 2000 Phone and Address Directory
- 1994 Phone and Address Directory
- Houston, Texas Directories, 1882-95
- 1898 Presbyterian Ministerial Directory
- Dallas, Texas Directory, 1889-94

www.censusfinder.com

- 1790-1830 census records at Ancestry
- 1835 statewide census (sic)
- 1880 census at Family Search
- Texas Death Records, 1964-1968
- Postmasters of Texas, statewide
- Military Land Grant Name Index

www.census-online.com

• **Online county-wide name lists** (no. of databases): Anderson (7); Andrews (3); Angelina (7); Aransas (0); Archer (8); Armstrong (3); Atascosa (7); Austin (4); Bailey (0); Bandera (3); Bastrop (31); Baylor (7); Bee (2); Bell (11); Bexar (5); Blanco (2); Borden (2); Bosque (4); Bowie (20); Brazoria (6); Brazos (8); Brewster (6); Briscoe (3); Brooks (0); Brown (7); Burleson (8); Burnet (3); Caldwell (6); Calhoun (3); Callahan (0); Cameron (1); Camp (0); Carson (1); Cass (35); Castro (0); Chambers (0); Cherokee (10); Childress (0); Clay (10); Cochran (9); Coke (14); Coleman (6); Collin (5); Collingsworth (0); Colorado (17); Comal (3); Comanche (1); Concho (4); Cooke (4); Coryell (11); Cottle (3); Crane (8);Crockett (20); Crosby (5); Culberson (1); Dallam (1); Dallas (4); Dawson (2); Deaf Smith (7); Delta (3); Denton (4); DeWitt (1); Dickens (3); Dimmit (6); Donley (1); Duval (1); Eastland (4); Ector (1); Edwards (2); El Paso (3); Ellis (11); Erath (3); Falls (1); Fannin (22); Fayette (6); Fisher (2); Floyd (0); Foard (0); Fort Bend (5); Franklin (0); Freestone (1); Frio (14); Gaines (1); Galveston (16); Garza (2); Gillespie (6); Glasscock (0); Goliad (6); Gonzales (43); Gray (3); Grayson (5);Gregg (15); Grimes (42); Guadalupe (4); Hale (0); Hall (7); Hamilton (7); Hansford (4); Hardeman (1); Hardin (6); Harris (3); Harrison (0); Hartley (2); Haskell (4); Hays (11); Hemphill (1); Henderson (41); Hidalgo (0); Hill (2); Hockley (12); Hood (1); Hopkins (1); Houston (6); Howard (4); Hudspeth (2); Hunt (0); Hutchinson (2); Irion (1); Jack (7); Jackson (9); Jasper (8); Jeff Davis (3); Jefferson (1); Jim Hogg (0); Jim Wells (0); Johnson (0); Jones (4); Karnes (1); Kaufman (6); Kendall (1); Kenedy (0); Kent (1); Kerr (15); Kimble (1); King (3); Kinney (1); Kleberg (0); Knox (3); La Salle (1); Lamar (8); Lamb (1); Lampasas (11); Lavaca (3); Lee (9); Leon (7); Liberty (7); Limestone (5); Lipscomb (1); Live Oak (6); Llano (8); Loving (0); Lubbock (7); Lynn (1); Madison (1); Marion (2); Martin (1); Mason (1); Matagorda (1); Maverick (0); McCulloch (1); McLennan (1); McMullen (7); Medina (23); Menard (1); Midland (11); Milam (8); Mills (0); Mitchell (2); Montague (5); Montgomery (3); Moore (5); Morris (2); Motley (2); Nacogdoches (22); Navarro (10); Newton (6); Nolan (1); Nueces (14); Ochiltree (1); Oldham (2); Orange (0); Palo Pinto (0); Panola (60); Parker (3); Parmer (1); Pecos (1); Polk (8); Potter (2); Presidio (6); Rains (8); Randall (5); Reagan (1); Real (1); Red River (4); Reeves (1); Refugio (7); Roberts (3); Robertson (20); Rockwall (0); Runnels (2); Rusk (53); Sabine (11); San Augustine (8); San Jacinto (0); San Patricio (6); San Saba (1); Schleicher (1); Scurry (0); Shackelford (0); Shelby (17); Sherman (1); Smith (22); Somervell (0); Starr (2); Stephens (20); Sterling (2); Stonewall (0); Sutton (1); Swisher (5); Tarrant (8); Taylor (1); Terrell (1); Terry (1); Throckmorton (4); Titus (3); Tom Green (0); Travis (0); Trinity (2) ; Tyler (20); Upshur (3); Upton (4); Uvalde (3); Val Verde (2); Van Zandt (16); Victoria (8); Walker (6); Waller (3); Ward (1); Washington (12); Webb (3); Wharton (2); Wheeler (2); Wichita (6); Wilbarger (5); Willacy (0); Williamson (4); Wilson (0); Winkler (2); Wise (24); Wood (0); Yoakum (5); Young (22); Zapata (3); and Zavala (6).

Jurisdictional History of the Indian Territory, Oklahoma Territory, and Oklahoma

Over the years, the term *Indian Country* was used to describe the western areas encompassing several Indian tribes, whether nations, reservations, or those roaming free over the Great Plains of the United States. The evolution of the Indian Country into an ***Indian Territory*** took place over the whole of the 19th Century. However, Indian Territory was never a territory in the official sense of the term. For the entire period of its existence, it never had a combined territorial government or a federally appointed territorial governor.

Soon after the 1803 Louisiana Purchase, Thomas Jefferson urged the resettling of tribes of the eastern United States on the new lands west of the Mississippi. In 1804, Congress passed legislation authorizing the negotiation of removal treaties with the eastern tribes, and over the next twenty years, several tribes or portions of tribes moved west.

This first phase of removal was mostly voluntary, and often conflicted with white settlers moving west of the Mississippi at the same time. For example, when Arkansas Territory was established in 1819, it included most of the area of present-day Oklahoma. And in 1821, Missouri was admitted to the Union, further reducing the perceived range of land that was to be dedicated to the relocation of eastern Indian tribes.

In 1828, the present western boundary of Arkansas was drawn, and for the first time, the law described the area west of that line as the exclusive domain of Indian tribes, or "Indian Country." Due to a misunderstanding of the Arkansas boundary, early white settlers north of the Red River (in present-day McCurtain County, Oklahoma) thought they were living in old Miller County, Arkansas Territory. Several hundred families were moved to areas south of the river to vacate the newly defined Indian Country. (Ironically, the resettled whites were moved to Mexican Texas, not Arkansas). This was a rare case in American history where whites were relocated to make room for Indians.

In the 1830s, forced removal of eastern Indian tribes began, the most notorious being the Cherokee removal, which history remembers as the "trail of tears."

In 1834, legislation defined the "Indian Country" as that portion of the western United States that was not part of any state or territory. The new law also regulated certain activities of non-Indians within the region and established judicial boundaries: the northern portion of the region (modern Kansas) was to be under the control of the federal courts of Missouri; the southern portion (modern Oklahoma), under the federal courts of Arkansas. Federal censuses in the Indian Country taken from 1820 through 1870 for non-Indians were under the jurisdiction of the Missouri and Arkansas federal marshals. (Indians were specifically excluded from the federal censuses, except those who lived off reservations and were subject to taxes like non-Indians.)

In the Indian Country, the most populous of the tribes were located in the southern portion, namely, the relocated Choctaw, Cherokee, Chickasaw, Creek, and Seminole Nations (the so-called Five Civilized Tribes). To the north in present-day Kansas were the reservations of numerous small Midwestern and plains tribes.

A second removal and concentration of Indian populations took place in 1854, when twelve treaties were negotiated with tribes living in the northern part of the territory. Together, these agreements opened most of present-day Kansas for white settlement. That same year Congress created Kansas Territory, which encompassed the remaining tribes and their diminished reservations. As a result, the Indian territory was reduced to the area of present-day Oklahoma (except for the Panhandle) with most of the land owned by the Five Civilized Tribes. Evidence of non-Indians living in the Indian Country can be seen in the 1860 federal census, where whites, blacks, adopted, or intermarried persons living on "Indian Lands West of Arkansas" were named and listed at the end of the Arkansas census schedules. Special censuses were taken periodically for Indians, and in the 1890 and 1900 federal censuses, Indian tribes were enumerated with population schedules added to the regular schedules for each territory or state (1890 lost, 1900 extant).

In 1865, because the governments of the Five Civilized Tribes had supported the South during the Civil War, the federal government declared its existing treaties with these tribes void. New treaties were negotiated the following year, in which the tribes either ceded the western portions of their lands to the federal government for the resettlement of more Indians, or, in the case of the Cherokees, provided for the sale of their western lands (the Cherokee Outlet) to friendly tribes.

With these newly ceded western lands of the Five Civilized Tribes available for Indian settlement, a third wave of removals began as the government started moving the remaining tribes from Texas, Kansas, Nebraska, and elsewhere into the territory. Between 1866 and 1885, the Cheyenne and Arapaho, the Comanche, Kiowa, and Apache, the Wichita and Caddo, the Potawatomi and Shawnee, the Kickapoo, the Iowa, the Sauk and Fox, the Pawnee, the Oto and Missouri, the Ponca, the Tonkawa, the Kaw, the Osage, the Peoria, the Wyandot, the Eastern Shawnee, the Modoc, and the Ottawa reservations were established in Indian Territory.

In the Osage Reservation Act of 1872, the law stated that the reservation was located in "Indian Territory," and all subsequent tribal agreements, executive orders, and other federal actions relative to the region referred to the area officially as ***Indian Territory***.

In 1887, Congress passed the General Indian Allotment Act, which initiated the process of dividing tribal property and dissolving tribal agreements. Subsequent allotment acts by 1906 had essentially ended tribal land ownership in present-day Oklahoma, with allotments of land divided among individual Indians. Records of the allotments, including a final "census" of the families involved, provides the most complete list of inhabitants of the Indian Territory for that time period.

In 1889, Congress established a separate federal court at Muskogee for Indian Territory, and for the first time it officially defined the area's boundaries: Indian Territory was the area bounded by the states of Kansas, Missouri, Arkansas, and Texas and the Territory of New Mexico. On April 22 the Unassigned Lands were opened to settlement by non-Indians in the first of the famous land runs. Over fifty thousand homesteaders settled in the region on that day.

In May 1890 Indian Territory was divided into Oklahoma Territory and Indian Territory. Oklahoma Territory was defined as incorporating the Unassigned Lands and all reservations, with the exception of those of the Five Civilized Tribes and the small reservations in the extreme northeastern portion of Indian Territory. While all of the reservations in the Cherokee Outlet were to be part of Oklahoma Territory, that portion of the Outlet still owned by the Cherokee Nation would remain as part of Indian Territory until purchased by the government. Almost immediately a special commission was organized to negotiate the allotment of the reservations in Oklahoma Territory and the sale of "surplus" (unallotted) lands so that they could be opened for non-Indian settlement. In 1893 the Cherokee sold their remaining portion of the Outlet, which was immediately incorporated into Oklahoma Territory and opened for settlement. Thus by 1893 Indian Territory had been reduced to just the reservations of the Five Civilized Tribes proper and the small reservations in the northeast.

Later in 1893, the Dawes Commission was created by Congress to negotiate agreements with the Five Civilized Tribes to allot their lands, and in 1898 the allotment process began in what remained of Indian Territory. In a futile attempt to maintain some semblance of continued Indian separation, leaders of the Five Civilized Tribes organized a constitutional convention in 1905, drew up a constitution, and asked to be admitted to the Union as the state of Sequoyah. Congress rejected the plan and in 1907 approved a statute that joined Indian Territory with Oklahoma Territory to create the new state of Oklahoma.

Censuses & Substitutes for Indian Territory, Oklahoma Territory, and Oklahoma

Several censuses were taken by the Five Civilized Tribes separate from the federal censuses or those taken by Oklahoma Territory. This included surviving censuses taken in 1880 and 1890 by the Cherokee government; an 1885 Choctaw census; and an 1890 census by the Chickasaw tribe. The Indian censuses identify both Indians and non-Indians living on their reservations.

The 1890 federal census included population schedules for the newly formed Oklahoma Territory, and added the Indian tribes of Indian Territory. Unfortunately, most of the 1890 federal censuses were burned or destroyed after a fire in the Commerce Building in Washington, DC in 1921. But some relief to the 1890 disaster exists, since Oklahoma Territory took a special territorial census in 1890 for its original seven counties (Beaver, Canadian, Cleveland, Kingfisher, Logan, Oklahoma, and Payne), which all survive.

The extant 1900 federal census for Oklahoma Territory also included population schedules for Indians. Both Soundex and Schedules are available for the 1900 federal census of Oklahoma Territory.

Upon statehood in 1907, the federal government sponsored a census for Oklahoma, however, of the 75 counties enumerated, only the name list for Seminole County survives at the National Archives.

A chronological list of censuses and substitutes taken by the Indian tribes, as well as those for Oklahoma Territory and the state of Oklahoma are identified below:

■ **1817-1900s.** See ***Cherokee Nation,*** microfilm of originals in the Oklahoma Historical Society, Indian Archives Division, Oklahoma City, OK. Includes correspondence, census records, enrollment records, laws and acts, journals, national council and senate records, court records, vital records, probate records, land and property records, school records, and other miscellaneous documents. Includes *Register of Persons...Under Treaty of 1817, Cherokee (Tahlequah) Census;* Includes *Cherokee Nation East, Roll of 1835; Cherokees Census of Flint District, With a Complete List of Names of Emigrants, 185;* Includes *Enrollments and Censuses, 1867-1920.; Supplemental Roll of Those Left Off the Rolls of 1880, Cherokee (Tahlequah), Per Capita;* and the *Hester Roll of Eastern Cherokees* (those living east of the Mississippi River in 1884). Filmed by the Oklahoma Historical Society, 1976, 129 rolls, beginning with FHL film #1666294. To locate all 129 rolls and the contents of each, visit the **www.familysearch.org** Web site. Go to Library, FHL Catalog, Film/Fiche Number search: 1666294.

■ **1830s-1900s Mississippi and Indian Territory.** See ***Choctaw Nation Records,*** microfilm of originals at the Oklahoma Historical Society, Indian Archives Division, Oklahoma City, OK. Includes census, Choctaw Indians, government records, correspondence, occupations, vital statistics, probate records, land and property, court records, military records, schools and other miscellaneous information. Filmed by the Oklahoma Historical Society, 90 rolls, beginning with FHL film #1666451 (Census and citizenship: Mississippi Choctaw census and citizenship 1830-1899. To locate all 90 rolls and the contents of each, visit the **www.familysearch.org** Web site. Go to Library, FHL Catalog, Film/Fiche Number search: 1666451.

■ **1830s-1920s.** See ***Sac and Fox, and Shawnee Nations,*** microfilm of originals in the Oklahoma Historical Society, Indian Archives Division, Oklahoma City, OK. Includes correspondence, census records, enrollment records, laws and acts, journals, national council and senate records, court records, vital records, probate records, land and property records, school records, and other miscellaneous documents. Filmed by the Oklahoma Historical Society, 1971, 64 rolls, beginning with FHL film #1671001. To locate all 64 rolls and the contents of each, visit the **www.familysearch.org** Web site. Go to Library / FHL Catalog / Film/Fiche Number search: 1671001.

■ **1830s-1900s.** See ***Indians and Intruders,*** compiled by Sharron Standifer Ashton, published by Ashton Books, Norman, OK, 1996-2002, 5 vols., index included in each volume. Contents: vol. 1: White intruders in the Old Creek Nation, 1831; intruders in the Choctaw Nation, 1882; 1860 Indian Territory slave schedules, Chickasaw District and Choctaw Nation; records of burials, baptisms, marriages and deaths at Fort Supply, Indian Territory; evidence of marriage in the Creek national records; Chickasaw traders in 1766; Cherokee Nation permits; intruders and non-citizens in the Creek Nation; vol. 2: Cherokee voters in the Old Cherokee Nation, 1835; Creek nation licenses and permits, 1875-1895; Choctaw Nation divorce records, 1875-1905; records of marriage in the Cherokee Nation, 1869-1895 and undated; Choctaw Nation marriages, 1889-1898; vol. 3: Creek Indian light horseman; Cherokee Civil War claims index; Chickasaw Nation citizenship records; Our brother in red, Indian Territory news, January 1890-May 1891; early Choctaw Mission students, 1823; map of Pushmataha District, Choctaw Nation; Choctaw Nation Court records, Blue County, 1852-1858; Peter James Hudson; Indian captives in the Southwest, 1870-1872; vol. 4: List of valuations of Cherokee improvements, 1835; roll of Pickens County, Chickasaw Nation, 1866; murder in the Choctaw Nation; Choctaw deaths, 1837-1854; Our brother in red, Indian Territory news, June 1891-August 1891; index to Chickasaw Nation record book, 1837-1855; abstracts from The Cherokee advocate, 1878; murders in the Cherokee and Choctaw Nations; register of Cherokee claims, 1842. Family History Library has bound v. 3-4 as one volume. FHL book 970.3 C424as, vols. 1-5, and FHL film #6002360-6002361.

■ **1831-1832.** See ***Register of Choctaw Emigrants to the West, 1831 and 1832,*** compiled by Betty C. Wiltshire, published by Pioneer Publ., Carrollton, MS, 199? 160 pages. FHL book 970.3 C451wb.

■ **1831-1847.** See ***Choctaw and Chickasaw Early Census Records,*** compiled by Betty Wiltshire, published by Pioneer Publ., Carrollton, MS, 199?, 173 pages. Includes index. Includes census of Choctaws, 1831 (Armstrong rolls) for the districts of Mushuluatubbee, Leflore and Natachache; muster rolls of Chickasaws, 1847; and rolls of Chickasaws, 1839. FHL book 970.1 W712c.

■ ***1837-1847 Chickasaw Indians Census Rolls, Indian Territory,*** abstracted and edited by Bennie Coffey Loftin and Johnny Cudd, published by the Pittsburg County Genealogical and Historical Society, McAlester, OK, 199?, 120 pages. FHL book 970.3 C432ci.

■ **1832-1900s Indian Territory,** See ***Creek Nation,*** microfilm of originals at the Oklahoma Historical Society, Indian Archives Division, Oklahoma City, OK. Includes census, correspondence, Creek Indians, Shawnee Indians, court records, government records, military records, land and property, vital statistics, schools, and other miscellaneous records. Filmed by the Oklahoma Historical Society, 1971, 51 rolls, beginning with FHL film #1666121. To locate all 51 rolls and the contents of each, visit the **www.familysearch.org** Web site. Go to Library, FHL Catalog, Film/Fiche Number search: 1666121.

■ ***1851 Cherokee Old Settlers' Annuity Roll,*** transcribed by Marybelle W. Chase, published by the author, Tulsa, OK, 1993, 132 pages. Includes Index. FHL book 970.3 C424cha. See also ***Cherokee Old Settler Roll, 1851,*** compiled and indexed by Larry S. Watson, published by

Histree, Yuma, AZ, 1993, 103 pages. FHL book 970.3 C424wa.

■ **1854-1934 Indian Territory.** See ***Kiowa Nation,*** microfilm of originals at the Oklahoma Historical Society, Indian Archives Division, Oklahoma City, OK. Includes census, enrollments, correspondence, court records, government relations, military history, history and culture, probate records, vital statistics, land and property, schools, Kiowa Indians, Comanche Indians, Apache Indians, Wichita Indians and affiliated bands, Caddo Indians, Delaware Indians, information on Quanah Parker and Cynthia Ann Parker, and other miscellaneous information. Filmed by the Oklahoma Historical Society, 1971, 116 rolls, beginning with FHL film #1666146. To locate all 116 rolls, visit the **www.familysearch.org** Web site. Go to Library, FHL Catalog, Film/Fiche Number search: 1666146.

■ ***1855 Census of Choctaw Nation, Indian Territory (Oklahoma),*** by Alma Mason, published by the author, McAlester, OK, 199?, 107 pages. Includes Apukshunnubbee District which is Cedar, Boktucklo, Eagle, Nashoba, Red River, Towson and Wade counties; Moshulatubbee District which is Gaines, San Bois, Skullyville, Sugar Loaf, and Tobucksy counties; and Pushmataha District which is Atoka, Blue, Jack's Fork, Kiamichi and Pushmataha counties. FHL book 976.6 X2m.

■ ***1860 Census of the Free Inhabitants of Indian Lands West of Arkansas,*** compiled Carole Ellsworth and Sue Emler, published by Oklahoma Roots Research, Gore, OK, 1984, 48 pages. Includes index. From intro: "Compiled from original microfilmed census published by the Nation Archives. This census is at the end of the 1860 census of Yell County, Arkansas. Film number M653-roll number 52. "This census was taken of the free inhabitants of the following Indian Nations: Creek, Cherokee, Chickasaw, Choctaw and Seminole. Enumeration includes whites, and those blacks who were considered free, living in Indian Nation. Included are surnames when given, age and sex, occupation and country or state of birth. In the Creek Nation, the census taker noted those citizens who were married to natives (Indians), and whether they had been adopted by one of the tribes. FHL book 976.6 X2e. Also on microfiche, filmed by the Genealogical Society of Utah, 1991, 2 microfiche; FHL film #6088844. See also ***Indian Lands West of Arkansas (Oklahoma): Population Schedule of the United States Census of 1860,*** compiled by Frances Woods, published by Arrow Print Co., 1964, FHL book 976.6 X2p 1860 and FHL film #1000357. The "Indian Lands West of Arkansas" name list was indexed and published with the misleading title, ***Oklahoma 1860 Census Index,*** compiled by Ronald Vern Jackson, et al, published by Accelerated Indexing Systems, 1984, 27 pages. FHL Book 976.6 X22j 1860.

■ **1860-1900.** See ***Notes on the Wyandotte's From Ohio to Indian Territory,*** by Toni Jollay Prevost, published by the author, Lake Mary, FL, 1992, 19 pages. Contains information about the Treaty of the 6th of April 1816 in Ohio concerning the Wyandottes; the Wyandotte land improvements in Ohio in 1843; Wyandotte children enrolled in the Shawnee Methodist Mission school in Kansas in 1851; Wyandottes who served in the Civil War from Wyandotte County, Kansas; Wyandottes on the 1860 and 1870 federal census of Wyandotte County, Kansas; abstracted index of the Wyandottes on the 1900 federal census in Indian Territory from Canada, Ohio, and Kansas; and biographical reference information on prominent Wyandotte families. FHL book 970.1 A1 No. 166 and FHL film #1697876.

■ **1864-1909 Indian Territory.** See ***Quapaw Nation,*** microfilm of originals at the Oklahoma Historical Society, Indian Archives Division, Oklahoma City, OK. Includes census; vital statistics; correspondence; Chippewa, Munsee or

Christian Indians; Citizen Potowatomi Indians; Delaware Indians; Kansas or Kaw Indians; Miami Indians; New York Indians; Nez Perce Indians; Oneida Indians; Modoc Indians; Ottawa Indians; Ponca Indians; Seneca Indians, Shawnee Indians; Tonkawa Indians: Peoria and Confederated tribes; Wyandot Indians; military history; court records; history; land and property; schools and other miscellaneous information. Filmed by the Oklahoma Historical Society, 25 rolls, beginning with FHL film #1671120. To locate all 25 rolls and the contents of each, visit the **www.familysearch.org** Web site. Go to Library / FHL Catalog / Film/Fiche Number search: 1671120.

■ **1863-1886 Indian Territory.** See ***Executive Department, Cherokee Nation G.W. Ross Sec'ty, October 24, 1865: Rebound Title Acts and Resolutions 1863-1886 Cherokee Nation,*** microfilm of originals in the Oklahoma Historical Society, Indian Archives Division, Oklahoma City, OK. Some text written in the Cherokee language. From intro: "This group of records includes various census rolls from 1835 through 1868, Civil War rosters of Indian Home Guards, claims for Civil War service being made in 1899, list of potential claimants who were supposed to be living in Indian Territory and some marriages (in the Cherokee language) performed by Reverend George Swimmer from 1864 to 1895. Also in the group are receipt rolls for a per capita payment under an act dated November 19, 1874 for Canadian and Tahlequah Districts and a census fragment 190-". Filmed by the Oklahoma Historical Society, 1976, 1 roll, FHL film #1666301.

■ **1867-1896 Indian Territory.** See ***List of Shawnee: Registered Members of the Shawnee Tribe 1867-1881 and Rolls of the Shawnee Tribe, 1896 Census,*** transcribed by Bobbie Dunbar, published by the author, Richland, MO, 1990, 24 pages. From intro: "Register of the name of the members of the Shawnee Tribe of Indians who have moved to and located in Cherokee Nation Indian Territory prior to the 10th day of June 1871 within two years from the 9th day of June 1869, in accordance with an agreement between the Shawnee Tribe Indians and the Cherokee Nation of Indians, by their delegations in Washington City, DC." FHL book 970.3 Sh28db.

■ **1869-1933 Indian Territory.** See ***Cheyenne and Arapaho Nations,*** microfilm of originals at the Oklahoma Historical Society, Indian Archives Division, Oklahoma City, OK. Includes census, correspondence, Cheyenne Indians, Arapaho Indians, Concho Indians, government relations, court records, military history, history and culture, probate records, land and property, schools and other miscellaneous information. Filmed by the Oklahoma Historical Society, 1971, 115 rolls, beginning with FHL film #1670886. To locate all 115 rolls and the contents of each, visit the **www.familysearch.org** Web site. Go to Library / FHL Catalog / Film/Fiche Number search: 1670886.

■ **1870-1930 Indian Territory and Oklahoma.** See ***Pawnee Agency,*** microfilm of originals at the Oklahoma Historical Society in Oklahoma City, Oklahoma. Includes Pawnee, Kaw, Ponca, Nez Perce, Oto, Missouri, and Tonkawa-Lipan Apache. Includes census, enrollments, council minutes, correspondence, court records, military records, history, cultural information, land and property, schools and other miscellaneous information. Filmed by the Oklahoma Historical Society, 55 rolls, beginning with FHL film #1671065 (Census and enrollment, letters and documents sent and received 4 June, 1894 through March 28, 1927; Census volumes and lists for the Nez Perce, Kaw, Tonkawa, Pawnee and Oto and Missouri 1880-1926).

■ **1874-1881 Indian Territory.** See ***Expanded Index of the Peoria Census, Annuity Rolls and Administrations, 1874-1881: With Undated Material, Quapaw Agency, Indian Territory,*** extracted from original records at the Oklahoma Historical Society, Indian Archives Division, Oklahoma City, OK, published by Gregath, Wyandotte, OK, 199?, 32 pages. FHL book 970.1 A1 No. 198.

■ **1874 Canadian District Per Capita Tax, Cherokee Nation**, in *The Cherokee Tracer*, Vol. 6, No. 3 (Summer 1996).

■ **1874 Cherokee Nation Receipt Roll**, in *The Cherokee Tracer*, Vol. 7, No. 1 (Winter 1997).

■ **1874 Tahlequah Receipt Roll, Cherokee Nation**, in *The Cherokee Tracer*, Vol. 10, No. 1 (Winter 2000).

■ **1878-1883 Indian Territory.** See ***Expanded Index of the Ottawa Census, Annuity Rolls and Administrations: 1878-1883, With Undated Material, Quapaw Agency, Indian Territory***, extracted from original records at the Oklahoma Historical Society, Indian Archives Division, Oklahoma City, OK, published by Gregath, Wyandotte, OK, 199?, 18 pages. FHL book 970.1 A1 No. 196.

■ ***1878 Annuity Rolls and 1890 Census of Chickasaw Nation, Indian Territory***, compiled by Joyce A. Rex, published McClain County Historical Society, Purcell, Oklahoma, 1990, 3 vols. Contents: vol. 1: 1878 annuity rolls and 1890 census of Pontotoc County now McClain County and portions of Grady, Garvin, Murray, Pontotoc, Johnston and Coal counties, Oklahoma; vol. 2: Pickens County now Carter, Love, Marshall counties, and portions of Garvin, Grady, Stephens, Jefferson, Murray, and Johnston counties, Oklahoma; vol. 3: Tishomingo and Panola counties, now Bryan county and portions of Johnston, Pontotoc and Murray counties, Oklahoma. FHL book 970.3 C432rj v. 1-3. Also available on 11 microfiche, FHL film #6125933-6125935.

■ ***1880 Cherokee Nation Census, Indian Territory (Oklahoma)***, from microfilmed originals at the National Archives, Ft. Worth, TX, both a book and CD-ROM publication, transcribed by Barbara Benge, published by Heritage Books, Bowie, MD, 2000, 596 pages. Includes index. Contains transcriptions of the original 1880 census of the Cherokee Nation, which is also available on FHL film #989204. Transcribed publication: FHL CD-ROM No. 1682 and FHL book 970.3 C424vLb.

■ **1880-1895 Tax Lists, Greer County, Texas (now Oklahoma),** in *Oklahoma Genealogical Society Bulletin*, Vol. 35, No. 4 (1990).

■ **1881-1886 Tax Records, Greer County, Texas (now Oklahoma),** in *Western Trails Newsletter*, Vol. 2, No. 4 (Oct 1989).

■ ***1880 and 1890 Census, Canadian District, Cherokee Nation, Indian Territory***, transcribed by Sharron Standifer Ashton, published by Oklahoma Genealogical Society, Oklahoma City, 1978, 90 pages. The Canadian District of the Cherokee Nation covered the area that is now Muskogee and McIntosh Counties, Oklahoma. FHL book 970.3 C424ash. Hester roll of Eastern Cherokees and census.

■ ***1885 Choctaw Census, Indian Territory***, transcribed by Monty Olsen, published by the Bryan County Heritage Association, 1996-2000, 4 vols. Index included in each volume. Contents: vol. 1: Blue County; vol. 2: Kiamitia County; vol. 3:. Pushmataha District: Atoka County [and] Jacks Fork County; vol. 4: Apukshunnubbee District: Cedar County, Wayne County, Boktoklo County, Towson County, Nashoba County, Eagle County and Red River County. The FHL has bound together all of Apukshunnubbee District including Eagle, Boktoklo, Towson, Nashoba, Eagle, Red River, Wade and Cedar Counties as one volume, and has bound together Atoka and

Jacks Fork Counties. FHL book 970.3 C451 v. 1-4. See also ***Index to the 1885 Choctaw Census,*** microfilm of original manuscript at the National Archives branch at Ft. Worth, TX. Filmed by the National Archives, 198?, series 75, 1 roll, FHL film #505975. See also ***The 1885 census of Atoka County, Choctaw Nation, Indian Territory,*** by James P. Cummings, published by the author, Mesquite, TX, 1976, 39 pages. FHL book 970.1 A1 No. 86.

■ **1885-1940 Indian Census Rolls,** microfilm of original records of the Bureau of Indian Affairs, now located at the National Archives, Washington, DC, Series M-595, 692 rolls. Copies at the Oklahoma Historical Society for 67 tribes of the Indian Territory are listed with name of tribe, roll number, and comments, and can be found at **www.ok-history.mus.ok.us/res/censusrolls.htm.** Contains census rolls that were usually submitted each year by agents or superintendents in charge of Indian reservations, as required by an act of 1884. The data on the rolls vary to some extent, but usually given are the English and/or Indian name of the person, roll number, age or date of birth, sex, and relationship to head of family. Beginning in 1930, the rolls also show the degree of Indian blood, marital status, ward status, place of residence, and sometimes other information. For certain years – including 1935, 1936, 1938, and 1939 – only supplemental rolls of additions and deletions were compiled. Most of the 1940 rolls have been retained by the Bureau of Indian Affairs and are not included in this publication. FHL has entire collection, but cataloged by the various Indian agencies or tribes that originally generated the census name lists. A descriptive bulletin was published by the National Archives, FHL's copy titled, ***Indian Census Rolls, 1885-1940: National Archives Microfilm Publications, Pamphlet Describing M595,*** 34 pages. FHL book 973 J53m no. 595.

■ **Indian Territory Records at the Oklahoma Historical Society**. See ***Catalog of Microfilm Holdings in the Archives & Manuscripts Division, Oklahoma Historical Society 1976-1989: Native American Tribal Records and Special Collections,*** published by the Oklahoma Historical Society, Indian Archives Division, Oklahoma City, OK, 1976-1989. Copy at FHL library, FHL book 970.1 Ok4cm.

■ **1886-1927 Indian Census Rolls, Ponca Agency,** microfilm of originals of the Bureau of Indian Affairs at the National Archives, Washington, DC., Includes the following: 1886: Ponca, Oto, Tonkawa 1887: Pawnee, Ponca, Tonkawa, Oto 1888: Ponca, Oto, Missouri, Tonkawa 1889-1890: Pawnee, Ponca, Oto, Tonkawa (not always in this order) 1891-1901: Ponca, Pawnee, Oto, Missouri, Tonkawa (not always in this order) 1902-1903: Tonkawa, Oto, Missouri, Ponca (not always in this order) 1904-1912: Ponca, Tonkawa (not always in this order) 1913: Ponca, Tonkawa, Kaw 1914: Ponca, Tonkawa 1915-1919: Ponca, Tonkawa, Kaw 1922-1924: Ponca, Tonkawa, Oto, Missouri (not always in this order) 1925-1927: Ponca, Oto, Tonkawa. Filmed by the National Archives, 1965, 6 rolls, beginning with FHL #580765 (Ponca 1886-1890).

■ **1887 Personal Property Tax Warrants, Garfield County, Oklahoma,** in *Four States Genealogist*, Vol. 2, No. 2 (Jan 1970).

■ ***1887-1939 Indian Census rolls, Cheyenne and Arapaho,*** microfilm of originals in the National Archives in Washington, DC. (part of series M595). Includes the following: 1887: Cheyenne, enlisted scouts, Arapaho 1888: Arapaho, Cheyenne, Fort Reno scouts, Cheyenne (other areas) 1889-1890: Missing 1891-1927: Arapaho, Cheyenne (not always in this order) 1928-1934: Alphabetical 1931: Supplemental rolls for births, deaths, adjustments 1932: Supplemental rolls for births, additions, deaths, adjustments 1933: Supplemental rolls for additions, deductions, adjustments, deaths 1934: Supplemental rolls for adjustments, additions, deductions, births, deaths, stillbirths 1935: Supplemental rolls only for adjustments 1936: Supplemental rolls only for adjustments, marriages 1937: Census rolls with supplemental rolls for births, deaths 1938: Supplemental rolls only for births, deaths, deductions, additions 1939: Supplemental rolls only for births, stillbirths, deaths, deduction, and adjustments. Filmed by the National Archives, 1965, 6 rolls, beginning with FHL film #574191. Selected census rolls extracted and published as ***Cheyenne Indian Census Rolls, Indian Territory, 1895-1900,*** compiled by Valorie Millican, publisher not noted, 2003, 226 pages. Includes a transcription of the census arranged alphabetically by name of individual, followed by a transcription arranged by household for each census year. FHL book 970.3 C429mv.

■ **1890 Oklahoma Territory.** See ***First Territorial Census of Oklahoma, 1890,*** microfilm of original schedules at the Oklahoma Historical Society in Oklahoma City, OK. Contains population schedules for the seven original counties of Logan, Oklahoma, Cleveland, Canadian, Kingfisher, Payne, and Beaver. Filmed by the Historical Society of Oklahoma, 1961, 1 roll, FHL film #227282. Partially indexed in ***1890 Oklahoma Territorial Census for the Counties of Kingfisher, Payne and Beaver,*** compiled by Vicki Sullivan and Mac R. Harris, published by Territorial Press, Oklahoma City, OK, 1977, No copy at FHL – check Oklahoma Historical Society Library.

■ **1890 Oklahoma Territory.** See ***Smith's First Directory of Oklahoma Territory, For the Year Commencing August 1st, 1890,*** by James W. Smith, originally published by the author, Guthrie, OK, 1890, 331 pages. FHL book 976.6 E4s 1890. Indexed in ***Basore's Name Finding List for Smith's First Directory of Oklahoma Territory August 1, 1890-1,*** by Brian Basore, published by the Oklahoma Historical Society, 2002, 128 pages. FHL book 976.6 E42b.

■ ***1890 Census of Chickasaw Nation, Indian Territory: And Other Records,*** by Joyce A. Rex, published by McClain County Historical & Genealogical Society, Purcell, OK, 1993, 3 vols., full-name index included in each volume. Contents: vol. 1: Pontotoc County (now McClain County and portions of Grady, Garvin, Murray, Pontotoc, Johnston and Coal Counties); vol. 2: Pickens County (now Carter, Love and Marshall Counties and portions of Garvin, Grady, Stephens, Jefferson, Murray and Johnston Counties); vol. 3: Tishomingo and Panola Counties (now Bryan County and portions of Pontotoc and Murray Counties). FHL book 970.3 C432 v.1-3.

■ ***1890 Census of the Cherokee Nation, Tahlequah District,*** microfilm of originals in the Oklahoma Historical Society, Indian Archives Division, Oklahoma City, OK. Some text written in the Cherokee language. Includes Tahlequah District census, schedule 1 in 7 volumes. In each volume abbreviations in columns 2 and 3 are "C" for Cherokee, "N" for native, "A" for adopted, "W" for white, "Col." Colored "D" for Delaware, "S" for Shawnee and "NC" for Native Cherokee. Filmed by the Oklahoma Historical Society, 1976, 2 rolls, as follows:

- Tahlequah District Census, schedule 1 1890 book 1 A-C, FHL film #1666299.
- Tahlequah District Census, schedule 1, 1890, book 2, C-F; book 3 F-H; book 4, H-M; book 5, N-R; book 6, R-T; book 7, T-Y; FHL film #1666300.

■ ***1890 Census of the Cherokee Nation, Sequoyah District,*** microfilm of originals in the Oklahoma Historical Society, Indian Archives Division, Oklahoma City, OK. Some text written in the Cherokee language. Includes Sequoyah District census. Schedule 1 is in 2 volumes. In each volume abbreviations in columns 2 and 3 are "C" for Cherokee, "N" for native, "A" for adopted,

"W" for white, "Col." for colored, "D" for Delaware, "S" for Shawnee, and "NC" for native Cherokee. Filmed by the Oklahoma Historical Society, 1976, 1 roll, FHL film #1666299.

■ ***1890 Census of the Cherokee Nation, Saline District,*** microfilm of originals in the Oklahoma Historical Society, Indian Archives Division, Oklahoma City, OK. Some text written in the Cherokee language. Includes Saline District census, schedule 1 is in 2 volumes. In each volume abbreviation in columns 2 and 3 are "C" for Cherokee, "N" for native, "A" for adopted, "W" for white, "Col" for colored "D" for Delaware and "S" for Shawnee, "NC" for Native Cherokee. Filmed by the Oklahoma Historical Society, 1976, 1 roll, FHL film #1666299.

■ ***1890 Census of the Cherokee Nation, Canadian District,*** microfilm of originals in the Oklahoma Historical Society, Indian Archives Division, Oklahoma City, OK. Some text written in the Cherokee language. Includes Canadian District census, schedule 1 is in 4 volumes. In each volume Abbreviations in columns 2 and 3 are "C" for Cherokee, "N" for native, "A" for adopted, "W" for white, "Col." for colored "D" for Delaware and "S" for Shawnee, "NC" for Native Cherokee. Filmed by the Oklahoma Historical Society, 1976, 1 roll, FHL film #1666296.

■ ***1891 Census Roll of Citizen Band of Potawatomi Indians Residing in Oklahoma, Indian Territory, Kansas, and Elsewhere,*** microfilm of handwritten records made by Samuel L. Patrick, U.S. Indian Agent, filmed by the Genealogical Society of Utah, 1979, 1 roll, FHL film #1036363.

■ **1891-1895 Tax rolls, Cleveland County, Oklahoma**, microfilm of original manuscripts at the Cleveland County Genealogical Society, Norman, OK. Lists are arranged by township and then alphabetically by surname. Filmed by the Genealogical Society of Utah, 1999, 2 rolls, FHL film #2168965 (vol. 1, 1891; vol. 2, 1892; vol. 3, 1893; and vol. 4, 1894) and FHL film #2168966 (vol. 5, 1895; and vol. 6, 1895). See also ***Cleveland County, Oklahoma Census of Taxpayers, 1891,*** compiled by the Cleveland County Genealogical Society, manuscript microfilmed by the Genealogical Society of Utah, 1977. Part one contains an alphabetical list of taxpayers which gives name, page number in original tax rolls, town or township where the property was located and a brief legal description of the property. Part two contains the same information transcribed in the order it appeared in the tax rolls. FHL film #2168969.

■ **1892 Canadian County Tax Rolls**, in *Canadian County Connections*, published serially beginning with Vol. 1, No. 1 (Feb 1978).

■ **1893-1966 Kay County**, see ***Old Census Records, Petition to Incorporate, 1893-1966,*** microfilm of originals at Kay County Clerk's Office, Newkirk, OK. Filmed by the Genealogical Society of Utah, 1996, 2 rolls: FHL film #2048208 (old census records, Town of Blackwell, 1893; Town of Braman, 1898; Town of Cross 1893; Town of Dilworth, 1917; Town of Kardy, 1906; Town of Kildare, 1902; Town of Nardin, 1898; Town of Kildare Census, 1894; Town of Newkirk, 1893; Town of Parker, 1893) and FHL film #2048209 (Town of Peckham, 1902; Town of Ponca city, 1893; Town of Tonkawa, 1894; Town of Washunga, 1923; Town of Uncas, 1966).

■ **1894-1907 Election Returns, Greer County, Texas (to 1896); Greer County, Oklahoma (after 1896).** Microfilm of originals in the Greer County courthouse in Mangum, Oklahoma. Filmed by the Genealogical Society of Utah, 1994, 1 roll, FHL film #1954679.

■ **1894-1922 Tax Records, Kay County, Oklahoma**, microfilm of originals at Kay County Courthouse in Newkirk, OK. Filmed by the Genealogical Society of Utah, 1996, 8 rolls, beginning with FHL film #2048694 (Personal Tax Rolls, 1894-1922).

■ **1895 Tax Receipts, Beaver County, Oklahoma,** in *Beaver County Heritage News*, Vol. 4, No. 4 (Oct 1996); and Vol. 5, No. 1 (Jan 1997).

■ **1895-1930 Indian Census Rolls,** microfilm of originals of the Bureau of Indian Affairs, now located at the National Archives, Washington, DC. Census rolls available for the following years and tribes:

- **1897-1898 Kechai Indian Census** at Anadarko Agency, Oklahoma Territory, FHL film #5765900.
- **1897-1898 Wacoe Indian Census** at Anadarko Agency, Oklahoma Territory, FHL film # 576900.
- **1897-1898 Tawakoni Indian Census** at Anadarko Agency, Oklahoma Territory, FHL film #576900.
- **1897-1898 Delaware Indian Census** at Kiowa Agency, Oklahoma Territory, FHL film # 576900.
- **1895-1934 Kiowa Indian Census** at Kiowa Agency, Oklahoma Territory, 7 rolls, beginning with FHL film #576900 (census of 1895).
- **1895-1915 Comanche Indian Census** at Anadarko Agency, Oklahoma Territory, 6 rolls, beginning with FHL film #576900 (census of 1895). Selected census years extracted and published as ***Comanche Indian Census Rolls, Indian Territory, 1900-1903,*** compiled by Valorie Millican, publisher not noted, 2003, 117 pages. Includes a transcription of the census arranged alphabetically by name of individual, followed by a transcription arranged by household for each census year. FHL book 970.3 C73m.
- **1896-1930 Apache Indian Census** at Kiowa Agency, Oklahoma Territory, 8 rolls, beginning with FHL film #576900 (census of 1896).
- **1895-1899 Caddo Indian Census** at Kiowa Agency, Oklahoma Territory, 6 rolls, beginning with FHL film #576900 (census of 1895).
- **1895-1924 Wichita Indian Census** at Anadarko, Oklahoma Territory, 6 rolls, beginning with FHL film #576900 (census of 1895).

■ **1896-1916 Tax Rolls, Greer County, Oklahoma,** microfilm of originals from the office of the County Clerk, Lawton, OK. Filmed by Southwest Oklahoma Genealogical Society, 198?, 20 rolls, beginning with FHL film #1324619 (1896).

■ **1896 Tax List, Greer County, Oklahoma,** published serially in *Western Trails Newsletter*, Vol. 10, No. 1 (Jan 1998) through Vol. 11, No. 3 (Jul 1998). See also "1896 Duke Township Tax Roll," in *Tree Tracers*, Vol. 4, No. 3 (Spring 1980).

■ **1896 Indian Territory.** See ***Index to Payment Roll For Old Settler Cherokee, 1896,*** transcribed by Marybelle W. Chase, published by the author, Tulsa, OK, 198?, 41 pages. Living persons were indexed separately from those who were dead at the date of payment. The payment roll of 1896 was prepared in accordance with an 1846 treaty which provided for payment of shares from funds established by the treaty to Cherokee Old Settlers in Indian Territory as original beneficiaries or as their legal heirs. The Old Settlers were Cherokees who began voluntary migration to land in what is now Arkansas after an 1817 treaty between the Cherokee Tribe and the United States. FHL book 970.3 C424cmwin. Also on microfiche, filmed by the Genealogical Society of Utah, 1993, 2 microfiche, #6101765.

■ ***1896 Tobucksy County, Choctaw Nation, Indian Territory,*** copied by Alma Burke Mason; typed by Bennie Lou Coffey Loftin, published by Pittsburg County Genealogical Society, McAlester, OK, 1988, 28 pages. FHL book 970.3 C451ma.

■ ***1896 Census of Citizens of Tahlequah District, Cherokee Nation,*** microfilm of original records in Tahlequah, OK. Alphabetically arranged by first letter of surname. Most of Tahlequah District, Cherokee Nation is now Cherokee County, Oklahoma. Filmed by the Genealogical Society of Utah, 1976, 1 roll, FHL film #989203.

■ **1896-1950 Seminole County, Konawa Area.** See ***They Came From Everywhere,*** by Arthur Ward Kennedy, published by Rapid Rabbit

Copy, Conway, AR, 1993, 3 vols. Contents: vol. 1: The people: census of Konawa and Avoca townships, 1896-1920; vol. 2: Part one of history, introduction, background and story of the Konawa area through 1930; vol. 3: Part two of history, the Konawa area during two decades of crises 1930-1950. FHL book 976.671 X2k, vol. 1-3.

■ **1896-1909: "The Dawes Rolls,"** See ***Applications for Enrollment of the Five Civilized Tribes, Dawes Commission, 1896-1909.*** microfilm of original Bureau of Indian Affairs records at the National Archives, Washington, DC. From introduction: "An act of Congress approved March 3, 1893 authorized the establishment of the Commission to negotiate agreements with the Cherokee, Choctaw, Chickasaw, Creek, and Seminole tribes providing for the dissolution of the tribal governments and the allotment of land to each tribal member. Senator Henry L. Dawes of Massachusetts was appointed Chairman of this Commission on November 1, 1893, after which it has commonly been referred to as the Dawes Commission. The Commission was authorized by an act of Congress approved June 28, 1898 to prepare citizenship (tribal membership) rolls for each tribe. These final rolls were the basis for allotment. Under this act, subsequent acts, and resulting agreements negotiated with each tribe, the Commission received applications for membership covering more than 250,000 people and enrolled more than 101,000. The Commission enrolled individuals as 'citizens' of a tribe under the following categories: citizens by blood, citizens by marriage, new born citizens by blood, minor citizens by blood, freedmen (former black slaves of Indians, later freed and admitted to tribal citizenship), new born freedmen, and minor freedmen. Delaware Indians adopted by the Cherokee tribe were enrolled as a separate group within the Cherokee. Within each enrollment category, the Commission generally maintained three types of census cards: 'Straight' cards for persons whose applications were approved, 'D' cards for persons whose applications were considered doubtful and subject to question, and 'R' cards for persons whose applications were rejected. Persons listed on 'D' cards were subsequently transferred to either 'Straight' or 'R' cards depending on the Commission's decisions. All decisions of the Commission were sent to the Secretary of the Interior for final approval. Filmed by the National Archives, 1983, series M1301, 468 rolls, beginning with FHL film #1439798 (Choctaws by blood 1-148). Locate all 468 rolls at the **www.familysearch.org** Web site. Go to Library / FHL library catalog / search by film/fiche Number: 1439798 (the first roll of film in the series).

■ **1896-1909 Dawes Commission, Published Report.** See ***The Final Rolls of Citizens and Freedmen of the Five Civilized Tribes in Indian Territory,*** prepared by the Dawes Commission and Commissioner to the Five Civilized Tribes, 1907, Government Printing Office, 2 vols., 1,267 pages. Reprinted by Genealogical Publishing Co., Inc., Baltimore, 2003, 2 vols., 633 & 635 pages. Includes Creek, Seminole, Cherokee, Choctaw, and Chickasaw Indian Rolls, vol. 1 is a combined index, "Index to the Final Rolls." FHL has the original book, FHL book 970.1 Un3c v. 1-2 and FHL film #962366 (vol. 1); FHL film #908371 (vol. 2). The index can be used as a finding aid to the Dawes Commission Allotments, 1896-1909, which includes a complete census listing of all Indian families involved in the allotments (over 250,000 applications and over 101,000 individuals enrolled). Look up a name and find their roll number in vol. 1, "Index to the Final Rolls of the Five Civilized Tribes." Then go to vol. 2, the "Final Rolls of the Five Civilized Tribes," to look up a membership roll number to get a census card number. To find the census cards see the "Dawes Rolls," *Applications for Enrollment of the Five Civilized Tribes, Dawes Commission, 1896-1909.*

■ **1897 Tax List, Washington County, Oklahoma,** in *Bartlesville Genealogical Society Newsletter*, July 1999 issue.

■ **1898-1914 Choctaw Finals Rolls.** See ***Indian Records, Choctaw by Blood: Choctaw Nation, Indian Territory, Final Rolls,*** transcribed, indexed and published by Arlene LeMaster, Family Heritage Resources, Poteau, OK, 1990, 3 vols. This is an extraction of the Choctaw applications for enrollment from the Dawes Rolls. FHL book 970.3 C451 vol. 1-3.

■ **1898-1914.** See ***Campbell's Abstract of Seminole Indian Census Cards and Index,*** compiled by John Bert Campbell, published by Oklahoma Print, Muskogee, OK, 1925, 120 pages. Appears to be an extract of Seminole census cards from the "Index to the Final Rolls." FHL book 970.3 Se52c. Also on microfiche, filmed by the Genealogical Society of Utah, 1995, 2 microfiche, FHL film #6111030.

■ ***Tribal Census for Annuity Rolls, 1897-1914,*** microfilm of originals at the Regional National Archives, Ft. Worth, TX. Filmed by the National Archives, 1978, 1 roll, FHL film #1028501.

■ **1897 Tax Roll, Greer County, Oklahoma,** in *Tree Tracers*, Vol. 5, No. 2 (Winter 1980).

■ **1897 Occupation Tax, Osage County, Oklahoma**, in *Bartlesville Genealogical Society Newsletter*, July 1999 issue.

■ **1898 Assessment Roll, Greer County, Oklahoma**, in *Oklahoma Genealogical Society Bulletin*, Vol. 16, No. 2 (Jun 1971); "1898 Delinquent Tax Payers," in *Western Trails Newsletter*, Vol. 10, No. 1 (Jan 1998).

■ **1898 Tax Assessment Roll, Jackson County, Oklahoma**, in *Oklahoma Genealogical Society Bulletin*, Vol. 15, No. 1 (Mar 1970) through Vol. 16, No. 1 (Jan 1971).

■ **1898 Indian Territory**. See ***Complete Delaware Roll 1898,*** by Dorothy Tincup Mauldin and Jeff Bowen, published by Native American Genealogical Research & Publishing, Hixson, Tennessee, 2001, 100 pages. Includes every name index. In 1867, Delaware tribal members who wished to preserve tribal membership when they were removed from Kansas to Indian Territory purchased 157,000 acres from the Cherokee in Indian Territory. This tract of land was large enough to provide 160 acres for each of the 985 members on the roll taken in Kansas. This 1898 roll was a list of the 1867 enrollees who were still living or their heirs and a list of their holdings. FHL book 970.3 D376m.

■ ***1900 Creek Nation Census,*** compiled by Carole Ellsworth and Sue Emler, published by Oklahoma Roots Research, 1984, FHL book 970.3 C861e and FHL film #6101319.

■ ***1900 U. S. Census of the Cherokee Indian Nation, Indian Territory,*** compiled by Carole Ellsworth and Sue Emler, published by Oklahoma Roots Research, 1982-1985, 5 vols. Extracted from National Archives microfilm, series T-623. Each volume includes a surname index. Contains separate sections of general population and Indian population. Contents: vol. 1: area now in Sequoyah and Muskogee Counties; vol. 2: area now part of Sequoyah County and town of Sallisaw; vol. 3: area now part of Sequoyah County; vol. 4: area now part of Muskogee and McIntosh Counties; vol. 5: area now part of Muskogee and Wagoner counties. FHL book 976.6 X2e 1900 vol. 1-5 and FHL film #6087401-6087405.

■ ***1900 Census of the Cherokee Nation, Indian Territory, now Sequoyah County, Oklahoma,*** read by Marie Sutton Stewart; typed by Donald J. Stewart, published by the Muldrow Genealogical Society, Muldrow, OK, 3 199?, 3 vols. Includes index. FHL book 970.3 C424sm vol.1-3.

■ ***1900 Census Index, Choctaw Nation, Indian Territory, Oklahoma,*** by Gloryann Hankins Young, published by the author, Wister, OK, 1991, 4 vols. Contents: Vol. 1: Le Flore county; vol. 2: Latimer-Pittsburg counties; vol. 3: Enumeration districts of Savanna, Hartshorne, Coalgate, Durant, Legal, Kiowa, Tuskohoma, Fanshawe, Caddo, Atoka, Wilson, Sterrett, Talihinia, Antlers, Eagletown, Gilmore, Good Water, and Nelson; vol. 4: Oak Hill - McCurtain counties. FHL book 976.6 X22y 1900 v. 1-4.

■ **1900 Census.** See ***LeFlore County, Oklahoma, Choctaw Nation, Indian Territory, 1900 Census,*** compiled and published by the Poteau Valley Genealogical Society, Poteau, OK, 1982-1983, 5 vols. Each volume includes an index. Contents: vol. 1: Oak Lodge, Mountain, Braden, Cedar, Pocola and adjoining areas; vol. 2: Spiro, Cowlington, Bokoshe, and surrounding areas; vol. 3: Cameron area; vol. 4: Poteau and Gilmore area; vol. 5: Monroe, Howe and Heavener area. FHL book 976.679 X2Lv.1-5.

■ **1900 Personal Property Tax, Canadian County, Oklahoma,** in *Oklahoma Genealogical Society Bulletin,* Vol. 17, No. 1 (Jan 1972); and Vol. 17, No. 2 (Jun 1972).

■ **1900-1906 Tax Rolls, Logan County, Oklahoma,** in *Logan County Genealogical Society News,* Vol. 5, No. 2 (Jan 1986) and Vol. 5, No. 4 (Jul 1986).

■ ***1901-1907 Native American Census: Seneca, Eastern Shawnee, Miami, Modoc, Ottawa, Peoria, Quapaw, and Wyandotte Indians (under Seneca School, Indian Territory),*** compiled by Jeff Bowen, published Mountain Press, Signal Mountain, TN, 199?, 223 pages. Includes index. These censuses were taken at the Seneca School in Indian Territory. Wyandotte (or Wyandot) Indians are included with the Huron Indian materials. FHL book 970.1 B675ba.

■ **1901-1920 Kay County.** See ***Treasurer's Tax rolls, 1901-1920,*** microfilm of original records at the Kay County Courthouse in Newkirk, OK. Includes some Kaw Indians, also known as the Kansa Indians, who lived on a reserve in the eastern portion of what is now Kay County. Filmed by the Genealogical Society of Utah, 1996, 37 rolls, beginning with FHL film #2056845 (Treasurer's tax rolls Ponca City, Parker, Waltham, Weston, 1901 Blackwell, Cross Cities; and railroads).

■ **1902-1903 Tax Rolls, Kiowa County, Oklahoma,** published serially in *Kiowa County Genealogical Society Newsletter,* beginning with Vol. 7, No. 1 (Feb 2000).

■ **1903 Tax List, Garfield County, Oklahoma,** published serially by township in *Garfield County Roots and Branches,* beginning with Vol. 9 No. 4 (Fall 1986).

■ ***1904-1915, Kiowa Indian Census,*** microfilm of original records at the Anadarko Philamanthic Museum, Anadarko, OK. Also contains records for Wichita, Caddo, Apache and Comanche tribes that were under the Kiowa Agency. Filmed by the Genealogical Society of Utah, 1996, 1 roll, FHL film #2031240.

■ **1905 Oklahoma Territory.** See ***Census of the Comanche Tribe of Indians, Kiowa Indian Agency, O. T., June 30, 1905,*** extracted from FHL film #576902, by Faye Riddles Washburn, published by Southwest Oklahoma Genealogical Society, 1990, 57 pages. FHL book 970.1 A1 no. 192.

■ **1905-1917.** See ***Garfield County, Oklahoma Taxpayers,*** compiled by Garfield County Genealogists, Inc., Enid, OK, 2000, 2 vols. Contains indexes to county tax records for 1905-1907 and an alphabetical list of taxpayers and their post office addresses copied from the R.L.

Polk City directory of Enid, Oklahoma, 1917. FHL book 976.628 R4g v. 1-2.

■ **1905-1906 Oklahoma City Directory**, R. L. Polk and Co., Dallas, TX. FHL book 976.638 E4p (book includes directories for 1916, 1941, 1960, 1969, 1975, and 1986, by various publishers. See also, FHL film #928379 (1905-1906 directory only).

■ **1905-1914 Tax Lists, Wagoner County, Oklahoma**, published serially in *Wagoner Genealogist*, beginning with Vol. 7, No. 2 (Jun 1987).

■ **1906 Tax List, Okmulgee County, Oklahoma**, in *Okmulgee County Genealogical Society Newsletter*, Vol. 9, No. 2 (May 1994).

■ **1907 Tax List, Garfield County, Oklahoma,** in *Garfield County Roots and Branches*, (1990 issue).

■ **1907 Tax List, Stephens County, Oklahoma,** published serially in *Foot Steps*, beginning with Vol. 1, No. 1 (Jan1986).

■ **1908 Tax List, Bryan County, Oklahoma**, in *Bryan County Heritage Quarterly*, Vol. 1, No. 3 (Feb 1985); May, August, and November issues, 1994; and Feb 1997 – Feb 2000).

■ **1908 Taxpayers, Coal County, Oklahoma**, in *Oklahoma Genealogical Society Bulletin*, Vol. 28, No. 2 (1983).

■ ***1908 Craig County, Oklahoma, First Tax List After Statehood: Beginning with 1908, roll books I, II, III, IV***, copied & indexed by Alta Mae Bowman and Mary Nell Bowman, published by the Craig County Genealogical Society, 1995, 96 pages. This index covers four volumes of Craig County tax records now in the Archives of the Vinita Public Library. FHL book 976.698 R42b.

■ **1908 Assessment Roll, Logan County, Oklahoma**, in *Logan County Genealogical Society News*, Vol. 20, No. 2 (Spring 2001).

■ **1908 Personal Property Tax List, Pontotoc County, Oklahoma**, published serially in *Pontotoc County Quarterly*, beginning with Vol. 4, No. 2 (Feb 1973).

■ **1908 Personal Property Tax List, McCain County, Oklahoma**, in *McClain County Oklahoma Historical & Genealogical Society Quarterly*, Vol. 17, No. 2 (Feb 2001) through Vol. 17, No. 4 (Aug 2001).

■ **1908 Indian Tax Rolls, (McCurtain County, Oklahoma),** compiled and published by the McCurtain County Genealogical Society, Idabel, OK, 1987, 10 pages. Includes history of the county and a list of cemeteries in the county. This is an index to taxation of Choctaw Indians in McCurtain County, Oklahoma, in 1908. FHL book 970.1 A1 no. 135. Originally published as part of "1908-1910 Tax Rolls, McCurtain County, Oklahoma," in *Intikba*, Vol. 2, No. 2 (Sep 1986).

■ **1908 Tax Roll, Muskogee County, Oklahoma,** microfilm of originals in the Muskogee County courthouse in Muskogee, OK. Filmed by the Genealogical Society of Utah, 1993, 1 roll, FHL film #1902077.

■ **1908-1921 Tax Lists, Tulsa County, Oklahoma**, published serially in *Tulsa Annals*, beginning with Vol. 3, No. 3 (Sep 1968).

■ **1909 Tax Sale of Delinquent Lands and Lots**, in *Leflore County Oklahoma Genealogist*, Vol. 1, No. 3 (Dec 1980).

■ **1910.** See ***McAlister, Pittsburg County, Oklahoma, an Extraction of Records From the Oklahoma State Prison in 1910: Copied From the***

Census Records of 1910, Indexed by Volume, extracted by John D. Woods, published by the author, Pleasant View, UT, 1993, 6 vols. FHL book 976.675 X28W 1910, vol. 1-6 and FHL film #1750784.

■ **1911 Property Assessment, Coal County, Oklahoma,** in *Oklahoma Genealogical Society Quarterly Newsletter,* published serially, beginning with Vol. 5, No. 4 (Dec 1998).

■ ***1911 Index to Tax Lists of Comanche County, Oklahoma, and Tax Information Extracted from R. L. Polk & Co.'s Lawton City Directory, 1911,*** compiled by Jewell (Rone) Tankersley, published by the author, Lawton, OK, 1984, 111 pages. FHL book 976.648 R4t .

■ **1911 Taxpayers, Comanche County, Oklahoma**, in *Tree Tracers,* Vol. 7, No. 3 (Spring 1983).

■ **1912-1936 Dewey County, Oklahoma.** See ***Scholastic Census, 1912-1936; and Pupil's High School Credit Records, 1901-1952,*** microfilm of original records of the Dewey County Superintendent of Schools, Taloga, OK. Most names arranged alphabetically within districts. Filmed by the Genealogical Society of Utah, 1989-1990, 25 rolls, beginning with FHL film #1664668 (1912).

■ **1912-1936 School District Enumeration Reports, Ellis County, Oklahoma,** microfilm of originals in the Office of the County Superintendent at the Ellis County courthouse in Arnett, Oklahoma. Ellis County was organized in 1907 from Woodward County and half of Day County (formerly known as "E" County in Oklahoma Territory). Filmed by the Genealogical Society of Utah, 1990, 12 rolls, beginning with FHL film #1065158 (1912-1914).

■ **1912-1934 Scholastic Enumeration Records, Major County, Oklahoma**, microfilm of originals in the Major County courthouse in Fairview, OK. Some books and years missing. Filmed by the Genealogical Society of Utah, 1991, 12 rolls, beginning with FHL film #1787502 (Enumeration records, 1912).

■ **1912-1926 School Censuses, Woodward County, Oklahoma,** microfilm of original records at the Woodward County Courthouse in Woodward, OK. Most volumes individually indexed. Filmed by the Genealogical Society of Utah, 1989, 11 rolls, beginning with FHL film #1639863 (1912-1913 enumerations).

■ **1916 County Register of Electors, Latimer County, Oklahoma,** microfilm of original records in the Latimer County Courthouse, Wilburton, OK. Contains an alphabetical list of registered voters including name, school district number, date of registration, age, residence, occupation, race, political affiliation, and registration certificate number. Filmed by the Genealogical Society of Utah, 1998, 1 roll, FHL film #2129955.

■ **1916 Taxpayers, Muskogee County, Oklahoma**, published serially in *Muskogee County Genealogical Society Quarterly,* beginning with Vol. 13, No. 4 (Dec 1996).

■ **1916 Taxpayers, Nash Township, Muskogee County, Oklahoma**, in *Fort Gibson Genealogical Society Newsletter,* Vol. 1, No. 6-9 (Sep 1985).

■ **1916 Farmers and Taxpayers, Okmulgee County, Oklahoma**, in *Okmulgee County Genealogical Society Newsletter,* Vol. 6, No. 1-2 (1991).

■ **1916-1946 Precinct Registers, Alfalfa County, Oklahoma**, microfilm of originals at Alfalfa County Museum, Cherokee, Oklahoma. Names in the register are listed alphabetically under each town. Information for each person listed in the register includes name, school district, date of registration, age, residence, occupation, race, color and political party. Precinct registers are not numbered. Filmed by the Genealogical Society of Utah, 1999, 1 roll, FHL film #2134766.

■ **1916-1920 County Register of Electors, Cotton County, Oklahoma,** microfilm of original records at the Cotton County Courthouse in Walters, OK. Names are listed under the first letter of the last name. Information includes name of voter; school district; date of registration; age, address and occupation of voter; occupation, race, color and political affiliation of voter and registration certificate number. Filmed by the Genealogical Society of Utah, 1998, 1 roll, FHL film #2109807.

■ **1916-1948 Greer County.** See ***Precinct Registers, 1916-1948; Register of Electors, 1916-1918, Greer County, Oklahoma,*** microfilm of originals in the Greer County courthouse in Mangum, OK. Most volumes individually indexed (formatted in the "ABC self-indexing format"). Some of the registers give birth dates as early as 1856. Filmed by the Genealogical Society of Utah, 1994, 1 roll, FHL film #1954680.

■ **1916-1922 Precinct Voting Registers, McClain County, Oklahoma,** microfilm of original records at the McClain County Clerk's office in Purcell, OK. Filmed by the Genealogical Society of Utah, 1997, 1 roll, FHL #2108408.

■ ***1916-1920 Census Records, Pawnee Agency,*** microfilm of originals at the Regional National Archives, Ft. Worth, TX. Filmed by the National Archives, 1978, 1 roll, FHL film #1249780.

■ **1916-1933 Voter Registration Records, Canadian County, Oklahoma,** microfilm of original records at the Canadian County Courthouse in El Reno, OK. Volume 2 is indexed. Index is at beginning of volume. Filmed by the Genealogical Society of Utah, 2001, 1 roll, FHL film #2257892.

■ ***1917 Comanche Indian Census, Kiowa Indian Agency, Anadarko, Caddo County, Oklahoma,*** compiled by Polly Lewis Murphy, et al, published by the authors, Anadarko, OK, 1990, 71 pages. FHL book 970.3 C73c.

■ **1917 Tax Assessment, Coal County, Oklahoma,** in *Oklahoma Genealogical Society Bulletin,* Vol. 28, No. 1 (1983).

■ **1917 Garfield County Taxpayers,** in *Garfield County Roots and Branches,* Vol. 21, No. 1 (Feb 1998) through Vol. 21, No. 3 (Aug 1998).

■ **1917 Taxpayers, Woods County, Oklahoma,** published serially in *Woods County Genealogists,* beginning with Vol. 9, No. 1 (Spring 1983).

■ ***1918 Kiowa County, Oklahoma Tax List,*** copied by Edna Howl Lauer, published by the Hobart Chapter of DAR, 32 pages. FHL book 976.6 A1 no. 21.

■ **1920 Personal Assessment, Seminole County, Oklahoma,** in *String of Beads,* Vol. 8, No. 2 (Dec 1999).

■ ***1922-1936 Tulsa County Voting Records,*** compiled from the original records by the Tulsa Genealogical Society, 15 vols., 1993-1996. FHL book 976.6 N4t vol. 1-15.

Online Censuses & Substitutes, Indian Territory & Oklahoma

Online Index: The printed ***Index to the Final Rolls*** is available online at the National Archives Web site. Go to **www.archives.govresearch_room/arc/arc_info/native_americans_final_rolls_index.html#list.**

■ **Online Census Databases, Oklahoma.** The following databases can be found at these sites:

www.ancestry.com

- 1890 OK Territorial Census
- 1900-1930 Federal Censuses
- 1907 OK – Seminole County
- Social Security Death Index
- Obituary Collection
- Dawes Commission Index, 1898-1914
- Dawes Commission Index, 1896
- Evening News, The (Ada, Oklahoma)
- Confederate States Field Officers

www.censusfinder.com

- 1890 Territorial Census Index – Statewide
- 1890 Territorial Oklahoma Census Records
- The 1890 Oklahoma City Directories
- Oklahoma State Databases of Census & Genealogy Records
- Search Oklahoma Census Records at Ancestry

www.census-online.com

- **Countywide census databases** (no. of databases): Adair (8); Alfalfa (0); Atoka (1); Beaver (1);l Beckham (6); Blaine (0); Bryan (0); Caddo (0); Canadian (1); Carter (0); Cherokee (0); Choctaw (0); Cimarron (0); Cleveland (2); Coal (0); Comanche (0); Cotton (0); Craig (0); Creek (0); Custer (1); Delaware (0); Dewey (1) ; Ellis (0); Garfield (0); Garvin (0); Grady (0); Grant (1); Greer (2); Harmon (2); Harper (0); Haskell (0); Hughes (0); Jackson (0); Jefferson (0); Johnston (0); Kay (1); Kingfisher (3); Kiowa (0); Latimer (0); Le Flore (0); Lincoln (1); Logan (1); Love (0); Major (0); Marshall (0); Mayes (4); McClain (1); McCurtain (0); McIntosh (9); Murray (0); Muskogee (0); Noble (0); Nowata (2); Okfuskee (0); Oklahoma (2); Okmulgee (0); Osage (0); Ottawa (1); Pawnee (0); Payne (1); Pittsburg (0); Pontotoc (0); Pottawatomie (0); Pushmataha (0); Roger Mills (0); Rogers (0); Seminole (0); Sequoyah (0); Stephens (0); Texas (0); Tillman (0); Tulsa (0); Wagoner (0); Washington (0); Washita (0); Woods (0); and Woodward (2).

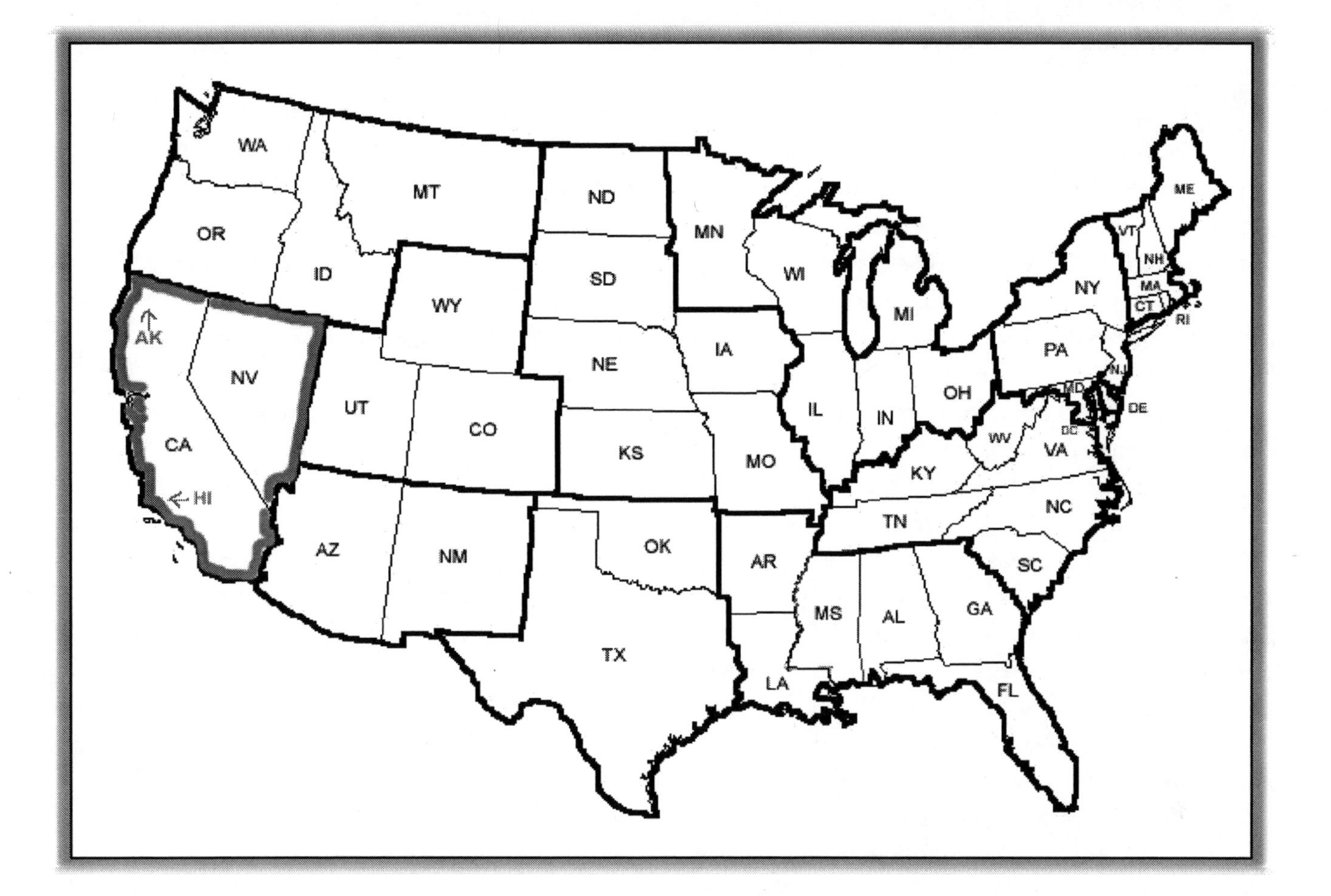

Chapter 2W – California & Nevada; Alaska & Hawaii

CALIFORNIA

History to 1850

The first European visitors to the Pacific coast of North America were convinced that California was really an island. The first claim began in 1542 when Juan Rodriguez Cabrillo anchored his ship in San Diego Bay and claimed the entire "island" for Spain, which he named California. One explanation for the name was that Cabrillo had been reading Ordoez de Montalvo's romance of chivalry, *Las Sergas de Esplandian* (Madrid, 1510), in which is told of black Amazons ruling an island of the name California near the Indies. No one can find any other reference to the name California before 1542, and it has no other known Spanish origin. If the California island story is really what happened, it would make Cabrillo quite a romantic.

Never one to cede anything to the Spanish, in 1579 Sir Francis Drake sailed up the Pacific coast beyond San Francisco Bay and claimed the entire region for England, naming the area New

Albion. But the British claim was never reinforced by colonization, and in 1602 Sebastian Vizcaíno charted the same coast and reconfirmed Spain's claim to the region, from the southern tip of present Baja California, Mexico to the northern tip of present Vancouver Island, British Columbia.

For the next two centuries, Baja (lower) California and Alta (upper) California were part of **New Spain**, which was a description of all Spanish claims in North America. During this time, California was mostly ignored by Europeans, except as a re-supply point for Spanish ships sailing from Manila and other Pacific outposts before returning to Spain. During the late 1600s a few presidios (forts) were established as protection for the re-supply ports, such as the presidios at Monterey Bay and San Diego Bay. The Spanish were reacting to the intrusion of Russian and English trading posts established just north of San Francisco Bay, but both intruders left California after only a few years.

The Spanish colonization of California did not really begin until the arrival of Junipero Serra in 1769. Serra was the Franciscan monk who founded the first nine California missions, ranging from San Diego Bay to San Francisco Bay. The Spanish were to establish a total of 21 missions, all connected with a wagon road called the El Camino Real (the Royal Road). For the most part, the Spanish missions were successful in converting the local Indians to Roman Catholicism, but a few California Indian tribes resisted by attacking and burning the missions. In response, the Spanish government provided military protection for the missions by establishing several more presidios, evenly distributed between the coastal missions. During the Spanish era, over 100 presidios were established.

Spanish pueblos (communal villages) were the first civilian towns in California. Mission workers were provided by the Catholic Church, while the presidios were manned by Spanish soldiers. But to provide civilian farmers and workers for the pueblos, incentives were required to get people to move there, and thus, a system of land grants, tax breaks, and other incentives was established. To attract settlers to the new towns, the Spanish government provided free land, livestock, farming equipment, and an annual allowance for the purchase of clothing and other supplies. In addition, the settlers were exempt from all taxes for five years. In return for this aid, the settlers were required to sell their surplus agricultural products to the presidios.

Three pueblos were created in California, the first was San José, founded in 1777. It was followed in 1781 by El Pueblo de Nuestra Señora la Reina de los Angeles del Río de Porciúncula. By 1790, the Los Angeles pueblo had 28 households and a population of 139. By 1800 Los Angeles had 70 households and a population of 315. The villa de Branciforte near present Santa Cruz was another pueblo established in 1797, developed primarily as a place for discharged soldiers from the presidios, but the Branciforte pueblo was never able to attract many soldiers and was abandoned in 1802. The San Jose and Los Angeles pueblos were still active when California became an American possession in 1848.

Colonial Spanish rule in California ended when Mexico gained independence from Spain in February 1821, but the Californios never heard about it until the new Mexican governor arrived in November 1822. At first, the transition of power had no change to the California way of life. But within just a few years, the mission system in California came to an end.

As early as 1826, Americans began visiting California after establishing overland routes from the Rocky Mountains. After some initial resistance, the Californios accepted their intrusion into the area. As an isolated province of Mexico, California had few manufactured goods, and the Americans were welcomed for the items they brought for trade.

By the early 1830s, the mission communities established by the Spanish were absorbed into the Mexican civilian government. The mission properties were distributed to soldiers in lieu of wages and to Mexican citizens in return for political favors. The local natives who remained were assimilated into the local society serving as laborers, household servants and vaqueros (cowboys).

The Mexican government continued the land grant process which the Spanish had initiated, and with the demise of the Mission system, California evolved into an isolated province dominated by a series of large ranchos, some as large as 100,000 acres in size. By 1840, huge cattle ranches stretched from San Diego Bay to San Francisco Bay, including the great Central Valley of California.

In 1841, the first wagon train left Missouri for California, even though the area was not part of the United States, and the settlers had no guarantee they would be able to stay. As more traders and settlers from the United States began to arrive, they sent back reports extolling the climate, long growing seasons, and the bounty one could gain from the California soil. During the 1840s, the American government was under the influence of an unofficial but practiced policy called "manifest destiny," meaning the U.S. believed they had the God-given right to take the entire continent by any means. Clearly, Americans began to covet the area of the southwest, and in fact, many historians feel that the annexation of Texas in 1845 led to a war that was as much to capture California and New Mexico from Mexico as it was to take the Rio Grande valley.

After the 1845 annexation of Texas, the U.S. honored the Republic of Texas claim to the Rio Grande Valley. This claim was the basis for the Mexican American War, which began in December 1845 when U.S. forces invaded the Rio Grande area and took possession of the area. In 1848, as part of the Treaty of Guadalupe Hidalgo ending the war with Mexico, the U.S. officially acquired the Rio Grande area, including the portion which extended into New Mexico. But in satisfaction of its "manifest destiny" urges, the U.S. also acquired the remainder of New Mexico, which included present Arizona; as well as present Colorado (west of the continental divide), and all of the present states of Utah, Nevada, and California. As compensation for the huge acquisition, the U.S. paid Mexico 15 million dollars for an area that was comparable in size to the Louisiana Purchase, and was over half of the Republic of Mexico.

Meanwhile, the U.S. had settled its long-held claim to the Oregon Country in 1846, establishing the 49th parallel as the northern boundary with British territory, and confirming the southern boundary of Oregon with California as the 42nd parallel. With the addition of the areas acquired from Mexico in 1848, the United States, for the first time, was a nation from "sea to sea," a goal of American expansionists dating back to George Washington and Thomas Jefferson. "Manifest destiny" was no longer a goal, it was a reality.

Immediately after becoming American territory in 1848, California was to rapidly expand, in fact the dramatic expansion was more than even the most ardent of the "manifest destiny" adherents could have foretold. Although California was never a territory, it quickly became a state in 1850. No other American territory or region had become a state so quickly.

The reason for California's sudden rise, of course, was that gold was discovered, creating a stampede of prospectors from all over the U.S. In just a few months, the population in California went from less than 2,000 Americans in December 1848 to nearly 93,000 by June 1850. Meanwhile, the State Constitutional Convention of 1849, followed by statehood in 1850, led to the establishment of a state government that rapidly organized the entire state into counties, taxing districts, and voting precincts.

The 1850 federal census taken in California was considered flawed due to the loss of the schedules for some of the most populous counties. The state of California authorized its own census in 1852 as a means of rectifying the problem. The 1852 census was the only state census taken in California and has its own problems due to faded and often illegible pages. But as census substitutes, California's many county-wide tax lists and voter registrations for every county document the population growth. More importantly for genealogists, they provide the actual names of the 19th century inhabitants of California in more detail than perhaps any other state in the Union.

Spanish & Mexican California Censuses & Substitutes

■ ***Census Records for Latin America and the Hispanic United States,*** by Lyman D. Platt, published by Genealogical Publishing Co., Baltimore, 1998, 198 pages. Survey of census records for Latin America, including Mexico, Guatemala, Peru, and other Latin American countries, and the Hispanic United States (including California, Arizona, New Mexico, Texas, Louisiana, and Florida). Includes a listing of the archives and publications where census records are available, as well as Family History Library film numbers. FHL book 980 X23pc.

■ ***The Decline of the Californios, a Social History of the Spanish-Speaking Californians, 1846-1890,*** by Leonard Pitt, published by the University of California Press, Berkeley, CA, 1965, 324 pages. FHL book 979.4 H2p.

■ **Ramo de Historia: 1522-1822,** microfilm of original manuscripts, Archivo General de la Nación, México, documenting the official records of the colonial provinces of Spain and Mexico. The "Historia" collection in the National Archive of Mexico includes copies of early conquest chronicles, historical accounts from the Vice-regal period, and other documents of an ecclesiastical, civic, military, and geographical nature. There are many pages of documents relating to the missions, presidios, and pueblos of California. Most of the volumes include an index. Filmed by the Genealogical Society of Utah, 1993-1994, 81 rolls, beginning with FHL film #1857411 (Colección de memorias de Nueva Espana [Memories of New Spain]).

■ **1752-1837 Early California.** See **Early California and Nogales, Arizona Lists of Expeditionary Members, Soldiers and Residents, 1752, 1775, 1781-1837: Material Emphasizes Santa Barbara, California,** microfilm of original manuscripts at the Santa Barbara Historical Society, Santa Barbara, California. Text in English and Spanish. Includes Santa Barbara censuses taken in 1834 and 1837. Includes lists of military personnel and other areas of California. Filmed by the Genealogical Society of Utah, 1988, 1 roll, FHL film #1548299.

■ **1770-1915 Mission Registers, Catholic Church, Mission San Carlos Burromeo de Carelo (Carmel, California),** microfilm of original records in the Diocesan Pastoral Office, Monterey and in the California State Archives, Sacramento, California. Includes baptisms, burials, marriages, confirmations, and miscellaneous business accounts. Filmed by the Genealogical Society of Utah, 1972, 10 rolls, beginning with FHL film #913159 (Index to baptisms and burials 1770-1885). A series of biographical sketches of clergy from 1817 is on FHL film #913167.

■ **1772-1906 Mission Registers, Catholic Church, Mission San Luis Obispo de Tolosa,** microfilm of original records in the Diocesan Pastoral Office, Monterey and in the California State Archives, Sacramento, California. Includes baptisms, burial, marriages, confirmations, and miscellaneous business accounts. Filmed by the Genealogical Society of Utah, 1972, 4 rolls, beginning with FHL film #913300 (Baptisms 1772-1821).

■ **1776-1912 Mission Registers, Catholic Church, Mission Santa Barbara,** microfilm of original records at the Mission Archives, Santa Barbara, California. Includes baptisms, burials, marriages, confirmations, and miscellaneous business accounts. Filmed by the Genealogical Society of Utah, 1972, 5 rolls, beginning with FHL film #913165 (Baptisms 1786-1858 Santa Barbara Indians).

■ **"1790 Padron (Census) of California,"** a typescript (photocopy) copied from Las Familias de California section in *Southern California Historical Society Quarterly*. Includes index. FHL book 979.4 A1 no. 67, and FHL film #1036747. See also ***California 1790 Census: Cities of Los Angeles, Monterey, San Diego, San Francisco, San Jose, and Santa Barbara,*** edited by Sue Powell Morgan. Published by Genealogical Services, West Jordan, UT, 1998, 63 pages. Contains transcripts of the 1790 censuses (padrones) of the pueblos, presidios, and missions for several colonial California cities. The census information includes the name of the head of household, age, occupation, previous residence or nativity, marital status, name of spouse, names and number of children and their ages. The heads of households are listed in alphabetical order. Includes surname index. FHL book 979.4 X29m.

■ **1797-1937 Mission Registers, Catholic Church, Mission San Miguel Arcangel (San Miguel, California),** microfilm of original records in the Diocesan Pastoral Office, Monterey, California. Includes baptisms, burials, marriages, confirmations, and miscellaneous business accounts. Filmed by the Genealogical Society of Utah, 1972, 3 rolls, beginning with FHL film #913312 (Baptisms 1797-1862, includes some marriages).

■ **1801 Santa Barbara Mission.** See **Estadística del Censo, 1801,** microfilm of original manuscript at the Mission Archives, Santa Barbara, California, including census statistics of the mission and town of Laguna 1801. Filmed by the Genealogical Society of Utah, 1972, 1 roll, FHL film #913167.

■ **1822 Mexican California Census.** See ***Chihuahua, Mexico Padrones / Census 1822: Para/for Babanoyava, San Andres, Santa Ysabel, Santa Cruz Tapacolmes, Satevo, Villa de Chihuahua y Quartels 1, 2, 3, 4, Ciudad de Chihuahua,*** by Patsy Mendoza Castro de Ludwig, published by the author, San Jose, CA, 1998, 473 pages. Extracts of microfilms #145 and #149, from the Bancroft Library, University of California at Berkeley, of the 1822 Padrones. Only legible entries were extracted. Text in Spanish and English. Includes index. FHL book 972.16 X22L.

■ **"1836 Mexican Census of Los Angeles and Orange County Area: Including the Rancho Santiago de Santa Ana After Which the Rancho Santiago Community Was Named,"** prepared from the 1836 Los Angeles Padron published in the *Southern California Historical Society Quarterly* in 1936 by Nanci Cole, Leonard Johnson, and Carol Swanson as a class project for Wayne Dell Gibson. Published by Santa Ana College Foundation Press, 1976, 104 pages. FHL book 979.4 X2mx. Also on microfilm, filmed by the Genealogical Society of Utah, 1987, 1 roll, FHL film #1320513.

■ **1836, 1844 Los Angeles Censuses.** See **Padrones de la Ciudad de Los Angeles, 1836, 1844,** microfilm of original records by the Genealogical Society of Utah, 1972, 1 roll, FHL film #913156.

■ ***Index to the Padrones,*** by Zoeth Skinner Eldredge, published by the Bancroft Library, University of California at Berkeley, Bancroft Library Series, Vol. III, 130 pages. This is an index to the Bancroft Library collection of 18th and 19th century padrones of residents of California. FHL book 979.4 X22e.

Spanish & Mexican Land Grants in California

As an example of the use of the California land grants as a genealogical resource, allow me to briefly tell the story of Andrew Jackson Dollarhide of Missouri. He came to California in 1849, initially to work the gold fields, but very soon after arriving, saw horse trading as a more profitable enterprise. Andrew and his brother Winfield began chasing down and taming wild horses left over from the Spanish era, and found themselves in the Pope Valley, an offshoot of Napa Valley, where Andrew did some business with a local cattle rancher. While there he became enamored with the rancher's daughter, and in 1852, Andrew married Delvina Pope, the daughter of Julian Pope, for whom Pope Valley was named. Julian Pope, born in Kentucky, came to California in 1830, became a citizen of Mexico and was given a land grant by the Mexican government in 1841. The land area of the grant was six miles long by three miles wide, or about 11,520 acres. After Julian Pope died in 1853, his daughter inherited her father's rancho. She died a few years later, which gave title of the land to her widower. Andrew Dollarhide became the sole owner of an original Mexican land grant, called *Rancho Locallome,* which Andrew changed to *Dollarhide Ranch.* Three generations of the Dollarhide family operated a large cattle ranch on the original property until the mid-1920s. Because of the existence of the original land grant cases, mostly residing in the National Archives (and microfilm at the Family History Library), the exact property can be traced to the original Mexican Land Grant of 1841, the confirmation of land ownership by a U.S. District Court in 1853, and a deed recorded at the Napa County Courthouse. Virtually all of the Spanish and Mexican land grants can be used the same way. Thus, the California land grants act as census substitutes, identifying many of the earliest inhabitants. By the way, the "Dollarhide Ranch" brand is on the label of an award winning Cabernet Sauvignon produced from vineyards on the same land, now owned by the St. Supéry Winery.

The following references may lead a researcher to a Spanish-Mexican Land Grant Holder:

■ **Spanish Archives, 1833-1845,** microfilm of original records at the California State Archives, Sacramento, CA. Additional indexes are filmed with each volume. Years are mixed within each volume. Written in Spanish and English. Filmed by the Genealogical Society of Utah, 1975. 14 rolls, beginning with FHL film #978888 (Index to Spanish archives).

■ ***Pueblo de Sonoma Court Records: Expedientes, 1841-1849,*** Translated, edited, and abstracted by Camelia Domenech O'Connor, published by Sonoma County Genealogical Society, 2003, 30 pages. From intro: "Historically, these records involve some of the first land grants made to private individuals in the area north of San Francisco. The petitions in this project were submitted to the court to document proof of ownership of these grants and to verify title. They also contain two land sales. However, these are not a complete listing of all the land grants in the North Bay area."

The court of record was in the city of Sonoma. Includes bibliographical references and a surname index. FHL book 979.418 R29o.

■ *Early Sonoma County, California, Land Grants 1846-1850,* Carmen J. Finley, projects director, Sonoma County Genealogical Society. Contains abstracts of original land grant records, arranged in alphabetical order by surname, showing name of grantee, description of property, acres, number of lots, cost, date of grant deed, authority, original deed book volume and page numbers. Also contains photocopies of original pages in grant deed books. Contents: Early history of the town of Sonoma (historical sketch) – Grants, vol. 2-A (includes alphabetical listing by surname of grantee, property description or lot number, acres, cost, date of grant deed, authority, book and page numbers), with photocopy of original record book -- Grants, book A, town lots (includes alphabetical listing of petitioners, giving lot numbers, cost, size in acres, date of petition and reference to volume and page numbers) – Grants, vol. B, town lots (includes alphabetical listing by surname of petitioners, giving lot nos. cost in dollars, size in acres, date of petition, and reference to volume and page number) with photocopy of original record book. Filmed by the Genealogical Society of Utah, 2002, 1 roll, FHL film #1440586.

■ *Spanish and Mexican Land Grants in California,* by Rose Hollenbaugh Aviña, published Arno Press, New York, 1976, 137 pages. FHL book 979.4 R2m.

■ *Ranchos of California, a List of Spanish Concessions, 1775-1822, and Mexican Grants, 1822-1846,* Robert Granniss Cowan, published Academy Library Guild, Fresno, CA, 1956, 151 pages. FHL book 979.4 R2cr.

■ *The History of San Diego County Ranchos: The Spanish, Mexican and American Occupation of San Diego County and the Story of the Ownership of Land Grants Therein,* by Robert W. Brackett, sponsored by the San Diego Historical Society, published by Union Title Insurance Co., 1960, 70 pages. FHL book 979.498 R2h.

■ *The Confirmation of Spanish and Mexican Land Grants in California,* by Ivy Belle Ross, reprint of thesis done in 1928 for the University of California, published by R. & E. Research Associates, 1974, 59 pages. FHL book 979.4 A1 No. 46.

■ *California Ranchos: Patented Private Land Grants Listed by County,* edited by Michael & Mary Burgess, published by Borgo Press, San Bernardino, CA, 1988, 144 pages. Includes index. Lists name of rancho, and to whom the patent was granted, including date and description of the location. FHL book 979.4 R2s.

■ **Private Land Grant Cases in the Circuit Court of the Northern District of California, 1852-1910,** microfilm of original records located in the National Archives, Washington, DC. The Circuit Court of the Northern District of California was abolished in 1911. The cases were given to the U.S. District Court for the Northern District of California, in 1912. Courts are located in San Francisco. The land grants were originally made from 1769-1846 by the Spanish and the Mexican governments, and later confirmed by the U.S. government from 1852-1910 through the Board of California Land Commissioners. Title to more than 8.8 million acres, nearly 14,000 square miles, of California land was based on 588 grants that were originally made by Spanish or Mexican authorities from 1769 to 1846 and later confirmed by the U.S. Government. Litigation concerning the land titles began immediately after the area was ceded by Mexico in 1848, and is continuing. Contains private land-grant case files, 1852-1910, of the Circuit Court of the Northern District of

California (abolished in 1911), which were given to the U.S. District Court for the Northern District of California in 1912. Filmed by the National Archives, series T1207, 28 rolls, beginning with FHL film #940180 (General index to cases).

■ **Index to Private Land Grant Cases, U.S. District Court, Southern District of California,** microfilm of original records located in the National Archives, Washington, DC. Contains index and dockets of land grant cases, arranged by docket number, for the years 1854-1878. Filmed by the National Archives, Series T1215, 1 roll, FHL film #940153. Another filming: FHL film #1415715.

■ **Index and Calendar to Private Land Grant Cases, U.S. District Court, Northern District of California, 1853-1904**, microfilm of original records located in the National Archives. Filmed by the National Archives, series T1214, 1 roll, FHL film #940151. Another filming: FHL film #1415714.

■ **Index by County to Private Land Grant Cases, U.S. District Court, Northern and Southern districts of California**, microfilm of original records located in the National Archives. Contains Spanish and Mexican land grants for ranchos listed by counties as the counties existed on Jan. 1, 1939. Arranged by county, rancho name, and includes name of claimant. Filmed by the National Archives, series T1216, 1 roll, FHL film #940152. Another filming: FHL film #1415716.

■ **Pre-statehood Records, 1838-1851, San Francisco County, California,** microfilm of original records at the San Francisco County courthouse. Indexes have been filmed at the end of some volumes. These are mostly land and property records; additional material may be found in the copies. Text in Spanish and English. Filmed by the Genealogical Society of Utah, 1975, 21 rolls, beginning with FHL film #974651 (Spanish blotters, 1839 & on).

California Censuses & Substitutes, 1850-1967

■ **1850 California Federal Census (Original Schedules),** microfilm of originals at the National Archives, part of series M432, 4 rolls, FHL has the following:

- Butte and Calaveras Counties, FHL film #2490.
- El Dorado County and Colusa County (part), FHL film #2491.
- Los Angeles, Marin, Mariposa, Mendocino, Monterey, Napa, Sacramento, Santa Barbara, Santa Cruz, San Diego, San Joaquin, and San Luis Obispo Counties; Shasta County (part), Shasta City (part), FHL film #2492.
- Solano, Sonoma, Sutter, Colusa (part), Shasta County (part), Shasta City (part), Trinity, Tuolumne, Yolo, and Yuba Counties, FHL film #442879.

■ **1850 California Federal Census (Indexes).** See ***Index to the 1850 Census of the State of California,*** compiled by Alan P. Bowman, published by Genealogical Publishing Co., Inc., Baltimore, 1972, 605 pages. Includes all California counties except Contra Costa, San Francisco, and Santa Clara Counties. FHL book 979.4 X2p. See also ***California 1850 Census Index,*** edited by Ronald Vern Jackson and Gary Ronald Teeples, published by Accelerated Indexing Systems, Bountiful, UT, 1978, 144 pages. FHL book 979.4X2j. See also ***California 1850 Census Index, A-Z,*** published by Heritage Quest, Bountiful, UT, 2001, 643 pages. FHL book 979.4 X22h. See also ***1850 U.S. Census Index, Western States: CA, NM, OR, TX, UT; Extracted From the Original U.S. Federal Census Schedules,*** CD-ROM publication by Heritage Quest, Bountiful, UT, 2000. Includes 332,865 records searchable by surname, given name, age, sex, race, birth place, state of census, county, locality, and National Archives microfilm roll number. The indexed names from the California 1850 federal census are complete for all counties except Contra Costa, San Francisco, and Santa Clara counties.

■ **1852 California State Census (Originals)**, microfilm of original schedules at the California State Archives, Sacramento. Filmed by the Genealogical Society of Utah, 1972, 6 rolls, as follows:

- Butte, Calaveras, Contra Costa, and El Dorado Counties, FHL film #909229.
- El Dorado, Los Angeles, Mariposa, Klamath, Mendocino, Monterey, Napa, Nevada, and Placer (part) Counties, FHL film #909230.
- Placer (part), Sacramento, San Diego, San Francisco (part) Counties, FHL film #909231.
- San Francisco (part), and San Joaquin (part) Counties, FHL film #909232.
- San Joaquin, San Luis Obispo, Santa Barbara, Santa Clara, Santa Cruz, Shasta, Sierra, Siskiyou, Solano, Sonoma, Trinity, and Tulare Counties, FHL film #909233.
- Tuolumne, Yolo, and Yuba Counties, FHL film #909234.

■ **1852 California State Census (Transcript).** See *California State Census, 1852*, microfilm of a typed transcript compiled in 1935 by the Daughters of the American Revolution. Includes index. Filmed by the DAR, 3 rolls, as follows:

- Butte, Calaveras, Colusa, Contra Costa, Eldorado, Klamath, Los Angeles, Marin, Mariposa, Mendocino, Monterey, Napa, Nevada, Placer, San Diego, and Sacramento Counties, FHL film #558285.
- San Diego, San Francisco, San Joaquin, San Luis Obispo, Santa Barbara, Santa Clara, Santa Cruz, and Shasta Counties, FHL film #558286.
- Sierra, Siskiyou, Solano, Sutter, Trinity, Tulare, Tuolumne, Yolo, and Yuba Counties, FHL film #558287.

■ **1852 California State Census (Index).** See *Index to the Gold Rush Census, California, 1852: An Every Name Index of the 1852 California Census Microfilm and the Subsequent 1935 D.A.R. Transcription,* CD-ROM publication prepared by the Southern California Genealogical Society, 2000, Burbank, CA. Windows format and Acrobat Reader 4.0 required. FHL CD No. 1017.

■ **1861-1865 California Union Soldiers.** See *Index to Compiled Service Records of Volunteer Union Soldiers Who Served in Organizations From the State of California,* microfilm of original records at the National Archives, Central Plains Branch, Kansas City, MO, Series M0533, filmed by the National Archives, FHL has 7 rolls, as follows:

- Surnames A-C, FHL film #881609.
- Surnames Co-Fos, FHL film #881610.
- Surnames Fot-I, FHL film #881611.
- Surnames J-McD, FHL film #881612.
- Surnames McE-P, FHL film #881613.
- Surnames Q-St, FHL film #881614.
- Surnames Su-Z, FHL film #881615.

The above publication included in **Index to Soldiers & Sailors of the Civil War**, a searchable name index to 6.3 million Union and Confederate Civil War soldiers now available online at the National Park Service Web site. A search can be done by surname, first name, state, or unit. California supplied 21,405 men to the war (all Union). To search for one go to the NPS Web site at **www.civilwar.nps.gov/cwss/.**

■ **1862-1866 Internal Revenue Assessment Lists for California,** microfilm of original records located in the National Archives, Washington, DC. Lists are arranged alphabetically by surname of those being assessed for each period. Filmed by the National Archives, 1988. FHL has 33 rolls, beginning with FHL film #1534664 (Annual lists, 1863).

■ ***The Foreign-born Voters of California in 1872: Including Naturalization Dates, Places, and Courts of Record,*** compiled by Jim Faulkinbury, published by the author, Sacramento, 1994. Arranged in two sections: the first containing nativity demographics for each county, listing the number persons from various countries; and the second containing an alphabetical listing by surname, showing name, age, nativity, date and place naturalized, name of court, remarks, year registered and county where registered. Information taken from the great registers for 1872 of each county entered by the county clerks. FHL has 6 microfiche, beginning with FHL fiche #6334778.

■ **1800s-1920 Vital Statistics Index,** microfilm of card file located at the Special Collections Unit, California State Library, Sacramento, CA. Card file arranged in alphabetical order by surname, of responses to vital records inquiries. Information includes the name and event in question, and applies to the state of California in general. Inquiries deal with births, marriages, deaths, naturalizations, etc., and responses include newspapers, county registers, California great register, and various other record sources throughout the state of California. Filmed by the Genealogical Society of Utah, 1991, 10 rolls, as follows:

- A - Brutt, J, FHL film #1711369.
- Brutt, J - Demont, A, FHL film #1711370.
- Demont, A - Gold, F, FHL film #1711371.
- Gold, F - Holman, N, FHL film #1711372.
- Holman, N - Landrum, R, FHL film #1711373.
- Landrum, R - Menne, A, FHL film #1711484.
- Menne, A - Peterson, A, FHL film #1711485.
- Peterson, A - Scott, C, FHL film #1711486.
- Scott, C - Vail, F, FHL film #1711487.
- Vail, F – Z, FHL film #1711488.

■ **Index to the California Information File, 1846-1986,** microfiche of index cards at the California State Library, Sacramento. Contains an index to the California Information File which contains 717,000 cards bearing about 1.4 citations to information in California periodicals, newspapers, manuscript collections, selected books, vertical file collections, county histories, government documents, theses, biographical encyclopedias, biographical files, etc. *A User's Guide to the California Information File,* is available under FHL call no. 979.4 A1 No. 127. Card file filmed by Commercial Microfilm Service, Bellevue, WA, 1986, 550 microfiche, beginning with FHL fiche #6333977 (A. – Adams, Charles). To locate film numbers for all 550 fiche, use the www.familysearch.org site. Go to Library / FHL Catalog / Film/Fiche Search: "6333977" (first film number in the series).

■ ***The California 1890 Great Register of Voters Index,*** compiled by volunteers of various California genealogical societies as part of a project for the California State Genealogical Alliance, Janice G. Cloud, editor, Margaret Goodwin, database manager, published by Heritage Quest, North Salt Lake, UT, 2001, 3 vols. Includes name of voter, age, birth place, current residence, county, registration date, naturalized, and page in original register. This work indexes 311,028 men living in California in 1890 and includes significant personal information useful to historians and genealogists. It goes far to replace lost 1890 federal census information. A citizen registering to vote in 1890 provided significant data: Name, Age, Birthplace, Occupation, Home address, and Naturalization information for immigrants. Given that approximately one third of the voters of California were immigrants, it is obvious that this information may be particularly useful. FHL book 979.4 N4c v.1-3.

■ ***1890 Great Registers,*** a CD-ROM publication by Heritage Quest, North Salt Lake, UT. This is a CD version of the 3-vol. index of the Great Registers prepared by the California State Genealogical Alliance Volunteers. CD not cataloged by the FHL as yet.

■ **1904-1949 San Francisco Newspapers Index,** microfiche of index cards located at the California State Library in Sacramento. The San Francisco Newspapers index is made up of three interfiled indexes covering the *San Francisco Call*, Jan. 1, 1904-Aug. 31, 1913, the *San Francisco Examiner*, Sept. 1, 1913-Sept. 23, 1928, and the *San Francisco Chronicle*, Sept. 1, 1913-Dec. 31, 1959. Includes an index which also has cross references to the subject headings or topics in the newspaper index. Includes a user's guide, compiled by Richard Terry, and published by the California State Library, Sacramento. FHL microfiche series contains 703 fiche, beginning with FHL fiche #6333980.

California Great Registers, by County

The extant Great Registers (voter registration lists) for all California counties were microfilmed by the Genealogical Society of Utah, from 1957 through 1994, including original manuscripts, printed reports, and duplicates found at county courthouses, local museums and libraries; or the California State Library (printed volumes) and the California State Archives (original manuscripts). The name lists from the Great Registers supply genealogists with the same details as a census, including name, age, nativity, naturalization status, marital status, etc. Most of the name lists are organized by year, then in alphabetical order by the first letter of the surname of the voter.

All 58 California counties are represented below. For those counties without microfilmed great registers (Only Imperial, Kings, and Riverside counties missing); tax lists, county deed indexes or city directories are indicated, so at least one census substitute for each county is shown:

■ **Alameda County Great Registers,** microfilm of original records at the California State Library, Sacramento, CA. Each year is alphabetically arranged by first letter of surname. Filmed by the Genealogical Society of Utah, 1975, 7 rolls, as follows:

- 1867, 1872-1873, 1875-1878, FHL film #976446.
- 1879-1880, 1882, 1884, 1886, 1888, FHL film #976447.
- 1890, 1892, FHL film #976448.
- 1894, FHL film #976449.
- 1896, FHL film # 976450.
- 1898, FHL film #976451.
- 1898 (supplement), FHL film #976452.

■ **Alameda County Great Registers, 1886-1900,** microfilm of original records at the Alameda County Clerk's office, Oakland, CA. Registers of voters alphabetically arranged by first letter of surname within each precinct. Filmed by the Genealogical Society of Utah, 1957, 1974, 3 rolls, as follows:

- 1896 Great register, FHL film #2502.
- 1892-1894 Great registers, FHL film #1000101.
- 1900 Great register, FHL film #1000102.

■ **Alpine County Great Registers, 1873-1890,** microfilm of original records at the Alpine County courthouse, Markleeville, CA. Includes the following years: 1873, 1875, 1876, 1877, 1879, 1886, 1888, 1890. Filmed by the Genealogical Society of Utah, 1975, 1 roll, FHL #976453.

■ **Alpine County Great Registers, 1866-1910; Indexes, 1908-1920,** microfilm of records located at the Alpine County Historical Records Commission, Markleeville, CA. Registers list registration number, name, age, occupation residence, precinct, country or state of nativity, post office address, date, place and court of naturalization, date of registration. Index to great registers are arranged by precinct number and give registration number, name, address, occupation and sometimes political party. Filmed by the Genealogical Society of Utah, 1993, 1 roll, FHL film #1888010 (Great registers and indexes).

■ **Amador County Great Registers,** microfilm of original records at the California State Library, Sacramento. Includes the following years: 1867, 1868, 1871, 1872, 1873, 1875, 1876, 1877, 1879, 1880, 1884, 1886, 1888, 1890, 1892, 1894, 1896, 1898. Filmed by the Genealogical Society of Utah, 1975, 1 roll, FHL film #976453.

■ **Butte County Great Registers and Indexes,** microfilm of original records located at the Meriam Library, California State University, Chico. Filmed by the Genealogical Society of Utah, 1990, 6 rolls, as follows:

- Index, Great Registers, 1866-1878, A-Z, FHL film #1685570.
- Index, Great Registers, 1884-1894, A-Z, FHL film #1685571.
- Great Registers, 1896, FHL film #1685572.
- Great registers, 1900, FHL film #1685573.
- Great registers, 1902-1909, FHL film #1685574.
- Great registers, 1906-1907, FHL film #1685575.

■ **Butte County Great Registers, 1867-1898,** microfilm of original records at the California State Library, Sacramento, CA. Each year is alphabetically arranged by first letter of surname. Filmed by the Genealogical Society of Utah, 1975, 2 rolls, as follows:

- 1867, 1872-1873, 1875, 1879-1880, 1882, 1886, 1890, 1892, 1894, and 1896, FHL film #976454.
- 1898, FHL film #976455.

■ **Butte County Great Register Index, 1898,** microfilm of card index located at the Paradise Genealogical Society Library, Paradise, California. Index gives name, place of residence, occupation, age, height, state of nativity or last residence. Filmed by the Genealogical Society of Utah, 1992, 2 rolls, FHL Film #1819679 (Index, A-M), and FHL film #1819680 (Index, Mc – Z).

■ **Butte County, California, Great Register: 1866-1878,** microfilm of typescripts located at the Paradise Genealogical Society Library, Paradise, California. Contains an extraction in chronological order, then alphabetical order by first letter only of surname of the great registers or voting registers of Butte County. Gives name, age, birth place, occupation, residence and date registered. Filmed by the Genealogical Society of Utah, 1992, 1 roll, FHL film #1831809.

■ **Butte County, California, Great Register: 1867-1908,** microfilm of a typescript located at the Paradise Genealogical Society Library, Paradise, California. Contains a listing by district and precinct of adult males over 21 years of age, giving name, age, state or country of nativity, occupation, local residence. Filmed by the Genealogical Society of Utah, 1992, 1 roll, FHL film #1831809.

■ **Calaveras County Great Registers, 1867-1898,** microfilm of original records at the California State Library, Sacramento, CA. Includes the following years: 1867, 1871, 1872, 1873, 1875, 1876, 1877, 1879, 1880, 1882, 1884, 1886, 1888, 1890, and 1892. Filmed by the Genealogical Society of Utah, 1975, 1 roll. FHL film #976456.

■ ***Colusa County Great Register, 1880,*** microfilm of original volume loaned for filming by Virginia Lee Stinchfield McKay, published by Addington & Green, county printers in 1880. Filmed by the Genealogical Society of Utah, 1981, 1 roll, FHL film #1035840.

■ **Colusa County Great Registers, 1866-1909,** microfilm of original records at the Colusa County Clerk's Office, Colusa, CA. Each year is alphabetically arranged by first letter of surname. Filmed by the Genealogical Society of Utah, 1989, 4 rolls, as follows:

- 1866-1877, FHL film #1666711.
- 1866-1890, 1890, A-L, FHL film #1666712.
- 1890, A-Z; 1892, A-Z, 1896, FHL film #1666724.
- 1900-1902, A-Z, 1904-1909, A-Z, FHL film #1666725.

■ **Colusa County Great Registers, 1871-1898,** microfilm of original records at the California State Library, Sacramento, CA. Filmed by the Genealogical Society of Utah, 1975. Includes the following years: 1871, 1872, 1873, 1875, 1876, 1880, 1886, 1890, 1892, 1894, 1896, 1898. FHL film #976457.

■ **Contra Costa County Great Registers, 1867-1898,** microfilm of original records at the California State Library, Sacramento, CA. Filmed by the Genealogical Society of Utah, 1975, 1 roll. Includes the following years: 1867, 1871, 1872, 1873, 1875, 1877, 1879, 1880, 1884, 1886, 1890, 1892, 1894, 1896, 1898, FHL film #976458.

■ **Del Norte County Great Registers, 1872-1898,** microfilm of original records at the California State Library, Sacramento, CA. Del Norte County absorbed part of old Klamath County in 1874. Includes the following years: 1872, 1875, 1876, 1878, 1886, 1890, 1892, 1894, 1896, 1898. Filmed by the Genealogical Society of Utah, 1975, 1 roll. FHL film #976459.

■ **El Dorado County Great Registers, 1867-1898,** microfilm of original records at the California State Library, Sacramento, CA. Includes the following years: 1867, 1868, 1872, 1873, 1875, 1876, 1877, 1878, 1879, 1880, 1882, 1886, 1888, 1890, 1892, 1894, 1896, 1898. Filmed by the Genealogical Society of Utah, 1975, 1 roll, FHL film #976460.

■ **Fresno County Assessment Rolls, 1862-1880,** microfilm of records located at the Fresno County Public Library, Fresno, CA. Rolls are arranged in alphabetical order by first initial of surname of owner. Contains record of assessments of real and secured personal property, showing name of owner, description of property, value, amount assessed and date paid, etc. Filmed by the Genealogical Society of Utah, 1994, 2 rolls, FHL film #1955259 (1862, 1872-1873 Assessment rolls), and FHL film #1955260 (1872-1880 Assessment rolls).

■ **Fresno County Great Registers, 1866-1908,** microfilm of records located at the Fresno County Public Library, Fresno, CA. Contains registers of legal voters giving name, age, occupation, country of nativity, post office address, naturalization court and place (if applicable), etc. Early registers from 1866 to 1895 are arranged alphabetically by surname. Registers from 1896 are arranged alphabetically by precinct name and then alphabetically by surname within the precinct. Filmed by the Genealogical Society of Utah, 1994, 16 rolls, as follows:

- 1866-1877, 1878-1887, 1887-1890, FHL film #1955187.
- 1887-1899, 1896-1899 Fresno City, FHL film #1955188.
- 1893-1895, 1873-1874, FHL film #1955717.
- 1896-1899, FHL film #1955189.
- 1896-1900, FHL film #1955190.
- 1900, FHL film #1955191.
- 1900-1902 , Fresno City, FHL film #1955193.
- 1902, FHL film #1955194.
- 1902, Fresno City, 1904 Precincts, FHL film #1955195.
- 1904 Precincts, FHL film #1955196.
- 1904 Precincts, 1904 Fresno City, FHL film #1955197.
- 1906 Precincts, FHL film #1955198.
- 1906 Precincts, FHL film #1955199.
- 1906 Fresno City, 1906 Precincts, 1908 Precincts, FHL film #1955257.
- 1908 Fresno County, FHL film #955258.
- 1908 Fresno Co., 1908 Fresno City, FHL film #1955259.

■ **Fresno County Great Registers, 1867-1898,** microfilm of original records at the California State Library, Sacramento, CA. Filmed by the Genealogical Society of Utah, 1975, 2 rolls, as follows:

- Great registers 1867, 1871-1873, 1875-1877, 1879-1880, 1884, 1886, 1890, FHL film #976461.
- Great registers 1892, 1894, 1896, 1898, FHL film #976462.

■ **Glen County Great Registers, 1892, 1894, 1896, 1898,** microfilm of original records at the California State Library, Sacramento, CA. Filmed by the Genealogical Society of Utah, 1975, 1 roll, FHL film #976463.

■ **Humboldt County Great Registers, 1871-1898,** microfilm of original records at the California State Library, Sacramento, CA. Each year is alphabetically arranged by first letter of surname. Filmed by the Genealogical Society of Utah, 1975, 2 rolls, as follows:

- Great registers, 1871-1873, 1875, 1879-1880, 1882, and 1890, FHL film #976464.
- Great registers, 1892, 1894, 1896, and 1898, FHL film #976465.

■ ***County of Humboldt Great Registers, 1866-1875,*** compiled by Marilyn Keach Milota, published by Humboldt County Genealogical Society, Eureka, CA, 1996, 322 pages. Contains an abstract of the original great register, arranged in alphabetical order by surname and giving complete name, registration number, age, place of nativity, occupation, place of residence and date of registration. FHL book 979.412 N48m 1866-1875.

■ ***County of Humboldt Great Register, 1896,*** compiled by Marilyn Keach Milota, published by Humboldt County Genealogical Society, Eureka, CA, 1996, 441 pages. Contains an abstract of the original great register, arranged in alphabetical order by surname and giving complete name, registration number, age, place of nativity, occupation, place of residence and date of registration. FHL book 979.412 N48m 1896.

■ ***List of the Names and Registration of the Domiciled Inhabitants of the County of Humboldt: Copied From the Great Register of Humboldt County, October 7th, 1884,*** by Louis T. Kinsey, County Clerk, photocopy of original published by L.T. Kinsey, County Clerk, 1884; published by Redwood Genealogical Society, Fortuna, CA, 1991, 68 pages. FHL book 979.412 N4L. See also ***List of the Names and Registration of the Domiciled Inhabitants of the County of Humboldt, Copied From the Great Register of Humboldt County, October 7th, 1884,*** compiled by Marilyn Keach Milota, published by Humboldt County Genealogical Society, Eureka, CA, 1997, 267 pages. Contains an abstract of the 1885 great register of voters, arranged in alphabetical order by surname and giving full name, age, place of birth, occupation, residence, date when sworn, number in register. FHL book 979.412 N48m.

■ ***Great Register and Supplement of the County of Humboldt, State of California, 1890: A Full, True, and Correct Transcript of the Registered Voters of Humboldt County, on the Sixth Day of October, A.D. 1890,*** microfilm of original register in possession of the Redwood Genealogical Society, Fortuna, California. Filmed by the Genealogical Society of Utah, 199?, FHL film #1750861. Book reprinted by the society, 130 pages, FHL book 979.412 N4h 1890.

■ **Imperial County Grantor and Grantee Indexes to Deeds, 1851-1907,** microfilm of records located at the Imperial County Recorder's Office, El Centro, CA. Filmed by the Genealogical Society of Utah, 1985, 1 roll, FHL film #1433101.

■ **Inyo County Great registers, 1871-1872, 1875, 1877, 1879-1880, 1882, 1884, 1886, 1890, 1892, 1894, 1896, 1898,** microfilm of original records at the California State Library, Sacramento, CA. Each year is alphabetically arranged by first letter of surname. Filmed by the Genealogical Society of Utah, 1975, 1 roll, FHL film #976466.

■ **Kern County Great registers, 1867-1898,** microfilm of original records at the California State Library, Sacramento, CA. Filmed by the Genealogical Society of Utah, 1975, 2 rolls, as follows:

- Great registers 1867, 1872-1873, 1873, 1877, 1879-1880, 1882, 1884, 1886, 1888, 1890, FHL film #976467.
- Great registers 1892, 1894, 1896, 1898, FHL film #976468.

■ ***The Great Register (Voter Registration), Kern County, California: A Partial Substitute for 1890 Census,*** data input and compilation by J. Hoyle Mayfield, published by Kern County Genealogical Society, Bakersfield, CA, 1995, 72 pages. Contains an alphabetical listing by surname of voters, showing name, age, state where born, occupation, residence, registration date, naturalization date, and remarks. FHL book 979.488 N4m.

■ ***Polk's Kings County (Kings County, California) City Directory: Including Avenal, Corcoran, Hanford and Lemoore,*** published by the R. L. Polk Co., FHL has 1955 and 1970 directories. FHL 979.485 E4p 1955 and 979.485 E4p 1970.

■ **Klamath County Great Registers, 1869, 1873,** microfilm of original records at the California State Library, Sacramento, CA. Each year is alphabetically arranged by first letter of surname. Klamath County was abolished in 1874, its area now in Del Norte County, northern Humboldt County, and western Siskiyou County. Filmed by the Genealogical Society of Utah, 1975, 1 roll, FHL film #976469.

■ **Lake County Great Registers, 1867-1894,** microfilm of records located at the Lake County Museum, Lakeport, CA. Contains registration information of voters, giving registration number, name, age, country of nativity, occupation, local residence, naturalization date, place, and court (if pertinent), date of registration, sworn, and cancellations. Names are arranged within alphabetical sequence (i.e., no strict order within each surname initial letter). Filmed by the Genealogical Society of Utah, 1991, 1 roll, FHL film #1750347.

■ **Lake County Great Registers, 1872-1873, 1875, 1879-1880, 1888, 1890, 1892, 1894, 1896, 1898,** microfilm of original records at the California State Library, Sacramento, CA. Each year is alphabetically arranged by first letter of surname. Filmed by the Genealogical Society of Utah, 1975, 1 roll, FHL film #976469.

■ **Lassen County Great Registers, 1866-1890, 1892-1894, 1896-1901,** microfilm of original records located at Lassen County Courthouse, Susanville, CA. Volumes arranged alphabetically by first letter of surname. Register includes name, age, occupation, county or state of nativity, local residence, naturalization (if applicable), etc. Filmed by the Genealogical Society of Utah, 1992, 1 roll, FHL film #1853495.

■ **Lassen County Great registers, 1868, 1873, 1877, 1879, 1886, 1890, 1898,** microfilm of original records at the California State Library, Sacramento, CA. Each year is alphabetically arranged by first letter of surname. Filmed by the Genealogical Society of Utah, 1975, 1 roll, FHL film #976470.

■ ***Census of the City and County of Los Angeles, California For the Year 1850, Together With an Analysis and an Appendix,*** by Maurice H. Newmark and Marco R. Newmark, published by the Los Angeles Times-Mirror Press, 1929, 139 pages. FHL book 979.493 X2p 1850.

■ **Los Angeles County Great Registers, 1873-1896,** microfilm of original records at the California State Library, Sacramento, CA. Each year is alphabetically arranged by first letter of surname. Filmed by the Genealogical Society of Utah, 1975, 6 rolls, as follows:

- Great registers 1873, 1875-1876, 1879-1880, 1882, 1884, 1886, FHL film #976928.
- Great registers 1888, 1890, FHL film #977994.

- Great registers 1892, 1894, FHL film #976929.
- Great registers, Los Angeles precincts 1-47, 1896, FHL film #976930.
- Great registers, Los Angeles precincts 48-74, 1896; precincts Acton – Pomona, 1-2, 1896, FHL film #976931.
- Great registers, Precincts, Pomona 3-4 – Wilmington, 1896, FHL film #976932.

■ ***Index to the 1890 Los Angeles County Great Register, State of California,*** compiled by Whittier Area Genealogical Society, 1993, 335 pages. Index includes register page, surname, given name, age, date of birth, residence, registration date. FHL book 979.493 N42w.

■ **1873-1935 Los Angeles City Directories,** microfilm of originals published by various publishers. Filmed by Research Publications, Woodbridge, CT, 1980-1984, FHL has 49 rolls, as follows:

- 1873, FHL film #1376980.
- 1875, 1878, 1879-1880, 1881-1882, FHL film #1376980.
- 1883-1884, 1884-1885, 1886-1887, 1887, FHL film #1376981.
- 1888, 1890, FHL film #1376982.
- 1890-1891, 1891, 1892, FHL film #1376983.
- 1893, 1894, FHL film #1376984.
- 1895, FHL film #1376985.
- 1896, FHL film #1376986.
- 1897, FHL #1376987.
- 1898, 1899-1900, FHL film #1376988.
- 1899-1900, FHL film #1376988.
- 1900-1901, FHL film #1376989.
- 1902, FHL #1611676.
- 1903 (A - Broadway), FHL #1611676.
- 1903 (Broadway - Z), FHL film #1611677.
- 1904, FHL film #1611677.
- 1905, FHL film #1611678.
- 1906, FHL film #1611679.
- 1906-1907, 1907 (A - Van Loan), FHL film #1611680.
- 1907 (Van Loan - Z), 1908, FHL film #1611681.
- 1909-1910, 1910 (A-Neicho), FHL film #1611682.
- 1910 (Neidermark - Z), 1911, FHL film #1611683.
- 1912, FHL film #1611684.
- 1913, FHL film #1611685.
- 1914, FHL film #1611686.
- 1915, FHL film #1611687.
- 1916, FHL film #1611688.
- 1917, FHL film #1611689.
- 1918, FHL film #1611690.
- 1920, FHL film #1611691.
- 1921, FHL film #1611692.
- 1922, (A-Z), FHL film #1611693.
- 1922, (Ads – END); 1923 (A-M) FHL film #1611694.
- 1923 (M-Z), FHL film #1611695.
- 1924 (A - Davis, C.R.), FHL film #1611695.
- 1924 (Davis C.R. Co. – Advertisements), FHL film #1611696.
- 1924 (advertisements - END), FHL film #1611697.
- 1925 (A - Lange, John), FHL film #1611697.
- 1925 (Lange, John C. - Z), FHL film #1611698.
- 1926, FHL film #1611699.
- 1926 (Moody, N. - Z), film #1611700.
- 1927 (A - Bruno, El.), FHL #1611700.
- 1927 (Bruno, Em. - Z), FHL film #1611701.
- 1928 (A - Parker), FHL film #1611702.
- 1928 (Paddack - Z), FHL film #1611703.
- 1929 (A - Eital R.), FHL film #1611703.
- 1929 (Eitel, H - Z), FHL film #1611704.
- 1930 (A - Morse, O.), FHL film #1611705.
- 1930 (Morse, P. - End), FHL film #1611706.
- 1931 (A - Etter, William A.), FHL film #1611706.
- 1931 (Etter, William K. - Z), FHL film #1611707.
- 1931 (Advertisements to END), FHL film #1611708.
- 1932 (A - Jackson-Post), FHL film #1611708.
- 1932 (Jackson, Pr. - Z), FHL film #1611709.
- 1933 (A - Smith, Geo.), FHL film #1611710.
- 1933 (Smith, Geo. - Z), FHL film #1611711.
- 1934 (A - Feldman, Chas.), FHL film #1611711.
- 1934 (Feldman, Chas. - Z), FHL film #1611712.
- 1935 (A - Lomile, M.), FHL film #1611713.
- 1935 (Lomis, J. - Z), FHL film #1611714.

■ **Madera County Great register, 1898,** microfilm of original records at the California State Library, Sacramento, CA. Alphabetically arranged by first letter of surname. Filmed by the Genealogical Society of Utah, 1975, 1 roll, FHL film #976933.

■ **Marin County Great Registers, 1866-1908,** microfilm of original records at the California State Archives, Sacramento, CA. Original register of printed copies in the State Library. Each year is alphabetically arranged by first letter of surname. Filmed by the Genealogical Society of Utah, 1975, 6 rolls, as follows:

- Great registers, 1866-1892, FHL film #980447.
- Great registers, 1892,1894, FHL film #980448.
- Great registers, 1896, FHL film #980449.
- Great registers, 1900, FHL film #980450.
- Great registers, 1902, 1904, FHL film #980451.
- Great registers, 1906, 1908, FHL film #980452.

■ **Marin County Great Registers, 1867-1868, 1873, 1875-1876, 1879-1888, 1886, 1888, 1890, 1892, 1894, 1896, 1898,** microfilm of original records at the California State Library, Sacramento, CA. Each year is alphabetically arranged by first letter of surname. Filmed by the Genealogical Society of Utah, 1975, 1 roll, FHL film #976933.

■ *Great Register of Marin County, 1890,* compiled by the Marin County Genealogical Society, Novato, CA, 1992, 52 pages. Indexed by John E. Hale. Indexed first in alphabetical order by surname, giving name, age, state where last resided, occupation, current residence, and if naturalized; indexed second by town of residence, occupation, where born, and name. FHL book 979.462 N42h 1890.

■ *Great Register of Marin County, California, 1892,* facsimile reproduction of original published 1892, published by the Marin County Genealogical Society, Novato, CA, 2002, 39 pages. FHL book 979.462 N4g 1892.

■ **Mariposa County Great Registers, 1872-1873, 1875-1877, 1879-1880, 1882, 1884, 1886, 1888, 1890, 1892, 1894, 1896, 1898,** microfilm of original records at the California State Library, Sacramento, CA. Each year is alphabetically arranged by first letter of surname. Filmed by the Genealogical Society of Utah, 1975, 1 roll, FHL film #976934.

■ *The Great Register of Mariposa County, California, 1890: Registered Voters of Mariposa County,* compiled and edited by Fresno Genealogical Society, Fresno, CA, 1992, 30 pages. Contains an alphabetical listing of registered voters, giving full name, age, birth place, residence, registration date, naturalization date, and occupation. FHL book 979.446 N4m.

■ **Mendocino, California Great Registers, 1866-1873, 1866-1879,** microfilm of registers located at Held Poage Memorial Home & Research Library, Mendocino County Historical Society, Ukiah, CA. Contains a register of voters, giving name, age, country of nativity, occupation, local residence, date, place and court when naturalized, and date of voter registration. Although the dates for both registers would seem to indicate duplicates, they are separate and not the same. The first register is missing surnames from A to D. Arranged in alphabetical order by surname initial. Filmed by the Genealogical Society of Utah, 1991, 1 roll, FHL film #1769135.

■ **Mendocino County Great Registers,** microfilm of original records at the California State Library, Sacramento, CA. Filmed by the Genealogical Society of Utah, 1960-1975, 2 rolls, as follows:

- Great registers for 1892, 1894, 1896, 1898, FHL film #976936.
- Great registers for 1867, 1871, 1873, 1875-1877, 1879-1889, 1882, 1884, 1886, 1888, 1890, FHL film #976935.

■ *Great Register of the County of Mendocino, California For the Year 1882,* microfilm of original published: Ukiah, Calif.: Mendocino Dispatch and Democrat, 1882, 49 pages. Filmed by the Genealogical Society of Utah, 1960, 1 roll, FHL film #207670.

■ ***Abstract From the 1890 Great Register of the State of California, County of Mendocino,*** by the Santa Barbara County Genealogical Society, 1998, 102 pages. Contains an alphabetical listing by surname, giving names, page no. in register, age, birth place, current residence, registration date, naturalization remarks (by code) if applicable. FHL book 979.415 N48a.

■ ***Great Register of Mendocino County, State of California, 1898,*** reprint of 1898 original by Pomo Chapter, Daughters of the American Revolution, 1979, 96 pages. FHL book 979.415 N4m.

■ **Merced County Great Registers, 1867, 1869, 1871-1872, 1875-1877, 1879-1880, 1890, 1892, 1894, 1896, 1898,** microfilm of original records at the California State Library, Sacramento, CA. Each year is alphabetically arranged by first letter of surname. Filmed by the Genealogical Society of Utah, 1975, 1 roll, FHL film #976937.

■ ***Merced County, California 1890 Great Register of Voters,*** compiled by members of the Merced County Genealogical Society, published Merced, CA, 1993, 59 pages. Includes alphabetized by surname voter registration for each precinct and a general index to voters. FHL book 979.458 N4m.

■ **Modoc County Great Registers, 1875-1876, 1879-1880, 1888, 1890, 1892, 1894, 1896, 1898,** microfilm of original records at the California State Library, Sacramento, CA. Includes a separate index for 1876-1879. Each year is alphabetically arranged by first letter of surname. Filmed by the Genealogical Society of Utah, 1975, 1 roll, FHL film #976938.

■ **Mono County Great Registers, 1872, 1875-1876, 1879-1880, 1882, 1884, 1886, 1888, 1890, 1892, 1894, 1896, 1898,** microfilm of original records at the California State Library, Sacramento, CA. Each year is alphabetically arranged by first letter of surname. Filmed by the Genealogical Society of Utah, 1975, 1 roll, FHL film #976939.

■ ***Great Register of the County of Mono, for the Year 1890,*** reprint of original volume, published by the Santa Barbara County Genealogical Society, 1991, 16 pages. Contains an alphabetical register (by first letter of surname only) of voters, giving voting number, name of voter, age, place of nativity, occupation, local residence, naturalized date, place and court, date of registration and if sworn. FHL book #979.4 A1 no. 220, and FHL film #2055286.

■ **Monterey County Great Registers, 1867, 1869, 1872, 1875-1876, 1879-1880, 1884, 1886, 1888, 1890, 1892, 1894, 1896, 1898,** microfilm of original records at the California State Library, Sacramento, CA. Each year is alphabetically arranged by first letter of surname. Filmed by the Genealogical Society of Utah, 1975, 1 roll, FHL film #977080.

■ ***Certified Copy of the Great Register of Monterey County, California, September 3, 1879,*** microfilm of original published by Monterey Democrat Book and Job Printing Office, Salinas City, CA, 1879, 31 pages. Contains registration information for 1866. Filmed by the Genealogical Society of Utah, 1976, 1 roll, FHL film #982110.

■ ***1890 Great Register of Monterey County, California,*** data extracted by volunteers from the Monterey County Genealogy Society, project coordinator, Karen Clifford; quality control editor, Bettyann Hedegard, published 1993, 114 pages. Arranged in alphabetical order by surname. From intro: "The following entries were extracted from the Great Register of Monterey County, a voter registration listing that can be used as a substitute of the missing

1890 federal census." Contains page number of original register, last and given names, age, where born, occupation, residence, naturalized plus date, place and court, and date registered. FHL book 979.476 N4g.

■ *Certified Copy of the Precinct Registers of Monterey County, California, 1896: Includes Information Transcribed From Other Sources and Submitted in Place of Missing Pages by the Staff Members of the Monterey, California Stake Branch Genealogical Library of the Church of Jesus Christ of L.D.S.* Transcript filmed by the Genealogical Society of Utah, 1976, 1 roll, FHL film #982110.

■ **Napa County Great Registers, 1867-1898,** microfilm of original records at the California State Library, Sacramento, CA. Includes the following years: 1867, 1872, 1875, 1880, 1888, 1890, 1892, 1894, 1896, 1898. Filmed by the Genealogical Society of Utah, 1975, 1 roll, FHL film #977081.

■ **Abstract of Napa County Great Registers: 1868-1905,** microfilm of records located at the Napa Valley Genealogical and Biographical Society, Napa, California. Copied by members of the society and arranged in alphabetical order for all Great Register years. Each entry contains name, age, nativity, date of registration, occupation, date of naturalization, residence and physical description of persons who registered to vote. Filmed by the Genealogical Society of Utah, 1997, 8 rolls, as follows:

- Great register, A to Buc, 1868-1905, FHL film #2074324.
- Great register, Buc to Far, 1868-1905, FHL film #2074354.
- Great register, Far to His, 1868-1905, FHL film #2074355.
- Great register, His to Mcc, 1868-1905, FHL film #2074356.
- Great register, Mcc to Ped, 1868-1905, FHL film #2074357.
- Great register, Ped to Ros, 1868-1905, FHL film #2074358.
- Great register, Ros to Vet, 1868-1905, FHL film #2074432.
- Great register, Vet to Zol, 1868-1905, FHL film #2074433.

■ **Nevada County Great Registers, 1867-1898,** microfilm of original records at the California State Library, Sacramento, CA. Filmed by the Genealogical Society of Utah, 1975, 2 rolls, as follows:

- Great registers 1867-1868, 1871, 1873 1875-1877, FHL film #977082.
- Great registers 1879-1880, 1882, 1884, 1886, 1888, 1890, 1892, 1894, 1896, 1898, FHL film #977083.

■ **Nevada County Great Registers, 1892-1908,** microfilm of records located at the Searls Historical Library, Nevada City, CA. Contains voting registers, showing voter's registration number, name, age, distinguishing physical marks or characteristics, occupation, country of nativity, place of residence, precinct, post office address, date, place and court of naturalization, date of registration. Filmed by the Genealogical Society of Utah, 1998, 3 rolls, as follows:

- Great registers, 1892-1894, FHL film #2132607.
- Great registers, 1900-1902, FHL film #2132608.
- Great registers, 1906-1908, FHL film #2132609.

■ *1890 Great Register of Nevada County, California Voter Registration List,* compiled by Emma Lee Price, published by Conejo Valley Genealogical Society, Thousand Oaks, CA, 1994, 96 pages. Shows page number in original register, an alphabetical listing by surname of voter, age, birthplace, precinct, date of registration and naturalization status. FHL book 979.437 N4p.

■ **Orange County Great Registers, 1892, 1894, 1896,** microfilm of original records at the California State Library, Sacramento, CA.

Filmed by the Genealogical Society of Utah, 1975, 1 roll, FHL film #977084.

■ ***The Great Register of Orange County, California, 1890,*** compiled by Orange County California Genealogical Society, Orange, CA, 1996, 48 pages. Contains a transcript of the original registers arranged in alphabetical order by surname, showing page and registration number, surname, given name, age, birthplace (state or country), occupation, residence, date, place and court where naturalized, and registration date. FHL book 979.496 N4o.

■ **Placer County Great Registers, 1867-1898,** microfilm of original records at the California State Library, Sacramento, CA. Each year is arranged alphabetically by the first letter of surname. Filmed by the Genealogical Society of Utah, 1975, 2 rolls, as follows:

- Great registers, 1867-1868, 1871-1873, 1876-1877, 1879-1880, 1882, FHL film #977085.
- Great registers, 1884, 1886, 1888, 1890, 1892, 1894, 1896, 1898, FHL film #977086.

■ **Plumas County Great registers, 1867-1898,** microfilm of original records at the California State Library, Sacramento, CA. Includes the following years: 1867-1869, 1871, 1872, 1875-1877, 1879-1880, 1884, 1886, 1888, 1890, 1892, 1894, 1896 & 1898. Filmed by the Genealogical Society of Utah, 1975, 1 roll, FHL film #977087.

■ **1905-1934 Riverside City/County Directories,** microfilm of original records located in various libraries and societies. Filmed by Research Publications, Inc., Woodbridge, CT, 1995, 6 rolls. FHL has the following:

- 1905, 1906, 1907, 1908 & 1910 Riverside City directories, FHL film #2308395.
- 1911, 1912, 1913 & 1914 Riverside city and county directories, FHL film #2308396.
- 1915, 1916, 1917 & 1918-1919 Riverside city and county directories. FHL film #2308397.
- 1921, 1923, 1925 & 1928 Riverside city directories, FHL film #2308398.
- 1927, 1929 & 1930 Riverside city directories, FHL film #2308399.
- 1931-1932 & 1934 Riverside city directories, FHL film #2308400.

■ **Sacramento County Great Registers, 1866-1901,** microfilm of original records at the California State Archives, Sacramento, CA. Each year is alphabetically arranged by first letter of surname. Contains original volumes of the printed copies in the State Library. Filmed by the Genealogical Society of Utah, 1975, 19 rolls, as follows:

- Great registers 1866, 1871, 1873, FHL film #978917.
- Great registers 1874-1880, FHL film #978918.
- Great registers 1880-1881, FHL film #978919.
- Great registers 1881-1888, FHL film #978920.
- Great registers 1882, 1884, 1886, FHL film #978921.
- Great registers 1888, FHL film #978922.
- Great registers 1890, FHL film #978923.
- Great registers, A-N 1890, FHL film #978924.
- Great registers, O-Z 1890, FHL film #978925.
- Great registers, 1892, FHL film #978926.
- Great registers, 1894, FHL film #978927.
- Great registers, 1895 (supplement), FHL film #978928.
- Great registers, A-K 1896, FHL film #978929.
- Great registers, L-Z 1896, FHL film #978930.
- Great registers 1897 (supplement), A-K 1898, FHL film #978931.
- Great registers, L-Z 1898, FHL film #978932.
- Great registers (supplement) 1898-1899, A-D 1900, FHL film #978933.
- Great registers, E-Q 1900, FHL film #978934.
- Great registers, R-Z 1900, 1900-1901 (supplement), FHL film #978935.

■ ***Great Register: Containing the Names and Registration of the Domiciled Inhabitants of the County of Sacramento, Qualified Electors and Legal Voters Thereof, 1866-1880,*** an apparent original volume, source and location unknown. Filmed by the Genealogical Society of Utah, 197?, 1 roll, FHL film #590424.

■ **Sacramento County Great Registers, 1867-1898,** microfilm of original records at the California State Library, Sacramento, CA. Each year is alphabetically arranged by first letter of surname. Filmed by the Genealogical Society of Utah, 1975, 3 rolls, as follows:

- Great registers, 1867-1868, 1872-1873, 1875-1877, 1879, FHL film #977088.
- Great registers, 1880, 1882, 1884, 1886, 1888, 1890, FHL film #977089.
- Great registers, 1892, 1896, 1898, FHL film #977090.

■ **Index to Sacramento County Voter Registrations: 1867 and 1872**, microfilm of card file located at the California State Library, Sacramento. Contains names of voters taken from the Great Register for Sacramento County, 1867 and 1872, arranged in alphabetical order by surname, giving name, age, nationality, occupation, location of residence, and date of registration. Filmed by the Genealogical Society of Utah, 1991, 7 rolls, as follows:

- 1867, A - Craw, A 1867, FHL film #1711488.
- 1867, Craw, A – Smith, A, FHL film #1711489.
- 1867, Smith, A - Z, FHL film #1711597.
- 1872, Clays - Hatch, C, FHL film #1711598.
- 1872, Hatch, C. - Mix, FHL film #1711599.
- 1872, Mix - Thomas, A, FHL film #1711600.
- 1872, Thomas, A - Z, FHL film #1711601.

■ *Supplement to the Great Register of the County of Sacramento for the Year 1882,* microfilm of original published by H.S. Crocker & Co., 1882, 12 pages. Alphabetically arranged. Filmed by the Genealogical Society of Utah, 1960, 1 roll, FHL film #207672.

■ **Sacramento County Great Register Index, 1890,** microfilm of original manuscript at the Sacramento County Clerk's Office. An alphabetical register of voters, by precinct, showing names and addresses of voters, with name and number of precinct, and may include name of court, with date and place of naturalization if foreign born. Filmed by the Genealogical Society of Utah, 2000, 1 roll, FHL film #2200427.

■ *1890 Great Register, Sacramento County, California,* transcribed & edited by Verna L. Benedict, published by the Genealogical Association of Sacramento, 1995. Includes district number, precinct number, surname, given names, age, birthplace, address of residence, registration date, naturalization date and location if applicable. Arranged in alphabetical order for voters. FHL has 6 microfiche:

- Aagaard – Chatterton, FHL fiche #6334616, fiche 1.
- Chenu – Gannon, FHL fiche #6334616, fiche 2.
- Garbarino – Kelly, FHL fiche #6334616, fiche 3.
- Kelly, T – Neubauer, FHL fiche #6334616, fiche 4.
- Neuhaus – Skelton, FHL fiche #6334616, fiche 5.
- Skidmore – Zora, FHL fiche #6334616, fiche 6.

■ **San Benito County Great Registers, 1875-1898,** microfilm of original records at the California State Library, Sacramento, CA. Includes the following years: 1875-1877, 1879-1880, 1882, 1884, 1886, 1890, 1892, 1894, 1896, 1898. Filmed by the Genealogical Society of Utah, 1975, 1 roll, FHL film #977091.

■ **San Bernardino County Great Registers, 1872-1898,** microfilm of original records at the California State Library, Sacramento, CA. Each year is alphabetically arranged by first letter of surname. Filmed by the Genealogical Society of Utah, 1975, 2 rolls, as follows:

- Great registers, 1872, 1876, 1879-1880, 1882, 1884, 1886, 1888, 1890, 1892, 1894, 1896, FHL film #977092.
- Great registers, 1898, FHL film #977093.

■ *Great Register of the County of San Bernardino, State of California: Uncanceled Entries Existing on Said Register the Ninth Day of October, A.D. 1882; Made and Done Pursuant of the Provisions of the Political*

Code, microfilm of original published by Times Print House, San Bernardino, CA, 1882, 16 pages. Filmed by the Genealogical Society of Utah, 1960, 1 roll, FHL film #207671.

■ *San Diego Census, 1850 Federal, 1852 California,* compiled by the San Diego Genealogical Society, 1984, 64 pages. FHL book 979.498 X2s.

■ *San Diego Taxpayers,* researched and typed by members of San Diego Genealogical Society, 1984, 48 pages. Contains various lists of assessments and tax rolls for San Diego City for the years 1850-1852. FHL book 979.498/S1 R4s.

■ *Great Register, San Diego County, 1866-1873,* researched and compiled by Patricia Sewell, published by the San Diego Genealogical Society, 1984, 203 pages. Contains a list of voters of San Diego County for the years 1866-1873. FHL book 979.498 N4s.

■ **San Diego County Great Registers, 1867-1898,** microfilm of original records at the California State Library, Sacramento, CA. Filmed by the Genealogical Society of Utah, 1975, 2 rolls, as follows:

- Great registers, 1867, 1871-1873, 1875-1877, 1879-1880, 1884, 1886, 1890, FHL film #977094.
- Great registers, 1892, 1894, 1896, 1898, FHL film #977095.

■ *San Francisco, California, 1890 Great Register of Voters,* edited by Jane Billings Steiner, published by Heritage Quest, North Salt Lake, 2001, 950 pages. Contains a transcript of the 1890 register, giving name of voter, age, birthplace, occupation, address of residence, naturalization details, date registered, district and precinct numbers. FHL book 979.461 N4s. (Also on CD-ROM, see page 44).

■ **San Francisco County Great Registers, 1866-1898; Indexes, 1866, 1888-1904,** microfilm of original records at the California State Library, Sacramento, CA. Filmed by the Genealogical Society of Utah, 1975, 184 rolls, beginning with FHL film #1001665 (Index, Abbe – Hamilton, C). To locate film numbers for all 184 rolls, use the www.familysearch.org site. Go to Library / FHL Catalog / Place Search: "California" / View Related Places: "San Francisco" / California, San Francisco, Voting Registers / "Great registers, 1866-1898; indexes, 1866, 1888-1904."

■ **San Francisco County Index of Naturalized Voters, 1850-1898,** microfilm of index cards located in the San Francisco Archives. Cards contain name of voter and date when voter was naturalized. Also includes number of voter's precinct and ward. Filmed by the Genealogical Society of Utah, 1983, 6 rolls, as follows:

- Voters index, A – C, FHL film #1378779.
- Voters index, C – H, FHL film #1378780.
- Voters index, H - McLeod, D, FHL film #1378781.
- Voters index, McLeod, A – R, FHL film #1378782.
- Voters index, R – V, FHL film #1378783.
- Voters index, V – Z, FHL film #1378784.

■ **San Joaquin County Great Registers, 1867-1898,** microfilm of original records at the California State Library, Sacramento, CA. Each year is alphabetically arranged by first letter of surname. Filmed by the Genealogical Society of Utah, 1975, 3 rolls, as follows:

- Great registers, 1867-1869, 1871-1873, 1875-1877, 1880, 1882, 1884, 1888, 1890, FHL film #977281.
- Great registers, 1892, 1894, 1896, FHL film #977282.
- Great registers 1898 - FHL film #977283.

■ **San Joaquin County Great Registers, 1900-1910,** microfilm of original records located at the Stockton-San Joaquin County Public Library, Stockton, CA. Includes name, age, nativity, place of residence, date and place of naturalization etc. Filmed by the Genealogical Society of Utah, 1992, 8 rolls, as follows:]

- Great registers, 1900, A-S, FHL film #1838363.
- Great registers, 1900, S-Z; 1902, A-M, FHL film

#1838465.
- Great registers, 1902, M-Z; 1904, A-H, FHL film #1838466.
- Great registers, 1904, H-Z; 1906, A-C, FHL film #1838467.
- Great registers, 1906, C-Y, FHL film #1838468.
- Great registers, 1906, Y-Z: 1908, A-Q, FHL film #1838584.
- Great registers, 1908, R-Z; 1910, A-K, FHL film #1838585.
- Great registers, 1910, L-Z, FHL film #1838675.

▪ **Precinct Index Great Register of San Joaquin County, 1904, 1908,** microfilm of original records located at the Stockton-San Joaquin County Public Library, Stockton, CA. Contains alphabetical listing of names for all precincts in San Joaquin County for 1904 and 1908. Filmed by the Genealogical Society of Utah, 1992, 1 roll, FHL film #1838362.

▪ ***San Luis Obispo County 1867 Great Register,*** reprint of 1867 original published by William B. Cook, San Francisco, CA, reprint by San Luis Obispo County Genealogical Society, 1994, 8 pages. Contains an alphabetical listing by surname of voters, showing name, age, occupation, citizenship status, residence and date of entry in register. FHL book 979.4 A1 No. 195 and FHL film #2055163.

▪ **San Luis Obispo County Great Registers, 1867-1868, 1871-1873, 1875, 1877, 1879-1880, 1884, 1886, 1888, 1890, 1892, 1898,** microfilm of original records at the California State Library, Sacramento, CA. Each year is alphabetically arranged by first letter of surname. Filmed by the Genealogical Society of Utah, 1975, 1 roll, FHL film #977284.

▪ ***Published by Authority, General List of Citizens of the United States Resident in the County of San Luis Obispo and Registered in the Great Register of Said County, August, 1871,*** reprint of original printed by A. L. Bancroft & Company, San Francisco, reprinted by San Luis Obispo County Genealogical Society, Atascadero, CA, 1977, 25 pages. Contains name of resident, age, occupation, citizenship status, place of residence, date of entry in register. FHL book 979.478 N4p. Another copy: FHL book 979.478 N4Ge.

▪ ***1890 Great Register With Index for San Luis Obispo County,*** compiled from originals in the possession of San Luis Obispo County Historical Society, San Luis Obispo, CA, by the San Luis Obispo County Genealogical Society, 1993, 60 pages. Includes surname index. Contains a register of voters showing name, age, country of nativity, occupation, local residence (town), naturalization date, place and court, date of registration. FHL book 979.478 N4e.

▪ ***Great Register, San Luis Obispo County, California, 1892,*** extracted by the California Central Coast Genealogical Society, San Luis Obispo, 197?, 186 pages. FHL book 979.478 N43c.

▪ ***Index to Great Register, San Luis Obispo County, 1902,*** microfilm of original published 1902. Filmed by the Genealogical Society of Utah, 1988, 1 roll, FHL film #1571207.

▪ ***San Luis Obispo County, CA, 1892 Great Register,*** compiled by Buelah Heidom and Helen Keller, published by the San Luis County Genealogical Society, Atascadero, CA, 1990, 2 vols.
Contents, vol. 1: A-K; vol. 2: K-Z. Gives name, age, height, complexion, color of eyes, color of hair, visible marks or scars (and location); occupation; country of nativity; place of residence; precinct; post office address; naturalized date, place, court; date registered in 1892. FHL book 979.478 N4g v. 1-2.

▪ **San Mateo County Great Registers, 1867-1869, 1871-1872, 1875-1877, 1879-1880, 1882,**

1884, 1886, 1890, 1892, 1894, 1896, 1898, microfilm of original records at the California State Library, Sacramento, CA. Each year is alphabetically arranged by first letter of surname. Filmed by the Genealogical Society of Utah, 1975, 1 roll, FHL film #977285.

■ ***Index to The Great Register of San Mateo County, 1890, California,*** compiled by The San Mateo County Genealogical Society, 1991, 37 pages. Includes persons name, age, birthplace, residence, if naturalized, and date of registration. FHL book 979.469 N4i.

■ ***Great Registers of the County of Santa Barbara, California, 1869-1911,*** microfilm of original published by Santa Barbara Press, 1869. Includes Great Registers for the years 1866-1869; 1867; 1875; 1877; 1879; 1880 (ms.); 1882; 1882 & 1884; 1886; 1886 with supplement of 1888; 1892; 1896; supplement to 1898 register; index to supplement to precinct, 1911. Names are in alphabetical order. Filmed by the Genealogical Society of Utah, 1988, 1 roll, FHL film #1548299. Another filming of 1879 vol., 1988, FHL film #1571207.

■ ***The Great Register of the County of Santa Barbara, California, 1890,*** photocopy of original by Santa Barbara County Genealogical Society, 1991, 67 pages. Contains a register in alphabetical order by surname, giving voting no., register no., name, age, country of nativity, occupation, local residence, if naturalized and date, place, by what court, date of registration and if sworn. FHL book 979.4 A1 No. 219 and FHL film #2055286.

■ **Santa Barbara County Great Registers, 1873-1875, 1877, 1879, 1890, 1892, 1894, 1896, 1898,** microfilm of original records at the California State Library, Sacramento, CA. Each year is alphabetically arranged by first letter of surname. Filmed by the Genealogical Society of Utah, 1975, 1 roll, FHL film #977286.

■ **Santa Clara County Great Register, 1892,** microfilm of original records, filmed by the Genealogical Society of Utah, 1957, 1 roll, FHL film #2502.

■ **Santa Clara County Great Registers, 1867-1896,** microfilm of original records at the California State Library, Sacramento, CA. Each year is alphabetically arranged by first letter of surname. Filmed by the Genealogical Society of Utah, 1975, 4 rolls, as follows:

- Great registers, 1867-1869, 1871- 1873, 1875-1876, 1879, FHL film #977287.
- Great registers, 1880, 1882, 1884, 1888, 1890, FHL film #977288.
- Great registers, 1892, 1894 (A-Bailey), FHL film #977289.
- Great registers, 1894 (B-Z), 1896, FHL film #977290.

■ ***Santa Clara County, California 1890 Great Register,*** published by the Santa Clara County Historical and Genealogical Society, Santa Clara, CA, 1999, 151 pages. Contains a transcription of the original register, arranged in alphabetical order by surname, giving registration number, name, age, country of nativity, occupation, local residence, naturalization date, place, court, and date of voting registration. FHL book 979.473 N4s.

■ **Santa Cruz County Great Registers, 1868-1869, 1871-1873, 1880, 1886, 1890, 1892, 1894, 1896, 1898,** microfilm of original records at the California State Library, Sacramento, CA. Each year is alphabetically arranged by first letter of surname. Filmed by the Genealogical Society of Utah, 1975, 1 roll, FHL film #978581.

■ **Shasta County Great Registers, 1867-1869, 1871-1873, 1875-1877, 1880, 1882, 1886, 1888, 1890, 1892, 1894, 1896,** microfilm of original records at the California State Library, Sacramento, CA. Each year is alphabetically arranged by first letter of surname. Filmed by the Genealogical

Society of Utah, 1975, 1 roll, FHL film # 978582.

■ *1890 Shasta County Great Register,* compiled and published by Joe Mazzini, Montgomery Creek, CA, 1996, 82 pages. Contains an abstract from the great register (voting registration) giving surname, given name, age, state where born, occupation, residence (town), date registered, if naturalized citizen, comments, register and page numbers.
Arranged in alphabetical order by surname. FHL book 979.424 N49m.

■ **Sierra County Great Registers, 1872-1898,** microfilm of original records at the California State Library, Sacramento, CA. Each year is alphabetically arranged by first letter of surname. Includes the following years: 1872-1873, 1875-1877, 1879-1880, 1884, 1886, 1890, 1892, 1894, 1896, 1898. Filmed by the Genealogical Society of Utah, 1975, 1 roll, FHL film #978583.

■ **Siskiyou County Great Registers, 1867-1898,** microfilm of original records at the State Library, Sacramento, CA. Each year is alphabetically arranged by first letter of surname. Includes the following years: 1867-1868, 1872, 1875, 1877, 1879-1880, 1886, 1890, 1892, 1894, 1896, 1898. Filmed by the Genealogical Society of Utah, 1975, 1 roll, FHL film #978584.

See *Klamath County Great Registers, 1869, 1873,* for the area of western Siskiyou County before 1874.

■ *The 1867 Great Register for Siskiyou County, California,* compiled by John A. Dye and Judy K. Dye, published by the authors, Kent, WA, 1988, 24 pages. Includes surname index. FHL book 979.421 X2d 1867.

■ *The 1892 Great Register for Siskiyou County, California,* compiled by John A. Dye and Judy K. Dye, published by the authors, Spokane, WA, 1986, 60 pages. Includes surname index. Register gives name of person, age, height, complexion, color of eyes, color of hair, visible marks, country of birth, precinct, P.O. address, occupation, date, place and court of naturalization, and date of registration. FHL book 979.421 X2d 1892.

■ *Solano County, California 1852 State Census Index,* compiled by Cordell Cowart, published by the Solano County Genealogical Society, Fairfield, CA, 1992, 60 pages. Index gives name of person, age, sex, occupation, birth state or country and page number in original census. FHL book 979.452 X22c.

■ **Solano County Great Registers, 1867-1898,** microfilm of original records at the California State Library, Sacramento, CA. Each year is alphabetically arranged by first letter of surname. Filmed by the Genealogical Society of Utah, 1975, 2 rolls, as follows:

- Great registers, 1867, 1872-1873, 1875-1880 1882, 1886, 1888, 1890, FHL film #978585.
- Great registers, 1892, 1894, 1896, 1898, FHL film #978586.

■ *Index to the 1890 Great Register of Solano County, California,* compiled by Cordell Coward, published by the Solano County Genealogical Society, Fairfield, CA, 1994, 97 pages. Contains an alphabetical listing by surname of persons, giving page number in original register, surname and first/middle names, age, birth place (state or country), current town of residence, date when registered, and if naturalized. FHL book 979.452 N42c.

■ *An Alphabetical Index and Reprint of the Schedules for the Residents of Sonoma County, California, June 21 - October 21, 1852,* edited by Dennis Harris, Redwood Empire Social History

Project, Department of History, Sonoma State University. Published by the Sonoma County Historical Records Commission, Santa Rosa, CA, 1983, 146 pages. FHL book 979.418 X22h 1852.

■ **Sonoma County Great Registers, 1867-1898,** microfilm of original records at the California State Library, Sacramento, CA. Each year is alphabetically arranged by first letter of surname. Filmed by the Genealogical Society of Utah, 1975, 3 rolls, as follows:

- Great registers, 1867, 1871-1873, 1875, 1879-1880, 1884, 1888, 1890, FHL film #978587.
- Great registers, 1892, 1894, 1896, FHL film #978588.
- Great register, 1898, FHL film #978589.

■ ***Great Register of Voters, Sonoma County, California, 1890,*** compiled by members of the Sonoma County Genealogical Society, published by the society, Santa Rosa, CA, 1989, 206 pages. FHL book 979.418 N4g.

■ **Stanislaus County Great Registers, 1867, 1869, 1871-1872, 1875, 1879-1880, 1886, 1888, 1890, 1892, 1894, 1896, 1898,** microfilm of original records at the California State Library, Sacramento, CA. Each year is alphabetically arranged by first letter of surname. Filmed by the Genealogical Society of Utah, 1975, 1 roll, FHL film #978590.

■ ***Great Register of the County of Stanislaus, State of California, 1890,*** compiled by Mileta Farr Kilroy and Bette Locke, published by the Genealogical Society of Stanislaus County, 1992. Transcript gives name, age, birthplace, residence and date of voter registration, occupation, and date of naturalization. FHL book 979.457 N4k and FHL film #1697906.

■ **Sutter County Great Registers, 1867-1898,** microfilm of original records at the California State Library, Sacramento, CA. Each year is alphabetically arranged by first letter of surname. Includes the following years: 1867, 1869, 1872-1873, 1875-1877, 1879-1880, 1882, 1886, 1888, 1890, 1892, 1894, 1896, 1898. Filmed by the Genealogical Society of Utah, 1975, 1 roll, FHL film #978591.

■ **Tehama County Great Registers, 1875-1896,** microfilm of original records at the California State Library, Sacramento, CA. Each year is alphabetically arranged by first letter of surname. Includes the following years: 1875, 1877, 1880, 1884, 1886, 1888, 1890, 1892, 1894, 1896. Filmed by the Genealogical Society of Utah, 1975, 1 roll, FHL film #978592.

■ **Trinity County Great Registers, 1867-1868, 1871-1873, 1875, 1877, 1879, 1888, 1890, 1892, 1894, 1896,** microfilm of original records at the California State Library, Sacramento, CA. Each year is alphabetically arranged by first letter of surname. Filmed by the Genealogical Society of Utah, 1975, 1 roll, FHL film #978593.

■ ***Certified Copies of All Poll Lists For Trinity County: As Transmitted to the County Clerk, for the General Election, to be Holden*** [sic] ***Tuesday, the Third Day of November, A.D. 1868,*** microfilm of original published by Gorden Printers, Weaverville, CA, 1868, 17 pages. Alphabetically arranged. Filmed by the Genealogical Society of Utah, 1960, 1 roll, FHL film #207673.

■ ***1890 Great Register of Trinity County, California: (Voter Registration List),*** compiled and edited by Delores V. Pederson, published by the Conejo Valley Genealogical Society, Thousand Oaks, CA, 1993, 30 pages. Shows page number in original register, name of voter (in alphabetical order by surname), age, birthplace, local residence, date of registration, and naturalization status. FHL book 979.414 N4p.

■ ***Trinity, 1967: Yearbook of the Trinity County Historical Society,*** edited by Pat Hamilton, published by the Trinity County Historical Society, Weaverville, CA, 1967, 60 pages. Contains historical information of the settlement and growth of Trinity County. Includes a transcript of the Trinity County great register for 1877. FHL book 979.4 A1 No. 185.

■ **Tulare County Great Registers, 1869, 1872, 1879-1880, 1882, 1884, 1886, 1888, 1890, 1892, 1894, 1896,** microfilm of original records at the California State Library, Sacramento, CA. Each year is alphabetically arranged by first letter of surname. Filmed by the Genealogical Society of Utah, 1975, 1 roll, FHL film #978594.

■ ***1898 Index, Voter Registration, Tulare County,*** FHL title: *1898 Tulare County Voters Register, Book One and Book Two,* copied by Jack and Alfreda Gilliam, published by the authors, 199?, 164 pages. Divided into three sections: index, transfers/cancellations, and corrections. Each section is in alphabetical order by name. Index gives name, number, precinct, age, and birthplace (state or country). Transfers-cancellations gives name, whether cancelled or transferred, from what precinct transferred, and to what precinct transferred. Corrections give name, corrected name, and precinct. Includes list of post offices listed in precincts. FHL book 979.486 N42g.

■ **Tuolumne County Great Registers, 1867, 1871, 1873, 1875, 1877, 1879-1888, 1882, 1884, 1886, 1888, 1890, 1892, 1894, 1896, 1898,** microfilm of original records at the California State Library, Sacramento, CA. Each year is alphabetically arranged by first letter of surname. Filmed by the Genealogical Society of Utah, 1975, 1 roll, FHL film #978595.

■ ***1890 Tuolumne County Great Register of Voters,*** excerpted by Viola McRae, Nell Holloway, and Dythe-Mary Egleston, published by the Tuolumne County Genealogical Society, Sonora, CA, 1993, 44 pages. Contains an alphabetical listing of voters copied from the original register, showing surname, given name, age, nativity, residence, date registered. FHL book 979.4 A1 No. 234.

■ **Ventura County Great Registers, 1875, 1877, 1879-1880, 1882, 1886, 1888, 1890, 1898,** microfilm of original records at the State Library, Sacramento, CA. Each year is alphabetically arranged by first letter of surname. Filmed by the Genealogical Society of Utah, 1975, 1 roll, FHL film #978596.

■ ***1890 Great Register of Ventura County, California: (Voter Registration List),*** compiled and edited
by Dolores V. Pederson, published by the Conejo Valley Genealogical Society, Thousand Oaks, CA, 1993, 69 pages. Shows page number in original register, names of voters (in alphabetical order by surname), age, birth place, precinct, date of registration, naturalization status. FHL book 979.492 N4p.

■ **Yolo County Great Registers, 1867-1898,** microfilm of original records at the California State Library, Sacramento, CA. Each year is alphabetically arranged by first letter of surname. Filmed by the Genealogical Society of Utah, 1975, 2 rolls, as follows:

- Great registers, 1867, 1871-1872, 1875, 1877-1880, 1882, 1886, 1888, 1890, FHL film #978597.
- Great registers 1892, 1894, 1896, 1898, FHL film #978598.

■ ***Great Register of Yolo County, 1890: Yolo County Index for the 1890 Great Register Project,*** compiled by J. E. Hale, published by the author, Kentfield, CA, 1992, 1 vol., various paging. The register has been abstracted and indexed in alphabetical order by surname in section one; by town in section two; and by precinct in section three of this compilation. From intro: "The 1890 great register project is designed to recreate a census of sorts to replace the U.S. census of 1890 that was lost in a fire. Since the great registers record only those eligible to vote it is not as broad a coverage as the U.S. census." FHL book 979.451 N48h.

■ **Yuba County Great Registers, 1867-1896,** microfilm of original records at the California State Library, Sacramento, CA. Each year is alphabetically arranged by first letter of surname. Includes the following years: 1867-1869, 1871-1873, 1875-1877, 1879-1880, 1882, 1884, 1888, 1890, 1892, 1894, 1896. Filmed by the Genealogical Society of Utah, 1975, 1 roll, FHL film #978599.

■ **Great Registers of Voters of Yuba County, 1896, 1900**, microfilm of records located at the John Q. Packard Library, Marysville, CA. Filmed by the Genealogical Society of Utah, 1991, 2 rolls, as follows:

- Great register, 1896, FHL film #1738594.
- Great register, 1900, FHL film #1738595.

California Online Census & Substitutes

The following databases can be found at these sites:

www.ancestry.com

- 1850 United States Federal Census
- 1860 Slave Schedules
- 1860 United States Federal Census
- 1870 United States Federal Census
- 1880 United States Federal Census
- 1900 United States Federal Census
- 1910 United States Federal Census
- 1920 United States Federal Census
- 1930 United States Federal Census
- California Census, 1790-1890 (AIS)
- Los Angeles City and County Census, 1850
- Monterey, California Census, 1850-60
- 1994 Phone and Address Directory
- 2000 Phone and Address Directory
- Los Angeles, California City Directories, 1888-90
- Nevada County, California Directory, 1895
- Ojai Valley, California Directory, 1938
- Pacific Coast Directory, 1867
- Pomona, California Directory, 1896-97
- Presbyterian Ministerial Directory 1898
- Protestant Episcopal Church Clerical Directory, 1898
- San Francisco, California Directories, 1889-91
- San Francisco Passenger Lists
- San Luis Obispo - Paso Robles Area, California City Directory, 1961
- Santa Barbara Area, California City Directory, 1972
- Santa Cruz Area, California City Directory, 1926
- Santa Maria and Lompoc Areas, California City Directory, 1963
- Santa Rosa Area, California City Directory, 1938
- Santa Rosa, California City Directory, 1968
- Santa Rosa, California City Directory, 1970
- Shafter and Wasco, California City Directory, 1969
- Shasta County, California Register, 1898
- Stockton and Lodi, California City Directory, 1952
- Stockton, California City Directory, 1958
- Stockton, California City Directory, 1967
- Vallejo and Fairfield, California City Directory, 1930-1931
- Yuba, Sutter, Colusa, Butte, and Tehama Counties, California Directory, 1885

www.censusfinder.com

- 1790-1890 Federal Census Records of California at Ancestry
- 1872 Foreign-Born Voters – Statewide Index
- 1880 Federal Census
- 1880 Federal Census Search at Family Search
- 1883 Pensioners on the Roll – Statewide
- 1886-1909 Notaries Public Statewide Index
- 1940-1997 California Death Records Search Engine
- California State Databases of Census & Genealogy Records

www.census-online.com

• **Countywide census databases** (no. of databases): Alameda (2); Alpine (10); Amador (1); Butte (2); Calaveras (0); Colusa (2); Contra Costa (0); Del Norte (1); El Dorado (2); Fresno (0); Glenn (0); Humboldt (2); Imperial (0); Inyo (1); Kern (2); Kings (0); Klamath (3); Lake (3); Lassen (5); Los Angeles (6); Madera (0); Marin (7); Mariposa (10); Mendocino (17); Merced (4); Modoc (0); Mono (0); Monterey (2); Napa (6); Nevada (3); Orange (0); Placer (1); Plumas (0); Riverside (0); Sacramento (0);

San Benito (0); San Bernardino (0); San Diego (2); San Francisco (14); San Joaquin (0); San Luis Obispo (9); San Mateo (7); Santa Barbara (6); Santa Clara (2); Santa Cruz (1); Shasta (38); Sierra (0); Siskiyou (0); Solano (1); Sonoma (10); Stanislaus (7); Sutter (0); Tehama (0); Trinity (2); Tulare (31); Tuolumne (0); Ventura (0); Yolo (1); and Yuba (0).

NEVADA

History to Statehood in 1864

The word "Nevada" is Spanish for "snow covered." It seems an apt description to anyone driving Nevada's I-80 today, where mountain after mountain reveal their snow caps to traveling genealogists.

The Spanish claim to what is now Nevada theoretically dates back to the conquest of Mexico in 1519. The first Spanish exploration of the area took place in 1540 when Melchi Diaz and party traveled through the southern part of present Nevada. Like most Spanish explorers for the first 200 years of New Spain, Diaz was looking for the "seven cities of gold," which the clever Nuevo Mexico natives had continually insisted were real, and kept the Spanish from staying in one place long enough to cause anyone harm. All the Indians had to do was tell the Spaniards that the cities of gold were just a few miles further on, and off they would go again. Had Diaz considered moving his expedition a bit further north, and changed his thinking to "mountains of silver," he might have had much more success in Nevada.

When Juan Rodriguez Cabrillo landed at San Diego Bay in 1542, he claimed California for Spain, and that claim technically included all of Nevada as well. But no further activity was recorded in Nevada until 1776, when Spanish Padre Garces, on a search for mission sites along the Old Spanish Trail to California, crossed the Colorado River into southern Nevada.

Apparently, Nevada was just a bit too far away from Mexico or California to attempt colonization – the Spanish never founded a single pueblo, mission, or presidio in Nevada. In fact, the first white settlements in the area came from the Americans, well after the Spanish era.

After independence from Spain in 1821, Mexico developed a little more interest in Nevada, but only as a means of getting to California. Like the Spanish, Mexico made no attempts to colonize the area.

In 1826, mountain man Jedediah Smith was the first American to cross Nevada's northern mountains, blazing a major section of a route that would become the primary California Trail. In 1828, Peter Ogden was the first to discover the Humboldt River, and immediately saw it as a route for traveling further west. A dozen explorers over the next several years tried to find the destination of the Humboldt, which as it turned out, ran out of water (by evaporation in the desert), ending at the Humboldt Sink, some 60 miles east of present Reno.

One notable Mexican trader, Antonio Armijo, led a party from Santa Fe to Los Angeles in 1829. He was traveling on what was to become known as the Old Spanish Trail. Passing through the southern desert of Nevada, his party found an abundance of artesian spring water that allowed travelers to cut directly through the vast desert to Los Angeles. The traders named the desert oasis Las Vegas, Spanish for "The Meadows."

Captain John C. Fremont, leader of several map-making expeditions for the U.S. Army, was very influential in the early discoveries of Nevada, particularly for the immigrant routes that would follow. In 1833, Fremont's expedition of about 25 men discovered a large fresh water lake, some 30 miles north of present Reno, which he named Lake Pyramid. John Fremont and his guide, Kit Carson, were the first Americans to see Lake Tahoe, and together they used the Pyramid Lake camp as a mustering point for later expeditions across the Sierra-Nevada Mountains into northern California and southern Oregon.

Moving on to California, Fremont became a player in the events leading up to the war with Mexico, and was a leader of the first attempt to declare California and Nevada as part of the United States.

In 1841, the first wagon train to California passed along the Humboldt River route through Nevada. This was the Bartleson-Bidwell party from Independence, Missouri, which crossed Nevada by way of the Humboldt, Carson Sink, and Walker River. Nevada and California were still part of Mexico – but Americans began to see the area as theirs, based on the "manifest destiny" attitude of the time. As it turned out, the war with Mexico, 1846-1848, was to be Nevada's ticket to become part of the United States.

The Mormons played a big role in early Nevada history, and contributed to the success of the American takeover of the Southwest. In 1847, the Mormons took possession of the Great Salt Lake Valley of Utah. At the time, they were in Mexican territory; but by special arrangements with the United States government, the Mormons had supplied a special battalion of soldiers to march on San Diego during the Mexican-American war, keeping them in alliance with the United States. In 1848, discharged soldiers of the Mormon Battalion in California had to find all new trails to rejoin their families back in Utah. In doing so, they established some of the first routes across the Sierra-Nevada Mountains into the Carson Valley of Nevada.

The treaty of Guadalupe Hidalgo ended the war with Mexico in 1848. As part of the treaty, the area of Utah, which included present Nevada, was added to the United States; along with the present states of Arizona, California, Colorado, and New Mexico. Of these areas, Nevada was the last to be settled by Americans.

The California gold rush brought thousands of prospectors through Nevada. One estimate was that in 1849, 24,000 people crossed the Sierra-Nevada mountains via the Carson Valley of Nevada. In 1850, some 45,000 people made the trek; and up to 52,000 in 1852. Yet, Nevada gained none of these folks – Nevada was seen only as a mustering point to cross the mountains and get to the gold fields of California. But, many of the same people who had ignored Nevada were to find themselves clamoring to get back there within just a few years.

Meanwhile, Brigham Young decided the Mormons should take advantage of the business opportunities from the thousands of prospectors crossing into Nevada. In 1851, Mormon settlers from Salt Lake began a trading post in the Carson Valley, which was called Reese's Station (or Mormon Station), which became the town of Genoa, the first white settlement in Nevada. In 1855, Brigham Young repeated the exercise and sent a party of 30 men who founded the "Mormon Fort," which became the town of Las Vegas, Nevada.

But the real interest in Nevada began with the discovery of silver and gold. In 1859, the largest known deposit of silver in the world was discovered, the Comstock Lode – an extremely rich four-mile-long lode near Virginia City, Nevada. The frenzy to mine the Comstock Lode essentially ended the California Gold Rush, because many of the California miners hurried back to Nevada to get in on the bonanza. The population of the Carson Valley exploded with thousands of prospectors arriving in a matter of a few weeks, and the rush continued for several more years. As a direct result, Nevada was organized as a territory in 1861, with Carson City as the capital. Nevada Territory's population was recorded at 14,404 persons, of which about 4,581 persons resided in and around Virginia City, site of the Comstock Lode mines.

At the height of the Civil War, the Comstock Lode exercised a far-ranging political and economic influence. Seeking to bolster the Union with another free state, President Lincoln encouraged Nevada to seek statehood at such a rapid pace that the state constitution had to be telegraphed to Washington.

The territory became the thirty-sixth state in October 1864.

Nevada State Censuses & Census Substitutes, 1864-1918

Politically, from 1848 to late 1850, the Nevada area was part of New Mexico and Utah Territories. Upon territorial status for Utah in 1850, Nevada was completely part of Utah Territory. The 1850 federal census for Utah Territory was taken with a census day of April 1, 1851. Although present Nevada was included in the area of Utah Territory, there was no recorded population there until June 1851 (Mormon Station).

The 1860 federal census for Utah Territory included five counties extended into Nevada country. Of these, three Utah counties had enumerated settlements in the Nevada area: St. Mary's, Humboldt, and Carson Counties. Over 80 percent of the Nevada area population was in Carson County, the scene of the Comstock Lode and associated mining camps. Carson County was established by Utah Territory in 1854, and encompassed all of what subsequently became the counties of Douglas, Lyon, Ormsby (now Carson City), Storey and portions of Washoe, Pershing, Churchill, Mineral, Esmeralda, and Nye in Nevada.

Upon territorial status for Nevada in 1861, the territorial legislature immediately authorized a census. Territorial censuses with various dates of 1861, 1862, 1863, and 1864 exist at the Nevada State Archives in Carson City, but may all be one census spread over time.

In the 1870 federal census, a few anomalies for southern Nevada exist. Several communities of Utah Territory were enumerated that were actually in Nevada. The state and county boundaries were not well marked or understood. The state of Nevada took one state census, that of 1875, which also survives. A bibliography of Nevada censuses and substitutes follows:

■ ***Early Nevada Records: Certificates of Survey, Carson Valley, 1856; 1862 Census of Churchill County; 1864; Census of Nye County,*** compiled by J.S. Thompson from various sources over a period of years. Microfilm of typescript, 17 pages (made in 1995). Contents: List of names found on certificates in Carson Valley 1856; alphabetical listing of 1862 census of Churchill County with name, age, gender, state of birth, occupation and residence; alphabetical list of names and age of those in Nye County census, 1864; list of names subscribed on 14 Feb. 1863 at a meeting in Virginia City to organize the Democratic party in Nevada. Filmed by the Genealogical Society of Utah, 1995, 1 roll, FHL film #1598348.

■ ***An Inventory & Index to the Records of Carson County, Utah & Nevada Territories, 1855-1861,*** compiled by Marion Ellison for the Carson Valley Historical Society in cooperation with the Nevada State Division of Archives & Records. Published by the Grace Dangberg Foundation, 1984, 438 pages. Includes index. Includes history of early Utah and Nevada Territories. Consists chiefly of land records. Contains probate records. FHL book 979.3 R2e.

■ **1861-1908 Naturalization Records, Washoe County, Nevada**, microfilm of original records at the San Bruno branch, National Archives. Includes partial index. Filmed by the Genealogical Society of Utah, 1975, 2 rolls, FHL film #977771 (Declarations of Intention, 1861-1906), and FHL film #977772 (Declaration of Intention, 1880-1906; 1906-1908; 1877-1906).

■ **1861-1865. Index to Compiled Service Records of Volunteer Union Soldiers Who Served in Organizations from the State of Nevada,** microfilm of original records in the National Archives, Washington, DC. Filmed by the National Archives, series M0548, 1 roll, FHL film #821939. This publication included in ***Index to Soldiers & Sailors of the Civil War,*** a searchable name index to 6.3 million Union and Confederate soldiers now available online at the National Park Service Web site. A search can be done by surname, first name, state, or unit.

Nevada supplied 1,684 men to the war (all Union). To search for one go to the National Park Service Web site at: **www.civilwar.nps.gov/cwss/.**

▪ **Nevada Territory Manuscript Census, 1861-1864; and Nevada State Manuscript Census for Washoe County, 1875,** microfilm of records located at Nevada State Library and Archives, Division of Archives and Records, Carson City, Nevada. Includes partial index to 1862 census for Storey and Ormsby Counties, Nevada Territory; census report of Henry DeGroot, 1861 (summaries only); Churchill County census report, 1862 (summaries only); Douglas County, 1862; Humboldt County, Buena Vista, 1862; Humboldt County, Echo township, 1862; Humboldt County, Humboldt township, 1862; Humboldt County, Prince Royal township, 1862; Humboldt County, Santa Clara township, 1862; Humboldt County, Star township, 1862; Lander County, 1863; Lyon County, Dayton, El Dorado Canyon, Palmyra, 1862; Lyon County, Silver City, 1862; Lyon and Churchill Counties, census report, 1863 (summaries only); Ormsby County, 1862; Storey County, Flowery District, 1862; Storey County, Gold Hill, 1862; Storey County, Virginia City, 1862; Washoe County, 1862; Washoe County, 1875. Filmed by the Nevada Division of Printing and Micrographics, 1991, FHL has 1 roll, FHL film #1689341.

▪ **1862 Census of Washoe County, Territory of Nevada,** microfilm of original records at the Nevada State Library, Division of Archives, Carson City, Nevada. Filmed 1983, 1 roll, FHL film #1705177.

▪ **1862 State Directory.** See ***First Directory of Nevada Territory: Containing the Names of Residents in the Principal Towns,*** compiled by J. Wells Kelly, published by Valentine, San Francisco, 1862. FHL book 979.3 E4v 1862. See also ***An Alphabetical Listing of the First Directory of Nevada Territory: Directory Compiled by J. Wells Kelly, circa 1861-1862, for the Towns of Aurora, Carson City, Dayton, Empire, Genoa, Gold Hill, Jack's Valley, Silver City, Virginia City, Washoe,*** microfilm of typescript, dated 1995, 120 pages. Filmed by the Genealogical Society of Utah, 1995, 1 roll, FHL film #1598348.

▪ **1862 Nevada Territorial Census,** name lists by towns, published in *Name Tracer,* a periodical of the Las Vegas Branch Library, Las Vegas, NV. For **Empire City, Genoa, and Washoe,** see Vol. 1, No. 1 (Jul 1997); **Aurora,** see Vol. 1, No. 3 (Sep 1967) and Vol. 1, No. 4 (Nov 1967); **Dayton,** see Vol. 1, No. 2 (Jul 1967) and Vol. 1, No. 3 (Sep 1967); **Virginia City**, see Vol. 2, No. 2 (Mar 1968) and Vol. 2, No. 3 (May 1968).

▪ **1862-1882 Nevada Territory & State Directories,** microfilm of originals published by various publishers. Filmed by Research Publications, Inc., Woodbridge, CT, 1980-1984. FHL has 4 rolls, as follows:

- **1862** First directory of Nevada Territory; **1863** Second directory of Nevada Territory; **1864-1865** Mercantile guide and directory for Virginia City, Gold Hill, Silver City and American City; **1866** Harrington's directory of the city of Austin; **1868-1869** The Nevada directory, FHL film #1377106.
- **1871-1872** Storey, Ormsby, Washoe and Lyon Counties directory; **1871-1873** The Pacific Coast business Directory; **1872** Wells, Fargo & Co.'s express directory; **1872** McKennys' gazetteer and directory of the Central Pacific Railroad and its branches; FHL film #1377107.
- **1873-1874** The Virginia City and Truckee railroad directory, **1875** A general business and mining directory of Storey, Lyon, Ormsby, and Washoe Counties, Nevada; Business directory of San Francisco and principal towns of California and Nevada; **1878** Business directory of the Pacific States and Territories; FHL film #1377108.
- **1878-1879** Bishop's directory of Virginia City, Gold Hill, Silver City, Carson City and Reno; **1880-1881** Pacific Coast directory, FHL film #1377109.

■ **1862-1929.** See **Storey County Records,** compiled by Nona Parkin, microfilm of typescript in the Nona Parkin collection of the Reno, Nevada Stake Family History Center, Reno, Nevada. Contents: vol. 1: Birth records/notices: Storey County records 1869-1912; Cemetery census: American Flat and Gold Hill with index, City of Gold Hill Cemetery record, Virginia City Cemetery with index; vol. 2: Death records/notices: Newspaper notices 1862-1912, Storey County death records 1887-1991 with index, Storey County records from 1875, Virginia City death records 1879-1890, Newspaper obituaries, Storey County 1922-1983, Storey County Coroner's records 1879-1887; vol. 3: Funeral home records: Register of funerals, Virginia City 1879-1914, Old mortuary records 1891-1918, Virginia City mortuary records 1879-1883 with index; City directories: American City, Gold Hill and Silver City 1864-1865; vol. 4: Marriage records/notices: Storey County marriage records 1862-1929 with index, Newspaper notices 1875-1912; vol. 5: Newspaper "scats", Pioneer families, Union membership rolls; vol. 6: Church records: Gold Hill Catholic Church, St. Paul's Episcopal Parish, Virginia City; vol. 7: Church records: Virginia City Catholic Church, St. Paul Episcopal Church. Includes some indexing. Filmed by the Genealogical Society of Utah, 1997, 2 rolls, FHL film #1598459 (Vols. 1-3); and FHL film #1598460 (Vols. 4-7).

■ **1862 Census of Washoe County, Territory of Nevada,** microfilm of original records at the Nevada State Library, Division of Archives, Carson City, Nevada. Filmed 1983, 1 roll, FHL film #1705177.

■ ***Lander County, Nevada 1863 Census,*** compiled by J.S. Thompson. Microfilm of typescript, 62 pages (made in 1995). Contents: part 1: Every-name index giving age (when known) and town; part 2: Alphabetical listing by surname in each town. Filmed by the Genealogical Society of Utah, 1995, 1 roll, FHL film #1598348.

■ **1863-1866 Internal Revenue Assessment Lists for the Territory and State of Nevada,** microfilm of original records at the National Archives, Washington, DC. Filmed by the National Archives, 1980, series M779, 2 rolls, FHL film #1578506 (District 1 Feb. 1863 - Nov. 1865), and FHL film #1578506 (District 1 Jan. - Dec. 1866).

■ ***1864-1983.*** *See* ***Esmeralda County Records,*** compiled by Nona Parkin, microfilm of typescript in the Nona Parkin collection of the Reno, Nevada Stake Family History Center, Reno, Nevada. Contents: vol. 1: Cemetery census: Index to Goldfield Cemetery; Goldfield Cemetery; vol. 2: Death records/obituaries: Esmeralda County death notices from newspapers 1864-1920, Goldfield newspaper obituaries 1922-1983, Newspaper notices 1864-1920; Marriage records/notices: Newspaper notices 1875-1916; Tax assessment records: Esmeralda County assessment roll 1864. Includes index. Filmed by the Genealogical Society of Utah, 1997, 1 roll, FHL film #1598448.

■ ***1869-1904 Election and Court Records of Humboldt County, Nevada,*** 12-page typescript, dated 1979. Includes election registers, 1869-1904 and justice court records. FHL book 979.3 A1 No. 27.

■ **1870 Federal Census, Rio Virgin and Washington County, Utah.** Microfilm of original schedules by the National Archives. Rio Virgin County was created in 1869 to gather outlying Mormon communities under Utah government. But the area of Rio Virgin County was actually in Nevada. The area should have been enumerated as part of Lincoln County, Nevada, but the Nevadans were less aware of the precise boundary with Utah, as were the Utahans with their boundary with Nevada or Arizona. In fact the Nevadans still thought of the area as "Pah-ute" County, left over from Arizona. The settlers in Panaca and Clover Valley within Lincoln County, Nevada were enumerated as part of

Washington County, Utah Territory. Names of residents of Rio Virgin communities can be found on FHL film #553110. (1870 Federal Census of Kane, Millard, Morgan, Piute, Rich, Rio Virgin, and Salt Lake Counties, Utah Territory). The Panaca and Clover Valley people were listed on FHL film #553112 (1870 Federal Census of Wasatch, Washington, and Weber Counties, Utah Territory).

■ **1871-1930**. See **Lincoln County Records,** compiled by Nona Parkin. Microfilm of typescript in the Nona Parkin collection of the Reno, Nevada Stake Family History Center, Reno, Nevada. Contents: vol. 1: Birth notices: Newspaper notices 1906-1912; Cemetery census: Caliente, Logandale, Panaca, Pioche; Death records/obituaries Newspaper notices 1871-1909, Panaca 1928-1978, Pioche 1922-1974, Pioche Daily Record 1906-1926; Jurors called for duty: Lincoln County 1876 & 1893; Marriage records/notices: Lincoln County records 1872-1915, Newspaper notices 1883-1900; Newspaper "scats"; vol. 2: Pioneer families; Registered voters: Buillionville 1876, Small precincts 1876 & 1890, Panaca 1890, Pioche 1876, 1886, 1888, 1890 & 1892; Tax assessment records: Lincoln County 1886, 1887, 1889, 1892; Pioche 1886, 1889-1893; Church records: Moapa Epiphany Mission 1930 (became St. Matthew's in 1931). Filmed by the Genealogical Society of Utah, 1997, 1 roll, FHL film #1598462.

■ **1871-1872**. See ***State of Nevada Directory,*** copied from the original by Nona Parkin. Original published Reno, NV, 1872. FHL book 979.3 E4pn and FHL film #1425608.

■ **1875 Nevada State Census.** See ***Census of the Inhabitants of the State of Nevada, 1875,*** microfiche of original published Carson City, Nevada: John J. Hill, State Printers, 1877, 2 vols. Filmed by Kraus-Thomson, Millwood, NY, 198?, 18 microfiche, as follows:

- Churchill, Douglas & Esmeralda Counties, FHL fiche #6016536.
- Elko (part), FHL fiche #6016537.
- Elko (part) & Eureka (part), FHL fiche # 6016538.
- Eureka (part), FHL fiche #6016539.
- Eureka (part), Humboldt & Lander (part), FHL fiche #6016540.
- Lander (part) & Lincoln (part), FHL fiche #6016541.
- Lincoln (part) & Lyon (part), FHL fiche #6016542.
- Ormsby (part) & Storey (part), FHL fiche #6016544.
- Storey (part), FHL fiche #6016545-6016550.
- Washoe (part), FHL fiche #6016551.
- Washoe (part) & White Pine (part), FHL fiche #6016552.
- White Pine (part), FHL fiche #6016553.

■ **1875 Nevada State Census - Name Index,** compiled by the Nevada State Library, ca 1900. Each county is separately indexed. White Pine County (film #6332701) is mislabeled as Hite County. Provides years, sex, race, occupation, vol. and page where complete census information for each name can be found. Filmed by the Nevada State Library, 14 fiche. FHL has the following:

- Churchill County, FHL fiche #6332696.
- Douglas County, FHL fiche #6332697.
- Elko County, FHL fiche #6332698.
- Esmeralda County, FHL fiche #6332699.
- Eureka County, FHL fiche #6332700.
- Humboldt County, FHL fiche #6332702.
- Lander County, FHL fiche #6332703.
- Lincoln County, FHL fiche #6332704.
- Lyon County, FHL fiche #6332705.
- Nye County, FHL fiche #6332706.
- Ormsby County, FHL fiche #6332707.
- Storey County, FHL fiche #6332708.
- Washoe County, FHL fiche #6332709.
- Hite (White Pine) County, FHL fiche #6332701.

■ *1875 Nevada State Census by County,* compiled by Nona Parkin, microfilm of typescript (2 volumes) in the Nona Parkin collection of the Reno, Nevada Stake Family History Center, Reno, Nevada. Contents: vol. 1: 1875 Nevada state census by county: Churchill, Douglas, Esmeralda, Elko, Eureka, Lyon, Lincoln,

Humboldt, Ormsby, Nye, Lander; vol. 2: Storey, Washoe, White Pine. Includes surname, age, sex, profession (for head of household) and birthplace arranged by household as abstracted from census. Filmed by the Genealogical Society of Utah, 1977, 1 roll, FHL film #1598455.

■ *Persons Living in Nevada Who Were Born in New Jersey, Extracted From Nevada State Census, 1875,* extracted and typed by Genevieve S. Jensen; a project of the Las Vegas, Nevada Multi-Regional Family History Center. Microfilm of typescript, 1994, 10 pages. Surnames are in alphabetical order. Includes name, age, sex, color, occupation, value of real estate, value of personal estate, place of birth, father of foreign birth, mother of foreign birth, county, volume and page. Filmed by the Genealogical Society of Utah, 1994, 1 roll, FHL film #1598226.

■ **1879-1916 Bunkerville Residents, Clark County, Nevada,** name list published in *Name Tracer*, Vol. 6, No. 4 (Oct 1972) through Vol. 7, No. 2 (Apr 1973). See also "1890 Bunkerville Residents," in Vol. 6, No. 3 (Jul 1972).

■ **1881 History.** See ***Reproduction of Thompson and West's "History of Nevada, 1881": With Illustrations and Biographical Sketches of its Prominent Men and Pioneers,*** with introduction by David F. Myrick. Includes history of Nevada and biographical sketches of some of the prominent men and pioneers and a patrons directory. Original published by Thompson & West, Oakland, CA, 1881, 680 pages. Reprint published by Howell-North, Berkeley, CA, 1958. FHL book 979.3 H2t. Indexed in ***Index to History of Nevada,*** by Helen J. Poulton and Myron Angel, published by the University of Nevada Press, Reno, NV, 1966, 148 pages. This index can be used with the original 1881 edition published by Thompson and West, and the 1958 reprint. FHL book 979.3 B4u v. 6.

■ ***1882 Lists of Registered Voters in Nevada, Various Precincts,*** typescript of extract of voter lists taken from the *Reno Evening Gazette* and *Nevada State Journal* of Reno. The places involved are: Wadsworth, Verdi Precinct, Franktown Districts, Buffalo Springs Precinct, Brown's Precinct, Glendale Precinct. FHL book 979.3 A1 No. 6, and FHL film #962208.

■ **1888-1892 Tax Lists, Eureka County, Nevada,** name lists to identify former Cornwall miners working Nevada mines, from an article published in *Cornwall Family Historical Society Journal* (Falmouth, Cornwall County, England), No. 71 (Mar 1994).

■ **1890-1926.** See ***Nevada Records of Marriages, Wills, and Miscellaneous Data,*** copied by the Daughters of the American Colonists (Nevada). Microfilm of typescript. Includes marriage records 1890-1896, First Presbyterian Church, Carson City, Nevada; abstracts of Wills 1906-1926, Fallon, Nevada; report of Stanton Post, No. 29, located at Carson City, County of Ormsby, Department of California, G.A.R. for third quarter of 1870; tax list of Lyon County, Nevada, for the year 1897. Includes a partial index. Filmed by the Genealogical Society of Utah, 1959, 1 roll, FHL film #176646.

■ **1913-1935 Reno City Directories.** microfilm of original records located in various libraries and societies. Filmed by Research Publications, Inc., Woodbridge, CT, 1995, 3 rolls, as follows:

- 1913-1914; 1917; 1920-1921; 1923 R.L. Polk & Co.'s Reno, Sparks and Washoe County directory, FHL film #2309382.
- 1925-1926, 1927-1928; 1930-1931 R.L. Polk & Co. of California, publishers, FHL film #2309383.
- 1932; 1933; 1935 Polk's Reno city directory, including Washoe County and Carson City, FHL film #2309384.

■ **1915-1981 Reno, Sparks, Washoe County, and Carson City Directory**, published by R. L. Polk and Company, Kansas City, MO. FHL has Library has: 1915 (photocopy), 1917, 1923, 1970, 1973, 1981. FHL book 979.35 E4pr 1915-1981.

■ **1917-1918 World War I Selective Service System Draft Registration Cards, Nevada,** microfilm of original records in the National Archives in East Point, Georgia. The draft cards are arranged alphabetically by state, then alphabetically by county or city, and then alphabetically by surname of registrants. Cards are in rough alphabetical order. Filmed by the National Archives, 1987-1988, 7 rolls, as follows:

- Churchill County; Clark County; Douglas County; Elko County, A-N; FHL film #1711534.
- Elko County, O-Z; Esmeralda County, Eureka County, Humboldt County, FHL film #1711535.
- Lander County; Lincoln County; Lyon County; Mineral County; Nye County, A-O; FHL film #1711536.
- Nye County, P-Z; Ormsby County; Storey County; Washoe County, A-M; FHL film #1711537.
- Washoe County, N-Z; White Pine County, A- J; FHL film #1711538.
- White Pine County, K- Z; FHL film #1711539.
- Indians, Prisoners, Insane, In Hospitals, Late Registrants, FHL film #2022391.

■ **1918 Lyon County.** See *Official List of Primary Voting Registration in Lyon County, Nevada: Taken from the Yerington Times, Yerington, Nevada, 1918,* copied by Nona Parkin, published by the author, 1964, 14 pages, FHL book 979.3 A1 No. 5.

Nevada Censuses & Substitutes Online

■ **1860, 1870, 1880, 1900, 1910, and 1920 Nevada Federal Censuses Online – Searchable Index and Full Extraction of Census Data, a** combined index sponsored by the Nevada State Historical Preservation Office. Every detail from a census entry for a person was extracted into a database that can be searched by county, first name, last name, age, occupation, and more. The system also allows a browse search to see the order in which the names were originally listed on a census page. No other state site has such complete census information online, and this database gives a researcher access to the names of virtually every resident of Nevada from 1860 through 1920. The censuses are online at the following Web site: **http://dmla.clan.lib.nv.us/docs/shpo/NVCensus/FindPeople/year.asp.**

The following online databases can be accessed at these sites:

www.ancestry.com

- 1860-1910 Nevada Censuses (AIS)
- 1870 Federal Census
- 1875 Nevada State Census
- 1880 Federal Census
- 1890 Veterans Schedules
- 1910 Federal Census
- 1920 Federal Census
- 1930 Federal Census

www.censusfinder.com (statewide)

- 1860-1920 Nevada Census Records Database
- 1860-1910 Nevada Census at Ancestry
- 1862 Nevada Directory
- 1863 Nevada Tax List
- 1880 Federal Census - images
- 1880 Federal Census Search at Family Search
- 1880 Federal Census of Norwegians

Countywide Census Records Online (CensusFinder):

Carson County

- 1870 Federal Census Mortality Schedule
- 1880 Federal Census Mortality Schedule
- 1883 Pensioners Census
- 1890 Special Census

Churchill County

- 1862 Territorial Census
- 1870 Federal Census Mortality Schedule
- 1890 Special Census

Clark County

- 1860 Washington County, UT Census - Now Clark Co., NV
- 1868 Census of St. Thomas
- 1870 Federal Census of Pah-Ute Co, NV, now Clark Co, NV
- 1870 Federal Census Mortality Schedule of Pah-Ute Co, now Clark Co
- 1880 Federal Census of Lincoln Co, NV, now Clark Co, NV

- 1880 Federal Census Mortality Schedule of Lincoln Co, now Clark Co
- 1890 Veterans and Widows Census of Lincoln Co, now Clark Co, NV
- 1900 Federal Census of Lincoln Co, NV, now Clark Co, NV
- 1910 Federal Census
- 1910 Federal Census ED 5
- 1910 Federal Census ED 6
- 1910 Federal Census ED 7
- 1910 Federal Census Records of Fort Mojave Indian Tribe
- 1920 Federal Census

Douglas County
- 1862 Territorial Census
- 1870 Federal Census Mortality Schedule
- 1880 Federal Census Mortality Schedule
- 1890 Veterans and Widows Census

Elko County
- 1870 Federal Census Mortality Schedule
- 1880 Federal Census Mortality Schedule
- 1883 Veterans and Widows Census

Esmeralda County
- 1870 Federal Census Index
- 1870 Federal Census
- 1870 Federal Census Mortality Schedule
- 1880 Federal Census Mortality Schedule
- 1883 Veterans and Widows Census
- 1890 Special Census

Eureka County
- 1880 Federal Census Mortality Schedule
- 1883 Veterans and Widows Census
- 1890 Special Census

Humboldt County
- 1870 Federal Census Mortality Schedule
- 1880 Federal Census Index
- 1880 Federal Census Mortality Schedule
- 1883 Veterans and Widows Census
- 1890 Special Census

Lander County
- 1870 Federal Census Mortality Schedule
- 1880 Federal Census Mortality Schedule
- 1883 Veterans and Widows Census
- 1890 Special Census

Lincoln County
- 1870 Federal Census
- 1870 Federal Census of Pah-Ute Co, later became Lincoln Co
- 1870 Federal Census Mortality Schedule of Pah-Ute, later became Lincoln Co
- 1880 Federal Census
- 1880 Federal Census Mortality Schedule
- 1883 Veterans and Widows Census
- 1890 Special Census
- 1900 Federal Census
- 1900 Indian Census

Lyon County
- 1870 Federal Census Mortality Schedule
- 1880 Federal Census Mortality Schedule
- 1883 Pensioners Census
- 1890 Special Census

Nye County
- 1870 Federal Census Mortality Schedule
- 1880 Federal Census Mortality Schedule
- 1883 Pensioners Census
- 1890 Special Census

Storey County
- 1880 Federal Census Mortality Schedule
- 1883 Pensioners Census
- 1890 Special Census

Washoe County.
- 1870 School Census
- 1883 Pensioners Census
- 1890 Special Census
- 1900 Federal Census
- 1900 Federal Census Partial
- 1870 Federal Census Mortality Schedule
- 1880 Federal Census Mortality Schedule

White Pine County
- 1870 Federal Census
- 1870 Federal Census Mortality Schedule
- 1880 Federal Census Mortality Schedule
- 1883 Pensioners Census
- 1887 Assessment Roll Book
- 1890 Assessment Roll Book
- 1890 Special Census

ALASKA

Historical Timeline

1725 - Peter the Great of Russia commissioned a Danish sea captain, Vitus Bering, to explore the Northwest coast of Alaska. This feat is credited with the "official" discovery by Russia and the first reliable information on the land. Bering established Russia's claim to Northwestern North America. Although the Russians visited Alaska with seal and fishing expeditions over the next fifty years, the first attempts at colonization did not begin until 1784.

1778. While searching for the elusive Northwest Passage, British Explorer Captain James Cook explored the waterway that downtown Anchorage now borders, Cook Inlet.

1784. Grigorii Shelikov establishes first white settlement at Three Saints Bay, Kodiak.

1795. The first Russian Orthodox Church established in Kodiak.

1799 - Alexander Baranov establishes Russian post known today as Old Sitka; trade charter grants exclusive trading rights to the Russian American Company.

1824. Russians begin exploration of mainland that leads to discovery of Nushagak, Kuskokwim, Yukon, and Koyokuk Rivers.

1867. Financial struggles force Russia to sell Russian America to the United States. Negotiated by U.S. Secretary of State William Seward, the treaty buys what is now Alaska for $7.2 million, or about 2 cents an acre. Alaska's value was not appreciated by most Americans, calling it "Seward's folly."

1868. Congress designates the Russian America purchase as the "Department of Alaska."

1872. Gold discovered near Sitka and in British Columbia.

1880. Richard Harris and Joseph Juneau, with the aid of local clan leader Kowee, discover gold on the Gastineau; Juneau is founded.

1896. Dawson City founded at mouth of Klondike River; gold discovered on Bonanza Creek.

1897-1900. Klondike gold rush.

1898. Skagway is largest city in Alaska; work starts on White Pass and Yukon Railroad; Congress appropriates money for telegraph from Seattle to Sitka; Nome gold rush begins.

1912. Alaska becomes a U.S. Territory. Alaska's population at 29,500 Eskimos, Indians and Aleuts; 4,300 "Caucasian Alaskans" and 26,000 Cheechakos (newcomers).

1913. First Alaska Territorial Legislature convenes. First law passed grants women voting rights.

1914. Congress authorizes the construction of the Alaska Railroad, clearing the way for the only railroad in history which would be owned and operated by the U.S. government. City of Anchorage born as construction campsite.

1924. Congress grants Native Americans the right to vote and U.S. citizenship.

1942. Japanese invade Alaska's Aleutian Islands. As part of the defense of the West Coast, the Alaska Highway is built in the amazingly short time of eight months and 12 days, linking Anchorage and Fairbanks with the rest of the nation. Anchorage enters the war years with a population of 7,724 and emerges with 43,314 residents.

1955. Constitutional Convention opens at University of Alaska.

1958. Statehood measure passes; President Eisenhower signs statehood bill.

1959. Statehood proclaimed; state constitution in effect.

Alaska Censuses and Substitutes

The act of 1912 making Alaska a territory prohibited the creation of counties without the approval of Congress. None were ever created, and Alaska remains the only state in the Union without counties.

Alaskan local governments function through incorporated cities, village governments, and various area-wide units such as judicial, election, school, recorder, and public utility districts. The modern Alaskan boroughs can cover large areas but are not analogous to counties, since they have the legislative powers of municipal governments.

Although Alaska was U.S. territory from 1867, a federal census for 1870 was not conducted there – except for a military tally of some of the inhabitants. Censuses exist for several local Alaskan jurisdictions from 1870 to 1880, many done as part of U.S. Government surveys of the seal and fishing industries. The extant name lists are included in the bibliography below.

Federal censuses came to Alaska in 1880, followed by 1890, but both were apparently statistical summaries only, since no name lists have been found. Without counties as the basic census units, the U.S. Census Bureau had to be creative in parceling out enumeration districts. The first full federal census was for 1900, which survives. In that year, the Census Bureau divided Alaska into Northern (Arctic), Southern (Kodiak Kuskokwim, Nushagak, Aleutian-Unalaska), and Southeastern (Sitka, Juneau) districts.

In the 1910, 1920, and 1930 censuses, Alaska was enumerated using four judicial districts, indicated by the location of the district courthouse as Division 1 (Juneau), Division 2 (Nome), Division 3 (Anchorage), and Division 4 (Fairbanks).

The following published censuses and census substitutes are available to Alaska researchers:

■ ***History of Russian America, 1732-1867,*** by Obshchei Redakt and N. N. Bolkhovitinova, written mostly in Russian, published by a Russian Institute, 3 vols., Includes bibliographical references and indexes. Details the history of Russian exploration and colonization of Alaska, the formation and history of the Russian-American Company, and the sale of Alaska to the United States in 1867. Text in Russian, with some in English. Contents: vol. 1: The establishment of Russian America, 1732-1799; vol. 2: The Russian-American Company, 1799-1825; vol. 3. Russian America: from its height to its decline, 1825-1867. FHL book 979.8 H2i v. 1-3.

■ ***History of the Russian Colonization in America,*** written in Russian by A. D. Drudzo and R. V. Kinzhalov, published Moscow, 1994, 379 pages. FHL book 947 W2d.

■ **1741-1867 Alaska**. See ***Russian America: A Biographical Dictionary,*** by Richard A. Pierce, published by Limestone Press, Kingston, Ontario, 1990, 555 pages. Table of contents serves as an index. Biographies deal largely with Russian immigrants to Alaska, 1741-1867. Canada and other areas are also represented. FHL book 979.8 D3p.

■ ***Alaska Census Records, 1870-1907,*** edited by Ronald Vern Jackson and Gary Ronald Teeples, published by Accelerated Indexing Systems, 1976, 68 pages. FHL book 979.8 X22j.

■ ***Enumeration of Sitka, Alaska Territory, 1870,*** microfilm of original published 1871, Government Printing Office. Some persons enumerated were Aleut Indians. Reproduced from Letter from the Secretary of War, in relation to the Territory of Alaska (House of Representatives Executive Document no. 5, 42nd Congress, 1st Session), published in the Serial Set of U.S. government documents, v. 1470. Filmed by the Genealogical Society of Utah, 1976, 1 roll, FHL film #982047.

■ ***Resident Natives of St. Paul Island, Alaska, July 1, 1870: Taken From Philip Volkov's Lists, August 8, 1873,*** microfilm of photocopy of original published by the Government Printing Office, 1884. Reproduced from Report on the Seal islands of Alaska (House of Representatives Miscellaneous Documents, vol. 13 no 42, pt. 8), published in the Serial Set of U.S. government documents, vol. 2136. Filmed by the Genealogical Society of Utah, 1976, 1 roll, FHL film #982046.

■ ***Census of Unalaska and Aleutian Villages, Alaska, March, 1878,*** typescript of government document. Includes the Aleutian Islands and the mainland Aleut Indian villages of Belkovsky, Nicholayevsk and Protossoff (also known as Morzovoy). FHL book 979.84 X2p. Filmed by the Genealogical Society of Utah, 1973, 1 roll, FHL film #908376.

■ ***Census of Sitka, Alaska Territory: Taken April 25, 1880, by Commander L. A. Beardslee, U.S.N.*** Microfilm of photocopy of original published by Government Printing Office, 1882. Reproduced from *Reports of Captain L. A. Beardslee, U. S. Navy, relative to affairs in Alaska,* (Senate Executive Document no. 71, 47th Congress, 1st session), published in the Serial Set of U. S. Government documents, vol. 1989. Includes only those inhabitants who were U. S. citizens by birth or naturalization, not the Aleut Indians who became citizens by treaty. Filmed by the Genealogical Society of Utah, 1976, 1 roll, FHL film #982047. See also **"Sitka, Alaska, 1881 Census,"** microfilm of original published in *Report of United States Naval Officers Cruising in Alaska waters, Jan. 24, 1882,* filmed by the Genealogical Society of Utah, 1976, 1 roll, FHL film #982047.

■ ***Approximate Census of Eskimos at the Cape Smythe Village: Weights and Measures of the Eskimos of Cape Smythe and Point Barrow [1885],*** microfilm of photocopy of original published by the Government Printing Office, 1885. Reproduced from *Report of the International Polar Expedition to Point Barrow, Alaska* (House of Representatives Executive Document no. 44, 48th Congress, 2nd session), published in the Serial Set of U.S. government documents, vol. 2298. Filmed by the Genealogical Society of Utah, 1976, 1 roll, FHL film #982047.

■ ***Tsimshian History Project: First Census of the Original Pioneers, Family Groups, 1887,*** by Tsimshian Studies Institute of Metlakatla, 7 pages. FHL book 979.8 A1 No. 6. Filmed by the Genealogical Society of Utah, 1991, 1 roll, FHL film #6093468.

■ ***Census of the Pribilof Islands of Alaska for 1890, 1891, 1892, 1893, 1894 and 1895; Births, Deaths, and Marriages on the Pribilof Islands, 1 June 1892 - 31 May 1893; 1 June 1893 - 31 May 1895,*** microfilm of photocopy of original published Government Printing Office, 1898, 60 pages. Reproduced from Seal and Salmon Fisheries and General Resources of Alaska, in Four Volumes. Volume 1 (House of Representatives Document no. 92, pt. 1, 55th Congress, 1st session), published in the Serial Set of U.S. government documents, vol. 3576. Filmed by the Genealogical Society of Utah, 1976, 1 roll, FHL film #982047.

■ ***Alaska Gold Rush, Extracted From the Original U.S. Federal Census Schedules: Alaska 1900 Census Index; Alaska 1910 Census Index; Alaska People Index; Alaska Polk Directories Index,*** a CD-ROM publication by Heritage Quest, North Salt Lake, 2001. (CD Available from **www.familyrootspublishing.com).** The CD has 105,574 names in the database., extracted from Alaska-Yukon Polk directories, 1902-1912. Also includes: History and timeline of the gold rush era, with population growth tables – articles from Heritage Quest Magazine: Genealogy Project in Alaska / by David A. Hales; *The Klondike Gold Rush - Finding Grandpa in the Crowd* / by Wenonah Finch Sharpe; *National Archives-Alaska Region* / by Patricia Brown Darling; *National Archives-Alaska Region* / by Donna Potter Phillips – Additional resources.

■ **Juneau, Alaska Naturalization Records, Oct. 1900-Sept. 1910,** microfilm of records located at the U.S. National Archives Branch, Seattle, WA (1988). Original records now located at the Anchorage branch, National Archives. Includes surname indexes. Contains declarations of intention, U.S. District Court, Juneau. Declarations are filed with the United States District Court located in the election district covering the towns or villages where the applicants reside. Each declaration or application will list the name of the town or place of residence. Filmed by the Genealogical Society of Utah, 1988, 1 roll, FHL film #1492069.

■ **Skagway, Alaska Naturalization Records, Mar. 1901 – Jan. 1917,** microfilm of records located at the National Archives, Anchorage branch. Includes surname indexes. Contains declarations of intention, U.S. District Court, Skagway. Declarations are filed with the United States District Court located in the election district covering the towns or villages where the applicants reside. Each declaration or application will list the name of the town or place of residence. Filmed by the Genealogical Society of Utah, 1988, 1 roll, FHL film #1492069.

■ ***Census of St. Paul Island, June 30, 1904: Births and Deaths of St. Paul Island, June 1903 - May 1904; School Report, St. Paul Island, Alaska, April 29, 1904; Census of St. George Island, Alaska, June 30, 1904; Census of St. Paul Island, June 30, 1905; Census of St. George Island, June 30, 1905,*** microfilm of photocopy of original published by Government Printing Office, 1906, 25 pages. Reproduced from *Letter from the Secretary of Commerce and Labor, Transmitting Copies of Certain Reports Relating to the Alaskan Seal Fisheries* (Senate Document no. 98, 59th Congress, 1st session), published in the Serial Set of U.S. government documents, vol. 4911. Filmed by the Genealogical Society of Utah, 1976, 1 roll, FHL film #982047.

■ ***Native Census, St. Paul Island, Alaska, Year Ended June 30, 1906; School Report, September 4, 1905 - April 30, 1906; Census of St. Paul Island, Alaska, Year Ended June 30, 1907; Record of Births and Deaths on St. George Island, June 1, 1906 - May 31, 1907; Census, St. George Island, June 30, 1907,*** microfilm of photocopy, originally published by the Government Printing Office, 1908, 11 pages. Reproduced from *Reports relating to Alaskan Seal Fisheries (Senate Document No. 376, 60th Congress, 1st session),* published in the Serial Set of U.S. government documents, vol. 5242. Filmed by the Genealogical Society of Utah, 1976, 1 roll, FHL film #982047.

■ **1902-1918.** See ***Alaska-Yukon Directories,*** microfilm of original records located in various libraries and societies. Filmed by Research Publications, Inc., Woodbridge, CT. FHL has 3 rolls, as follows:

- 1902 1903, 1905-1906 (2) Alaska-Yukon directories, FHL film #2308320.
- 1907, 1908, 1909-1910, 1911-1912 Alaska-Yukon directories, FHL film #2308321.

- 1915-1916, 1917-1918 Alaska-Yukon directories, FHL film #2308322.

■ **1903-1907.** See ***An Index to the Early History of Alaska as Reported in the 1903-1907 Fairbanks Newspapers,*** compiled and edited by David A. Hales, published by the University of Alaska, 1980, 28 pages. FHL book 979.86 B32e.

■ ***Index to the Seward Gateway, a Newspaper, 1904-1910,*** by Mike Stallings, published by the Seward Community Library, 1983, FHL book 979.83 B32s.

■ ***Nome Telephone Directory for 1905,*** facsimile reprint of original published for the Alaska Telephone and Telegraph Co.: Nome, Alaska: Alaska Printing Co., 1905, 28 pages. Reprint by Shorey Publications, Seattle, 1971. FHL book 979.8 A1 No 5.

■ ***Alphabetical Index of Alien Arrivals at Eagle, Hyder, Ketchikan, Nome, and Skagway, Alaska, June 1906-August 1946,*** compiled by Claire Prechtel-Kluskens, published by the National Archives, 1997. May include name, age, nationality or citizenship, names of persons accompanying the individual, and port of entry. Arranged in reverse alphabetical order with some cards out of order. Filmed by the National Archives, series M2016, 1 roll, FHL film #2138428.

■ **1908-1914.** See ***Name Authority File for Fairbanks, Alaska Newspapers, 1908-February 1914,*** published by Alaska Historical Commission, 1986, 52 pages. Contains an index to 2,500 names of individuals whose names appeared in the Fairbanks newspapers from 1908 to Feb. 19, 1914. FHL book 979.86 B32n.

■ **1910-1929 Fairbanks, Juneau, and Skagway Naturalization Records,** see **Declaration of Intention, 1910-1929; Naturalization Records, 1910-1929; Indexes, 1901-1929,** microfilm of originals at the National Archives Branch in Seattle, WA (1989). Originals now at the Anchorage branch, National Archives. The Fairbanks naturalization records do not show an exact date for applying for citizenship. The date is from the stamp on the declaration of intention (when it was received). The records do not show if a person was accepted as a citizen of the United States in all the applications. The records also do not always show if or when a file was closed. Filmed by the Genealogical Society of Utah, 1988-1989, 6 rolls, as follows:

- Juneau & Skagway indexes to declarations of intention, 900-1929, 1901-1917, FHL film #1605522.
- Juneau & Skagway indexes to declarations of intention 1900-1929, 1901-1917 (another filming), FHL film #1445999.
- Juneau declaration of intention, 1910-1929, FHL film #1492132.
- Fairbanks naturalization records No. 1-290, FHL film #1492133.
- Fairbanks naturalization records No. 290-550, FHL film #1492134.
- Fairbanks naturalization records no. 551-699, 1922-1924, FHL film #1492135.

■ ***Index to the Petersburg Newspapers, 1913-1916,*** by Celia Forrest, published by the Alaska Historical Commission, 1984, 133 pages. Indexes the *Petersburg Progressive* (January 8, 1913-1915) and the *Petersburg Weekly Report* (1915). FHL book 979.82 B32f.

■ **1917-1918 Alaska, World War I Selective Service System Draft Registration Cards,** microfilm of original records at the National Archives branch in East Point, Georgia. The draft cards are arranged alphabetically by Alaskan city draft boards, and then alphabetically by surname of the registrants. Filmed by the National Archives, series M1509. FHL has 4 rolls, as follows:

- Anchorage City, A – Z; Cordova City, A – Z; Douglas City, A – Z; Eagle City, A – Z; Fairbanks City, A - Kalzer, Albert Maximilian, FHL film #1473296.

- Fairbanks City, Kaakinen, Alexander – Z; Haines City, A – Z; Iditarod City, A – Z; Juneau City, A – Z; Ketchikan City, A – Z, FHL film #1473297.
- McCarthy City, A – Z; Nenana City, A – Z; Nome City, A – Z; Petersburg City, A – Z; Ruby City, A – Z; Seward City, A – Z; Sitka City, A – Z; St. Michael, A – Z; Skagway, A – Z, FHL film #1473298.
- Tanana City, A – Z; Valdez City, A – Z; Wrangell, A – Z, FHL film #1473299.

■ ***Juneau and Douglas Telephone Directory, July 1947,*** microfilm of original published by Juneau & Douglas Telephone Co., 1947. Filmed by the Genealogical Society of Utah, 1988, 1 roll, FHL film #1320749.

■ ***Sitka Telephone Directory, January 1950,*** by Sitka Telephone. Filmed by the Genealogical Society of Utah, 1988, 1 roll, FHL film #1320749.

■ **1959-1986.** See ***Fairbanks (Alaska) City Directory: Contains Buyers' Guide and a Complete Classified Business Directory,*** published by R. L. Polk and Co., Kansas City, MO. FHL has directories for 1959, 1965, 1970, 1975, 1979, 1984, and 1986. FHL book 979.86 E4p 1959-1986.

■ **1960-1985.** See ***Anchorage (Alaska) City Directory: Including Advertising Section and a Complete Classified List,*** published by R. L. Polk and Co., Kansas City, MO. FHL has directories for 1960, 1965, 1969-70, 1980, 1985. FHL book 979.83/A1 E4p 1960-1985.

■ **1962-1984.** See ***Ketchikan (Alaska) City Directory: Contains Buyers' Guide and a Complete Classified Business Directory,*** published by R. L. Polk and Co., Kansas City, MO. FHL has directories for 1962, 1966, 1970, 1976, 1980, and 1984. FHL book 979.82/K1 E4p 1962-1984.

■ **1965-1981.** See ***Juneau (Alaska) City Directory: Including Auke Bay and Douglas, Contains Buyers' Guide and a Complete Classified Business Directory,*** published by R. L. Polk and Co., Kansas City, MO. FHL has directories for 1965, 1971, 1975, and 1981. FHL book 979.82 E4p 1965-1981.

Alaska Online Censuses & Substitutes

A few census databases are available online at the following sites:

www.ancestry.com
- 1900 United States Federal Census
- 1910 United States Federal Census
- 1920 United States Federal Census
- 1930 United States Federal Census
- Alaska Census, 1870-1907 (AIS)

www.censusfinder.com
- Alaska Statewide Databases of Census & Genealogy Records
- WWI Draft Registration Cards – files arranged alphabetically

www.census-online.com
- Matanuska-Susitna census

Alaska Historical Collections of the Alaska State Library are described at their Web site at:
http://library.state.ak.us/hist/hist.html.
As an example of historical resources, see ***Alaska Newspapers on Microfilm, 1866-1998,*** a 301-page guide with 994 entries with holdings information and chronologies for Alaskan newspaper locations. Copies were distributed to libraries and museums throughout Alaska, to other state libraries and to the Library of Congress. Most of the microfilm listed in the publication is available for use through Interlibrary Loan. Contact your local library to initiate a request.

HAWAII

Historical Timeline

300 - 900 A.D. Polynesians arrive at the Hawaiian Islands by outrigger canoe from Tahiti.

1627. Spanish sailors visit Hawaii, describe volcanic eruption in ship's log

1778. On an expedition to China, British sea captain James Cook discovers the Hawaiian Islands. He names them the Sandwich Islands after the Earl of Sandwich, one of the expedition's sponsors.

1780s. Other European and U.S. trading ships began to arrive on their way to China. Disease brought from other parts of the world killed many of the Hawaiians.

1794. Hawaii is placed under the protectorate of Great Britain by Capt. George Vancouver.

1795. King Kamehameha I unifies Hawaiian Islands.

1821. Protestant missionaries arrive. Many Hawaiians converted to Christianity.

1831. Catholic missionaries that arrived during the late 1820s were forced to leave or be imprisoned in 1831.

1835. The first sugar plantation is established on Kauai Island

1839. Roman Catholics receive religious freedom

1840. Hawaii adopted its first constitution.

1842. First House of Representatives is called to order; first class begins at Punahou, the new private school.

1843. Lord George Paulet seizes Hawaii in the name of England.

1848. A law passes that divided the land between the king and his chiefs. Most of the chiefs gave their land to the government, which in turn sold land to the Hawaiian people.

1852. First steam-powered ship is used in inter-island service.

1853. Smallpox epidemic takes the lives of over 5,000 Hawaiians.

1865. First immigrant plantation workers depart from Yokohama, Japan for Hawaii.

1878. First telephone is in operation, two years after Alexander Graham Bell's patent.

1879. First steam locomotive pulled its first train load of sugarcane on Maui.

1882. Iolani Palace first occupied by the Hawaii royalty. During the reign of King Kalakaua, 1874-1891, many Hawaiian customs that had been discouraged by earlier rulers became popular again. He became known as the "Merry Monarch."

1883. Electricity arrives as five arc lamps are strung around Iolani Palace; Great Chinatown Fire, losses exceeded $1,455,000.

1887. To enhance trade with the United States, King Kalakaua allowed them exclusive use of Pearl Harbor as a naval base.

1890s. Several U.S. and European settlers had begun planting pineapples. Sugarcane planting also became an important industry. Thousands of workers were needed for these plantations; many came from China, Japan and the Philippines.

1891. Upon the death of King Kalakaua, his sister, Emma, becomes Hawaii's only ruling queen and last Hawaiian monarch. As Queen Liliuokalani, she tries to maintain Hawaii's culture against the large influx of Americans and Europeans who now control the economy.

1893. A trumped up revolution brings forth the American and British inspired Republic of Hawaii, sometimes called "Dole's Republic." Queen Liliuokalani is overthrown, but remains an important influence among the Hawaiian people. Over the next few years, she is successful in convincing President Grover Cleveland that an annexation of Hawaii to the United States should not take place without the approval of the Hawaiian native population.

1898. Hawaiian Islands annexed to the United States.

1900. Hawaii becomes a U.S. territory. The federal census of 1900 was taken with a census day of 1 June 1900, and Hawaii was included, becoming a territory on 14 June 1900 while the census was still in progress. Population: 154,001. No counties existed yet, and the census was divided into five districts including all islands.

1901. The Hawaiian Pineapple Company, now Dole, is established.

1905. The five original counties of Hawaii created: Hawaii, Honolulu, Kalawao, Kauai, and Maui. There have been no new counties or changes since 1905. Kalawao County comprised only the Kalaupapa Leper Colony on Molakai Island. The de facto county stills exists, although the entire area is now part of a National Historical Park.

1910. Hawaii Territory population of 191,874 enumerated in the federal census of 1910.

1920. Hawaii Territory population of 255,881 enumerated in the federal census of 1920.

1934. President Roosevelt was the first U.S. President to visit Hawaii.

1941. After the historic Japanese bombing of Pearl Harbor and Oahu on Dec. 7, 1941, the United States declared war on Japan and entered World War II.

1959. Hawaii became the 50th state on Aug. 21, 1959.

Hawaii Censuses and Substitutes

For centuries, the Hawaiian Islands were governed by tribal chiefs, generally for each of the eight main islands. All island tribes were first unified under King Kamehameha I in 1795. On and off from that time forward, Hawaii came under jurisdiction of the British and others, but the islanders never tolerated any outside rulers for very long, revolted frequently, and generally went back to their own form of self-government whenever it suited them. Yet, the Hawaiians were always ready to adopt any European culture that improved their lives – and within three or four generations of their first contact with Europeans, the native Hawaiians were as well educated and "civilized" as any culture of Europe.

The Kingdom of Hawaii sponsored several census-like tabulations taken for all of the islands from as early as 1795, but only a few name lists for the censuses from about 1840 forward have survived. The Kingdom of Hawaii took three censuses in 1878, 1890, and 1896, but the territory and state of Hawaii has not taken a census separate from the federal censuses.

Private land ownership has existed in Hawaii since the reign of Kamehameha III, who, at the urging of the growing number of Europeans in Hawaii, instituted a land system of Royal grants and private land sales in 1848. Many of the early land records still exist, and the records can often serve as census substitutes. In 1898, when Hawaii was annexed to the United States, virtually all of the arable lands were in the hands of private ownership, or held by the local governments. When Hawaii became a territory in 1900, it maintained ownership of its public land – the only U.S. territory to do that. Clear title to the land was another matter, however, and after decades of cross-claims and litigation, the Hawaiian royal lands confiscated by the Republic of Hawaii were finally returned to the Hawaiian Territorial or State government. As a result, most island mountains, forests, and beaches are owned by the state of Hawaii today.

In spite of the convoluted land claims from 1898 forward, tracing land sales in Hawaii is an important source for genealogical information, by using the records of the original land grants (patents) and subsequent land sales (deeds).

The following published censuses and substitutes are available for Hawaii:

■ **1789-1843.** See ***The American Frontier in Hawaii: The Pioneers, 1789-1843,*** by Harold Whitman Bradley, original published by Stanford University Press, 1942, reprinted by Peter Smith, Gloucester, MA, 1968, 488 pages. Includes index. FHL book 996.9 H2b.

■ **1836-1855 Award Books,** (Record of land transfers from the Hawaiian Royalty to private companies and individuals). Microfilm of original manuscripts at the Department of Land and Natural Resources, Honolulu. Filmed by the Genealogical Society of Utah, 1964, 12 rolls, as follows:

- Award book, vol. 1, 1836-1849, FHL film #571189.
- Award book, vol. 2, 1848-1852, FHL film #571190.
- Award book, vol. 2, 1848-1852, FHL film #571191.
- Award book, vol. 3, 1846-1854, FHL film #571192.
- Award book, vol. 4, 1850-1852, FHL film #571193.
- Award book, vol. 5,1851-1853, FHL film #571194.
- Award book, vol. 6, 1851-1853, FHL film #571195.
- Award book, vol. 6, 1851-1853, FHL film #571196.
- Award book vol. 7, 1852-1854, FHL film #571197.
- Award book, vol. 8, 1852-1853, FHL film #571198.
- Award book, vol. 9, 1852-1855, FHL film #571199.
- Award book, vol. 10, 1852-1855, FHL film #571200.

■ ***Hawaii 1840-1843 Territorial Census Records,*** edited by Ronald Vern Jackson, published by Accelerated Indexing Systems, North Salt Lake, UT, 1986. Mr. Jackson was famous for his creative titles – Hawaii did not become part of the U.S. until 1898 and a territory in 1900. The source of these "Territorial Census Records" are presumably from the original censuses of the Kingdom of Hawaii now located at the Archives of Hawaii and microfilmed by the Genealogical Society of Utah. FHL book 996.9 X22j 1840.

■ **1840-1866; 1847-1896 Census Files,** microfilm of originals from the Hawaiian Bureau of Customs, now located at the Archives of Hawaii, Honolulu. Chronologically arranged. Records consist of school census statistics, population census statistics, and summaries of births, marriages and deaths. Includes four pages of the original 1866 census of Hawaii, and loose sheets of corrections to a later (apparently the 1896) census on Oahu. Filmed by the Genealogical Society of Utah, 1976, 1 roll, FHL film #1009896. (1840-1866, items 1-2; 1847-1896, items 3-4).

■ **1843 History.** See ***History of the Hawaiian or Sandwich Islands: Embracing Their Antiquities, Mythology, Legends, Discovery by Europeans Sixteenth Century, Re-discovery by Cook, With Their civil, Religious and Political History, From the Earliest Traditionary period to the Present Time,*** by James Jackson Jarves, microfilm of original book published by Tappan & Dennet, Boston, 1843. Filmed by the Genealogical Society of Utah, 1985, 1 roll, FHL film #1425609.

■ **1844-1900 Deeds and Other Records; 1845-1917 Grantee-Grantor Index to Deeds,** microfilm of original records at the Department of Land and Natural Resources in Honolulu. Text in Hawaiian and English. Includes deeds for all islands/counties. Filmed by the Hawaii Dept.

of Land and Natural Resources, 1975. FHL has 108 rolls, beginning with FHL film 986199 (Oahu grantee index, A-Z, 1845-1869). To locate places, years, and film numbers for all 108 rolls, use the **www.familysearch.org site**. Go to Library / FHL Catalog / Film/Fiche Search: "986199" (first film number in the series).

■ **1847-1961 Patents Upon Confirmation of Land Commission,** microfilm of original records at the Hawaii Department of Land and Natural Resources, Honolulu. Filmed by the Genealogical Society of Utah, 1964, 19 rolls. The first roll in the series is a name index to all patent holders, FHL film #571219. To locate places, years, and film numbers for all 19 rolls, use the **www.familysearch.org site** site. Go to Library / FHL Catalog / Film/Fiche Search: "571219" (first film number in the series).

■ ***Indices of Awards Made by the Board of Commissioners to Quiet Land Titles in the Hawaiian Islands,*** microfilm of original published: Honolulu, Hawaii: Office of the Commissioner of Public Lands of the Territory of Hawaii, 1929. 1 vol. Filmed by the Genealogical Society of Utah, 1987, 1 roll, FHL film #1321397.

■ **1878, 1890 & 1896 Hawaii Census Records,** microfilm of originals from the Hawaiian Bureau of Customs, now located at the Archives of Hawaii, Honolulu. Filmed by the Genealogical Society of Utah, 1977, 8 rolls, as follows:

- **1878** census records, island of Hawaii: town of Hilo, FHL film #1010681.
- **1878** census records, island of Hawaii: town of Hilo, FHL film #1010682.
- **1890** census records, island of Hawaii: town of Hilo, FHL film #1010683.
- **1890** census records, island of Hawaii: town of Hilo, FHL film #1010684.
- **1890** census records, island of Hawaii: town of Puna, No. Kohala, and So. Kohala; island of Kauai: town of Lihue, Koloa, and Waimea (Kekaha, Mana, Waimea, and Makaweli), FHL film #1010685.
- **1890** census records, island of Molokai and Maui; island of Oahu: towns of Koolaupoko and Waialua, FHL film #1010686.
- **1896** census records, island of Oahu: district of Kona (Honolulu), FHL film #1010687.
- **1896** census records, island of Oahu: district of Waikahalulu (Honolulu), FHL film #1010688.

■ **1884-1936 Honolulu and Hawaii Territory Directories,** microfilm of originals by various publishers in various libraries and societies, filmed by Research Publications, Woodbridge, CT, 1980-1995. FHL has 18 rolls, as follows:

- **1884** city directory of Honolulu and island of Oahu; **1890** directory, Kingdom of Hawaii; **1892** directory and hand-book of Honolulu and the Hawaiian Islands, FHL film #2156544.
- **1898** directory and hand-book of Honolulu and the Hawaiian Islands; **1900-1901** directory of Honolulu and Hawaii Territory, FHL film #2156545.
- **1902, 1903-1904** and **1904-1905** directories of Honolulu and the territory of Hawaii, FHL film #1759763.
- **1905-1906, 1907** and **1908** directories of Honolulu and the territory of Hawaii, FHL film #1759764.
- **1909** and **1910** directories of Honolulu and the territory of Hawaii, FHL film #1759765.
- **1911** and **1912** directories of Honolulu and the territory of Hawaii, FHL film #1759766.
- **1913** and **1914** directories of Honolulu and the territory of Hawaii, FHL film #1759767.
- **1915 and 1916** directories of Honolulu and the territory of Hawaii, FHL film #1759768.
- **1917** and **1918** directories of Honolulu and the territory of Hawaii, FHL film #1759769.
- **1919** and **1920** directories of Honolulu and the territory of Hawaii, FHL film #1759770.
- **1921** directory of Honolulu and the territory of Hawaii, FHL Film #1759771.
- **1922** directory of Honolulu and the territory of Hawaii, FHL film #1759772.
- **1923** and **1924** directories of Honolulu and the territory of Hawaii, FHL film #1759773.
- **1925** and **1926** directories of Honolulu and the territory of Hawaii, FHL film #1759774.
- **1927 and 1928-1929** directories of Honolulu and the territory of Hawaii, FHL film #1759775.
- **1929-1930** and **1930-1931** directories of Honolulu

and the territory of Hawaii, FHL film #1759776.

- **1931-1932** and **1932-1933** directories of the city and county of Honolulu and the territory of Hawaii, FHL film #1759777.
- **1934-1935** and **1935-1936** directories of the city and county of Honolulu and the territory of Hawaii, FHL film #1759778.

■ **1885 History**. See ***An Account of the Polynesian Race, its Origin and Migrations and the Ancient History of the Hawaiian People to the Times of Kamehameha I,*** by Abraham Fornander, original published 1885-1887, 3 vols. Reprint published by Tuttle, Rutland, VT, 1969, 3 vols. in 1 and includes ***Index to The Polynesian Race,*** by Abraham Fornander, FHL book 996 H6f.

■ **1887 Register of Voters, Hawaiian Islands, 1888 Register of Voters, Island of Oahu,** microfilm of original records of the Hawaiian Inspector of Elections, now located at the Archives of Hawaii in Honolulu. Contains a list of voters for all islands/districts. This register is a list of persons who took the oath to support the Constitution and laws, and registered and voted at the General Election of September 12th, 1887 and (on the Island of Oahu) Special Election of August 22nd, 1888. Records arranged by island, district, ward or precinct, then alphabetically by name of voter. Includes information on age, place of birth, occupation, local residence, registration date, entitled to vote for nobles (ownership of property required), and remarks. Includes Supplemental register of voters for nobles in wards of district of Honolulu. Filmed by Archives of Hawaii, 1992, 1 roll, FHL film #1674473.

■ **1800s.** See **Hawaiian Genealogies in Bishop Museum,** microfilm of original manuscripts at the Bernice P. Bishop Museum Archives in Honolulu, Hawaii. Text in Hawaiian and English. Most genealogies were recorded in the 1800s, but deal with ancestors for many hundreds of years before that time. Filmed by the Genealogical Society of Utah, 1978, 7 rolls, beginning with FHL film #1025948 (genealogy of Hawaiian chiefs, Queen Liliuokalani, et al.). To locate contents, Hawaiian and European family names, types of collections, and film numbers for all 7 rolls, use the www.familysearch.org site. Go to Library / FHL Catalog / Film/Fiche Search: "1025948" (first film number in the series).

■ **1890 Hawaiian Kingdom Census**, microfilm of photocopy made 1990 in Hawaii. Contains index (typescript) and extract (handwritten) of the 1890 Census of Hawaii for the districts or islands: Hilo – Kau – Hamakua – Kau, contains Bureau of Conveyance adoption index, 1847-1899; 3rd Circuit Court probate index, pkt. 1-522, approx. 1850-1899; 1910 census extract & index of Kau – Kohala (south & north) – Puna – Kauai – Maui – Molokai – Oahu. Includes index in each volume. Filmed by the Genealogical Society of Utah, 1990, 1 roll, FHL film #1675447.

■ **1917-1918 World War I Selective Service System Draft Registration Cards, Hawaii,** microfilm of original records in the National Archives in East Point, Georgia. The draft cards are arranged by county or city draft board, and then alphabetically by surname of the registrants. Cards are in rough alphabetical order. Filmed by the National Archives, 1987-1988, 14 rolls, as follows:

- Hawaii County, No. 1, A - S, Kami, FHL film #1452025.
- Hawaii County, No. 1, T. Kamich – M. Seyas, FHL film #1452026.
- Hawaii County, No. 1, C. Shao – Z; Hawaii County, No. 2, A – M, FHL film #1452027.
- Hawaii County, No. 2, N - Z Honolulu City, No. 1, A – J, FHL film #1452095.
- Honolulu City, No. 1, K - P. Sampson, FHL film #1452096.
- Honolulu City, No. 1, P. San – Z; Honolulu City, No. 2, A - E. Contreras, FHL film #1452097.
- Honolulu City, No. 2, A. Cook - V. Kawai, FHL film #1452098.
- Honolulu City, No. 2, J. Kawaihea – N, FHL film #1452099.

- Honolulu City, No. 2, 0 - J. Texeira, FHL film #1452100.
- Honolulu City, No. 2, W. Thayer – Z; Kauai County, A - G, FHL film #1452101.
- Kauai County, H – V, FHL film #1452102; Kauai County, W – Z; Maui County, A – Z, Miazato, FHL film #1452103.
- Maui County, N. Michikawa – Z, FHL film #1452104.
- National Guard, A – Z, FHL film #1452105.

■ **1917-1977.** See ***Directory of the City and County of Honolulu, Hawaii: Including Island of Oahu, Contains Buyers' Guide and a Complete Classified Business Directory,*** published by R. L. Polk and Company, Honolulu, HI. FHL has original directory books for 1917, 1938-39, 1940-41, 1959-60, 1963-64, and 1977. FHL book 996.93 E4p 1917-1977.

■ **1920-1966 Honolulu City-County Voter Registrations.** See ***Affidavit on Application For Registration of Voters, ca1920-1966,*** microfilm of original records from the city and county of Honolulu and stored at the Honolulu Hawaii West Stake Center Records are arranged by the first two or more letters of the surname; therefore several different surnames may appear to be misfiled. The first name is not considered in the arrangement. Name, address, age, birth date and place, and occupation are included in the information. Filmed by the Genealogical Society of Utah, 1990, 104 rolls, 16mm film, beginning with FHL film #1653824 (surnames Aa – Ahs). To locate the remaining alphabetical break-down, and the film numbers for all 104 rolls, use the **www.familysearch.org** site. Go to Library / FHL Catalog / Film/Fiche Search: "1653824" (first film number in the series).

Hawaii Online Censuses & Substitutes

A few census databases are available online at the following sites:

www.ancestry.com
- 1900 Federal Census
- 1910 Federal Census
- 1920 Federal Census
- 1930 Federal Census

www.censusfinder.com
- 1900-1910 Hawaii Census Search at Ancestry
- 1941 Pearl Harbor Casualty List

Honolulu County
- 1920 Federal Census of Midway Island
- 1800s Obituaries from The Sandwich Isle Gazette
- 1800s Obituaries from The Ka Hae Hawaii Newspaper
- 1800s Obituaries from The Hawaiian Gazette
- 1896-1909 Territory of Hawaii Births (partial)
- Genealogy of The Chiefs of Na Lani Kamehameha
- Portuguese Ships Lists to Hawaii

Kalawao County
- 1920 Federal Census Index
- 1920 Federal Census Transcription – pp 1A-5A
- 1920 Federal Census Transcription – pp 5B-9B
- 1920 Federal Census Transcription – pp 10A-14A
- 1920 Federal Census of Kalaupapa

Hawaiians Found in Washington State
- Forgotten Hawaiian who left Hawaii for Washington State
- Hawaiians listed on Washington State Census Records
- 1839-1853 Birth and Deaths at Fort Vancouver in Washington State

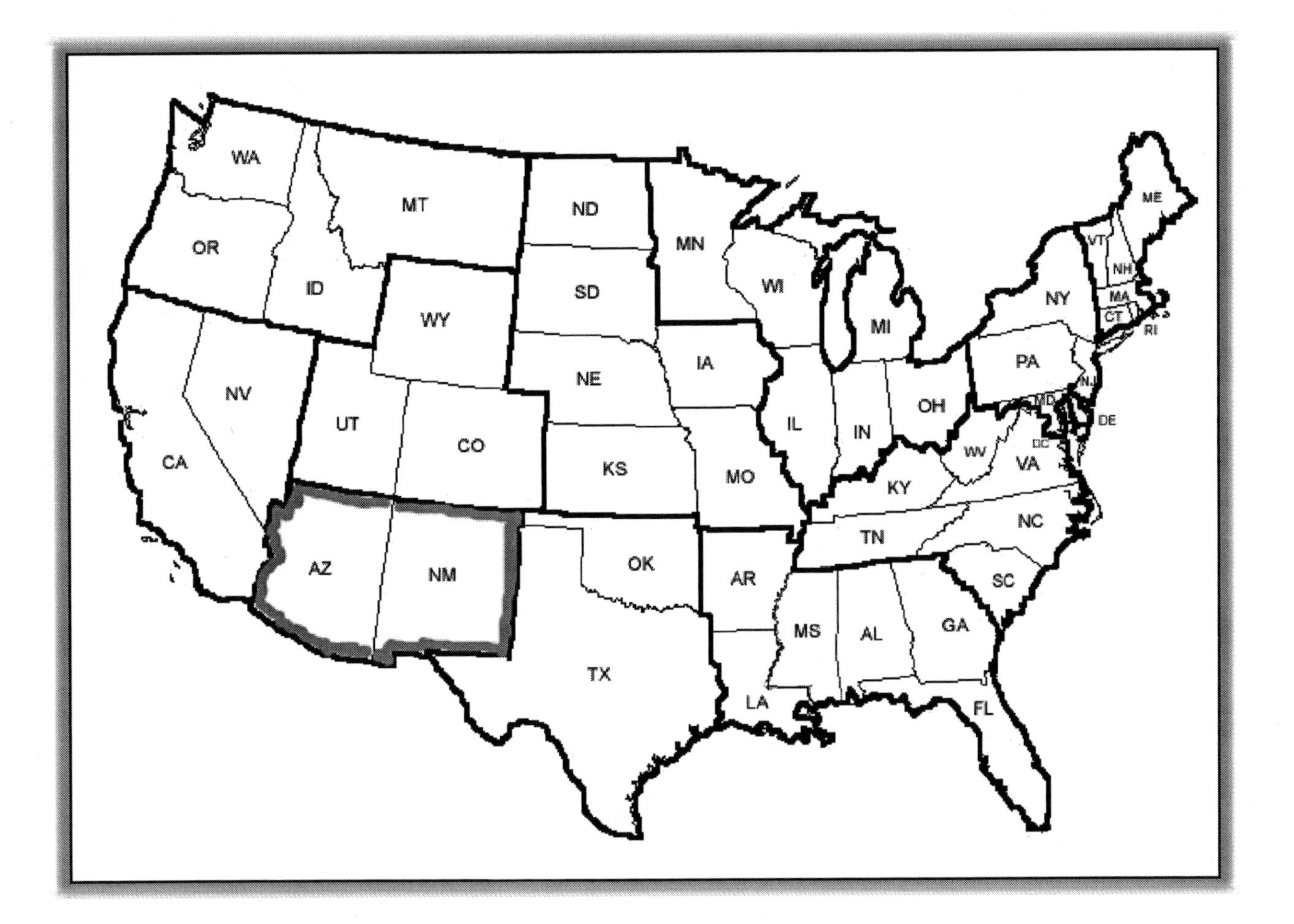

Chapter 3W – Nuevo Mexico

Arizona and New Mexico

Historical Timeline, Arizona & New Mexico

1536. Spanish explorer Cabeza de Vaca enters New Mexico via Texas. He is credited with starting the story of the Seven Cities of Cibola, supposedly made of gold. The local Indians perpetuate the rumor, by continually telling the Spaniards that the cities of gold were just a little further away. This ploy works for nearly 60 years, keeping the Spanish soldiers from staying very long in one place.

1539. Franciscan friar Marcos de Niza and companion Esteban explore New Mexico looking for the Seven Cities of Cibola. They reach the Zuni village of Hawikuh where Esteban is killed.

1540. Francisco Vasquez de Coronado of Spain came searching for the Seven Cities of Cibola. Coronado never finds the cities of gold, but does find the Gulf of California, Colorado River, Grand Canyon, and areas in present Colorado and Kansas. He claims the entire region as part of New Spain.

1590. First attempt to colonize Nuevo Mexico made by Spaniard Gaspar de Sosa.

1598. Juan de Oñate founds the first permanent Spanish colony at San Juan de los Caballeros (near present-day Espanola, New Mexico). San Juan becomes the first capital of the Province of Nuevo Mexico.

1600. San Gabriel is founded at the confluence of the Rio Grande and Chama Rivers. San Gabriel becomes the second capital of Nuevo Mexico.

1609. Governor Pedro de Peralta founds Santa Fe as the new capital of the Spanish Province of Nuevo Mexico.

1680. The Pueblo Indians revolt and drive the Spanish out of northern New Mexico, who flee to El Paso del Norte.

1692. Diego de Vargas conquers New Mexico (again) for Spain. Jesuit father Kino founds the Guevavi mission near present Nogales, Arizona.

1700. Founding of the San Xavier del Bac mission (White Dove of the Desert), near present Tucson, Arizona.

1706. Villa de Albuquerque founded.

1743. French trappers reach Santa Fe and begin trade with the Spanish.

1752. After many revolts from the Pima and Papago tribes, a Spanish settlement was established at Tubac Pueblo, about 45 miles south of present Tucson, Arizona.

1776. A Spanish presidio (fort) is built at Tucson. – A route from Santa Fe to Los Angeles is explored, which becomes known as the Old Spanish Trail.

1800. The Spanish population of Nuevo Mexico at about 20,000.

1804. hearing of an intrusion of Americans into their territory, Spanish troops are dispatched from Santa Fe to intercept the Lewis and Clark Expedition, but fail to find them.

1807. U.S. Army officer Zebulon Pike leads the first American expedition into Nuevo Mexico. The published report of his expedition is the first written English description of the Spanish culture in North America.

1821. Mexico gains independence from Spain and exerts military control of Nuevo Mexico. That same year, trappers and traders from the United States come into the area via a new route which will become known as the Santa Fe Trail.

1829. The first commercial caravan along The Old Spanish Trail from Santa Fe to Los Angeles was led by Mexican trader Antonio Armijo. He is best known for naming an artesian spring in the desert just west of Arizona (Las Vegas).

1836. The new Republic of Texas claims all land to the Rio Grande, including the eastern half of present New Mexico, and a portion of southern Colorado.

1841. Texas soldiers invade New Mexico but they are held at bay by Mexican troops under the command of Governor Manuel Armijo.

1845. Texas annexed to the U.S. The U.S. honors the Texas claim to the Rio Grande, but Mexico warns that a war will result from such an action.

1846. Mexican-American War begins. U.S. Forces take control of the Rio Grande Valley. The captured area from the Texas line to the Rio Grande is annexed to the United States, based on the acquired Texas claim. A provisional government is set up by General Stephen Watts Kearny. This provisional "New Mexico

Territory" operates until replaced by the expanded New Mexico territorial government in 1850.

1848. As part of the Treaty of Guadalupe Hidalgo ending the war with Mexico, the United States gains ownership to the remainder of New Mexico west of the Rio Grande (including present Arizona), present Colorado (west of the continental divide), a portion of present southwestern Wyoming; and all of present California, Utah and Nevada. In compensation, the U.S. paid Mexico a sum of 15 million dollars for an area which was over half of the Republic of Mexico, and was comparable in size to the Louisiana Purchase.

1850. June 1, **Federal Census**. The provisional Territory of New Mexico included the original seven counties of Bernalillo, Rio Arriba, Santa Ana, Santa Fe, San Miguel, Taos, and Valencia counties. Taos County included an area of all or part of 13 modern Colorado counties. The area of present Arizona north of the Gila River was also part of New Mexico Territory, but no population was enumerated there.

1850. September 9, California admitted into the Union as the 31st state; and on the same day, Congress established both Utah Territory and New Mexico Territory.

1852. Doña Ana County established, stretching across the southern portion of New Mexico Territory, well into the area that later became Arizona.

1853 Gadsden Purchase. Seeking access for a southern railroad route, the U.S. pays Mexico a sum of 10 million dollars to purchase a 45,000 square mile tract of land south of the Gila River. The purchase was negotiated by James Gadsden, minister to Mexico, who, along with Jefferson Davis, had earlier proposed a plan to build a transcontinental railroad that would link the southern states to the Pacific leading to a southern-confederate dominance of the region. The area of the Gadsden Purchase was added to New Mexico Territory, which immediately expanded Doña Ana County to include the entire area.

1859. New Mexico Territory creates Arizona County from Doña Ana, the Gadsden Purchase area of present Arizona south of the Gila River.

1860 Federal Census. New Mexico's population of 93,516 people was enumerated in areas of present southern Colorado, and all of present Arizona and New Mexico. Arizona's enumeration was in Arizona County, New Mexico Territory, including the few settlements just north of the Gila River; plus Fort Mojave on the Colorado River, technically in New Mexico's Valencia County.

1861. Confederate troops from Texas invade New Mexico.

– The Confederate Territory of Arizona is declared with the capital at La Mesilla.

– The U.S. Territory of Colorado created by Congress. New Mexico loses the northern-most parts of Taos and Mora counties to the new territory.

1862. Battle of Velvarde and Glorieta Pass fought. Confederate occupation of New Mexico ends.

– Arizona County, New Mexico abolished, its area returned to Doña Ana County.

1863. Arizona Territory created by Congress, with Prescott as the capital. The northern boundary of Arizona Territory extended west to the California line, and included all of present Clark County, Nevada. When Congress divided New Mexico Territory on the same meridian as Colorado's western line, the resulting map created the "four corners" of Colorado, Utah,

Arizona, and New Mexico, still the only point in the U.S. where four states touch at their corners.

1864. Arizona Territorial census taken, mandated by the federal act under which the territory was formed, and enumerated within three judicial districts.

1866. Arizona Territorial census taken, authorized by the territorial legislature, including the five original counties of Mohave, Pah-Ute, Pima, Yavapai and Yuma.

1867. Arizona territorial capital moved to Tucson.

1869. John Wesley Powell and party explore the Grand Canyon by boat.

1870 Federal Census. New Mexico Territory's population at 91,874. Arizona Territory's population at 9,658. The 1870 Mortality Schedule for Tombstone, Arizona Territory listed the name, age, nativity, and cause of death of all persons who died between June 1, 1869 and May 31, 1870. Most of the deaths were the result of gunshot wounds or knife wounds, with a couple of hangings, and one rattlesnake bite. At the end of the schedules, the census enumerator wrote a few words of explanation, saying that most of Tombstone's young men settled their differences of opinion in the street.

1879. The first railroad crosses New Mexico Territory.

1880 Federal Census. New Mexico Territory's population at 119,565. Arizona Territory's population at 40,440. After microfilming, the National Archives gave away the original 1880 census schedules for both New Mexico Territory (3 vols.) and Arizona Territory (1 vol.). They are now located at the DAR Library in Washington, DC.

1881. The first railroad crosses Arizona Territory. – On October 26, Wyatt Earp, Doc Holliday, and three more Earp brothers were involved in a gunfight at Tombstone's OK Corral. According to the last ten movies depicting the event, the Earps were usually the good guys.

1885. New Mexico Territorial census taken with federal assistance.

1886. After leaving his hideout in Arizona, the great Apache Chief Geronimo surrenders to soldiers on September 4, marking the end of the Indian wars in the West.

1889. Arizona territorial capital moved to Phoenix.

1912. (Jan. 6th), New Mexico becomes the 47th state, with Santa Fe as the state capital.

1912. (Feb. 14th, Valentines Day), Arizona becomes the 48th state, with Phoenix as the state capital.

ARIZONA

Statewide Censuses & Substitutes

■ **1801 Mexican Census**. See ***Mexican Census Pre-territorial: Pimeria Alta, 1801,*** transcribed by Eugene L. Sierras, published by the Arizona State Genealogical Society, Tucson, AZ, 1986, 61 pages, FHL book 979.1 X2s 1801. Pimeria Alta was an area of land now stretching from Sonora, Mexico to Pima, Cochise, and Santa Cruz Counties, Arizona.

■ **1831 Mexican Census**. See ***Mexican Census Pre-territorial: Tucson, Tubac & Santa Cruz, 1831,*** transcribed by Eugene L. Sierras, published by the Arizona State Genealogical Society, Tucson, AZ, 1986, 30 pages. From page 7: "The National Republican Congress at Mexico City in 1824 combined the provinces of Sonora and Sinaloa under the name Estado Interno de Occidente (Interior State of the West). In 1830, the Congress divided Occidente, Sonora, and southern Arizona was again independent. The following year, 1831, a census was taken. This is the only name by name census of the Sonoran Desert for 1831. The census includes Tucson, Tubac and Santa Cruz." FHL book 979.1 A1 no. 62. See also, ***Index to the 1831 Census of Arizona and Sonora***, compiled by Instituto Genealógico e Histórico Latinoamericano, published by the Institute, Highland, UT, 1983, 30 pages. Includes name (listed alphabetically by surname), biographical information (relationships), house no., and reference to census. FHL book 979.1 A1 no. 87. Also on microfilm, filmed by the Genealogical Society of Utah, 1990, 1 roll, FHL film #1697282.

■ **1852 Mexican Census**. See ***Mexican Census Pre-territorial: Pimeria Alta, 1852***, transcribed by Eugene L. Sierras, published by the Arizona State Genealogical Society, Tucson, AZ, 1986, 104 pages. FHL book 979.1 X2se 1852.

■ **1860-1993 Arizona Obituary Card Index**, microfilm of card index at the Mesa Family History Center, Mesa, Arizona. Organized in alphabetical order by the name of deceased person. Filmed by the Genealogical Society of Utah, 1993, 39 rolls, as follows:

- Aarni, John C. - Andrews, William A, FHL film #1877927.
- Andreyka, Theodore E. - Ballard, William Henry, FHL film #1892217.
- Ballato, Thomas L. - Berridge, Sally, FHL film #1892218.
- Berringer, Ida M. - Branche, Louise, FHL film #1892219.
- Brand, Frank B. - Burnum, Fannie, FHL film #1892220.
- Buros, Arline - Casey, William, FHL film #1892221.
- Cash, Aubrey O. - Cole, William, FHL film #1892222.
- Coleman, J. J. - Crismon, William Alma, FHL film #1892400.
- Crisp, Arnold - Dennis, William, FHL film #1892401.
- Dennison, Annie Mae - Earp, Wyatt, FHL film #1892402.
- Earps - Ferguson, Willie Leon, FHL film #1892403.
- Fergusson, Erna - Fulton, William Shirley, FHL film #1892404.
- Fults, Lawrence A. - Goetz, William F., FHL film #1892476.
- Geoury, Perle - Gurley, William Donald, FHL film #1892477.
- Gurnee, Hazel - Hatton, William, FHL film #1892478.
- Hatz, Albert - Hirn Esther B., FHL film #1892479.
- Hirose, Elki - Huskey, Mark, FHL film #1892480.
- Huskinson, Della Eliza - Jones, Jerry William, FHL film #1892481.
- Jones, Jesse - Kirby, Wesley Daniel, FHL film #1892482.
- Kirchback, Myrtle Briner - Leibovitz, Minnie, FHL film #1892483.
- Leibsohn, Mayer - Lujan, Yrene, FHL film #1892787.
- Lujar, M. - Matlock, W. W., FHL film #1892788.
- Matlow, Lester - McNelly, William T., FHL film #1892789.
- McNelty, Frank H. - Monck, Fred L., FHL film #1892790.
- Moncrief, John - Nail, Pete, FHL film #1892791.
- Naile, Emma Elvira - O'Neal, W. J., FHL film #1892792.
- O'Neall, Elva - Pena, Virginia, FHL film #1892793.
- Penberthy, Ann Seely - Prescott, Thomas J., FHL film #1892794.
- Presley, Charles - Reynolds, June, FHL film #1893098.
- Reynolds, Kate - Roseveare, Joseph, FHL film #1893099.
- Rosin, Henry E. - Schneidewind, Naomi E., FHL film #1893100.
- Schneidmiller, Ann - Sims, Willis W., FHL film #1893101.
- Simser, Morris N. - Staff, Mabelle E., FHL film #1893102.
- Stafford, Annette - Swanson, William, FHL film #1893437.

- Swanty, Elva B. - Toth, Twyla, FHL film #1893438.
- Totress, Ferdinand - Vining, Edith R., FHL film #1893439.
- Vinnedge, Sadie H. - West, William D., FHL film #1893440.
- Westall, Daniel Edward - Wilson, Zula Jane, FHL film #1893441.
- Wilstach, Emma M. - Zynda, Keith R., FHL film #1893442.

■ **1860, 1864, and 1870 Censuses**. See *Federal Census – Territory of New Mexico and Territory of Arizona: Excerpts from the Decennial Federal Census, 1860, for Arizona County in the Territory of New Mexico, the Special Territorial Census of 1864 Taken in Arizona and Decennial Federal Census, 1870, for the Territory of Arizona,* Government Printing Office, Washington, DC, 1965, 253 pages. Arranged in alphabetical order by surname. May list name, age, sex, occupation, value of property, and state or country of birth. FHL book 979.1 X2pa.

■ **1861-1865 Arizona Territory Union and Confederate Soldiers**. See *Index to Compiled Service Records of Volunteer Union Soldiers Who Served in Organizations From the Territory of Arizona,* microfilm of original records in the National Archives, Washington, DC, filmed by the National Archives, 1 roll, FHL film #881608. See also, *Index to Compiled Service Records of Confederate Soldiers Who Served in Organizations from the Territory of Arizona,* microfilm of original records in the National Archives, Washington, DC. Filmed by the National Archives, series M375; FHL has 1 roll, FHL film #821837. Both of these publications included in *Index to Soldiers & Sailors of the Civil War,* a searchable name index to 6.3 million Union and Confederate Civil War soldiers now available online at the National Park Service Web site. A search can be done by surname, first name, state, or unit. Arizona Territory supplied 926 men to the war (655 Union, 271 Confederate). To search for one go to the NPS Web site: **www.civilwar.nps.gov/cwss/.**

■ **1864 Territorial (Federal) Census of Arizona,** microfilm of original records at the Arizona Department of Libraries, Archives & Public Records in Phoenix, Arizona. This census was provided for in the federal organic act establishing Arizona Territory, one of only three such censuses ever dictated by the federal government between decennial census years. (The others were the 1857 Minnesota Territory and 1907 Oklahoma)). The results of the enumeration were used in forming judicial districts and for the election of members to the territorial legislature and other offices. The census schedule questions include a person's name, age, sex, marital status, where born, how long a local resident, citizenship status, occupation, residence of all married individuals, and value of personal and real estates. Filmed by the Arizona Department of Libraries, Archives & Public Records, 1997. FHL has 1 roll, FHL film #2114989. See also ***The 1864 Census of the Territory of Arizona,*** extracted by the Historical Records Survey, division of Women's and Professional Projects, Works Progress Administration, 1938, 210 pages, FHL book 979.1 X2p 1864. Also on microfilm, filmed by the Genealogical Society of Utah, 1973, 1 roll, FHL film #897437.

■ **1866 Arizona Territorial Census**, microfilm of original records at the Arizona Department of Libraries, Archives and Public Records, Phoenix, Arizona. This was the only census authorized by the territorial legislature. (The 1864 territorial census was a federal enumeration). Includes schedules for all five counties in place in 1866: Mohave, Pah-Ute, Pima, Yavapai and Yuma counties. Filmed with ***An Index to the 1866 Census of Arizona Territory,*** by Jim Schreier. Filmed by the Genealogical Society of Utah, 1976, 1 roll, FHL film #928107. See also ***Arizona 1866 Territorial*** [Index], edited by Ronald Vern

Jackson, et al., published by Accelerated Indexing Systems, North Salt Lake, 1982, 64 pages, FHL book 979.1 X2j 1866.

■ *Arizona 1867 Census Index,* by Ronald Vern Jackson, et al., published by Accelerated Indexing Systems, Salt Lake City, UT, 1983, 54 pages. This was taken from what appears to be a census of Pima County (Tucson) only. FHL book 979.1 X2j 1866.

■ *Arizona 1869 Territorial Census Index,* by Ronald Vern Jackson, et al., published by Accelerated Indexing Systems, Salt Lake City, UT, 1983, 100 pages. No territorial census was taken in Arizona in 1869. This appears to be a county census taken in Yavapai County only. FHL book 979.1 X22a.

■ **Arizona Naturalizations, 1882-1912; Index, 1864-1911**, microfilm of original records at the National Archives, Pacific Southwest Region, Laguna Niguel, California. Volumes include indexes. The Second Judicial District court sat at Tucson, Pima County, and also at Tombstone, Cochise County. Filmed by the Genealogical Society of Utah, 1989, 4 rolls, as follows:

- Index of naturalizations, 1864-1911; Declarations of Intention, 1881-1906 FHL film #1638109.
- Record of naturalizations, 1882-1898, FHL film #1638403.
- Final record of naturalizations, 1903-1906; 1904-1906, FHL film #1638404.
- Petitions for naturalization, 1907-1910; 1909-1912, FHL film #1638405.

■ **Manifests of Alien Arrivals at Douglas, Arizona, September 10, 1906-October 10, 1955,** microfilm of original records at the National Archives, College Park, MD. Includes over 65,000 manifests of permanent, temporary, statistical, and non-statistical alien arrivals at Douglas, Arizona, September 1906 - October 1955. Some U.S. citizen arrivals are also included, as well as some records of aliens excluded from admission. Filmed by the National Archives, 2000, 13 rolls, series M1760, beginning with FHL film #2241356.

■ **1917-1918 World War I Selective Service System Draft Registration Cards, Arizona,** microfilm of original records at the National Archives in East Point, Georgia. The draft cards are arranged alphabetically by state, then alphabetically by county or city, and then alphabetically by surname of the registrants. Filmed by the National Archives, Series M1509, 20 rolls, cataloged by the FHL as follows:

- Apache County; Cochise County, A - Escalnate, Juan, FHL film #1473300.
- Cochise County, Eades, W. O. - McCutchan, K. C., FHL film #1522202.
- Chochise County, McAhay, William E. - Skea, T., FHL film #1522201.
- Chochise County, Skea, Thomas – Z; Coconino County, A - Lasa, Feliciano, FHL film #1522348.
- Coconino County, Labate, Gila County, A – Gillienore, John Matthew, FHL film #1522399.
- Gila County, Gabbert, Paul - Ramirez, Louis, FHL film #1522641.
- Gila County, Rabago, Alexander - Z; Graham County, FHL film #1522605.
- Greenlee County, A - Salsido, Amado, FHL film #1522447.
- Greenlee County, Saavedra, Alejandra - Z; Maricopa County, A - Fair, Fred Buiel, FHL film #1522450.
- Maricopa County, Fabaniso, F. - Maher, A., FHL film #1522449.
- Maricopa County, Mabin, William J.- Taylor, R., FHL film #1522456.
- Maricopa County, Tabana, Franaseu - Z; Mohave County, FHL film #1522646.
- Navajo County, Pima County, A - Grijalva, Francisce, FHL film #1522647.
- Pima County, Gabriel, Aaron D. Valles, Jose, FHL Film #1522648.
- Pima County, Vagaste, Jesus - Z; Pinal County, A - Peace, William F., FHL film #1522649.
- Pinal County, Pachecs, Domingo - Z; Santa Cruz County, FHL film #1522650.

- Yavapai County, A - Miller, Hugo Alvin, FHL film #1522651.
- Yavapai County, Mead, Oren Graham - Z, FHL film #1522652.
- Yuma County, FHL film #1522653.
- Indians, Prisoners, Insane, In Hospitals, Late Registrants, FHL film #2022330.

■ **Statewide Arizona Census Records and Substitutes Online**. These databases available online via a direct link from **www.censusfinder.com**:

- Arizona Census, 1831-1880 at Ancestry
- 1864 Territorial Census Partial
- 1864 Territorial Census - First Judicial District
- 1880 Federal Census - Images
- 1880 Federal Census Records Search at Family Search
- 1883 Pensioners on the Roll for Arizona Territory
- 1911-2000 Arizona Pioneers' Home Index
- RootsWeb Search
- Arizona Statewide Databases of Census & Genealogy Records

ARIZONA Countywide Censuses & Substitutes

Statewide censuses & substitutes for Arizona need to be supplemented by the many resources available at the county level. The censuses, tax lists, and voter registrations available for each Arizona county are shown below:

Apache County

■ **1882-1895 Tax Assessment Rolls, Apache County, Arizona**, microfilm of original records located at the Arizona Department of Libraries, Archives & Public Records, Phoenix, Arizona. Arranged in alphabetical order by surname. Includes name of tax payer, description of property, value of property, amount of tax, and when paid. Filmed by the Genealogical Society of Utah, 2002, 3 rolls, as follows:

- **1882-1889** tax assessment rolls, A-C, FHL film #2293303.
- **1889** tax assessment rolls, C-Z; **1894** tax assessment rolls, A-U, FHL film #2293304.
- **1894** tax assessment rolls, U-Z; **1895** tax assessment rolls, FHL film #2293305.

■ **1882-1920 Great Registers, Apache County, Arizona**, microfilm of original records at the Apache County Courthouse in St. Johns, Arizona. Each voter register lists name, place of birth, date of naturalization, and date of registration. Filmed by the Genealogical Society of Utah, 2002, 3 rolls, as follows:

- **1882-1884** great register, FHL film #2297313.
- **1884** great register; **1916** great register, Adamana precinct – Vernon precinct, A-Mc, FHL film #2297314.
- **1916** great register, Vernon precinct, Mc-Z thru Concho precinct; **1920** great register; **1888-1898** great registers, duplicate typed and published copy, FHL film #2320534.

Cochise County

■ **1881-1910 & 1912-1926 Great Registers, and 1922-1932 Index to Great Registers, Cochise County, Arizona**, microfilm of originals and photocopy of typescript at the Cochise County Courthouse in Bisbee, Arizona. The Great Register for 1898 is missing and was not filmed. Lists name, age, country of nativity, occupation, local residence, date and court of naturalization, date of voter registration, date of cancellation, if any; height, weight, color of eyes and hair, race, and political party. Some precincts are not listed in alphabetical order. Filmed by the Genealogical Society of Utah, 1997, 18 rolls, as follows:

- **1881, 1882, 1884, 1886, 1888, 1890, 1892, 1894, 1896, 1900, 1902** great registers, FHL film #2079898.
- **1902, 1904, 1906, 1908, 1909, 1910** great registers, FHL film #2079899.
- **1910, 1912** great registers, FHL film #2079900.
- **1913** supplement & **1914** ledger, FHL film #2080412.
- **1914** county register, FHL film #2080413.

- **1914** & **1916** county registers, FHL film #2080414.
- **1916** & **1918** great registers, FHL film #2080415.
- **1918** great registers, FHL film #2080416.
- **1918** great register, Douglas, FHL film #2080417.
- **1920** great register, FHL film #2080418.
- **1920** & **1922** great registers, FHL film #2080450.
- **1922** great register, FHL film #2080451.
- **1922** & **1924** great registers, FHL film #2080452.
- **1924** & **1926** great registers, FHL film #2080453.
- **1926** great register, FHL film #2080454.
- **1926** great register; **1922** & **1924** Index to great registers, FHL film #2080455.
- **1924, 1926, 1928, 1930** Index to great registers, FHL #2080456.

Coconino County

■ **1894-1911 Great Registers, Coconino County, Arizona**, microfilm of original records at the Arizona Department of Libraries, Archives & Public Records, Phoenix, Arizona. Includes Great Registers for 1894, 1902, 1906, 1908, 1910, and 1911 supplement. Lists name, age, country of birth, place of residence, naturalized (date, place, court), date of registration and number, and voter number. Filmed by the Arizona Dept. of Libraries, Archives & Public Records, 1998. FHL has 1 roll, FHL film #2111296.

Gila County

■ **1881-1895 Duplicate and Original Assessment and Delinquent Tax Records, Gila County, Arizona**, microfilm of original records at the Arizona Department of Libraries, Archives & Public Records located in Phoenix, Arizona. Includes name of taxpayer, description of property, value of personal and real property, amount of tax, total value and remarks. Filmed by the Genealogical Society of Utah, 2002, 3 rolls, as follows:

- **1881-1890** duplicate and original assessment rolls, (A-K), FHL film #2293846.
- **1890** duplicate and original assessment rolls (cont., K-Z); **1895** duplicate and original assessment rolls; **1887-1892** tax collector's record of property sold for delinquent taxes, FHL film #2293847.
- **1893-1895** tax collector's record of property sold for delinquent taxes, FHL film #2293848.

■ **1881-1920 Great Registers and Census of Gila County, Arizona**, microfilm of original records at the Arizona Department of Libraries, Archives & Public Records located in Phoenix, Arizona. Includes the Gila County census of 1882, the great register for 1888 which also is listed as the jury list for 1890, and the great registers for 1894, 1896, 1898, 1900, 1902, 1904, 1906, 1908, and 1910. Lists name of voter, age, country of birth, local city of residence, date-place-court of naturalization, and date of registration to vote. Filmed by the Genealogical Society of Utah, 1998, 2002, 6 rolls, as follows:

- **1881, 1888, 1894-1910** great registers, **1882** census, **1890** jury list, FHL film #2321349.
- **1890, 1892, 1894, 1896, 1898, 1900, 1902, 1904, 1905, 1906, 1908, 1910, 1912** great registers, FHL film #2321350.
- **1912, 1914, 1916** county registers, FHL film #2321404.
- **1916, 1918** general registers, FHL film #2321405.
- **1918, 1920** general registers, FHL film #2321406.
- **1920** register of electors, FHL #2321407.

■ **1890 Great Register Census, Gila County, Arizona Territory**, in *Gila Heritage*, a publication of the Northern Gila County Genealogical Society, Payson, AZ, Vol. 14, No. 4 (Nov 1996).

■ **1908-1910**. See ***Great Register of Gila County, Territory of Arizona, 1908-1910***, microfilm of original printed volume published by Silver Belt Print, Globe, AZ, 1910, 76 pages. Certified by E.T. Stewart, County Recorder. Includes naturalization information. Filmed by the Genealogical Society of Utah, 1987, 1 roll, FHL film #1421818.

Graham County

■ **1881-1900 Assessment and Tax Rolls, Graham County, Arizona**, microfilm of original records at the Graham County Courthouse in

Safford, Arizona. May include name of taxpayer, description of property, and total tax amount. Filmed by the Genealogical Society of Utah, 1999, 3 rolls, as follows:

- **1881-1891** assessment and tax rolls, FHL film #2133939.
- **1892-1898** assessment and tax rolls, FHL film #2133940.
- **1899-1900** assessment and tax rolls, FHL film #2134263.

■ **1882-1920 Great Registers and 1882 Census of Graham County, Arizona**, microfilm of original records at the Arizona Department of Libraries, Archives & Public Records located in Phoenix, Arizona, and at the Graham County Recorder's Office in Safford, Arizona. Lists information for the 1882 census. May list the following information on the great register: name, age, place of birth, and residence, date and place of naturalization, and date of registration; and lists statistics of Graham County for acres of land cultivated, acres of wheat-barley-corn-or potatoes raised, number of horses, mules, cattle, calves, hogs, and sheep. Filmed by the Arizona Dept. of Libraries, Archives & Public Records, 1998-1999, and by the Genealogical Society of Utah, 6 rolls, as follows:

- **1882** great register, FHL film #2111296.
- **1882-1888, 1890-1898** great registers, FHL film #2134224.
- **1892-1898, 1890-1898, 1904** great registers, FHL film #2134264.
- **1882** census, **1894, 1902, 1906-1908, 1910, 1912, 1914** great registers, FHL film #2134422.
- **1916, 1918** general registers, FHL film #2134265.
- **1920** great register, FHL film #2134266.

Greenlee County

■ **1910 Great Register of Greenlee County, Arizona**, microfilm of original records at the Arizona Department of Libraries, Archives & Public Records located in Phoenix, Arizona. Lists information for the 1910 great register of Greenlee County, Arizona. Lists name, age, place of residence, naturalized, register and voter number. Filmed by the Arizona Dept. of Libraries, Archives & Public Records, 1998, 1 roll, FHL film #2111296.

■ **1912-1926 General County Register, Greenlee County**, Arizona, microfilm of original records at the Arizona Department of Library, Archives and Public Records in Phoenix, Arizona. May include date of registration, name, occupation, age, country of birth, declaration of naturalization, city of residence, signature of elector and recorder, and remarks. Arranged in register by first letter of surname. Filmed by the Genealogical Society of Utah, 1999, 4 rolls, as follows:

- **1912, 1913, 1914, 1916** general county register, FHL film #166322.
- **1916, 1918, 1920** general register, FHL film #2166323.
- **1922, 1924, 1926** general register, FHL film #2166324.
- **1926** general register, Franklin (A-Z), Blue, Eagle precincts; **1918** Official military register of electors, FHL film #2166489.

La Paz County

La Paz County, Arizona, created in 1983, was the last county formed in the United States. As yet, no county records have been published or microfilmed, but a couple of databases for La Paz County areas have been made available online:

■ **Census Records and Substitutes Online, La Paz County, Arizona**. These databases available online via a direct link at **www.censusfinder.com**:

- 1863 Mine Deeds and Claims
- 1920-1922 Students at Bouse Elementary School

Maricopa County

■ **Official Registers of Electors for Maricopa County, 1876-1932**, microfilm of original records at the Department of Libraries, Archives and

Public Records, Phoenix, Arizona. Usually filed chronologically, arranged somewhat alphabetically in registration years. Some rolls include missed records or retakes in an appendix at the end. Filmed by the State Library & Archives, 1984, 33 FHL rolls: Great Registers, Maricopa County, Arizona:

- **1876-1890, 1894-1895**, FHL film #1405007.
- **1894-1895, 1904-1906**, FHL film #1405008.
- **1904-1906** (cont.), **1906-1908, 1902, 1909-1911** Electors: **1910-1911, 1912** (A-B), FHL film #1405009.
- **1912-1913** (C-Z), FHL film #1405010.
- **1913, 1914**, FHL film #1405011.
- **1914,** FHL film #1405012.
- **1914,** FHL film #1405013.
- **1914, 1916,** FHL film #1405014.
- **1916**, FHL film #1405015.
- **1916, 1918**, FHL film #1405016.
- **1918**, FHL film #1405017.
- **1918**, FHL film #1405018.
- **1918**, FHL film #1405019.
- **1918, 1920**, FHL film #1405020.
- **1920**, FHL film #1405021.
- **1920**, FHL film #1405022.
- **1920**, FHL film #1405023.
- **1920, 1922**, FHL film #1405024.
- **1922**, FHL film #1405025.
- **1922**, FHL film #1405026.
- **1922**, FHL film #1405027.
- **1922, 1924**, FHL film #1405028.
- **1924**, FHL film #1405029.
- **1924**, FHL film #1405030.
- **1924**, FHL film #1405031.
- **1924**, FHL film #1405032.
- **1924, 1926**, FHL film #1405033.
- **1926**, FHL film #1405034.
- **1926**, FHL film #1405035.
- **1926**, FHL film #1405036.
- **1926**, FHL film #1405037.
- **1926, 1928, 1930**, FHL film #1405038.
- **1930, 1932**, FHL film #1405039.

■ **1882 Delinquent Tax List, Maricopa County, Arizona Territory**, name list in *Desert Tracker*, a publication of the West Valley Genealogical Society, Sun City, AZ, Vol. 14, No. 2 (Summer 1993).

■ **1903-1935 City Directories, Phoenix & Maricopa County, Arizona**, microfilm of originals published by various publishers. Filmed by Research Publications, Woodbridge, CT, 1980-1984, 6 FHL rolls, as follows:

- **1903** A. P. Skinner's Phoenix city directory, by A. P. Skinner; **1912** Phoenix city and Salt River valley directory, including Phoenix, Glendale, Mesa and Tempe; **1913** Phoenix city and Salt River valley directory, including Phoenix, Buckeye, Glendale Mesa and Tempe; **1915** Phoenix city and Salt River valley directory, including Phoenix, Buckeye, Glendale, Mesa and Tempe; **1916** Phoenix city and Salt River valley directory, including Phoenix, Buckeye, Chandler, Glendale, Mesa and Tempe, FHL film #1843284.
- **1917** Phoenix city and Salt River valley directory, including Phoenix, Chandler, Glendale, Mesa and Tempe; **1918** Phoenix city and Salt River valley directory, including Phoenix, Chandler, Glendale, Mesa and Tempe, by Arizona Directory Co.; **1919** Phoenix city and Salt River valley directory, including Phoenix, Chandler, Gilbert, Glendale, Mesa and Tempe, FHL film #1843285.
- **1920** Phoenix city and Salt River valley directory of Phoenix, Chandler, Gilbert, Glendale, Mesa and Tempe; **1921** Phoenix city and Salt River valley directory, including Phoenix, Chandler, Gilbert, Glendale, Mesa and Tempe; **1923** Phoenix city and Salt River valley directory, including Phoenix, Chandler, Gilbert, Glendale, Mesa and Tempe, FHL film #1843286.
- **1925** Phoenix city and Salt River valley directory, including Phoenix, Chandler, Gilbert, Glendale, Mesa and Tempe; **1928** Phoenix city and Salt River valley directory, including Phoenix, Buckeye, Chandler, Gilbert, Glendale, Mesa, Peoria, Scottsdale and Tempe, FHL film #1843287.
- **1929** Arizona Directory Co.'s Phoenix city and Salt River Valley directory, including Phoenix, Buckeye, Chandler, Gilbert, Glendale, Mesa, Peoria, Scottsdale and Tempe; **1930** Arizona Directory Co.'s Phoenix city and Salt River valley directory, including Phoenix, Buckeye, Chandler, Gilbert, Glendale, Mesa, Peoria, Scottsdale and Tempe, FHL film #1843288.
- **1931** Phoenix city and Salt River valley directory, including Phoenix, Buckeye, Chandler, Gilbert, Glendale, Mesa, Peoria, Scottsdale and Tempe;

1932 Phoenix city and Salt River valley directory, including Phoenix, Chandler, Gilbert, Glendale, Mesa, Peoria, Scottsdale and Tempe; **1935** Phoenix city directory, FHL film #1843289.

■ **Census Records and Substitutes Online, Maricopa County, Arizona.** These databases available online via a direct link at **www.censusfinder.com:**

- 1880 Federal Census Part 1
- 1880 Federal Census Part 2
- 1880 Federal Census Part 3
- 1912-1925 Business Directory Transcriptions

Mohave County

■ **1872, 1882 Census, Mohave County, Arizona,** microfilm of original records in the Mohave County Courthouse in Kingman, Arizona. Arranged in by first letter of surname. Filmed by the Genealogical Society of Utah, 2002, 1 roll, FHL film #2295145 (Mohave County census, 1872, and Mohave County census, 1882).

■ **1876-1899 Tax Rolls and Property Sold for Taxes, Mohave County, Arizona,** microfilm of original records located in the Mohave County Courthouse in Kingman, Arizona. Lists name, description of property, value, amount of tax and if paid. Filmed by the Genealogical Society of Utah, 2002, 3 rolls, as follows:

- **1876-1886** tax assessment rolls, FHL film #2295146.
- **1887-1895** tax assessment rolls; **1876-1880** delinquent tax rolls, FHL film #2295358.
- **1888-1895** delinquent tax rolls; **1881-1899** record of property sold for delinquent taxes, FHL film #2295147.

■ **1876-1920 Great Registers of Mohave County, Arizona,** microfilm of original records at the Mohave County Courthouse in Kingman, Arizona. Some pages are dark and may be hard to read. Lists name, age, country or state of birth, local residence, date and place of naturalization if listed, and date of registration. Filmed by the Genealogical Society of Utah, 2002, 4 rolls, as follows:

- **1876-1890** great registers, FHL film #2295022.
- **1892-1914** great registers, FHL film #2295141.
- **1914** great registers, cont.: **1918** great registers, precincts A-F, FHL film #2295142.
- **1918** great registers, cont., precincts F-Z; **1920** great registers, FHL film #2295143.

■ **Census Records and Substitutes Online, Mohave County, Arizona.** These databases available online via a direct link at **www.censusfinder.com:**

- 1870 Federal Census Images
- 1870 Federal Census Index
- 1870 Federal Census Transcription
- 1870 Federal Census Transcription of Town of Hardyville
- WWII Honor List
- 1900-1917 Pioneer Grave Book

Navajo County

■ **1895-1932 Great Registers and Registration of Electors, Navajo County, Arizona,** microfilm of original manuscripts at the Arizona Department of Libraries, Archives & Public Records, Phoenix, Arizona. Filmed by the state archives, 1984, 8 FHL rolls, as follows:

- **1895-1898** great registers, FHL film #1405040.
- **1895-1898** great registers (another filming), FHL film #833351.
- **1900-1904, 1906, 1908, 1910, 1912-1914, 1916** great registers, FHL film #1405041.
- **1918, 1920**, registration of electors, FHL film #1405042.
- **1906-1911** registers & supplemental records, FHL film #1405043.
- **1922, 1924** registers, FHL film #1405044.
- **1924, 1926, 1928, 1930**, FHL film #1405045.
- **1932** registers, FHL film #1405046.

■ **1896-1902 Tax Sale Certificates, Navajo County, Arizona,** microfilm of original records at the Navajo County Courthouse in Holbrook, Arizona. Lists description of property, date of sale, name of person who owed assessed tax, name of purchaser, assessed value, amount paid, date to which taxes have been paid, and remarks. Filmed by the Genealogical Society of Utah, 2002, 1 roll, FHL film #2296955 (Tax sale certificates, 1896-1902).

■ **1918 Official Military Register of Electors, Navajo County, Arizona**, microfilm of original records at the Navajo County Courthouse in Holbrook, Arizona. Lists name, military command, post office address, and legal residence. Filmed by the Genealogical Society of Utah, 2002, 1 roll, FHL film #2297104 (Official military register of electors, 1918).

Pah-Ute County

Pah-Ute County was one of five original counties created by Arizona Territory in 1864.The original area spanned the Colorado River, east to the present Mohave-Yavapai line, and west to the 1863 border with California. The latter portion included the area west of the Colorado River now part of Clark County, Nevada, including the present city of Las Vegas. When the Nevada-Arizona boundary was adjusted in 1869 to the Colorado River, a remnant of old Pah-Ute east of the river was still part of Arizona Territory. In the 1870 federal census, people living in the original Pah-Ute area were enumerated within Nevada's Lincoln County and Utah's Rio Virgin County. The latter county was erroneously established by Utah Territory entirely within Nevada and not abolished until 1872. Pah-Ute county was officially abolished in 1871, the remnant area incorporated into Mohave County. No county records for Pah-Ute County exist, but at least one census was taken under the name Pah-Ute: See **1866 Arizona Territorial Census**, microfilm of original records at the Department of Libraries, Archives and Public Records, Phoenix, Arizona. This was the only census authorized by the territorial legislature. Includes schedules for all five counties in place in 1866: Mohave, Pah-Ute, Pima, Yavapai and Yuma counties. Filmed with ***An Index to the 1866 Census of Arizona Territory***, by Jim Schreier. Filmed by the Genealogical Society of Utah, 1976, 1 roll, FHL film #928107. See also ***Arizona 1866 Territorial*** [Index], edited by Ronald Vern Jackson, et al., published by Accelerated Indexing Systems, North Salt Lake, 1982, 64 pages, FHL book 979.1 X2j 1866.

Pima County

■ **1797 Tucson Census**, name list published in *Revista,* a publication of the Instituto Genealógico e Histórico Latinoamericano, Highland, Utah, Vol. 1, No. 3 (July 1989).

■ **1831 Tucson Census, Civilian Households**, in *Copper State Bulletin*, Vol. 16, No. 1 (Spring 1981); and **1831 Military Households**, in Vol. 16, No. 2 (Summer 1981).

■ **1866, 1867, 1872, 1874, 1876, and 1882 Censuses for Pima County, Arizona**, microfilm of original manuscripts at the Arizona Department of Libraries, Archives and Public Records in Phoenix, Arizona. Includes name, residence, whether head of family, number of single persons over 21, number between 10 and 21, number under 10, and remarks. 1882 lists name only. Filmed by the Genealogical Society of Utah, 1999, 1 roll, FHL film 2155710.

■ **1876-1881 Great Registers for Pima County, Arizona**, microfilm of original records at the Arizona Department of Libraries, Archives and Public Records in Phoenix, Arizona. Filmed by State Library and Archives, 1984, 1 FHL roll, FHL film #1405047.

■ **1879-1894 Assessment Rolls; 1898 Assessment and Tax Roll, Pima County, Arizona**, microfilm of original records at the Arizona Department of Libraries, Archives and Public Records in Phoenix, Arizona. Includes name of taxpayer, description of property, value of land and improvements and personal property, poll tax, and total volume. The assessment roll information is repeated in the tax roll books with the indication whether the tax has been paid or not paid. The county sheriff was also the county assessor. Some records are light and may be hard to read. Filmed by the Genealogical Society of Utah, 1999, 5 rolls, as follows:

- **1879-1883** assessment and tax rolls, A-S, FHL film #2148738.
- **1883** assessment and tax rolls, T-Z, FHL film #2148739.
- **1886-1890** assessment and tax rolls, FHL film #2148740.
- **1890-1892** assessment rolls, FHL film #2171017.
- **1893-1894** assessment rolls, and **1898** assessment and tax roll of the city of Tucson, FHL film #2171018.

■ **1882-1926 Great Registers for Tucson & Pima County, Arizona,** microfilm of original records at the Arizona Department of Libraries, Archives and Public Records in Phoenix, Arizona. May include name, age, country of birth, precinct, occupation, political party, naturalization information, address, height and weight, signature and date of registration. Filmed by the Genealogical Society of Utah, 1999, 2002, 9 rolls, as follows:

- **1882-1901** great register, FHL film #2169803.
- **1901** great register, FHL film #2148436.
- **1912** great register, **1914** great register, FHL film #2148437.
- **1914** great register, **1920** (Tucson precincts 1-5), FHL film #2148438.
- **1916** general register, Pima County, FHL film #2293854.
- **1920** great register, Tucson precincts 6-10; **1920** Outside precincts: Ajo 1, Ajo 2, Arivaca, Condon, Continental, Cottonwood, Ft. Lowell, Greaterville, Helvetia, Indian Oasis, Langhorn, Olive Camp, Pantano, Quijotoa, Reddington, Sahuarita, San Xavier, Silverbell, Tanque Verde, Twin Buttes, Vail; **1922** great register, Tucson, precincts 1-5; **1922** Outside precincts: Pastime Park, Ajo, Continental, Langhorn, FHL film #2148439.
- **1922** outside precincts: Fort Lowell, Greaterville, Twin, Buttes, Silverbell, Pantano, Cottonwood, Helvetia, Arivaca, Sahuarita, Olive Camp, San Xavier, Condon, Tanque Verde, Reddington, Quijotoa, Indian Oasis, Vail, FHL film #2148628.
- **1924** great register, Tucson precincts 1-11, FHL film #2148628.
- **1924** great register, outside precincts; **1926** great register, Tucson precincts, 1-6; FHL film #2148629.
- **1926** great register, outside precincts; **1926** great register, Tucson precincts 7-11, FHL film #148630.

■ ***Directory of the City of Tucson for the Year 1881: Containing a Comprehensive List of Inhabitants With Their Occupations and Places of Residence,*** compiled by G. W. Barter, published by H. S. Crocker & Co., San Francisco, 1881, 114 pages. Filmed by Xerox University Microfilms, Ann Arbor, MI, 197?. FHL has 1 roll, FHL film #1299604.

■ **1899-1935 City Directories, Tucson, Arizona,** microfilm of originals published by various publishers. Filmed by Research Publications, Woodbridge, CT, 1980-1984. FHL has 5 rolls, containing the following:

- **1899-1900, 1901** Tucson City Directories, FHL film #2258272.
- **1902, 1912, 1913, 1914, 1917, 1918, 1919, 1920** Tucson City Directories, FHL film #1843290.
- **1921, 1921, 1922, 1924, 1926** Tucson City Directories, FHL film #1843291.
- **1927, 1928, 1929, 1930, 1931** Tucson City Directories, FHL film #1843292.
- **1932, 1933, 1934, 1935** Tucson City Directories, FHL film #1843293.

■ **Census Records and Substitutes Online, Pima County, Arizona.** These databases available online via a direct link at **www.censusfinder.com:**

- 1870 Federal Census (images & index)
- 1880 Federal Census Index - Surnames A-Mon
- 1880 Federal Census Index - Surnames Moor-Y
- 1880 Federal Census Pages 145B-150B
- 1880 Federal Census Pages 151A-156A
- 1880 Federal Census Pages 156B-160A

Pinal County

■ **1876-1920 Great registers, Pinal County, Arizona**, microfilm of original records in the Pinal County Courthouse in Florence, Arizona. Lists name, age, country of nativity, local residence, date, place and court of naturalization, date of registration to vote and remarks. Filmed by the Genealogical Society of Utah, 2003, 3 rolls, as follows:

- **1876-1894** great registers, FHL film #2321650.
- **1882-1894, 1890, 1892, 1894, 1896-1911, 1912, 1916** great registers, FHL film #2321651.
- **1916** duplicate, **1918, 1920** great registers, FHL film #2321652.

■ **Census Records and Substitutes Online, Pinal County, Arizona**. These databases available online via a direct link at **www.censusfinder.com:**

- 1877-1910 Birth Records
- 1887-1908 Death Records
- 1920-1929 Fisher Funeral Home Records

Santa Cruz County

■ **1831 Mexican Census, Civilian Households, (now Santa Cruz County, New Mexico)**, in *Copper State Bulletin*, Vol. 17, No. 1 (Spring 1982) through Vol. 17, No. 4 (Winter 1982).

■ **1900-1920 Great Registers of Santa Cruz County, Arizona,** microfilm of original records at the Arizona Department of Libraries, Archives & Public Records, Phoenix, Arizona. Includes name, age, country of birth, local residence, date, place and court of naturalization, and date of registration to vote. Beginning in 1912 at statehood, the occupation and signature of elector was added. Filmed by the Genealogical Society of Utah, 2002, 3 rolls, as follows:

- **1900-1914** great registers, FHL film #2317753.
- **1914** great registers (cont'd); **1918** great register, FHL film #2317754.
- **1920** great registers, FHL film #2317755.

■ ***1904 Great Register of Santa Cruz County, Arizona, Territory of Arizona,*** published by authority; made and done pursuant to the Revised Statutes of Arizona, microfilm of original great register of Santa Cruz County, Territory of Arizona, 1904, 11 pages. Filmed by the Genealogical Society of Utah, 1994, 1 roll, FHL film #1750769, item 5.

■ **Census Records and Substitutes Online, Santa Cruz County, Arizona**. These databases available online via a direct link from **www.censusfinder.com:**

- 1904 Great Register
- WWII Honor List

Yavapai County

■ ***An Index to the 1869 Census of Yavapai County, Territory of Arizona,*** by Jim and Mary Schreier, published by Arizona Territorial Censuses, 1976, 21 pages. Copy at the Arizona Department of Libraries, Archives and Public Records, Phoenix, Arizona.

■ **1873-1927 Teacher's Monthly Reports and School Census Marshal's Report, Yavapai County, Arizona**, microfilm of original records at the Arizona Department of Libraries, Archives and Public Records, Phoenix, Arizona. Includes name and age of student and names of parents. Filmed by the Genealogical Society of Utah, 2002, 4 rolls, as follows:

- **1873-1874, 1877-1885** teacher's monthly report, **1895** – June **1902** school census marshal's report, FHL film #2293497.
- **1902-1915** school census marshal's reports, FHL film #2293498.
- **1915, 1920** school census marshal's reports, FHL film #2293499.
- **1920, 1927** school census marshal's reports, FHL film #2293500.

■ ***Arizona Territorial Poll Tax Records, 1873-1876, Yavapai County, Prescott, Arizona,*** compiled by Dora M. Whiteside, published 1984,

40 pages. Includes surname index. From preface: "The book from which these records were extracted is located in the Sharlot Hall Museum and Archives in Prescott." FHL book 979.1 A1 no. 21, and FHL film #1698293.

■ **1873 Territorial Poll Tax Records, Yavapai County, Arizona Territory**, name list in *Family Connections,* a publication of the Family History Society of Arizona, Phoenix, AZ, Vol. 3, No. 1 (Winter 1986).

■ ***Arizona Territorial Great Register of 1876, Yavapai County, Arizona,*** by Dora M. Whiteside, published 1987, 28 pages. From Intro: "In 1876 Yavapai County included what was later to be Coconino, Apache, Navajo, a portion of the northern parts of Gila, Maricopa, Graham, and Greenlee Counties." FHL book 979.1 A1 no. 68, and FHL film #2055163.

■ **1875-1932 Official Electors Registers, Yavapai County, Arizona**, microfilm of records at Yavapai County Recorder's Office, Prescott, Arizona. Records sometimes titled "Great Register" or "Precinct Register." Filmed by the Genealogical Society of Utah, 1995, 13 rolls, as follows:

- **1875, 1884, 1881, 1875-1899** election registers, FHL film #1299283.
- **1916** election register, FHL film #1299282.
- **1920** election register, FHL film #1299279.
- **1920** & **1922** election register (Ashfork to Date Creek), FHL film #1299280.
- **1922** election register, FHL film #1299281.
- **1900-1902, 1904-1908, 1910-1913** great registers, FHL film #1299284.
- **1914, 1916, 1918** great registers, FHL film #1299285.
- **1924, 1926** election registers, FHL film #1299286.
- **1920, 1922, 1924** election registers, FHL film #1299287.
- **1924** election register, FHL film #1299288.
- **1930, 1932, 1876, 1882, 1884, 1886, 1886** supplement, **1890, 1892, 1894, 1896, 1898, 1900, 1902, 1904, 1906** great registers, FHL film #1299289.
- **1924** election register, FHL film #1299290.
- **1930, 1932** register, FHL film #2028173.

■ **1878-1895 Tax Assessment and Delinquent Tax Rolls, Yavapai County, Arizona**, microfilm of original records at the Arizona Department of Libraries, Archives and Public Records, Phoenix, Arizona. A couple of volumes include indexes. Filmed by the Genealogical Society of Utah, 2002, 7 rolls, as follows:

- **1878-1881** tax rolls, A-K, FHL #2293306.
- **1881** tax rolls, K-Z; **1885**, A-S, FHL film #2293307.
- **1885** tax, S-Z; **1889** tax rolls, A-P, FHL film #2293308.
- **1889** tax rolls, P-Z; **1893** tax rolls, A-M, FHL film #2293309.
- **1893** tax rolls, M-Z; **1895** tax rolls; **1878-1881** delinquent tax rolls, FHL film #2293495.
- **1882-1891** delinquent tax rolls, FHL film #2293496.
- **1892-1895** delinquent tax rolls, FHL film #2293497.

■ **Census Records and Substitutes Online, Yavapai County, Arizona**. These databases available online via a direct link at **www.censusfinder.com:**

- 1870 Federal Census Index - Surnames A-L
- 1870 Federal Census Index - Surnames M-Z
- 1870 Federal Census Transcription – pp 82A- 90B
- 1870 Federal Census Transcription – pp 91A-96B
- 1870 Federal Census Transcription – pp 97A-104A
- 1870 Federal Census Transcription – pp 104B-111B
- 1870 Federal Census Transcription – pp 112A-114B
- 1870, 1880, 1900 & 1920 Census Index Search
- 1880 Federal Census Mortality Schedule

Yuma County

■ ***Surname Index for the Arizona Sentinel, 1875-1905,*** [Yuma, Arizona], compiled and published by the Genealogical Society of Yuma, Arizona, 1997, 244 pages. Arranged in alphabetical order by surname. Lists name, description, subject, page number, and date. FHL book 979.171 B32g.

■ **1902-1918 Great Registers of Yuma County, Arizona**, microfilm of original records located at the Arizona Department of Libraries, Archives and Public Records, Phoenix, Arizona. Lists name, age, country of birth, local residence, date, place, and court of naturalization, and date of registration. After statehood in 1912, the occupation and signature were added. Filmed by the Genealogical Society of Utah, 2002, 3 rolls, as follows:

- **1902-1914** great registers, FHL film #2318335.
- **1914 & 1918** great registers, FHL film #2318336.
- **1918** great registers, FHL film #2318337.

■ **1881, 1888-1902 Tax Assessment Records, Yuma County, Arizona Territory**, microfilm of original records located at the Arizona Department of Libraries, Archives and Public Records, Phoenix, Arizona. Includes name of taxpayer, description of property, value of property and personal property, total value, year and remarks. Filmed by the Genealogical Society of Utah, 2002, 1 roll, FHL film #2293272.

■ **Census Records and Substitutes Online, Yuma County, Arizona**. These databases available online via a direct link at:

www.censusfinder.com

- 1870 Federal Census Index - Surnames A-O
- 1870 Federal Census Index - Surnames P-Z
- 1870 Federal Census Transcription, pp 115A-120B
- 1870 Federal Census Transcription, pp 121A-126B
- 1870 Federal Census Transcription, pp 127A-133A
- 1870 Federal Census Transcription, pp 133B-134B

www.census-online.com

- 1865 Territorial Census - First Judicial District
- 1883 Pensioners on the Roll
- Late 1800s Federal Censuses, Searchable

NEW MEXICO

Spanish-Mexican Censuses & Substitutes, 1681-1846

■ **1681-1846 Vigil's Index**, microfilm of original records at the U.S. Bureau of Land Management, Santa Fe, New Mexico. General index of all the [land] documents from the time of the Spanish and Mexican governments until the year 1846. Text in Spanish. Filmed by the University of New Mexico Library, Albuquerque, NM, 1955-1957. FHL has 1 roll, FHL film #1016949.

■ **1705 Santa Fe Presidial Soldiers and Citizens**, in *Herencia* a publication of the Hispanic Genealogical Research Center, Albuquerque, NM, in Vol. 6, No. 3 (Jul 1998).

■ **1710-1860 Santa Fee Church Records**. See ***Santa Cruz de la Cañada, Baptisms, 1710-1860: Baptism Database of Archives Held by the Archdiocese of Santa Fe and the State Archives of New Mexico***, database entry by Thomas D. Martinez, Benito Estevan Montoya and Rosina Lasalle (nee Vigil), published San Jose, CA, 1993, 498 pages. Includes name, date of baptism, name of parents and godparents if recorded. Arranged in alphabetical order by surname. FHL book 978.956 K2ms.

■ **1726-1956 San Juan Pueblo, (Catholic Church Records)**, microfilm of original records at the San Juan de los Caballeros Church, San Juan, New Mexico. Text in Spanish and English. Includes indexes. Church may also be known as St. John the Baptist. The church directory lists this as the head church of Chamita parish. Retakes are located at the end of the film roll.

Filmed by Golightly, El Paso, TX, 1956, 7 rolls, as follows:

- Baptisms 1726-1837, FHL film #16981.
- Baptisms 1849-1898, FHL film #16976.
- Baptisms 1899-1956, FHL film #16977.
- Marriages 1726-1776,1830-1836,1850-1855 (marriages 1777-1829 are not available); Deaths, 1726-1857, FHL film #16982.
- Confirmations, 1887-1954, FHL film #16978.
- Marriages, 1857-1956, FHL film #16979.
- Deaths, 1857-1956, FHL film #16980.

■ ***1728-1857 New Mexico Marriages - Santa Fe - St. Francis Parish and Military Chapel of Our Lady of Light (La Castrense)***, extracted by Marie J. Roybal and Lila Armijo Pfeufer; compiled by Margaret Leonard Windham and Evelyn Lujan Baca, published by the New Mexico Genealogical Society, Albuquerque, NM, 1997, 417 pages. Includes several indexes. FHL book 978.956 K28r.

■ ***1736-1873 New Mexico Baptisms - San Buenaventura de Cochiti Church***, extracted by Donald Dreesen and Evelyn Lujan Baca; compiled by Margaret Leonard Windham and Evelyn Lujan Baca, published by the New Mexico Genealogical Society, Albuquerque, NM, 2000, 409 pages. FHL book 978.957 K2d.

■ **1747-1851 Santa Fe Church Records.** See ***New Mexico Baptisms of Santa Fe: Parroquia de San Francisco de Assisi (Parish of Saint Francis of Assisi)***, compiled by Margaret Leonard Windham and Evelyn Lujan Baca, published by the New Mexico Genealogical Society, Albuquerque, NM, 2002, 4 vols. Includes bibliographic references. Includes indexes for baptisms, parents, godparents, grandparents and others. Contents: vol. 1: 5 September 1747 to 17 July 1791; vol. 2: 15 August 1796 to 30 December 1822; vol. 3: 1 January 1823 to 26 June 1833; Castrense register, 9 June 1798 to 26 June 1833; vol. 4: 18 February 1839 to 17 July 1851. FHL book 978.956/S1 K2w v. 1-4. See also **1747-1851 Santa Fe Baptisms**, database of archives held by the archdiocese of Santa Fe and the state archive of New Mexico, database entry by Thomas D. Martinez, Benito Estevan Montoya, Rosina Lasalle (nee Vigil), published San Jose, CA, 1993, 606 pages. FHL book 978.956 K2m.

■ ***1747-1763; 1753-1770 Births or Christenings, San Francisco de Assisi (Cathedral), Santa Fe, New Mexico***, computer printout; births or christenings, compiled by the Genealogical Department, The Church of Jesus Christ of Latter-day Saints. Filmed by the Genealogical Society of Utah, 1977, 2 rolls, FHL film #1205005 (1747-1763), and FHL film #12005472 (1753-1770).

■ ***1750-1830 Spanish and Mexican Censuses of New Mexico***, compiled by Virginia Langham Olmsted, published by the New Mexico Genealogical Society, Albuquerque, NM, 1981, 305 pages. All items except names are in English. Includes index. FHL book 978.9 X2ov.

■ **1764 & 1765 Census, San Gabriel**, in *Herencia*, a publication of the Hispanic Genealogical Research Center, Albuquerque, NM, in Vol. 5, No. 2 (Apr 1997).

■ **1790 Census of the Presidio of Santa Fe**, in *Nuestras Raices*, a publication of the Genealogical Society of Hispanic America, Denver, CO, in Vol. 8, No. 3 (Fall 1996).

■ **1790 Spanish of Taos**, in *New Mexico Genealogist*, Vol. 21, No. 3 (Sep 1982). See also "**1790 Taos Census**," in *Herencia*, Vol. 5, No. 3 (Jul 1997).

■ **1790-1841 Censuses.** See ***Early Taos Censuses and Historical Sources***, compiled by Julián Josué Vigil, microfilm of original published by J. J. Vigil, 1983, 172 pages. Includes index. Contains: 1790 census for Taos (incomplete); "Spaniards from the jurisdiction of Taos" Militia muster rolls, 1806 for Taos (incomplete); 1841 census for Taos; Ranchos de Taos Appendices: Taos genealogical materials in the archives of the Archdiocese of

Santa Fe, microfilm edition; Taos materials in Fr. Angélico Chávez, "Archives of the Archdiocese of Santa Fe" (1957). Taos priests to 1850. (starts in 1701); Taos materials in Twitchell's "Spanish archives of New Mexico," vol. 1-2. Above documents in "Calendar of microfilm edition of the Spanish archives of New Mexico, 1621-1821"; Additional Taos materials in above "Calendar" (no Twitchell numbers). Early Taos materials in the Ritch Collection, Huntington Library, plus on Bancroft Library item. Taos materials listed in "Calendar of the microfilm edition of the Mexican archives of New Mexico" (1970). Filmed by the New Mexico State Archives, 1983, 4 fiches, FHL fiche #6331382.

■ **1793 & 1795 Census Surnames**, in *Herencia*, a publication of the Hispanic Genealogical Research Center, Albuquerque, NM, in Vol. 3, No. 4 (Oct 1995).

■ **Early Censuses For Middle Rio Grande**, in the *Albuquerque Genealogical Society Quarterly*, Vol. 5, No. 2 (Aug 1980).

■ ***1811-1849; 1861-1864, 1892 Records of the Sandia Mission: Located in the Vicinity of Albuquerque, New Mexico***, typescript translated into English and typed by the Genealogical Society of Utah, 1963-1965, 302 pages. Includes marriage records from Sandia, Bernalillo, Los Corrales, Los Algodones, Albuquerque, Santa Fe and Cienaga, New Mexico for the years 1811-49, 1861-64, 1892; as well as a list of donors to the Sandia Mission. FHL book 978.9 K2 sp. Also on microfilm, filmed by the Genealogical Society of Utah, 1972, 1 roll, FHL film #874356 Item 1.

■ **Tax Revolt of 1816 (Taos)**, in *Ayer Y Hoy En Taos*, a periodical of the Taos County Historical Society, Taos, NM, Vol. 26 (Spring 1999).

■ **1818 Military Census, Santa Fe**, in *Herencia*, a publication of the Hispanic Genealogical Research Center, Albuquerque, NM, in Vol. 4, No. 3 (Jul 1996).

■ **1821-1846 Mexican Archives.** See ***Calendar of the Microfilm Edition of the Mexican Archives of New Mexico, 1821-1846***, by Myra Ellen Jenkins, a microfilm project sponsored by the National Historical Publications Commission, published by the New Mexico Records Center, Santa Fe, 1970, 144 pages. The records identified are at the New Mexico State Archives in Santa Fe. FHL book 978.9 A3nn and FHL film #962164.

■ **1821 Santa Fe Census**, in *Herencia*, a publication of the Hispanic Genealogical Research Center, Albuquerque, NM, in Vol. 2, No. 3 (Jul 1994).

■ **1821 Santa Fe Census**, see ***New Mexico Province, Santa Fe Parish, Census of 1821***, compiled by Patricia Black Esterly, published by the New Mexico Genealogical Society, Albuquerque, NM, 1994, 165 pages. Includes index. Contains Santa Fe with barrios of San Francisco, Torreon, San Miguel and Nuestra Senora de Guadalupe and outlying districts with partidos of Rio Tesuque, Galisteo and Cienega y Ranchos. FHL book 978.956 X2e.

■ **1830 Santo Domingo Census**, in the *New Mexico Genealogist*, a periodical of the New Mexico Genealogical Society, Albuquerque, NM, in Vol. 33, No. 1 (Mar 1994) through Vol. 33, No. 3 (Sep 1994).

■ ***New Mexico Censuses of 1833 and 1845: Socorro and Surrounding Communities of the Rio Abajo***, by Teresa Ramírez Alief, Jose Gonzales, Patricia Black Esterly, published by the New Mexico Genealogical Society, Albuquerque, NM, 1994, 153 pages. Includes index. FHL book 978.962 X2a.

■ **1839 Census, Males Capable of Bearing Arms (Valencia)**, in *New Mexico Genealogist*, Vol. 20, No. 2 (Jun 1981).

NEW MEXICO
Statewide Censuses & Substitutes, 1850-1945

■ **Territorial Tax Rolls**, in *New Mexico Genealogist*, Vol. 17, No. 3 (Sep 1978).

■ **1850 Federal Census, Territory of New Mexico**, microfilm of original records at the National Archives, Washington, DC. The seven original counties of the provisional Territory of New Mexico were enumerated with a census day of June 1, 1850. Congress created the Territory of New Mexico September 9, 1850, replacing the provisional government. Filmed by the National Archives, 1964, 4 FHL rolls, as follows:

- Bernalillo and Rio Arriba Counties, FHL film #16603.
- Santa Ana and Santa Fe Counties, FHL film #443666.
- San Miguel and Taos Counties, FHL #443667.
- Valencia County, FHL film #443668.

■ ***New Mexico 1850 Territorial Census***, (printed extract & index), transcribed by the New Mexico Genealogical Society; edited by Margaret Leonard Windham, published by the New Mexico Genealogical Society, Albuquerque, NM, 4 vols., 1976. Contents: vol. 1: Valencia County; vol. 2: Rio Arriba and Santa Ana Counties; vol. 3: Taos and San Miguel Counties; vol. 4: Bernalillo and Santa Fe Counties. Includes index. FHL book 978.9 X2p v.1-4. See Also ***New Mexico 1850 Census Index***, edited by Ronald Vern Jackson and Gary Ronald Teeples, published by Accelerated Indexing Systems, Bountiful, UT, 1978, 54 pages. FHL book 978.9 X2j.

■ **1852-1951 New Mexico Naturalization Records**, microfilm of original records at the New Mexico State Archives in Santa Fe, New Mexico. Various Naturalization Records for Colfax County, Valencia County, 1852-1951. Filmed by the Genealogical Society of Utah, 2004, 1 roll, FHL film #2392555.

■ ***Federal Census – Territory of New Mexico and Territory of Arizona: Excerpts From the Decennial Federal Census, 1860, for Arizona County in the Territory of New Mexico, the Special Territorial Census of 1864 Taken in Arizona and Decennial Federal Census, 1870, for the Territory of Arizona***, Government Printing Office, Washington, DC, 1965, 253 pages. Arranged in alphabetical order by surname. May list name, age, sex, occupation, value of property, and state or country of birth. FHL book 979.1 X2pa.

■ **1860 Federal Census, New Mexico Territory**, microfilm of originals at the National Archives, Washington, DC, The 1860 census was filmed twice. The second filming (2nd) is listed first and is usually easier to read. However, since some of the records were faded or lost between the first and second filmings, search the first filming (1st) whenever the material on the second filming (2nd) is too light or missing. In 1860 the area of Arizona was part of the New Mexico Territory, with most of the population in Arizona County. Filmed by the National Archives, 1950, 1967, 6 rolls, as follows:

- New Mexico: (2nd) Arizona, Bernalillo, Dona Ana, and Rio Arriba Counties, FHL film #803712.
- New Mexico: (2nd) San Miguel County, FHL film #803713.
- New Mexico: (2nd) Santa Fe and Socorro Counties, FHL film #803714.
- New Mexico: (2nd) Taos County, FHL film #803715.
- New Mexico: (2nd) Santa Ana, Mora, and Valencia Counties, FHL film #803716.
- New Mexico: (1st) Entire territory, FHL film #16602.

■ **1861-1865 Civil War Soldiers & Sailors.** See ***Index to Soldiers & Sailors of the Civil War***, a searchable name index to 6.3 million Union and Confederate Civil War soldiers available online at the National Park Service Web site. A search can be done by surname, first name, state, or unit. New Mexico Territory supplied 12,970 men to the war (all Union). To search for one go to the NPS Web site: **www.civilwar.nps.gov/cwss/.**

■ **1862-1874 Internal Revenue Assessment Lists** for the Territory of New Mexico, microfilm of originals in the National Archives in Washington, DC. Filmed by the National Archives, series M0782, 1988. FHL has 1 roll, FHL film #1578508.

■ **1870 Federal Census, New Mexico Territory**, microfilm of original records in the National Archives, Washington, DC. The 1870 census was filmed twice. The second filming (2nd) is listed first and is usually easier to read. However, since some of the records were faded or lost between the first and second filmings, search the first filming (1st) whenever the material on the second filming (2nd) is too light to read. Filmed by the National Archives, 1962, 1968, 7 rolls, as follows:

- New Mexico: (2nd) Bernalillo, Colfax, Dona Ana, and Grant Counties, FHL film #552392.
- New Mexico: (2nd) Lincoln, Mora, and Rio Arriba Counties, FHL film #552393.
- New Mexico: (2nd) San Miguel and Santa Ana Counties, FHL film #552394.
- New Mexico: (2nd) Santa Fe, Socorro, and Taos Counties, FHL film #552395.
- New Mexico: (2nd) Valencia County, FHL film #552396.
- New Mexico: (1st) Mora, Lincoln, Dona Ana, Grant, Colfax, Bernalillo, and Valencia Counties, FHL #16606.
- New Mexico: (1st) Rio Arriba, San Miguel, Santa Ana, Santa Fe, Socorro, and Taos Counties, FHL film #16607.

■ ***Over 1400 Naturalization Records for Various Courts of New Mexico: 1882-1917***, extracts of original records at the National Archives, Denver Regional branch. Compiled and published by the Foothills Genealogical Society of Colorado, 1998, 84 pages. Includes index. Includes name of individual, county applied in, date of application, book and page number, country of birth, and court where recorded. FHL book 978.9 P48f.

■ **1885 New Mexico Territory Census (Federal Duplicate Originals),** microfilm of federal copy at the National Archives, Washington, DC, series M846, 6 rolls. Film may be viewed at many NARA affiliated facilities, including the New Mexico State Archives, but there is no film of the federal copy at the Family History Library in Salt Lake City, Utah. An 1885 census was taken with partial federal funding only in Colorado, Dakota Territory, Florida, Nebraska, and New Mexico Territory. The 1885 census included population schedules, agricultural schedules, industry & manufacturers schedules, and mortality schedules. Two complete sets of the census schedules were prepared, one which was sent to the Census Office in Washington, DC, the other retained at the state/territory. New Mexico Territory's federal set is complete for all counties in place in 1885, the originals now located at the National Archives. The territory's duplicate original set is located at the University of New Mexico, Albuquerque, and is missing four counties.

■ **1885 New Mexico Territory Census (Territory's Duplicate Originals)**, microfilm of duplicate originals at the University of New Mexico, Special Collection Library, Albuquerque, New Mexico. Missing population schedules: Bernalillo, Rio Arriba, Santa Fe, and San Miguel Counties. Filmed by Golightly-Payne-Coon Co., El Paso, TX, 1957. FHL has 2 rolls, as follows:

- Bernalillo, Colfax, Dona Ana, Santa Fe (mortality schedules only), Sierra, Socorro, Mora and Rio Arriba (mortality schedules only), FHL film #16610.
- Taos, Valencia, Grant and Lincoln counties, FHL film #16611.

■ **1885 Census of Albuquerque, New Mexico**, microfilm of territory's duplicate originals at the New Mexico State Archives in Santa Fe, New Mexico. Lists date, name, occupation, age, sex, and remarks. Filmed by the Genealogical Society of Utah, 2004, 1 roll, FHL film #2203769. See also ***Territorial Census and Surname Index of the City of Albuquerque, Territory of New Mexico: Books 1,2, and 3 - Book 4 is not extant, April 1885,*** Howard W. Henry, editor and compiler, published by the Genealogy Club of Albuquerque, 2000, 81 pages. Index lists name, page and line number. Includes photocopy of census from microfilm. FHL book 978.961/A1 X2h 1885.

■ **Delayed Certificates of Birth**, microfilm of records at New Mexico Department of Public Health, Santa Fe, New Mexico. Organized by county, then by date of birth. A delayed birth certificate was issued to those who visited the courthouse of residence, filed affidavits and documents attesting to the information, confirmed by witnesses. Many of these delayed birth certificates were issued after 1935, and were used by those near or over 65 years old who needed proof of birth to apply for Social Security benefits. Filmed by the Genealogical Society of Utah, 1995, 5 rolls, as follows:

- Bernalillo County, 1871-1895; Catron County, 1881-1895; Chaves County, 1897-1895; and Colfax County, 1873-1893, FHL film #1991905. Another filming of Bernalillo, Catron, Chaves, and Colfax, plus DeBaca, Eddy, and Dona Ana, FHL film #1991647.
- Colfax County (cont.), 1893-1895; Curry County, 1891; De Baca County, 1882-1892; Eddy County, 1880-1895; Dona Ana County, 1868-1895; and Grant County (part), 1873-1895, FHL film #1992055.
- Grant county (cont.), 1895; Guadalupe County, 1870-1895; Harding County, 1882-1895; Hidalgo County, 1883-1895; Lincoln County, 1876-1895; Luna County, 1882-1895; McKinley County, 1882-1895; Mora County, 1876-1895; Otero County, 1866-1895; Quay County, 1887-1895; and Rio Arriba County, 1871-1895; FHL film #1992056.
- Roosevelt County, 1891; Sandoval County, 1876-1895; San Miguel County, 1873-1895; San Juan County, 1877-1895; and Santa Fe County, 1869-1895; FHL film #1992057.
- Sierra County, 1867-1895; Socorro County. 1867-1895; Taos County, 1866-1895; Torrance County, 1877-1893; Union County, 1873-1895; and Valencia County, 1866-1895, FHL film #1992058.

■ **1889-1942 Certificate and Record of Death**, microfilm of records at Bureau of Vital Records & Health, Department of Health, Santa Fe, New Mexico. May include deceased's name, sex, color or race, marital status, date and place of birth, age, occupation, date, place and cause of death, place of burial and undertaker, length of residence where death occurred, name and birthplace of father, name and birthplace of mother, and name of person providing information. Organized by county/city, in chronological order by date of death. Filmed by the Genealogical Society of Utah, 1996, 29 rolls, as follows:

- Albuquerque (city) 1889-1907, FHL film #2032734.
- Curry County, 1909-1919; De Baca County, 1917-1919; Doña Ana County, 1907-1913; and Chaves County 1907-1915, FHL film #2032740.
- Chaves County, 1916-1919; Colfax County, 1907-1913; Doña Ana County, 1914-1919; Eddy County, 1908-1919; and Grant County, 1907-1914, FHL film #2032741.
- Lincoln County, 1910-1919; Luna County, 1907-1919; McKinley County, 1904-1919; and Mora County, 1907-1919, FHL film #2032742.
- Otero, Quay counties; 1907-1919; and Albuquerque (city), 1907-1910, FHL film #2032743.
- Albuquerque (city), 1910-1913; and Colfax County, 1913-1914, FHL film #2032876.
- Sierra County, 1907-1919; Socorro County, 1907-1919; Taos County, 1908-1919; Torrance County, 1908-1919; Union County, 1910-1920; Valencia County, 1899-1919; and Albuquerque (city), 1914-1915, FHL film #2032877.

- Albuquerque (city), 1916-1917; Colfax County, 1915-1917; Rio Arriba County, 1906-1918; Roosevelt County, 1910-1919; Sandoval County, 1916-1919; San Juan County, 1907-1919; and Santa Fe County, 1907, FHL film #2032878.
- Colfax County, 1918-1919; Grant County, 1915-1917; Guadalupe County, 1914-1919; and Harding County, 1897-1918, FHL film #2032879.
- Santa Fe County, 1908-1919; Sierra County, 1901-1913; and Albuquerque (city), 1919, FHL film #2032880.
- Albuquerque (city), 1920; Bernalillo County, and Chaves-Grant counties, 1920, (De Baca County missing), FHL film #2032881.
- McKinley-Otero, Guadalupe, 1920; Hidalgo, Luna, Lincoln, Lea - Quay, and Valencia counties, (Harding County missing), FHL film #2032882.
- Bernalillo-Luna counties, 1921; FHL film #2032883.
- McKinley-Valencia counties, 1921; Bernalillo County, Jan-Jul 1922, FHL film #2032884.
- Bernalillo County, Aug-Dec 1922; Catron-Quay counties, 1922, FHL film #2032885.
- Rio Arriba-Valencia counties, 1922; Bernalillo, Jan-Jun 1923, FHL film #2032886.
- Bernalillo County, Jul-Dec 1923; Catron-Harding counties, 1923, FHL film #2032887.
- Hidalgo-Union counties, 1923, FHL film #2032888.
- Valencia County, 1923; Bernalillo-Guadalupe counties, 1924, FHL film #2032889.
- Harding-Valencia counties, 1924, FHL film #2032890.
- Bernalillo-Eddy counties, 1925; Grant County, Jan-Mar 1925, FHL film #2032891.
- Grant County, Apr-Dec 1925; Guadalupe-Sierra counties, 1925, FHL film #2032892.
- Socorro-Valencia counties, 1925; Bernalillo-DeBaca counties, 1926, FHL film #2032893.
- Doña Ana-Sandoval counties, 1926, FHL film #2032894.
- San Juan-Valencia counties, 1926, FHL film #2032895.
- Indian death certificates: Bernalillo, McKinley, Otero counties, 1920-1927, FHL film #2032896.
- Indian death certificates: Rio Arriba, Sandoval, San Juan, Santa Fe, Taos counties, 1919-1927; Taos County, 1937-1938; Valencia County, 1920; Bernalillo County, 1927; Chaves, Lincoln, Grant counties, 1926; Hidalgo, Otero counties, 1938, FHL film #2032897.
- Bernalillo County, 1939-1942; McKinley County, 1926-1933; Santa Fe County, 1926-1942; Socorro County, 1936-1942; Taos County, 1927-1942; Union County, 1933; Valencia County, 1922-1942, FHL film #2032898.
- McKinley County, 1934-1942; Otero County, 1928-1942; Rio Arriba County, 1927-1942; Sandoval, San Juan counties, 1927-1942, FHL film #2032899.

■ **1927-1945 New Mexico Death Certificates,** microfilm of original records at the New Mexico Department of Health, Vital Records & Health Statistics, Santa Fe, New Mexico. Arranged chronologically in each county by date of death. Filmed by the NM Dept. of Health, 1978, 46 rolls, cataloged by the FHL as follows:

- Bernalillo - Doña Ana counties, 1927, FHL film #1913277.
- Eddy - San Juan counties, 1927 San Miguel County, Jan-Jul 1927, FHL film #1913278.
- San Miguel County, 1927; Santa Fe - Valencia counties, 1927, FHL film #1913279.
- Bernalillo - Doña Ana counties, 1928, FHL film #1913280.
- Eddy - Sandoval counties, 1928, FHL film #1913281.
- San Juan - Valencia counties, 1928, FHL film #1913282.
- Bernalillo - Grant counties, 1929, FHL film #1913283.
- Guadalupe - Sandoval counties, 1929, FHL film #1913284.
- Rio Arriba - Valencia counties, 1929, FHL film #1913285.
- Bernalillo - De Baca counties, 1930, FHL film #1913286.
- Dona Ana - Rio Arriba counties, 1930, FHL film #1913287.
- Roosevelt - Valencia counties, 1930, FHL film #1913288.
- Bernalillo - Grant counties, 1931, FHL film #1913289.
- Guadalupe - Socorro counties, 1931, FHL film #1913290.
- Taos - Valencia counties 1931; Bernalillo - Dona Ana counties, 1932, FHL film #1913291.
- Eddy - San Miguel counties, 1932, FHL film #1913292.

- Santa Fe - Valencia counties, 1932; Bernalillo – Colfax counties, 1933, FHL film #1913293.
- Curry - San Juan counties, 1933, FHL film #1913294.
- San Miguel – Valencia, 1933; Bernalillo 1934, FHL film #1913295.
- Catron - Otero counties, 1934, FHL film #1913296.
- Quay - Valencia counties, 1934, FHL film #1913297.
- Bernalillo - Grant counties, 1935, FHL film #1913298.
- Guadalupe - Santa Fe counties, 1935, FHL film #1913299.
- Sierra - Valencia counties, 1935; Bernalillo - Colfax counties, 1936, FHL film #1913300.
- Curry - Roosevelt counties, 1936, FHL film #1913301.
- Sandoval - Valencia counties; 1936; Bernalillo County, 1937, FHL film #1913302.
- Bernalillo County, 1937; Catron - Harding counties, 1937, FHL film #1913303.
- Hidalgo - Santa Fe counties, 1937, FHL film #1913304.
- Sierra - Valencia 1937; Bernalillo, Curry, De Baca, and Dona Ana counties, 1938, FHL film #1913305.
- Catron - Colfax counties, 1938; Eddy - San Juan counties, 1938, FHL film #1913306.
- San Miguel - Valencia counties, 1938; Bernalillo County, 1939, FHL film #1913307.
- Catron - Quay counties, 1939, FHL film #1913308.
- Rio Arriba - Valencia counties, 1939, FHL film #1913309.
- Bernalillo - Grant counties, 1940, FHL film #1913310.
- Guadalupe - San Miguel counties, 1940, FHL film #1913311.
- Sierra - Valencia counties, 1940; Bernalillo - Colfax counties, 1941, FHL film #1913312.
- Curry - Sandoval counties, 1941, FHL film #1913313.
- San Juan - Valencia counties, 1941; Bernalillo County 1942, FHL film #1913314.
- Catron - Quay counties, 1942, FHL film #1913315.
- Rio Arriba - Valencia counties, 1942, FHL film #1913316.
- Bernalillo - Grant counties, 1943, FHL film #1913317.
- Guadalupe - Santa Fe counties, 1943, FHL film #1913318.
- Sierra - Valencia counties, 1943; Bernalillo - De Baca counties, 1944, FHL film #1913319.
- Doña Ana - San Juan counties, 1944, FHL film #1913320.
- San Miguel - Valencia counties, 1944; Bernalillo County, 1945, FHL film #1913321.
- Catron - Quay counties, 1945, FHL film #1913322.

■ **1880-1920**. See ***Some Marriage Records of the State of New Mexico: (ca. 1880-1920)***, typescript compiled by members of the Daughters of the American Revolution (New Mexico), published by the DAR, 1971-1973, 2 vols. Includes index. Contents: vol. 1: Bernalillo Co.; vol. 2: Chaves Co, Eddy Co., San Juan Co., Otero Co., Quay Co., Roosevelt Co., and Curry Co. FHL book 978.9 V25d v. 1-2. Also on microfilm filmed by the Genealogical Society of Utah, 2 rolls, FHL film 908289 (vol. 1), and FHL film #928026 (vol. 2).

■ **Statewide New Mexico Census Records and Substitutes Online**. These databases available online via a direct link at **www.censusfinder.com:**

- New Mexico Census, 1831-80 at Ancestry
- 1540 Coronado Expedition Muster Roll
- 1598-1608 Onate Expedition Muster Roll
- 1600 New Mexico Settlers List
- 1880 Federal Census of Norwegians
- 1880 Federal Census - Images
- 1880 Federal Census Search at Family Search
- 1899-1940 New Mexico Death Index
- Early Settlers of Taos Valley
- New Mexico State Databases of Census & Genealogy Records

NEW MEXICO Countywide Censuses & Substitutes

Statewide censuses & substitutes for New Mexico need to be supplemented by the many resources available at the county level. The censuses, tax lists, and voter registrations available for each New Mexico county are shown below:

Arizona County

■ **1860 Federal Census, Arizona County, Territory of New Mexico.** Arizona County was created by New Mexico Territory, taken from Doña Ana County in 1859 from the area of the Gadsden Purchase. Arizona County was abolished in 1862, the area returned to Doña Ana County. For the only census under the name Arizona County, see the following:

- 1860 Federal Census, New Mexico Territory, (2nd filming), Arizona, Bernalillo, Doña Ana, and Rio Arriba counties, FHL film #803712.

Bernalillo County

■ **1882 Voter Registration Lists, Bernalillo County, New Mexico,** microfilm of original records at the New Mexico State Archives in Santa Fe, New Mexico. Text in Spanish and English. Filmed by the Genealogical Society of Utah, 2004, FHL film #2203770.

■ **1870-1918 Probate Records, Bernalillo County, New Mexico,** microfilm of original records at the New Mexico State Archives in Santa Fe, New Mexico. Some pages are light and may be hard or difficult to read. Includes index in some volumes. Includes items covered during regular terms and special sessions of probate court. Filmed by the Genealogical Society of Utah, 2004, 3 rolls, as follows:

- Probate records, vol. 1-2 (p. 1-219, cont.), 1870-1893, FHL film #2203766.
- Probate records, vol. 2 (cont., p. 218-end) – vol. 4, 1893-1910, FHL film #2203767.
- Probate claim docket, vol. 1, 1894-1897; Estate docket, 1906-1918, FHL film #2203769.

■ **1877 List of Special US Tax Payers, Bernalillo County, New Mexico Territory,** in *New Mexico Genealogist*, Vol. 28, No. 2 (Jun 1989).

■ **1882 Delinquent Tax Payers, Bernalillo County, New Mexico Territory,** in *New Mexico Genealogist*, Vol. 28, No. 2 (Jun 1989).

■ **1888-1896 Newspaper Index,** see ***Surname Index of the Daily Citizen, Albuquerque, New Mexico***, compiled by Laurel E. Drew, editor; Howard W. Henry, compiler; Eldon W. Pierce, technical director, published by the Genealogy Club of Albuquerque, New Mexico, 1994-2001. In September 1892, the masthead of the newspaper started carrying the name, *The Evening Citizen*, but the ownership block on the succeeding pages never changed from *The Daily Citizen*. The newspaper index books for New Mexico newspapers continued to carry the name of *The Daily Citizen* as the name of the newspaper. Contents: 1888, 1889.1890, 1891, 1892, 1893, 1894, 1895, 1896. Arranged alphabetically by surname for each year. FHL Library has 1888-1893, 1896, 1893 bound as one volume. 1896 bound as one volume. FHL book 978.961/A1 1888-1896.

■ ***Index of the Vital Records in the Albuquerque Journal, Albuquerque, New Mexico,*** Laurel E. Drew, editor; Howard W. Henry, compiler; Eldon W. Pierce, technical director; John M. Puckett, compiler; et al., published by the Genealogy Club of Albuquerque, PAF Users Group, 1994. Title varies slightly as newspaper changed its name. Index compiled on an annual basis with some events carried over to the next year especially if it occurred toward to the latter months of the year. Names are alphabetical by surname with date of event and page where it appeared. Contents: 1918, 1920, 1921, 1922, 1923, 1924, 1925, 1926, 1936, 1937, 1939, 1940, 1942, 1943, 1944, 1947, 1948, 1949 & 1955. FHL Library has bound 1921-1922, 1924-1926, and 1939-1940 together. FHL book 978.961/A1 B32h 1918-1955. See also, ***Index to Obituary Notices and Death Articles: In the Albuquerque Journal, Albuquerque, New Mexico***, compiled by Hugh M.

Bivens, et al., published by the Genealogy Club of Albuquerque, 1997-2000, 2 vols. Listed in alphabetical order by surname for each year. Lists name, date and page number of the newspaper. Contents: vol. 1: 1960, 1961, and 1962; vol. 2: 1963, 1964, and 1965, 1951, 1999, 2000, 2001. FHL book 978.961/A1 V4b 1951-2001.

■ ***Albuquerque and Las Vegas Business Directory for 1883***, microfilm of original directory published by Armijo Brothers & Borradaile, 1883, 97 pages. Filmed by University Microfilms International, Ann Arbor, MI, 1970, FHL film #1303032 (Albuquerque and Las Vegas Business Directory for 1883).

■ **1905-1935 City Directories, Albuquerque, New Mexico**, microfilm of originals published by various publishers. Filmed by Research Publications, Woodbridge, CT, 1980-1984, 7 rolls, as follows:

- 1905-1906, 1907, 1908-1909, 1909-1910, 1910-1911, FHL film #1843249.
- 1912, 1913, 1914, 1915, 1916, FHL film #1843250.
- 1917, 1918, 1919, 1920, FHL film #1843251.
- 1921, 1922, 1923, 1924, FHL film #1843252.
- 1925, 1926, 1927, 1928, FHL film #1843253.
- 1929, 1930, 1931, 1932, FHL film #1843254.
- 1933, 1934, 1935, FHL film #1843255.

■ **Census Records and Substitutes Online, Bernalillo County, New Mexico**. These databases available online via a direct link from **www.censusfinder.com:**

- 1930 Federal Census Records Index, Surnames A-L
- 1930 Federal Census Records Index, Surnames M-Z
- 1934 La Reata, Albuquerque High School Students

Catron County

■ **Census Records and Substitutes Online, Catron County, New Mexico**. These databases available online via a direct link from **www.censusfinder.com:**

- 1930 Federal Census Records Index, Surnames A-Cordova
- 1930 Federal Census Records Index, Surnames Cordova-Key
- 1930 Federal Census Records Index, Surnames Ki-Pera
- 1930 Federal Census Records Index, Surnames Per-Z

Chaves County

■ **1882-1935 Reverse Deed Index; Deed Releases, Chaves County, New Mexico**, microfilm of originals at the New Mexico State Archives in Santa Fe, New Mexico. Lists date, name of grantee and grantor, type of land transaction, book and page number. Filmed by the Genealogical Society of Utah, 2004, 2 rolls, as follows:

- Reverse deed index, releases, etc., 1882-1935, A-DeWett, FHL film #2205611.
- Reverse deed index, releases, etc., Dibrell-McWilliam, FHL film #2203649.

■ ***New Mexico, Chaves County, Reverse Deed Index, Releases, Etc., 1882-1935***, (printed extract), compiled and published by the Roswell Chapter New Mexico, Daughters of the American Revolution, 11 vols., FHL book 978.943 R22n A-Z. Also on microfilm, filmed by the Genealogical Society of Utah, 1982-1983, 1989, 1992, 1998, 9 rolls, beginning with FHL film #1320810 (Al-Az).

■ **1891 Tax Assessment Roll, Chaves County, New Mexico Territory**, in *New Mexico Genealogist*, Vol. 18, No. 3 (Sep 1979) and Vol. 18, No. 4 (Dec 1979).

■ **Census Records and Substitutes Online, Chaves County, New Mexico**. These databases available online via a direct link from **www.censusfinder.com:**

- 1930 Federal Census Index.
- 1903-1907 Birth Records
- 1903-1907 Death Records
- 1903-1907 Victims of Disease in Chaves County
- 1908 Birth Records
- 1908 Death Records
- 1909 Birth Records

Cibola County

Cibola County was the second to last county created in the United States, created from Valencia in 1981. There are no published or microfilmed county records yet, but at least one genealogical list was produced for the area:

■ **1907 Annual Genealogical Report (Form E),** microfilm of original records at the LDS Church Archives, Salt Lake City. Includes genealogical information for members of The Church of Jesus Christ of Latter-day Saints in present Cibola County, New Mexico. St. Johns Stake records are on pp. 1185-1284. St. Johns Stake includes the Alpine, Bluewater, Branch, Eagar, Greer, Luna, Nutrioso, Ramah, and St. Johns Wards. May print only direct ancestor and those born 95+ years ago. All other information must be crossed out. Filmed by the Genealogical Society of Utah, 1956, 1 roll, FHL film #774320.

Colfax County

■ **1870, 1926 Voter Registration List, Colfax County, New Mexico,** microfilm of original records at the New Mexico State Archives in Santa Fe, New Mexico. Filmed by the Genealogical Society of Utah, 2004, 1 roll, FHL film not cataloged yet.

■ ***1891 Assessment Roll for Colfax County, Territory of New Mexico: Names of Property Owners,*** transcribed by Nancy Robertson, published by Friends of Raton Anthropology, Raton, NM, 1980, 17 pages. Arranged alphabetically within precincts of Elizabethtown, Ute Park, Cimarron, Rayado, Elkins, Raton, Folsom, Madison, Chico, Pena Flor, Ponil Park, Springer, Cimilario, Clayton, Red Lake, Blossburg, Ponil, Maxwell City, Colmor, Buena Vista Raton, Gladstone, Black Lakes, Carrizo Frampton, Road Canon, Catskill, and Mesa. FHL book 978.9 A1 No. 103.

■ ***Every Name Index, Colfax County, New Mexico, 1910 Territorial Census,*** Howard W. Henry, editor and project coordinator; Eldon W. Pierce, technical advisor, published by the Genealogy Club of Albuquerque, 2000, 149 pages. FHL book 978.922 X22h.

Curry County

■ ***Marriage Records (1909-1915), Curry County Courthouse, Clovis, New Mexico,*** compiled by Louise E. and Robert J. Reithel, published under the auspices of the Curry County Genealogical Society of New Mexico, Clovis, NM. The book has alphabetized listings for groom and bride for each year. Each entry gives groom's name, bride's name, date, book number and page number. Book filmed by the Genealogical Society of Utah, 1990, FHL film #1597655.

■ ***Marriages in Curry County, New Mexico, Before 1921,*** by Walter Conner; assisted by Louise Smith and Wanda Dunn, published 1987, from the original records in the Curry County Court House, Clovis, New Mexico. Contents: vol. 1, pt. 1: Alphabetically by the groom; vol. 1, pt. 2: Alphabetically by the bride, FHL 978.927 V22c.

■ ***Marriages Performed in the Area of Curry County, New Mexico, 1905-1908, When it Was Still a Part of Roosevelt County, New Mexico Territory,*** copied by Sallie Foster and Louise Reithel, published by the Curry County Genealogical Society of New Mexico, 1985, 8 pages. Transcripts are in the Curry Courthouse located in Clovis, New Mexico. Includes groom's name, bride's names, date, book number, page number, and brides' index. FHL book 978.9 A1 No. 18.

■ ***Every Name Index, Curry County, New Mexico, 1910 Territorial Census,*** Howard W. Henry, editor and project coordinator; Eldon W. Pierce, technical advisor, published by the Genealogy Club of Albuquerque, 2000, 112 pages. Includes name, city, county, page and line number. Arranged in alphabetical order by surname. FHL book 978.927 X22h.

■ *Curry County, New Mexico, Registration for the Draft For World War I: Published by the Clovis Journal, Thursday, July 26, 1917,* edited by the Clovis Branch Family History Center, microfilm of original published: Clovis, New Mexico: Clovis Branch Family History Center, 1996. 17 leaves. Includes the July 26, 1917 registration list of young men between the ages of 21-31, and an alphabetical list which includes home town. On April 6, 1917, the United States declared war on Germany. By June 30, 1917 New Mexico had contributed 1,239 soldiers, and by June 1918 New Mexico had enlisted 10,000 young men between the ages of 21 to 31 in the armed services of the United States. Population of Curry County at that time was approximately 10,000. Filmed by the Genealogical Society of Utah, 1996, 1 roll, FHL film #1598430.

■ *Men in U.S. Military service, WWII: As Listed in the Clovis News Journal, Curry County, New Mexico, July 15, 1942; Taken from the Wednesday, July 15, 1942, "Heroes Edition" (Section 2), Over 700 Curry County Men Are Now in the Armed Forces,* transcribed by Don McAlavy, microfilm of original and photocopies: [Clovis, New Mexico: D. McAlavy, 2000, 23 pages. Filmed by the Genealogical Society of Utah, FHL film #1573646.

De Baca County

■ *A Genealogical Index of Early De Baca County, New Mexico, Deeds, 1917 thru 1929,* compiled by Morton L. Ervin; Mae Allen Form, published by Ervin Publishing, Albuquerque, NM, 2000, 2 vols. Lists name of grantor and grantee, type of instrument, and date recorded. Contents: vol. 1: Grantor index; vol. 2: Grantee index. Arranged in alphabetical order by surname. FHL book 978.944 R22e v. 1-2.

■ **1928 History.** See ***Living Water: Our Mid-Pecos History: the Families & Events – From Fort to Future,*** published by Mid-Pecos Historical Foundation, Inc., Bob Parsons, editor, microfilm of original published 1928, 304 pages. Includes history of De Baca County, New Mexico and biographies of some of the families that lived there. Filmed by the Genealogical Society of Utah, 2000, 1 roll, FHL film #1425223. Indexed in ***Living Water Index For the De Baca County, NM History Book,*** by Harold Kilmer, published 1999, Clovis, NM, 39 pages. Filmed by the Genealogical Society of Utah, 2000, 1 roll, FHL film #1425223.

Doña Ana County

■ **1868-1922 Registered Voters, Doña Ana County, New Mexico,** microfilm of original records at the New Mexico State Archives in Santa Fe, New Mexico. Text in English and Spanish. Filmed by the Genealogical Society of Utah, 2004, 1 roll, FHL film 2203944.

■ **1870-1871, 1875 Assessment Records, Doña Ana County, New Mexico,** microfilm of original records at the New Mexico State Archives in Santa Fe, New Mexico. Text in English and Spanish. Filmed by the Genealogical Society of Utah, 2004, 1 roll, FHL film #2203945.

■ *A Genealogical Index of Early Doña Ana County, New Mexico, Deeds, 1847-1907,* compiled by Morton L. Ervin, published by Ervin Publishing, Albuquerque, NM, 2002, 2 vols. Contents: vol. 1: Grantor name; includes index to grants and patents; vol. 2. Grantee name. Arranged in alphabetical order by surname. FHL Library has bound vol. 1-2 together. FHL book 978.966 R22e vol. 1-2.

■ ***1966, 1967, 1985 Greater Las Cruces (Dona Ana County, New Mexico) City Directory: Including Mesilla, Mesilla Park and University Park, Contains Buyers' Guide and a Complete Classified Business Directory,*** R. L. Polk and Company, Dallas, TX. FHL has 1966, 1967, 1985 directories. FHL book 978.966 E4p 1966-1985.

■ **Census Records and Substitutes Online, Doña Ana County, New Mexico.** These databases available online via a direct link from **www.censusfinder.com:**

- 1860 Federal Census Records of Moury City Part 1
- 1860 Federal Census Records of Moury City Part 2
- 1900 Federal Census Images
- 1930 Federal Census Index.
- Voters List

Eddy County

■ **Tax Payers, June 1900, Eddy County, New Mexico Territory,** in *Pecos Trails,* a publication of the Eddy County Genealogical Society, Carlsbad, NM, in Vol. 7, No. 1 (May 1987).

■ **1904 Census, Weed, Pinon, Avis & McDonald Flats, Eddy County, New Mexico,** name lists published in *Pecos Trails,* in Vol. 3, No. 1 (May 1983) through Vol. 4, No. 1 (May 1984).

■ **1892-1921 Marriage Certificates, Eddy County, New Mexico,** microfilm of original records at the New Mexico State Archives in Santa Fe, New Mexico. Filmed by the Genealogical Society of Utah, 2004, 1 roll, FHL film #2203937.

■ **Marriage Indexes for Eddy County, New Mexico, Bride and Groom Indexes, for the years 1889 to 1985,** computer generated typescript, 6 vols., 1,500 pages. Index was compiled and produced by the Eddy County Clerk's Office, Eddy County Courthouse, in Carlsbad, New Mexico. Contents: vol. 1: Grooms. A - Gonyea; vol. 2: Grooms. Gonzales-Orozco, Enrique; vol. 3: Grooms. Orozco, Florencio - Z; vol. 4: Brides. A-Goodman, Nancy; vol. 5: Brides. Goodman, Norma-Owens, Dorothy; vol. 6: Brides. Owens, Effie-Z. Dates refer to date license was purchased, not date of marriage. Indexes are arranged in alphabetical order by name and give the date of issue, the groom's and bride's names, book number, and page number. FHL book 978.942 V22e v.1-6. Also on microfilm, filmed by the Genealogical Society of Utah, 1990, 1 roll, FHL film #1697323.

■ ***A Genealogical Index of Early Eddy County, New Mexico Deeds: 1884 to 1905,*** compiled by Morton L. Ervin, Doris Ann Ervin, Barbara Duckworth, published by Ervin Publishing, Albuquerque, NM, 1998, 204 pages. Includes index to grantees. May include name of grantor and grantee, type of instrument, date of instrument, and recording date. FHL 978.942 R22e.

■ **Census Records and Substitutes Online, Eddy County, New Mexico.** These databases available online via a direct link at **www.censusfinder.com:**

- 1930 Federal Census Index.
- Early Birth Records
- Early Death Records
- Military Records
- 1887-2000 Probate Records
- 1900-1999 Military Discharge Records.
- 1910-1918 Artesia Funeral Records
- 1918-1925 Artesia Funeral Records

Grant County

■ **1870-1987 Death Index, Grant County, New Mexico,** compiled by Carl W. Scholl, published by the LDS Family History Center, Silver City, NM, 1993, microfilm of original arranged in alphabetical order by name and gives name of deceased, cemetery name with notes, location in cemetery (section, block, plot), state and city, birth date and death date. Information is sometimes incomplete. Contents: vol. 1: A-F; vol. 2. G-M; vol. 3; N-Z. From Intro: "This list of over 28,000 names consists of cemetery, sexton and funeral home records as well as New Mexico death certificates. As a result there is information on persons who died here but are buried elsewhere. The Lordsburg, NM cemetery is also included." Death dates cover ca. 1870-1987. Filmed by the Genealogical Society of Utah, 1993, 29 microfiches, FHL fiche #6075941 (vol. 1, 9 fiches); FHL fiche #6075942 (vol. 2, 10 fiches); FHL fiche #6075943 (vol. 3, 10 fiches).

■ **1895 Silver City Tax Roll, Grant County, New Mexico Territory**, in *New Mexico Genealogist*, Vol. 17, No. 1 (Mar 1978) through Vol. 17, No. 3 (Sep 1978).

■ **1898 Silver City Tax Roll, Grant County, New Mexico Territory**, in *New Mexico Genealogist*, Vol. 17, No. 3 (Sep 1978).

■ **Census Records and Substitutes Online, Grant County, New Mexico**. These databases available online via a direct link at **www.censusfinder.com:**

- 1860 Federal Census Records of Moury City Part 1
- 1860 Federal Census Records of Moury City Part 2
- 1870 Federal Census Records Transcription
- 1880 Federal Census Extraction of "Buffalo Soldiers"
- Death and Cemetery Records - Over 55,000 Records
- 1935 Grant County Ranches

Guadalupe County

■ ***A Genealogical Index of Early Guadalupe County, New Mexico Deeds, 1891 to 1916***, compiled by Morton L. Ervin, published by Ervin Publishing, Albuquerque, NM, 1999, 159 pages. Includes separate index to grantor and index to grantee. Arranged in alphabetical order by surname. Grantor index for USA is located between grantor and grantee index. FHL book 978.925 R22e. Also on microfilm, filmed by the Genealogical Society of Utah, 2001, 1 roll, FHL film 1440328.

■ **Census Records and Substitutes Online, Guadalupe County, New Mexico**. These databases available online via a direct link from **www.censusfinder.com:**

- 1930 Federal Census Index.

Harding County

■ **1894-1956 San Jose Catholic Church Records**, microfilm of original records at the San Jose Church, Mosquero, Harding County, New Mexico. Includes indexes. Filmed by Golightly, El Paso, TX, 1956, 4 rolls, as follows:

- Baptisms 1894-1914, FHL film #16833.
- Baptisms 1925-1956, FHL film #16834.
- Marriages 1894-1955, FHL film #16835.
- Deaths 1931-1956; Confirmations 1921-1954, FHL film #16836.

■ **1918-1956 Holy Family Catholic Church Records**, microfilm of original records at Holy Family Church, Roy, Harding County, New Mexico. Includes indexes. Contents: Baptisms, 1918-1956; Marriages, 1918-1956; First Communion, 1926-1949; Confirmations, 1920-1954; Deaths, 1918-1956. Filmed by Golightly, El Paso, TX, 1956, 1 roll, FHL film #16880.

Hidalgo County

■ **1916-1956 St. Joseph's Catholic Church Records**, microfilm of original records in St. Joseph's Church, Lordsburg, Hidalgo County, New Mexico. Includes indexes. Contents: Baptisms, 1916-1956; Communions, 1921-1956; Confirmations, 1919-1955; Marriages, 1916-1956; Deaths, 1921-1956. Filmed by Golightly, El Paso, TX, 1956, 1 roll, FHL film #16801.

■ **Census Records and Substitutes Online, Hidalgo County, New Mexico.** These databases available online via a direct link from **www.censusfinder.com:**

- 1930 Federal Census Records Index, Surnames A-Cruz

- 1930 Federal Census Records Index, Surnames Cu-Hynds
- 1930 Federal Census Records Index, Surnames I-M
- 1930 Federal Census Records Index, Surnames N- Sh
- 1930 Federal Census Records Index, Surnames Si-Z
- Hidalgo County School Records

Lea County

■ *A Genealogical Index of Early Lea County, New Mexico Deeds: 1900-1917*, compiled by Morton L. Ervin; Doris Ann Ervin; Barbara Duckworth, published by Ervin Publishing, Albuquerque, NM, 1999, 93 pages. May include name of grantee and grantor, type of instrument, date of instrument, and filing date. Arranged in alphabetical order by surname. FHL book 978.933 R22e.

■ *Lea County, New Mexico, Marriage Book 1, 07 August 1917-12 June 1930 With Groom's and Bride's Indexes*, copied by members of the Southeastern New Mexico Genealogical Society, published by the society, Hobbs, NM, 1991, 72 pages. Includes indexes. Arranged in order by date of marriage and gives the names of groom and bride, date and place of marriages, and page number. FHL book 978.933 V2L.

■ **1938-1956 St. Helena Catholic Church Records**, microfilm of original records at the St. Helena Church, Hobbs, Lea County, New Mexico. Includes indexes. Contents: Communions, 1938-1941; Confirmations, 1943; Baptisms, 1939-1954; Marriages, 1940-1956; Deaths 1940-1956; Confirmations, 1940; Baptisms, 1951-1956; Confirmations, 1951-1954; Communions, 1951- 1956. Filmed by Golightly, El Paso, TX, 1956. FHL film #16778.

■ **Census Records and Substitutes Online, Lea County, New Mexico**. These databases available online via a direct link at: **www.censusfinder.com:**

- 1930 Federal Census Index, surnames A-Chaney
- 1930 Federal Census Index, surnames Chap-Flem
- 1930 Federal Census Index, surnames Flet-J
- 1930 Federal Census Index, surnames Jackson-New
- 1930 Federal Census Index, surnames Ni-Sl
- 1930 Federal Census Index, surnames Sm-Will
- 1930 Federal Census Index, surnames Wils-Z

Lincoln County

■ *A Genealogical Index of Early Lincoln County, New Mexico, Deeds, 1869 to 1893*, compiled by Morton L. Ervin and Doris Ann Ervin. Published by Ervin Publishing, Albuquerque, NM, 1999, 143 pages. Lists name of grantor and grantee, instrument type and date, recording date. Arranged in alphabetical order by surname. FHL book 978.964 R22e.

■ *Some Early Death Records in Lincoln County, New Mexico: From File found in the Tucumcari Mortuary of Quay County, New Mexico*, copied by Charles Barnum, published 2000, 12 pages. FHL book 978.926/T1 V3b. Also on microfilm, filmed by the Genealogical Society of Utah, 2001, 1 roll, FHL film #1145773 Item 11.

■ **Census Records and Substitutes Online, Lincoln County, New Mexico**. These databases available online via a direct link from **www.censusfinder.com:**

- 1860 Federal Census Records Transcription at Lincoln Co. USGenWeb
- 1860 Federal Census of Village of Lincoln and Fort Stanton
- 1880 Federal Census Extraction of "Buffalo Soldiers"
- 1890 Special Veterans Census
- 1900 Federal Census Records Index
- First Families of Lincoln County

- 1876-1975 Delayed Birth Records
- 1898-1944 Catholic Funeral Records of St. Rita Church at Carrizozo
- 1913-1919 Death Index
- 1938 WPA Biographies

Los Alamos County

Los Alamos County was created in 1949 under the urging of the U.S. government, mainly as a means of gathering certain defense activities into a single civilian jurisdiction. No known county records have been published or microfilmed yet, except for some church records:

■ **1946-1956 Immaculate Heart of Mary Catholic Church Records,** microfilm of original records in the Immaculate Heart of Mary Church, Los Alamos, Los Alamos County, New Mexico. Includes indexes. Contents: Baptisms, 1946-1956; Confirmations, 1950-1954; Marriages, 1946-1956; Deaths, 1946-1956. Filmed by Golightly, El Paso, TX, 1956. FHL film #16805.

Luna County

■ ***Inventory of the County Archives of New Mexico, No. 15, Luna County (Deming),*** prepared by the New Mexico Historical Records Survey, Service Division, War Services Section, Work Projects Administration, 1942, 306 pages. This is an inventory of all county records at the Luna County Courthouse in Deming, New Mexico as of 1942. FHL book 978.968 A3h. Also on microfilm, filmed by the Genealogical Society of Utah, 1993, 1 roll, FHL film #1697891.

■ ***Every Name Index, Luna County, New Mexico, 1910 Territorial Census,*** Howard W. Henry, editor and project coordinator; Eldon W. Pierce, technical advisor, published by the Genealogy Club of Albuquerque, 2000, 36 pages. Includes name, city, county, page and line number. Arranged in alphabetical order by the surname. FHL book 978.968 X22h.

■ **Census Records and Substitutes Online, Luna County, New Mexico**. These databases available online via a direct link at **www.censusfinder.com:**

- 1910 Federal Census Records, Transcription of Deming Village:
- 1913 Census of Columbus
- 1919 Census of Columbus
- 1930 Federal Census Records Index – Surnames A-Chancey
- 1930 Federal Census Records Index – Surnames Chandler-Garrett
- 1930 Federal Census Records Index – Surnames Garv-Kre
- 1930 Federal Census Records Index – Surnames Kri-Parc
- 1930 Federal Census Records Index – Surnames Parg-Smiley

McKinley County

■ ***Index of Death Register for McKinley County, New Mexico, 1907-1935,*** compiled by Joyce V. Hawley Spiros, published by Verlene Publishing, Gallup, NM, 1982, 43 pages. This index does not include dates. It refers to page numbers in the original records. FHL book 978.983 V22s. Also on microfilm, filmed by the Genealogical Society of Utah, 1988, 1 roll, FHL film #1320699.

■ ***McKinley County, New Mexico Index of Probate Court Records and Wills,*** compiled by Joyce V. Hawley Spiros, published by the author, Gallup, NM, 1980, 48 pages. FHL book 978.983 P2sp. Also on microfilm, filmed by the Genealogical Society of Utah, 1988, 1 roll, FHL film #1421875.

■ **Census Records and Substitutes Online, McKinley County, New Mexico**. These databases available online via a direct link from **www.censusfinder.com:**

- 1930 Federal Census Index. Surnames starting with: [A-Case] [Casey-Gene] [George-Kuhn] [Kuipers-Nielson] [Nieto-Silva] [Silversmith-Zuniga]

Mora County

■ **1872-1956 Santa Clara Catholic Church Records, Wagon Mound, Mora County, New Mexico**, microfilm of original records at the Santa Clara Church, Wagon Mound, New Mexico. Text partly in English and partly in Spanish. Includes indexes. Includes information from surrounding missions of Cimarron, Ocate, Watrous (formerly La Junta), and others. Filmed by Golightly, El Paso, TX, 1956, 6 FHL rolls, as follows:

- Baptisms, 1872-1894 (Cimarron and Ocate); Baptisms, 1897-1901 (Ocate), FHL film #17035.
- Baptisms, 1873-1903 (Watrous); FHL film #17036.
- Baptisms, 1905-1920 (Watrous); FHL film #17037.
- Baptisms, 1920-1956 (Wagon Mound and missions), FHL film #17038.
- Confirmations, 1920-1955 (Wagon Mound and missions), FHL film #17039.
- Marriages, 1872-1889,1893-1894 (Cimarron and Ocate); Marriages, 1873-1908 (Watrous and Ocate); Marriages, 1908-1956 (Wagon Mound and missions); Deaths, 1873-1956 (Wagon Mound and missions), FHL film #17040.

■ **1892-1899 Presbyterian Church Records, Ocate, Mora County, New Mexico**, microfilm of original records at the Presbyterian Historical Society in Philadelphia, Pennsylvania. Text in Spanish. Filmed by the Genealogical Society of Utah, 1966, 1 rolls, FHL film #504311 (Session minutes, 1892-1899).

Otero County

■ **Census Records and Substitutes Online, Otero County, New Mexico**. These databases available online via a direct link at **www.censusfinder.com:**

- 1910 Federal Census of Avis
- 1930 Federal Census Index. Surnames starting with: [A-Brau] [Braz-Cory] [Cou-Galla] [Galle-Hit] [Hix-Mac] [Mad-Ne] [Ni-Robe] [Robi-S] [T-Z]

■ ***A Personalized History of Otero County, New Mexico***, by Emily Kalled Lovell, published by Star Pub., Alamogordo, NM, 1963, 39 pages. Includes towns of Alamogordo, Avis, Bent, Boles Acres, Cloudcroft, Elk, High Rolls-Mountain Park, La Luz, Mayhill, Orogrande, Pinon, Sunspot, Tularosa and Weed. FHL book 978.9 A1 No. 120.

Quay County

■ **Census Records and Substitutes Online, Otero County, New Mexico**. These databases available online via a direct link at **www.censusfinder.com:**

- 1930 Federal Census Index. Surnames starting with: [A-Brion] [Bris-Cre] [Cri-Galla] [Galle-Harm] [Harn-Kelle] [Kelly-Mays] [Mc-Os] [Ot-Roq] [Ros- Summ] [Sumr-Willh] [William-Z]

■ ***Tucumcari (Quay County, New Mexico) City Directory***, R. L. Polk and Company, Dallas, TX, 1957-1988. FHL has directories for the years 1957, 1967, and 1988. FHL book 978.926 E4h 1957-1988.

■ ***Some Early Death Records in Lincoln County, New Mexico: From File found in the Tucumcari Mortuary of Quay County, New Mexico***, copied by Charles Barnum, published 2000, 12 pages. FHL book 978.926/T1 V3b. Also on microfilm, filmed by the Genealogical Society of Utah, 2001, 1 roll, FHL film #1145773 Item 11.

Rio Arriba County

■ ***Index to New Mexico Territory Deed Record Book, Rio Arriba County, 1852-1854***, by Elias P. Clark, published by the author, no date, 11 pages. Families which occur most often in the index and transactions are Archuleta, Borrego, Clark, Lucero, Gallegos, Martinez, Martin, and Valdez. FHL book 978.9 A1. Also on microfilm, filmed by the Genealogical Society of Utah, 1982, 1 roll, FHL film #1035969.

■ **1726-1956 San Juan Pueblo, (Catholic Church Records, Rio Arriba County, New Mexico)**, microfilm of original records in the San Juan de los Caballeros Church, San Juan, New Mexico. Text in Spanish and English. Includes indexes. Church may also be known as St. John the Baptist. The church directory lists this as the head church of Chamita parish. Retakes are located at extreme end of film. Filmed by Golightly, El Paso, TX, 1956, 7 rolls, as follows:

- Baptisms 1726-1837, FHL film #16981.
- Baptisms 1849-1898, FHL film #16976.
- Baptisms 1899-1956, FHL film #16977.
- Marriages 1726-1776,1830-1836,1850-1855 (marriages 1777-1829 are not available); Deaths, 1726-1857, FHL film #16982.
- Confirmations, 1887-1954, FHL film #16978.
- Marriages, 1857-1956, FHL film #16979.
- Deaths, 1857-1956, FHL film #16980.

■ **Census Records and Substitutes Online, Rio Arriba County, New Mexico**. These databases available online via a direct link from **www.censusfinder.com:**

- 1930 Federal Census Records Index – Surnames A-Fl
- 1930 Federal Census Records Index – Surnames Fr-Loo
- 1930 Federal Census Records Index – Surnames Lopez-Montoya
- 1930 Federal Census Records Index – Surnames Morris-Schl
- 1930 Federal Census Records Index – Surnames Schu-Z

Roosevelt County

■ *50 Years of Marriages in Roosevelt County, NM,* compiled by the Roosevelt County Searchers Genealogical Society, Portales, NM, 2001, 330 pages. Includes name of bride and groom, marriage date, book and page number. Arranged in alphabetical order in two sections by the last name of groom and by the last name of the bride. FHL book 978.932 V2f. Also on microfilm, filmed by the Genealogical Society of Utah, 2001, 1 roll, FHL film # 1440533.

■ ***Marriages Performed in the Area of Curry County, New Mexico, 1905-1908, When it Was Still a Part of Roosevelt County, New Mexico Territory,*** copied by Sallie Foster and Louise Reithel, published by the Curry County Genealogical Society of New Mexico, 1985, 8 pages. Transcripts are in the Curry Courthouse located in Clovis, New Mexico. Includes groom's name, bride's names, date, book number, page number, and brides' index. FHL book 978.9 A1 No. 18.

■ **1903 Tax List, Roosevelt County, New Mexico Territory**, in *Roosevelt County Searchers Genealogical Society,* Vol. 1, No. 2 (Aug 1998) through Vol. 2, No. 2 (Apr 1999).

■ **Census Records and Substitutes Online, Roosevelt County, New Mexico**. These databases available online via a direct link from **www.censusfinder.com:**

- Early Settlers in the Long Community
- 1910 Federal Census Images
- 1920 Federal Census Images
- 1909-1918 Death Register
- 1915-1920 Long Mercantile Ledger
- 1930 Federal Census Index. Surnames starting with: [A-Breshears] [Breshears-Cot] [Couch-Finley] [Finley-Hallford] [Halloway-Johnson] [Johnson-Lowe] [Loy-Morris] [Morrison-Rawley][Ray-Smith] [Smith-Usrey] [Usrey-Z]

Sandoval County

■ ***Inventory of the County Archives of New Mexico, No. 23, Sandoval County (Bernalillo),*** prepared by the New Mexico Historical Records Survey, Service Division, War Services Section, Work Projects Administration, 1939, 180 pages. This is an inventory of all county records at the Sandoval County Courthouse in Bernalillo, New

Mexico as of 1939. FHL book 978.957 A3h. Also on microfilm, filmed by the Genealogical Society of Utah, 1993, 1 roll, FHL film #1697891, item 7.

■ ***1736-1873 New Mexico Baptisms - San Buenaventura de Cochiti Church***, extracted by Donald Dreesen and Evelyn Lujan Baca; compiled by Margaret Leonard Windham and Evelyn Lujan Baca, published by the New Mexico Genealogical Society, Albuquerque, NM, 2000, 409 pages. FHL book 978.957 K2d.

■ **1830 Santo Domingo Census**, in the *New Mexico Genealogist*, a periodical of the New Mexico Genealogical Society, Albuquerque, NM, in Vol. 33, No. 1 (Mar 1994) through Vol. 33, No. 3 (Sep 1994).

■ **1903-1937 Deeds, 1903-1926 Deed Indexes, Sandoval County, New Mexico**, microfilm of original records at the Sandoval County Courthouse in Bernalillo, New Mexico and at the New Mexico State Archives in Santa Fe, New Mexico. Some of the warranty deeds are recorded in English and Spanish. Some of the typed sheets have "bleed thru" and the records may be hard to read. Filmed by the Genealogical Society of Utah, 2003-2004, 9 rolls, beginning with FHL film #2203679.

■ **Census Records and Substitutes Online, Sandoval County, New Mexico.** These databases available online via a direct link from **www.censusfinder.com:**

- 1930 Federal Census Index. Surnames starting with: [A-B] [B-C] [C-D] [D-G] [G-H] [H-L] [L-M] [M] [M-Q] [Q-S] [S-T] [T-Z]

San Juan County

■ ***Early Marriage Records, San Juan County, New Mexico, 1887-1912***, compiled and published by the Totah Tracers Genealogical Society, Farmington, New Mexico, no date, 57 pages. From Preface: "The early San Juan County marriage records were recorded in two books. These two books have been combined into one publication divided into two sections, with each section indexed separately. Our publication shows the date of marriage and the name of the bride and groom." Includes indexes. FHL book 978.9 A1 No. 112.

■ ***1910 Census Records, Farmington Precinct, San Juan County, New Mexico***, presented by Norma H. Jameson and presented through the Daughters of the American Revolution. Desert Gold Chapter, San Juan County, New Mexico. Arranged in alphabetical order and gives name, page number and precinct number. Farmington precinct seems to be precinct 5. FHL book 978.9 A1 No. 60. Also on microfiche, filmed by the Genealogical Society of Utah, 1996, 1 fiche, FHL fiche #6125696.

■ **1919-1927 Probate Records, San Juan County, New Mexico**, microfilm of original records at the New Mexico State Archives in Santa Fe, New Mexico. Filmed by the Genealogical Society of Utah, 2004, 1 roll, FHL film #203672.

San Miguel County

■ ***Inventory of the County Archives of New Mexico, No. 24, San Miguel County (Las Vegas)***, prepared by the New Mexico Historical Records Survey, Service Division, War Services Section, Work Projects Administration, 1941, 267 pages. This is an inventory of all county records at the San Miguel County Courthouse in Las Vegas, New Mexico as of 1941. FHL book 978.955 A3h. Also on microfilm, filmed by the Genealogical Society of Utah, 1993, 1 roll, FHL film #1697891, item 8.

■ ***Albuquerque and Las Vegas Business Directory for 1883***, microfilm of original directory published by Armijo Brothers & Borradaile, 1883, 97 pages. Filmed by University Microfilms International, Ann Arbor, MI, 1970, FHL film

#1303032 (Albuquerque and Las Vegas Business Directory for 1883).

■ **Census Records and Substitutes Online, San Miguel County, New Mexico**. These databases available online via a direct link from **www.censusfinder.com:**

- 1930 Federal Census Index. Surnames starting with: [A-Arch] [Arch-Bare] [Bare-Cari] [Carl-Dear] [Dear-Euch] [Euci-Gall] [Gall-Gomez] [Gomez-Gran] [Grand-Herr] [Herr-Law] [Lay-Luc] [Luc-Mae] [Mae-Mar] [Mar-Mon] [Mon-Ortiz] [Mon-Ortiz] [Ortiz-Peters] [Peters-Raybal] [Raybal-Ruiz] [Ruiz-Sas] [Sast-Spo] [Spr-Tru] [Tru-Varela] [Vas-Z]

Santa Ana County (1850-1876)

An original county of New Mexico Territory in 1850, Santa Ana was annexed by Bernalillo County in 1876. Censuses under the name Santa Ana County exist for the 1850, 1860, and 1870 federal censuses of New Mexico Territory, as follows:

- **1850** Federal Census, New Mexico Territory, Santa Ana and Santa Fe Counties, FHL film #443666.
- **1860** Federal Census, New Mexico Territory (2nd filming) Santa Ana, Mora, and Valencia Counties, FHL film #803716.
- **1870** Federal Census, New Mexico Territory (2nd filming) San Miguel and Santa Ana Counties, FHL #552394.

Santa Fe County

■ **1710-1860 Santa Fe Church Records**. See *Santa Cruz de la Cañada, Baptisms, 1710-1860: Baptism Database of Archives Held by the Archdiocese of Santa Fe and the State Archives of New Mexico*, database entry by Thomas D. Martinez, Benito Estevan Montoya and Rosina Lasalle (nee Vigil), published San Jose, CA, 1993, 498 pages. Includes name, date of baptism, name of parents and godparents if recorded. Arranged in alphabetical order by surname. FHL book 978.956 K2ms.

■ *1728-1857 New Mexico Marriages - Santa Fe - St. Francis Parish and Military Chapel of Our Lady of Light (La Castrense)*, extracted by Marie J. Roybal and Lila Armijo Pfeufer; compiled by Margaret Leonard Windham and Evelyn Lujan Baca, published by the New Mexico Genealogical Society, Albuquerque, NM, 1997, 417 pages. Includes several indexes. FHL book 978.956 K28r.

■ **1747-1851 Santa Fe Church Records.** See *New Mexico Baptisms of Santa Fe: Parroquia de San Francisco de Assisi (Parish of Saint Francis of Assisi)*, compiled by Margaret Leonard Windham and Evelyn Lujan Baca, published by the New Mexico Genealogical Society, Albuquerque, NM, 2002, 4 vols. Includes bibliographic references. Includes indexes for baptisms, parents, godparents, grandparents and others. Contents: vol. 1: 5 September 1747 to 17 July 1791; vol. 2: 15 August 1796 to 30 December 1822; vol. 3: 1 January 1823 to 26 June 1833; Castrense register, 9 June 1798 to 26 June 1833; vol. 4: 18 February 1839 to 17 July 1851. FHL book 978.956/S1 K2w v. 1-4. See also **1747-1851 Santa Fe Baptisms,** database of archives held by the archdiocese of Santa Fe and the state archive of New Mexico, database entry by Thomas D. Martinez, Benito Estevan Montoya, Rosina Lasalle (nee Vigil), published San Jose, CA, 1993, 606 pages. FHL book 978.956 K2m.

■ *1747-1763; 1753-1770 Births or Christenings, San Francisco de Assisi (Cathedral), Santa Fe, Santa Fe, New Mexico*, computer printout; births or christenings, compiled by the Genealogical Department, The Church of Jesus Christ of Latter-day Saints. Filmed by the Genealogical Society of Utah, 1977, 2 rolls, FHL film #1205005 (1747-1763), and FHL film #12005472 (1753-1770).

■ **1821 Santa Fe Census,** see ***New Mexico Province, Santa Fe Parish, census of 1821,*** compiled by Patricia Black Esterly, published by the New Mexico Genealogical Society, Albuquerque, NM, 1994, 165 pages. Includes index. Contains Santa Fe with barrios of San Francisco, Torreon, San Miguel and Nuestra Senora de Guadalupe and outlying districts with partidos of Rio Tesuque, Galisteo and Cienega y Ranchos. FHL book 978.956 X2e.

■ **1868-1922 Mortgage Records, Santa Fe County, New Mexico,** microfilm of original records at the Santa Fe County Courthouse in Santa Fe, New Mexico. Some of the records are recorded in Spanish. Some pages are light and faded and may be hard or difficult to read. The office of Probate Clerk and Recorder were held by the same person. Salt Lake City, Utah: Filmed by the Genealogical Society of Utah, 2004, 9 rolls, beginning with FHL film #2312938 (Mortgage records, Vol. A-B, 1869-1881).

■ **1900-1951 Marriage Records, Santa Fe County, New Mexico,** microfilm of original records at the Santa Fe County Courthouse in Santa Fe, New Mexico. The office of Probate Clerk and Recorder were held by the same person. Includes index in each volume. The marriage books change from page numbers to certificate numbers. Filmed by the Genealogical Society of Utah, 2004. 12 rolls, beginning with FHL film #2312279 (Marriages, 1900-1910).

■ **1928-1935 Santa Fe (New Mexico) City Directories,** microfilm of original records located in various libraries and societies. Microfilm of original records by various publishers. Filmed by Research Publications, Woodbridge, CT, 1990, 1 roll, FHL film #2309618 (contains 1928-1929, 1930-1931, 1932-1933, and 1934-1935 directories).

■ **Census Records and Substitutes Online, Santa Fe County, New Mexico.** These databases available online via a direct link from **www.censusfinder.com:**

- 1900 Federal Census Records Index for Precinct 1 – Pojoaque
- 1900 Federal Census Records for Precinct 1 – Pojoaque - Pages 1A-4B
- 1900 Federal Census Records for recinct 1 – Pojoaque - Pages 5A-8B
- 1900 Federal Census Images
- 1930 Federal Census Index. Surnames starting with: [A-Bald] [Bali-Cate] [Catr-Dom] [Don-Garas] [Garcia-Gonzales] [Gonzalez-Jimenes] [Jimenez-Luh] [Luj-Martin] [Martinez-Montez] [Monto-Oro] [Ort-Per] [Pet-Rod] [Roe-Salav] [Salaz-Star] [Stas-Vie] [Vig-Z]

Sierra County

■ ***Inventory of the County Archives of New Mexico, No. 26, Sierra County,*** prepared by the New Mexico Historical Records Survey, Service Division, War Services Section, Work Projects Administration, 1942, 272 pages. This is an inventory of all county records at the Sierra County Courthouse in Hot Springs (now Truth or Consequences), New Mexico as of 1942. FHL book 978.967 A3h. Also on microfilm, filmed by the Genealogical Society of Utah, 1993, 1 roll, FHL film #1697891, item 4.

■ **1884-1948 Marriage Records, Sierra County, New Mexico,** see ***Sierra County, New Mexico, Marriage Records,*** originally compiled by Iva Hartsell Weiss; expanded and augmented by Elinor Weiss Peacock; edited by Tillie Torres Candelaria, et al., published by the Sierra County Genealogical Society, Truth or Consequences, NM, 1990, 1998, 3 vols. Includes groom and bride indexes. Arranged in alphabetical order by groom's name and gives the names of the groom and bride, their birthdates, birth places, ages, date and place of marriage, name and title of official, book and page number, filing date, and remarks. Information is not always complete. Contents: vol. 1: 1884 to 1920; vol. 2: 1918-1938 (books 2-3); vol. 3: 19 Apr 1938-30 Oct 1948 (books 4-5). FHL book 978.967 V2w vol. 1-4.

■ **Census Records and Substitutes Online, Sierra County, New Mexico**. These databases available online via a direct link at: **www.censusfinder.com:**

- 1930 Federal Census Index. Surnames starting with: [A- Chaves] [Chaves – Heath] [Heath-Miranda] [Miranda-Sedillos] [Sedillos-Zook]
- Founding Families of Rio Abajo Database

Socorro County

■ **1821-1853 Marriage Records, Socorro County, New Mexico**, see ***San Miguel del Socorro, New Mexico Marriage Records, 1821-1853,*** extracted by Joe Sanchez III; edited by Antoinette Duran Silva, published by J. Sanchez, Whittier, CA, 1999, 112 pages. Information was extracted from marriage books A & B. Includes index. FHL book 978.962/S1 K2s.

■ **1821-1956 Socorro Church Records**, microfilm of original records in the San Miguel Catholic Church, Socorro, New Mexico. Text partly in English and partly in Spanish. Includes indexes. Includes information from the San Marcial Mission and other nearby churches. Filmed by Golightly, El Paso, TX, 1957, 5 FHL rolls, as follows:

- Baptisms, 1821-1850, FHL film #16993.
- Baptisms, 1865-1931; Confirmations, 1877-1919; Baptisms 1894-1921 (San Marcial), FHL film #16994.
- Baptisms, 1921-1934 (San Marcial); Marriages, 1921-1931 (San Marcial); Deaths, 1921-1933 (San Marcial); Confirmations, 1926 (San Marcial); First communion, 1940-1944 (San Marcial), Baptisms, 1932-1956; Confirmations, 1900-1955, FHL film #16995.
- Marriages, 1821-1853; Deaths, 1821-1853, FHL film #16996.
- Marriages, 1882-1956; Marriages, 1883-1921 (San Marcial); Deaths, 1913-1956; Baptisms, 1869-1885 (San Marcial); Confirmations, 1869-1872 (San Marcial), FHL film #16997.

■ ***New Mexico Censuses of 1833 and 1845: Socorro and Surrounding Communities of the Rio Abajo,*** by Teresa Ramírez Alief, Jose Gonzales, Patricia Black Esterly, published by the New Mexico Genealogical Society, Albuquerque, NM, 1994, 153 pages. Includes index. FHL book 978.962 X2a.

■ **Census Records and Substitutes Online, Socorro County, New Mexico**. These databases available online via a direct link from **www.censusfinder.com:**

- Sierra, Socorro & Valencia Counties Database
- 1819 Militia List for Sabinal / Belen

Taos County

■ ***1770-1860 Index to Taos Marriages,*** extracted by David Salazar, indexed by Bill Trujillo. Published by the Genealogical Society of Hispanic America, Southern California Branch, Santa Fe Springs, CA, 1994, 152 pages. Arranged in alphabetical order by surname. May include name, relationship, page number, and date of marriage. FHL book 978.953 VC22s.

■ ***Early Taos Censuses and Historical Sources, 1790-1841,*** compiled by Julián Josué Vigil, microfilm of original published by J. J. Vigil, 1983, 172 pages. Includes index. Contains: 1790 census for Taos (incomplete); "Spaniards from the jurisdiction of Taos" Militia muster rolls, 1806 for Taos (incomplete); 1841 census for Taos; Ranchos de Taos Appendices: Taos genealogical materials in the archives of the Archdiocese of Santa Fe, microfilm edition; Taos materials in Fr. Angélico Chávez, "Archives of the Archdiocese of Santa Fe" (1957). Taos priests to 1850. (starts in 1701); Taos materials in Twitchell's "Spanish archives of New Mexico," v. 1-2. Above documents in "Calendar of microfilm edition of the Spanish archives of New Mexico, 1621-1821"; Additional Taos materials in above "Calendar" (no Twitchell numbers). Early Taos materials in the Ritch Collection, Huntington Library, plus one Bancroft Library item. Taos materials listed in "Calendar of the microfilm edition of the Mexican archives of New Mexico" (1970). Filmed by the New Mexico State Archives, 1983, 4 fiches, FHL fiche #6331382.

■ **1701-1956 Church Records, Our Lady of Guadalupe Catholic Church, Taos, New Mexico**, microfilm of original records in the Our Lady of Guadalupe Church, Taos, New Mexico. Text partly in English and partly in Spanish. Includes indexes. Filmed by Golightly, El Paso, TX, 1957, 14 rolls, as follows:

- Baptisms, 1701-1837, FHL film #17020.
- Baptisms, 1837-1850, FHL film 17021.
- Baptisms, 1850-1879, FHL film #17010.
- Baptisms, 1866-1871,1880-1887, FHL film #17011.
- Baptisms, 1887-1915, FHL film #17012.
- Baptisms, 1915-1925, FHL film #17013.
- Baptisms, 1925-1933, FHL film #17014.
- Baptisms, 1933-1956, FHL film #17015.
- Confirmations, 1894-1955, FHL film #17016.
- Marriages, 1777-1856, FHL film #17022.
- Marriages, 1856-1895, FHL film #17017.
- Marriages, 1895-1956, FHL film #17018.
- Deaths, 1827-1850, FHL film #17023.
- Deaths, 1850-1956, FHL film #17019.

■ **1852-1869 Church Records, Our Lady of Sorrows Church, Arroyo Hondo, New Mexico**, microfilm of original records in the Our Lady of Sorrows Church, Arroyo Hondo, Taos County, New Mexico. Text in Spanish. Contents: Baptisms, 1852-1869; Marriages, 1852-1869; Deaths, 1852-1869. There are confirmations with the baptisms. Filmed by Golightly, El Paso, TX, 1956. FHL film #16622.

■ ***Abstract of Title to the Entire Sangre de Cristo Grant, 1853-1920***, typescript, author-publisher-date not noted, 14 pages. Shows the chain of title to the entire Sangre de Cristo grant, from the original source of title to Morton C. Fisher, and the chain of title to the original Costilla Estate from Morton C. Fisher to the United States Freehold Land and Emigration Company. FHL book 978.9 A1 No. 5 and FHL film #962324.

■ **Census Records and Substitutes Online, Taos County, New Mexico**. These databases available online via a direct link at **www.censusfinder.com:**

- 1701-1709 Baptisms
- 1710-1719 Baptisms
- 1720-1726 Baptisms
- 1775-1777 Baptisms
- 1777-1779 Baptisms
- 1779-1828 Baptisms at Picuries Catholic Church
- 1832-1857 Baptisms
- 1860 Federal Census Records
- 1885 Veterans Census Records
- 1885 Census Mortality Schedules
- 1910 Federal Census Records Index
- 1917-1918 Draft Registrations
- 1918-1919 Deaths Caused by the Spanish Flu Epidemic

Torrance County

■ ***Inventory of the County Archives of New Mexico, No. 29, Torrance County (Estancia)***, prepared by the Historical Records Survey, Division of Professional and Service Projects, Works Progress Administration, 1939, 181 pages. This is an inventory of all county records at the Torrance County Courthouse in Estancia, New Mexico as of 1939. FHL book. 978.963 A3h.

■ **1858-1956 Church Records, Our Lady of Sorrows Catholic Church**, microfilm of original records in the Our Lady of Sorrow Church, Manzano, Torrance County, New Mexico. Text partly in English and partly in Spanish. Includes indexes. Filmed by Golightly, El Paso, TX, 1956, 2 FHL rolls, as follows:

- Baptisms, 1867-1956, FHL film #16845.
- Deaths, 1858-1946; Confirmations, 1868-1955; Marriages, 1876-1956; Deaths, 1946-1956, FHL film #16846.

■ ***A Genealogical Index of Early Torrance County, New Mexico, Deeds: 1903 to 1920***, compiled by Morton L. Ervin; Doris Ann Ervin; Barbara Duckworth, published by Ervin Publishing, Albuquerque, NM, 1998, 241 pages. Includes index to grantors. May include name of grantor and grantee, date of instrument, type of instrument, and date of recording. Arranged in alphabetical order by surname of grantee. FHL book 978.963 R22e.

■ **1912-1956 Church records, St. Alice Mission Catholic Church**, microfilm of original records in the St. Alice Mission, Mountainair, Torrance County, New Mexico. Text partly in English and partly in Spanish. Includes indexes. Filmed by Golightly, El Paso, TX, 1956, 2 rolls, as follows:

- Baptisms, 1912-1956, FHL film #16847.
- Confirmations, 1917-1955; Marriages, 1915-1956; Deaths, 1929-1956, FHL film #16848.

■ **Census Records and Substitutes Online, Torrance County, New Mexico**. These databases available online via a direct link from **www.censusfinder.com:**

- 1930 Federal Census Index. Surnames starting with: [A-Bowden] [Bowden-Colb] [Cole-Garcia] [Garcia-Irwin] [Isenhart-Maes] [Maest-Otero] [Otero-Sanchez] [Sanchez-Tapia] [Tapia-Z]
- First Families of Torrance County

Union County

■ ***New Mexico Marriages, Union County***, extracted by June Lofgreen; edited by Margaret Leonard Windham, published by the New Mexico Genealogical Society, Albuquerque, NM, 1994, 1998, 3 vols. Includes index. Contents: vol. 1: 1893-1940; vol. 2: 1941-1955; vol. 3: 1956-1990. Arranged in alphabetical order by surname of groom. FHL has bound vols. 1-3 together, FHL book 978.923 V28L vol. 1-3.

■ **Union County, New Mexico Death Records**, compiled by June Lofgreen, microfilm of information gathered from Union County newspaper death notices and obituaries, cemetery inscriptions, mortuary records, and some death certificates. Includes index. Includes Clayton, New Mexico burials: Clayton Cemetery, IOOF Cemetery, Clayton Memorial Cemetery, and Old Clayton Cemetery; Miscellaneous burials: Burial place unknown, cremated, ranch burials, and war causalities; Union County burials out of Clayton; New Mexico burials out of Union County; Burials outside of New Mexico. Filmed by the Genealogical Society of Utah, 1995, 1 roll, FHL film #1750790.

■ **1907-1956 Catholic Church Records, Clayton, New Mexico**, microfilm of original records in the St. Francis Xavier Church, Clayton, New Mexico. Text in Spanish and English. St. Francis Xavier was formerly Our Lady of Sorrows. Includes indexes. Includes baptisms of the St. Joseph of Nazareth Hospital, Clayton, Union, New Mexico. Also includes baptisms and confirmations of the St. Joseph Church, Folsom, Union, New Mexico. Filmed by Golightly, El Paso, TX, 1956, 2 rolls, as follows:

- Baptisms, 1907-1930 (St. Joseph); Baptisms, 1927-1955 (St. Francis Xavier); Baptisms, 1922-1938 (St. Joseph of Nazareth); Confirmations, 1921-1941 (St. Joseph); Confirmations, 1946-1956 (St. Francis Xavier), FHL film #16750.
- Marriages, 1907-1956 (St. Francis Xavier); Deaths, 1907-1956 (St. Francis Xavier); Confirmations, 1909 (St. Francis Xavier), FHL film #16751.

■ **Census Records and Substitutes Online, Union County, New Mexico**. These databases available online via a direct link at **www.censusfinder.com:**

- Early Residents, Settlers and Homesteaders
- 1930 Federal Census Index. Surnames starting with: [A-Bowen] [Bowers- Coster] [Coston-Fitz] [Fla-Hardin] [Hardw-Kiser] [Kite- McKas] [McKay-Palm] [Par-Sala] [Sals-Str] [Stu-Weh] [Wei-Z]

Valencia County

■ ***New Mexico Baptisms [Tome, Valencia County]: Nuestra Señora de la Inmaculada Concepción de Tomé***, extracted by Margaret L. Buxton, et al.; compiled by Margaret Leonard Windham and Evelyn Lujan Baca, published by the New Mexico Genealogical Society, Albuquerque, NM, 1998. Includes index. Contents: vol. 1: 22 March 1793-8 May 1853. FHL book 978.992 K2b.

■ **Deed records, 1873-1922, 1930-1964; Indexes, 1873-1925, Valencia County, New Mexico,** microfilm of original records at the Valencia County Court House in Los Lunas, New Mexico. Deeds may be recorded in English or Spanish. The County Clerk also acted as the County Recorder. Some pages are faded and light and may be hard and difficult to read. The Old Spanish Grants, Inc., was a corporation organized in California and had its main offices in Los Angeles, California. It sold property within the exterior boundaries of the Nicholas Duran de Chavez Grant or San Clemente Grant in Valencia County, New Mexico. The corporation also sold property within the town of Dalies, Valencia County, New Mexico. Some volumes also contain bonds and oaths of office, notary public, etc. Some volumes include separate indexes. Filmed by the Genealogical Society of Utah, 1988, 2004, 13 rolls, beginning with FHL film #2388332 (Indirect index to real property, grantee, 1873-1926).

■ **1877 Tax Payers, Valencia County, New Mexico Territory**, in *New Mexico Genealogist*, Vol. 34, No. 3 (Sep 1995).

■ **1890 Poll Tax List, Valencia County, New Mexico Territory**, in *New Mexico Genealogist*, Vol. 37, No. 3 (Sep 1998).

■ **1905-1950 Marriage Records, Valencia County, New Mexico**, microfilm of original records at the Valencia County Courthouse in Los Lunas, New Mexico. Includes index in each volume. Filmed by the Genealogical Society of Utah, 2004, 7 rolls, as follows:

- Marriage records, vol. 1, 1905-1910, FHL film #2388039.
- Marriage records, vol. 2-4, 1910-1921,FHL film #2388189.
- Marriage records, vol. 5-7, 1921-1931, FHL film #2311199.
- Marriage records, vol. 8-10, 1931-1937, FHL film #2388190.
- Marriage records, vol. 11-13, 1937-1942, film #2388191.
- Marriage records, vol. 13-15, 1942-1947, film #2388192.
- Marriage records, vol. 16-17, 1947-1950, FHL film #2388330.

■ **1907-1928 Register of Deaths, Valencia County, New Mexico**, microfilm of original records in the Valencia County Courthouse in Los Lunas, New Mexico. Includes index. Lists name of deceased, date of death, place of death, sex, race, occupation, age, cause of death, place of burial, and other information. Filmed by the Genealogical Society of Utah, 2004, 1 roll, FHL film #2388039.

■ **Census Records and Substitutes Online, Valencia County, New Mexico**. These databases available online via a direct link from **www.censusfinder.com:**

- 1750 Spanish Colonial Census Records for Belen
- 1930 Federal Census Index. Surnames starting with: [A-Awe] [Awl-Blia] [Block- Chaves] [Chavez-Contr] [Contu-Gallegos] [Gallegos-Gonzales] [Gonzales-Jaramillo] [Jaramillo-Louis] [Louis-Mason] [Mason-Oliguin] [Oliguin-Perea] [Perez-Romero] [Romero-Sanchez] [Sanchez-Silva] [Silva-Tucker] [Tucker-Zwick]
- Sierra, Socorro & Valencia Counties Database
- Original Settlers of Village of Belen
- 1825 Residents of Belen (source is 1825 tax list)

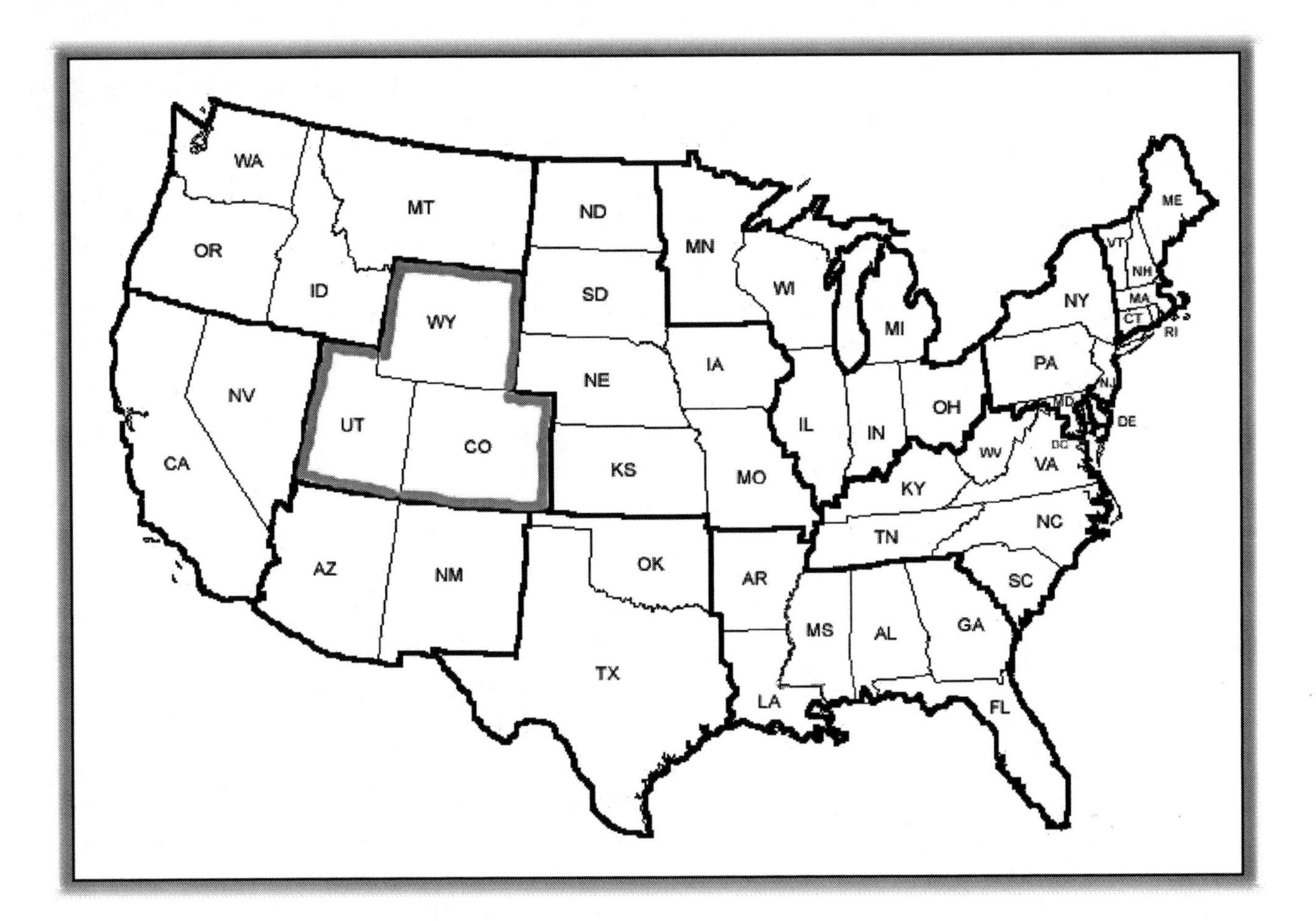

Chapter 4W – The Mountain West

Colorado, Utah, and Wyoming

Colorado

Timeline, 1541-1900

1541. After months of searching for the Seven Cities of Cibola as far north as Kansas, Spanish Conquistador Vasquez de Coronado finally gave up, and headed back to Mexico via the southeastern corner of present Colorado. The route Coronado followed would later be called the Santa Fe trail.

1682. French explorers Cavalier and La Salle erect a cross near the mouth of the Mississippi River, claim the entire Mississippi Basin for France, and name the region Louisiana after King Louis XIV. The Louisiana area included all of present Colorado east of the Rocky Mountains.

1763. Treaty of Paris ending the French and Indian War in North America removes France from Louisiana. The area west of the Mississippi River becomes Spanish territory, the area east of the river becomes British territory.

1765. Spanish explorer Juan Maria Rivera leads an expedition into the San Juan and Sangre de Cristo Mountains in search of gold and silver.

1776. Fathers Silvestre Velez de Escalante and Francisco Atanasio Dominguez seek a new route from New Mexico to California, explore present Colorado and Utah.

1802. Napoleon defeats Spain in battle. As spoils of war, he takes ownership of Louisiana again in exchange for a couple of duchies in northern Italy.

1803 Louisiana Purchase. The United States acquires Louisiana from Napoleon, a vast area which had as a legal description, "the drainage of the Mississippi and Missouri rivers," including all of Colorado east of the Rocky Mountains. However, Spain disagrees with that description and still claims most of the Louisiana tract, including present Colorado. From their base in Santa Fe, the Spanish vow to vigorously defend the area from any American intruders.

1804. Lewis and Clark's Corps of Discovery leave St. Louis via the Missouri River in search of a passage to the Pacific Ocean. Soon after, Spanish troops were dispatched from Santa Fe to Colorado to intercept and arrest them, but Lewis and Clark found the route north of Colorado to be more easily crossed. They were well into present South Dakota by the time the Spanish troops finally gave up looking for them.

1806. Lieutenant Zebulon Pike and a small party of U.S. soldiers sent to explore routes across the Louisiana Purchase to the Rocky Mountains. Pike discovers a peak that now bears his name, but fails in an effort to climb it. The party reached the headwaters of the Arkansas River near present Leadville, Colorado.

1807. Pike crosses the Sangre de Cristo Mountains to the Conejos River in the San Luis Valley and builds Pike's Stockade. He is soon placed under arrest by Spanish troops and taken to Santa Fe; but he and his men are released after a few days. Pike's written account of his expedition was the first English language description of the Spanish culture in North America.

1819. Spanish-American treaty (often called the Adams-Onís treaty) sets the boundary between the United States and Spanish territory, which included the Red River as the boundary between Spanish Texas and Arkansas Territory, and the Arkansas River as the division between the Spanish Province of Nuevo Mexico with Missouri Territory. As a result of the treaty, only the northeastern section of present Colorado remained in the United States (the area east of the Continental Divide and north of the Arkansas River).

1820. Major Stephen H. Long sent by President Monroe to explore the Colorado region of the Louisiana Purchase. Long's party came up the South Platte River. Long's Peak named for him. Dr. Edwin James, historian of Long's expedition, leads the first recorded ascent of Pike's Peak. James Peak, west of Denver, was named for him.

1821. Mexico gains independence from Spain and reaffirms the 1819 Spanish-American treaty line as the now Mexican-American boundary. Mexico holds lands from Texas to present New Mexico, Arizona, and California; plus southern and western Colorado, and all of Utah and Nevada. Also in 1821, the first traders from the United States came into the Mexican Province of Nuevo Mexico via southeastern Colorado on what would become known as the Mountain Route of the Santa Fe Trail.

1825. Fur-traders, trappers and Mountain Men begin operations in present Colorado, including the Bent brothers, Ceran St. Vrain, Louis Vasquez, Kit Carson, Jim Baker, James Bridger, Thomas Fitzpatrick, "Uncle Dick" Wooten, and Jim Beckworth. The first trading posts they established were located in the Arkansas and South Platte Valleys.

1832. Bent's Fort is built by the Bents and St. Vrain near the present city of La Junta. For those following the Arkansas River from Fort Dodge, Bent's Fort becomes an important stop on the Mountain Route of the Santa Fe Trail.

1836. The new Republic of Texas asserts a claim to all land east of the Rio Grande through present New Mexico and a narrow strip of mountain territory extending into Colorado as far north as the 42nd parallel. In 1841, Texas soldiers invaded the area, but were never successful in taking political control away from Mexico.

1842. Lieutenant John C. Fremont undertakes the first of his five exploration trips into the Rocky Mountains and beyond.

1845. As a condition of the annexation of Texas to the United States, the Texas Claim to parts of New Mexico and Colorado is purchased by the United States. A war with Mexico results from this action.

1846. General Stephen W. Kearney leads troops along the Santa Fe Trail through southeastern Colorado en route to the conquest of New Mexico during the Mexican War. Kearney establishes the provisional New Mexico Territory, which operates under U.S. protection until officially established by Congress in 1850. New Mexico Territory included a portion of present Colorado south of the Arkansas River.

1848. At the Treaty of Guadalupe Hidalgo ending the war with Mexico, the United States annexes the area of present California, Nevada, Utah, Arizona (north of the Gila River), New Mexico, and that part of Colorado west of the Continental Divide. The U.S. paid Mexico a sum of fifteen million dollars for an area that was over half of the Republic of Mexico and comparable in size to the Louisiana Purchase.

1850. Federal Census taken in New Mexico Territory (Jun 1850) and Utah Territory (Apr 1851). New Mexico Territory included present Colorado south of the Arkansas River, Utah Territory included present western Colorado; while most of eastern Colorado was in the "Unorganized Territory" of the great plains. Although there may have been upwards of 2,000 Mountain Men roaming the Rocky Mountain Range, no population was recorded in any of the Colorado areas.

1851. First permanent non-Indian settlement in Colorado is founded at Conejos in the San Luis Valley; irrigation is begun; Fort Massachusetts is established.

1853. Captain John W. Gunnison leads exploring party across southern and western Colorado. Also in this year, John C. Fremont's last expedition, seeking a feasible railroad route through the mountains, follows Gunnison's route through the San Luis Valley and into the Gunnison River country.

1854. Kansas and Nebraska Territories established. Both extend from the Missouri River to the Continental Divide. The area of present Colorado is now within four U.S. Territories: Utah, New Mexico, Kansas, and Nebraska.

1858. Green Russell's discovery of placer gold deposits near the confluence of the South Platte River and Cherry Creek, precipitates a gold rush from the East. The "Pikes Peak or Bust" slogan begins. Montana City, St. Charles, Auraria, and Denver City are founded. Pueblo founded as Fountain City. Arapahoe County, Kansas Territory is organized.

1859. Jefferson Territory organized to govern mining camps and first towns of present Colorado; officers are elected, and several counties established. The territorial government is never sanctioned by the U.S. Congress, but operates with the consent of the local population. Also in this year, prospectors spread through the mountains and establish camps at Boulder, Colorado City, Gold Hill, Hamilton, Tarryall, and Pueblo. Gold is found by George A. Jackson along Chicago Creek on present site of Idaho Springs. John Gregory makes famous gold-lode strike on North Clear Creek, stimulating a rush of prospectors, who establish camps of Black Hawk, Central City and Nevadaville.

1860 Federal Census. The U.S. Census Office ignores Jefferson Territory, but includes an enumeration of the inhabitants of present Colorado as part of four U.S. territories: 1) Utah Territory: no Colorado population; 2) New Mexico Territory: the settlements in the San Luis Valley of Mora County; 3) Kansas Territory: the mining camps and towns in Arapahoe County; and 4) Nebraska Territory: Boulder, Altoona, and other northwestern towns at the end of the Nebraska census schedules labeled as *Unorganized Area West of 101°30′*. Also in 1860, rich placer discoveries cause a stampede of miners to California Gulch at the present site of Leadville. The Colorado region continues to be administered by Jefferson Territory officials, and Miners' and People's Courts.

1861. After a successful invasion of the Rio Grande Valley by Confederate troops, the Confederate Territory of Arizona is declared with the capital at La Mesilla. The territory included the southern half of present New Mexico and Arizona.

1861 Colorado Territory. Partly in reaction to the confederate incursion into New Mexico, Colorado Territory is established by the U.S. Congress with the same boundaries as the present state, ending the ephemeral reign of Jefferson Territory. The first Colorado Territorial Assembly meets, creates 17 counties, authorizes a university, and selects Colorado City as the capital. As part of the organic act creating Colorado Territory, a territory-wide census was required. In late 1861, the territory conducted a census as part of an election poll taken by each of the county assessors, the combined county name lists now called the *1861 Poll Book for Colorado*.

1862. Colorado troops are instrumental in defeating Confederate General Henry H. Sibley's Army at La Glorieta Pass. The confederate control of New Mexico/Arizona ends, and the U.S. Territory of New Mexico continues. The Colorado Territorial capital moved to Golden.

1866. Colorado Territorial Census/Poll List taken by county assessors. List includes names of males over 21. Only two county lists survive.

1867. Denver established as the new capital of Colorado Territory.

1870 Federal Census. Population of Colorado Territory at 39,864. Also in 1870, the Denver and Pacific Railroad is constructed to connect Denver with the Union Pacific at Cheyenne, Wyoming Territory.

1876. Colorado is admitted to the Union as the 38th State, one hundred years after the Declaration of Independence of the United States, hence, Colorado's nickname becomes "The Centennial State."

1880 Federal Census. Population of Colorado at 194,327.

1885. Colorado State Census taken with federal assistance.

1900 Federal Census. Population of Colorado at 539,700. In 1900, Gold production reaches a peak of more than $20,000,000 annually at Cripple Creek, the second richest gold camp in the world.

COLORADO

Censuses & Substitutes, 1859-1935

The Territory of Colorado conducted censuses in 1861 and 1866. The 1861 name lists survive (as poll lists) and have been extracted and indexed as the *1861 Colorado Poll Book.* Although there is evidence that the statistics of the 1866 census was in fact reported by the Governor to the state legislature, there is no record of the 1866 name lists ever being collected at the state level. The 1866 census was similar to the 1861, in that it was a list of males over 21, taken as a poll list by each of the county assessors. Only a couple of countywide name lists appear to be extant.

The State of Colorado took only one statewide census, that of 1885. This census was suggested by the United State Census Office, and some federal funds were used to assist in conducting the census, but the 1885 remains a state census, not a federal census. Similar forms used for the 1880 federal census were printed and provided by the Census Office for the 1885 Colorado State Census, and the Census Office asked for a duplicate copy of the statewide schedules. The state's microfilmed copy has numerous missing counties, but using both the federal and state copies together allows for a complete set for all but one missing county (Garfield).

The following census name lists and substitutes are available for Colorado:

■ **1859 – 1875 Denver City Directories** (with other Colorado cities), microfilm of originals published by various publishers. Filmed by Research Publications, Woodbridge, CT, 1980-1984, 1 microfiche, 1 microfilm roll, cataloged by the FHL as follows:

- **1859** Directory, Denver City and Auraria, FHL fiche #6043861.
- **1866** – *History of the City of Denver, From its Earliest Settlement to the Present Time; to Which is Added a Full and Complete Business Directory of the City;* **1871** – *The Rocky Mountain Directory and Colorado Gazetteer With a Complete and Accurate Directory of Denver, Golden City, Black Hawk, Central City, Nevada City, Idaho Springs, Georgetown, Boulder, Greeley, Colorado City, Pueblo, Trinidad, etc.;* and **1873, 1874, 1875** Denver City Directories, FHL film #1376794.

■ ***Colorado 1860 Census Index,*** edited by Ronald Vern Jackson, published by Accelerated Indexing Systems, Bountiful, UT, 1981, 56 pages. From the title page: "This index includes every given name on the census record." FHL book 978.8 X22j. There was no "Colorado" until Colorado Territory was established in 1861. Ronald Jackson was famous for creating census indexes to phantoms. No where does the index tell you the source of the names, whether Arapahoe County, Kansas Territory, western Nebraska Territory, or northern New Mexico Territory. At the time of the 1860 federal census, the area of present Colorado was part of four U.S. territories. See the Colorado Timeline entry for the 1860 Federal Census for a further explanation.

■ ***Index to Gilpin County, Colorado 1860 U.S. Census, Extracted From the 1860 U.S. Census of Arapahoe County, Kansas Territory,*** by Alan Granruth, published by the Foothills Genealogical Society, Lakewood, CO, 1995, 134 pages. This is an alphabetized extract of the census including dwelling number, name, age, sex, color, occupation, personal property, & birthplace. FHL book 978.862 X28g. Also on microfilm, FHL film #2055223.

■ **1860, 1870, 1880 Federal Censuses; and 1885 State Census, Boulder County, Colorado.** See ***Alphabetized Listing of Census Returns and Mortality Schedules for Boulder County, Colorado, 1860-1885,*** by Sanford Charles Gladden, published by the University of Colorado Libraries, Boulder, CO, 1978. FHL purchased microfilm from the author in 1981, 1 roll, FHL film #1294357.

■ ***Colorado Voters in the 1861 Territorial Election for a Delegate to the 37th Congress,*** an extraction of the original name lists at the Colorado State Archives by the Computer Interest Group of the Colorado Genealogical Society, Denver, CO, 1996, 156 pages. Includes index. FHL book 978.8 N4c. Also on microfilm, FHL film #1750820. This series of countywide name lists is titled ***1861 Poll Book for Colorado*** at the Colorado State Archives. In satisfaction of the requirement for a territorial census to be taken by the organic act of 1861 in which the Territory of Colorado was created, the territory incorporated the names of males over 21 as part of the assessor's polls for the first territorial election.

■ **1861-1865 Colorado Civil War Soldiers.** See ***Civil War Index Cards, 1861-1865,*** microfilm of original records at the Colorado State Archives, Denver, CO. Each card gives name, rank, age, organization, when and where enrolled, by whom enrolled, when and where mustered, by whom mustered, book and page numbers, and other information. Filmed by the Genealogical Society of Utah, 1992, 4 rolls, as follows:

- Civil War index cards: A – Franklin, Ashley M., FHL film #1862946.
- Civil War index cards: Franklin, Ashley M. – McFadden, Owen, FHL film #1862947.
- Civil War index cards: McFadden, Owen – Shock, Adam L., FHL film #1862948.
- Civil War index cards: Shock, Adam L. – Z, FHL film #1862949.

See also, ***Index to Compiled Service Records of Volunteer Union Soldiers Who Served in Organizations From the Territory of Colorado,*** microfilm of original records at the National Archives, Washington, DC, filmed by the National Archives, Series M0534, 1964, 3 rolls, as follows:

- Index, A-Hap, 1861-1865, NARA M534 roll 1, FHL film #821998.
- Index, Har-O, 1861-1865, M534 roll 2, FHL film #821999.
- Index, P-Z, 1861-1865, M534 roll 3, FHL film #822000.

The above indexed names included in ***Index to Soldiers & Sailors of the Civil War,*** a searchable name index to 6.3 million Union and Confederate Civil War soldiers now available online at the National Park Service Web site. A search can be done by surname, first name, state, or unit. Colorado Territory supplied 8,461 men to the war (all Union). To search for one go to the NPS Web site at: **www.civilwar.nps.gov/cwss/.**

■ **1862-1866 Internal Revenue Lists for the Territory of Colorado,** microfilm of originals at the National Archives, Washington, DC. Filmed by the National Archives, 1968, Series M0757, 3 rolls, as follows:

- Revenue name lists, divisions 1-14 Annual, monthly, special 1862-1863 (NARA M757 roll 1), FHL film #1578500.
- Revenue name lists, divisions 1-14 Annual, monthly, special 1864 (NARA M757 roll 2), FHL film #1578501.
- Revenue name lists, divisions 1-14 Annual, monthly, special 1865-1866 (NARA M757, roll 3), FHL film #1578502.

■ **1865-1867 Taxpayers, Clear Creek County, Colorado Territory,** name list published in *Foothills Inquirer,* Vol. 16, No. 1 (Spring 1996) through Vol. 16, No. 3 (Fall 1996), a publication of the Foothills Genealogical Society of Colorado, Lakewood, CO.

■ **1866 Heads of Families, Jefferson County, Colorado Territory,** name list published in *Foothills Inquirer,* Vol. 17, No. 3 (Fall 1997) and Vol. 18, No. 4 (Winter 1998), a publication of the Foothills Genealogical Society of Colorado, Lakewood, CO.

■ **1870 Colorado Territory Federal Census,** microfilm of original schedules at the National Archives, Washington, DC, filmed twice by the National Archives, 1962, 1968. The 2nd filming (on 2 rolls) is listed first and is usually easier to read. However, since some of the records were faded or lost between filmings, search the 1st filming (on 1 roll) whenever the material on the 2nd is too light to read:

- **1870,** 2nd filming, Arapahoe, Bent, Boulder, Clear Creek, Summit County (part) Includes Breckenridge, folio 146 only, Conejos, Costilla, Douglas, and El Paso, FHL film #545593.
- **1870,** 2nd filming, Fremont, Gilpin, Greenwood, Huerfano, Jefferson, Lake, Larimer, Las Animas, Park, Pueblo, Saquache, Summit (part), and Weld Counties, FHL film #545594.
- **1870,** 1st filming, Arapahoe, Bent, Boulder, Clear Creek, Conejos, Costilla, Douglas, El Paso, Summit, Fremont, Gilpin, Greenwood, Huerfano, Jefferson, Lake, Larimer, Las Animas, Park, Pueblo, Saquache, and Weld Counties, FHL #2686.

■ ***Colorado Territory Census Index, 1870,*** compiled and published by the Weld County Genealogical Society, Greeley, CO, 1977, (?? pages). FHL book 978.8 X2w 1870 index. Also on microfilm, filmed by the Genealogical Society of Utah, 1978, 1 roll, FHL film #1036745. See also, ***Colorado 1870 Census Index,*** edited by Ronald Vern Jackson, published by Accelerated Indexing Systems, North Salt Lake, UT, 1981, 55 pages. FHL book 978.8 X22j 1870. See also, ***Colorado 1870 Census Index, A-Z,*** edited by Raeone Christensen Steuart, published by Heritage Quest, Bountiful, UT, 2000, 131 pages. FHL book 978.8 X22c 1870.

■ **1870-1880 Colorado Federal Mortality Census Schedules and Related Indexes,** microfilm of original records at the DAR Library, Washington, DC. Each year includes an index prepared by the DAR. Filmed by the National Archives, 1962, 1 roll, Series T0655. FHL film #422411. See also, ***Colorado 1870 Mortality Schedule,*** edited by Ronald Vern Jackson, et al, published by Accelerated Indexing Systems, Bountiful, UT, 1981, 20 pages. FHL book 978.8 X28j 1870. And see also, ***Colorado 1880 Mortality Schedule,*** edited by Ronald Vern Jackson, et al, published by Accelerated Indexing Systems, Bountiful, UT, 1981, 34 pages. FHL book 978.8 X28j 1880.

■ ***Index to Gilpin County, Colorado 1870 U.S. Census,*** by Alan Granruth, published by the Foothills Genealogical Society, Lakewood, CO, 1995, 146 pages. The alphabetical listings include house and family numbers, name, age, sex, color, occupation, real estate, personal property, and birth place. FHL book 978.862 X28g. Also on microfilm, FHL film #2055223.

■ **1870-1900 Federal Censuses, and 1885 Census,** included in ***Archuleta County Records,*** transcribed by the Archuleta County Genealogical Society, Pagosa Springs, CO, ca1985-ca1995, 3 vols., Contents: vol. 1. Maps (1850 Iron County, Utah; 1860 Iron and Washington Counties, Utah; 1870, 1883 Conejos County, Colorado) and census records (1880 Conejo County, Colorado; 1885 Archuleta County, Colorado); vol. 2: Deaths (cemetery records, 1885 mortality schedule, misc. obituaries); vol. 3. 1900 census. Vol. 1 and 2 bound together by library. Includes indexes. FHL book 978.832 H2a v. 1-3. Also on microfiche, FHL fiche #6104872.

■ **1876-1935 Denver City Directories,** microfilm of originals published by various publishers. Filmed by Research Publications, Woodbridge, CT, 1980-1984, 45 microfilm rolls, cataloged by the FHL as follows:

- **1876, 1877, 1878, 1878,** and **1879** Denver City Directories, FHL film #1376795.
- **1880, 1881, 1882, 1883,** and **1884** Denver City Directories, FHL film #1376796.
- **1885, 1886,** and **1887** Denver City Directories, FHL film #1376797.
- **1888** and **1889** Denver City Directories, FHL film #1376798.
- **1890** Denver City Directory, FHL film #1376799.
- **1891** Denver City Directory, FHL film #1376800.
- **1892** Denver City Directory, FHL film #1376801.
- **1893** Denver City Directory, FHL film #1376802.
- **1894** and **1895** Denver City Directories, FHL film #1376803.
- **1896** and **1897** Denver City Directories, FHL film #1376804.

- **1898** and **1899** Denver City Directories, FHL film #1376805.
- **1900** Denver City Directory, FHL film #1376806.
- **1901** Denver City Directory, FHL film #1376807.
- **1902** and **1903** Denver City Directories, FHL film #1611467.
- **1904** Denver City Directory, FHL film #1611468.
- **1905** Denver City Directory, FHL film #1611468.
- **1906** Denver City Directory, FHL film #1611469.
- **1907** Denver City Directory, (Abair to Miller, O.), FHL film #1611469.
- **1907** Denver City Directory, (Miller, P. to Zwitz), and **1908** Denver City Directory, FHL film #1611470.
- **1909** Denver City Directory, FHL film #1611471.
- **1910** Denver City Directory, FHL film #1611472.
- **1911** Denver City Directory, FHL film #1611473.
- **1912** Denver City Directory, FHL film #1611474.
- **1913** Denver City Directory, FHL film #1611475.
- **1914** Denver City Directory, FHL film #1611476.
- **1915** Denver City Directory, FHL film #1611477.
- **1916** Denver City Directory, FHL film #1611478.
- **1917** Denver City Directory, FHL film #1611479.
- **1918** Denver City Directory, FHL film #1611480.
- **1919** Denver City Directory, FHL film #1611481.
- **1920** Denver City Directory, FHL film #1611482.
- **1921** Denver City Directory, FHL film #1611483.
- **1922** Denver City Directory, FHL film #1611484.
- **1923** Denver City Directory, FHL film #1611485.
- **1924** Denver City Directory, FHL film #1611486.
- **1925** Denver City Directory, FHL film #1611487.
- **1926** Denver City Directory, FHL film #1611488.
- **1927** Denver City Directory, FHL film #1611489.
- **1928** Denver City Directory, FHL film #1611490.
- **1929** Denver City Directory, FHL film #1611491.
- **1930** Denver City Directory, FHL film #1611492.
- **1931** Denver City Directory (p.1608-1653 missing; omits names between Macris, Jas. and Mays, Inez), FHL film #1611493.
- **1932** Denver City Directory, FHL film #1611494.
- **1933** Denver City Directory, FHL film #1611495.
- **1934** Denver City Directory, FHL film #1611496.
- **1935** Denver City Directory, FHL film #1611497.

■ **1880 Colorado Federal Census: Soundex and Population Schedules,** microfilm of original records at the National Archives, Washington, DC, filmed by the National Archives, 14 FHL rolls, beginning with FHL film #377999 (1880 Soundex A160 – C415); and FHL film #1254087 (1880 Population Schedules, Arapahoe Co.). See also, ***Colorado, 1880, Census Index,*** an every-name index to Colorado's population of 39,864 people, edited by Ronald Vern Jackson, published by Accelerated Indexing Systems, Bountiful, UT, 1981, 470 pages. FHL book 978.8 X22j 1880.

■ ***Clear Creek County, Colorado Census of 1880,*** a transcript of the original "1880 Short Form" records at the Clear Creek County Courthouse, compiled by Dorothy Kyler and Fae Tarrant, published by the Foothills Genealogical Society of Colorado, Lakewood, CO, 1987, 305 pages. An every-name index, arranged in alphabetical order by first letter of surname, age, color, and sex. From introduction: "On the completion of the 1880 Federal Census, some Colorado counties prepared lists of persons residing in the individual counties from the census schedule. Clear Creek County was one of the counties to prepare such a list." (Editor's comment: Actually, every county in the United States compiled the 1880 Short Forms, but few of them still survive). See FHL book 978.861 X2k. Also on microfilm, 1 roll, FHL film #1425410.

■ **1880-1910 Federal Censuses and 1885 State Census, Gunnison County,** See ***Census Records, Gunnison County, Colorado, Present Precinct 2,*** copied by Oscar D. McCollum, Jr., for Marble Historical Society, Marble, CO, 1983, 50 pages. Includes index. Includes 1880 census, Rockland Dainage; 1885 census, Crystal City and Scofield; 1900 census, Marble Village and Crystal; 1910 census, several localities in and near Crystal and Marble. Portions of Precinct 2 were formerly in Precincts 10, 22, and 24. FHL book 978.841 X2c Also on microfilm, FHL film #1321014.

■ **1885 Colorado State Census.** In 1885, the US government offered federal assistance to any state or territory who wished to take a census. Only five states or territories took up the government's offer: Colorado, Dakota Territory, Florida, Nebraska, and New Mexico Territory.

Each state/territory was to supply the federal government with a duplicate original (federal) copy of the census schedules for all counties, and retain a duplicate (state) copy. For Colorado, both the federal copy and the state copy were microfilmed, but the federal set was much more complete. The federal set microfilmed by the National Archives is missing Fremont and Garfield counties, while the state copy has Fremont, but is missing Garfield and eighteen other counties. Although territorial censuses were taken in 1861 and 1866, the 1885 census was the only state census taken in Colorado.

Copies of the microfilmed state and federal sets are available from the Family History Library in Salt Lake City and thousands of branch Family History Centers, as follows:

■ **1885 Colorado State Census (State Copies),** microfilm of the state's duplicate originals at the Colorado State Archives, Denver, CO. Filmed by the Colorado State Archives Microfilm Department, ca1957, 4 rolls, as follows:

- **1885** State Census (state copy), Arapahoe County, FHL film #929067.
- **1885** State Census (state copy), Chaffee, Conejos, Custer, Delta, Dolores, Douglas, Eagle, El Paso, Fremont, Gilpin, Gunnison, Huerfano, Jefferson Counties, FHL film #929068.
- **1885** State Census (state copy), Lake, Las Animas, Mesa, Park, Rio Grande, Weld counties, FHL film #929069.
- Another filming of Fremont County original at the Local History Center, Canon City Public Library in Canon City Colorado, filmed 1998, FHL film #2109433.

■ **1885 Colorado State Census (Federal Copies),** microfilm of the duplicate originals at the National Archives, Central Plains Region, Kansas City, MO, filmed by the National Archives, 1949, Series M0158, 8 rolls, as follows:

- **1885** State Census (federal Copy), Arapahoe, vol. 1, FHL film #498503.
- **1885** State Census (federal copy), Archuleta – Clear Creek vol. 2, FHL film #498504.
- **1885** State Census (federal copy), Conejos – Elbert, vol. 3, FHL film #498505.
- **1885** State Census (federal copy), El Paso – Huerfano, vol. 4, FHL film #498506.
- **1885** State Census (federal copy), Jefferson – La Plata, vol. 5, FHL film #498507.
- **1885** State Census (federal copy), Larimer – Ouray, vol. 6, FHL film #498508.
- **1885** State Census (federal copy), Park – Routt, vol. 7, FHL film #498509.
- **1885** State Census (federal copy), Saguache – Weld, vol. 8, FHL film #498510.

■ ***1885 Colorado State Census, Arapahoe County: Including the City of Denver and Portions of Present- Day Adams and Arapahoe Counties,*** a CD-ROM publication compiled and published by the Colorado Genealogical Society, Denver, CO, 2002, FHL CD-ROM No. 1442.

■ ***Bent County, Colorado, 1885 State Census,*** compiled and published by the Southeastern Colorado Genealogical Society, Pueblo, CO, 51 pages. Includes index. FHL book 978.897 X2b.

■ ***Clear Creek County, Colorado Census Index, 1885,*** copied by Dorothy Kyler & Fae Tarrant, a photocopy of the original census book at the Clear Creek County Courthouse in Georgetown, CO, published by the Foothills Genealogical Society of Colorado, Lakewood, CO, 1988, 162 pages. FHL book 978.861 X2k. See also ***Combined 1885 Clear Creek County, Colorado State Census: Being a Comparison of the Clear Creek County, Colorado Census Book and the State Census on Microfilm,*** compiled and published by the Foothills Genealogical Society of Colorado, Lakewood, CO, 1994, 213 pages. Includes index. The comparison is between the county's original census book and the federal copy on microfilm. The county's copy was not microfilmed as part of "1885 Colorado State Census (State Copies)," cited above. FHL book 978.861 X2c. Also on microfilm, 1 roll, FHL film #1698163.

■ *Custer County, Colorado, Census Index: 1885 State Census, 1900 & 1910 Federal Census,* extracted by members of the Southeastern Colorado Genealogy Society, Inc., published by the society, 1987, 106 pages. Includes excerpts of births, marriages and deaths from several newspapers and lists of towns still in existence and extinct. Maps on covers. The 1885 state census is printed in full with an index and followed by indexes to the 1900 and 1910 federal census records. FHL book 978.852 X2c. Also on microfiche, FHL fiche #6087804.

■ *The 1885 Census of Delta County, Colorado (Delta County's First Census),* transcribed by John W. Lynn, published by Lynn Research, Grand Junction, CO, 1987, 40 pages. FHL book 978.8 A1 No. 46.

■ *The 1885 Census of Dolores County, Colorado (Dolores County's First Census),* transcribed by John W. Lynn, published by Lynn Research, 1987, 22 pages. FHL book 978.8 A1 No. 47.

■ *Index for the Colorado – El Paso County – 1885 Census,* indexed by members of the Pikes Peak Genealogical Society, published by the society, Colorado Springs, CO, 1992, 176 pages. FHL book 978.856 X2i. Also on microfilm, FHL film #1425410.

■ *Gilpin County, Colorado 1885 State Census,* computerized by Julie McKeown, published by the Foothills Genealogical Society, Lakewood, CO, 1992, 332 pages. Includes family/dwelling no., name, color, age sex, relationship, marital status, occupation, birth place of individual and parents. FHL book 978.862 X28m. Also on microfilm, FHL film #2055223.

■ *1885 Census, Huerfano County, Colorado,* abstracted by Noreen I. Riffe, published by the Southeastern Colorado Genealogy Society, Pueblo, CO, 1994, 135 pages. Contains a list from Colorado postal history. The Post Offices, by William H. Bauer, James L. Ozment, and John H. Willard, 1885 mortality 1885 mortality schedule and 1885 census listings for Huerfano County, Colorado. Includes index. Map on cover. FHL book 978.851 X2.

■ *1885 Colorado State Census, Jefferson County,* compiled and published by the Foothills Genealogical Society of Colorado, Lakewood, CO, 1998, 214 pages. Includes index. FHL book 978.884 X2c. Also on microfilm, FHL film #1425184.

■ *Larimer County, Colorado 1885 State Census,* compiled and published by the Larimer County Genealogical Society, Ft. Collins, CO, 2000, 215 pages, FHL book 978.868 X2L.

■ *The 1885 Census of Mesa County, Colorado (Mesa County's First Census),* transcribed by John W. Lynn, published by Lynn Research, Grand Junction, CO, 1987, 52 pages. FHL 978.8 A1 No. 48.

■ *Park County, Colorado: 1885 state Census,* computerized by Opal Kendall Langino, published by the Foothills Genealogical Society of Colorado, 1995, (?? Pages). FHL book 978.859 X28L. Also on microfilm, FHL film #2055223.

■ *1885 Census, Pueblo County, Colorado,* abstracted by Noreen Riffe and Betty Polunci, published by the Southeastern Colorado Genealogical Society, Pueblo, CO, 1995, 397 pages. FHL book 978.855 X28r.

■ *The 1885 State Census of Weld County, Colorado: With Index,* copied and compiled by Jacquelyn Gee Glavinick, published by the Weld County Genealogical Society, Greeley, CO, 1984, 408 pages. FHL book 978.872 X28g.

■ **1900 Colorado Federal Census, Soundex and Population Schedules,** microfilm of original records at the National Archives, Washington, DC, filmed by the National Archives, 83 FHL rolls, beginning with FHL film #1242399 (1900 Soundex A000 – A450); and FHL film #1240117 (Population schedules: Arapahoe Co., City of Denver (ED's 1-37).

■ ***Boulder County, Colorado, 1900 Census Index,*** prepared under the direction of Lois Wescott and Mary McRoberts for the Boulder Genealogical Society, Boulder, CO, 1986, 187 pages, FHL book 978.863 X22b.

■ ***Index to Twelfth Census of the United States: 1900, Weld County, Colorado,*** copied compiled by Jacquelyn Gee Glavinick, published by the Weld County Genealogical Society, Greeley, CO, 1992, 163 pages. FHL book 978.872 X22g. Also on microfilm, FHL film #2055249.

■ ***Statewide Marriage index, 1900-1939, 1975-1992,*** microfilm of original records of the Colorado Department of Health now at the Colorado State Archives, Denver, CO, filmed by the archives, 1975-1992. The card index is arranged alphabetically by groom's name and gives county, names of husband and wife, their ages, race, date and place of marriage, certificate number, and other information. The computer print-out gives the names of the groom and bride, the county, and date of ceremony. These films are the best copies available. Original cards have been destroyed. The index is in two formats: 1900-1939 is a card index and 1975-1992 is a computer print-out. The card index was created by the Division of Vital Statistics which was under the Department of Health in Colorado. There are no statewide indexes for pre-1900 and 1940-1974. Researchers should check indexes in each county. The index for 1900-1939 has omitted many names, has poor alphabetizations and many cards are out-of-order. FHL has 106 microfilm rolls, beginning with FHL film #1690047 (Colorado Statewide Marriage Index, 1900-1939 Aab, Alexandra - Allen, Edgar J.).

■ ***Statewide Divorce Index, 1900-1992,*** microfilm of original records of the Colorado Health Department now at the Colorado State Archives, Denver, CO, filmed by the archives, 1975-1992. Card index gives names of plaintiff and defendant, county, date and place of marriage, names and ages of minor children, date of decree, name of court, and docket number. Computer print-out gives the names, decree date and type, and docket number. These films are the best copies available. Original cards have been destroyed. Index is in two formats: 1900-1939 is a card index and 1975-1992 is a computer print-out. Card index was created by the Division of Vital Statistics which is a section of the Department of Health in Colorado. There are no statewide indexes for pre-1900 and 1940-1974. Researchers should check indexes in each county. The index for 1900-1939 has omitted many names, has poor alphabetizations and many cards are out-of-order. FHL has 14 rolls, beginning with FHL film #1690153 (Colorado Divorce Records Index, 1900-1939 Aaby, Catherine - Bechwith, Maggie).

■ **1910 Colorado Federal Census, Population Schedules,** microfilm of original records at the National Archives, Washington, DC, filmed by the National Archives, 17 FHL rolls, beginning with FHL film #1374125 (1910 population schedules, Adams, Arapahoe, Archuleta, Baca, Bent, Chaffee, Cheyenne, and Clear Creek Co. (National Archives Series T624 roll 112). See also ***Colorado 1910 Census Index,*** compiled and published by Heritage Quest, division of ProQuest Information and Learning Company, North Salt Lake, UT, 2002, 3 vols. From introduction: "Only Heads-of-Household are extracted with the following exceptions: 1). Someone residing within the home who has a different surname, regardless of age. 2). All individuals living in an institution such as an orphanage, hospital, or poorhouse." Contents: vol. 1: A – Got; vol. 2: Gou – Oku; vol. 3: Ola – Z. FHL book 978.8 X22cc 1910 v. 1-3. See also ***Colorado, Montana and Wyoming 1910 U.S. Federal Census Index,*** a CD-ROM publication compiled and published by Heritage Quest, North Salt Lake, UT, 2002. FHL CD-ROM No. 1164. The Colorado name list is the same database as the published book shown above.

▪ ***1910 United States Population Census, 1910 Index, Baca County, Colorado and 1890 Tax Assessment Roll, Baca County, Colorado,*** compiled by Valorie Millican, published by V. Millican, Campo, CO, 1998, 45 pages. Names are listed alphabetically; 1890 listing is alphabetical by location. 1910 listing includes names, age, sex, etc.; 1890 listing is name only. FHL book 978.899 X22m.

▪ ***Boulder County, Colorado, 1910 Census Index,*** by Mary McRoberts, published by the Boulder Genealogical Society, Boulder, CO, 1989, 150 pages. Index is alphabetical arranged by name and includes name, age, enumeration district, sheet and line number. FHL book 978.863 X22m.

▪ ***Weld County, Colorado, Index to Thirteenth Census of the United States, 1910,*** compiled by Jacquelyn Glavinick, published by the Weld County Genealogical Society, Greeley, CO, 1993, 358 pages. FHL book 978.872 X22w. Also on microfilm, FHL film #1750772.

▪ **1920 Colorado Federal Census, Soundex and Population Schedules,** microfilm of original records at the National Archives, Washington, DC, filmed by the National Archives, Series 99 rolls, beginning with FHL film #1823723 (Soundex, A000 Frank thru A424), and National Archives Series T625, roll 155, FHL film #1820155 (Population schedules: Adams Co., Bent Co., Alamosa Co., Arapahoe Co., and Boulder Co.).

▪ **Map of Denver Showing 1920 Census Enumeration Districts.** See ***Beeler's Official Map of the City and County of Denver: Approved by the City Engineers,*** original published 1921 by the Beeler Map Co., Denver. This is a photocopy of the original map annotated by the Census Bureau, located at the National Archives, Central Plains Region, Kansas City, MO to show 1920 U.S census enumeration districts for the city of Denver in four parts, scale 1:12,000. Contents: part 1: E.D.'s 1-27, 101-136, 143-184, 195-198, 206-214, 221-237, 250-261,305-313; part 2: E.D.'s 137-142, 185-194, 199-205, 215-220, 262-270, 292-301; part 3: E.D.'s 27-51, 55-71, 75-102, 258-261, 275-286; part 4: E.D's 40-41, 52-54, 72-74, 244, 262-274, 287-294. FHL map 978.883 E7b part 1-4 (Map Case). Also on microfiche, FHL fiche #6117550.

▪ **1930 Colorado Federal Census, Population Schedules,** microfilm of original records at the National Archives, Washington, DC, 24 rolls, beginning with National Archives Series T626, roll 2291, FHL film #2339964 (Population schedules: Adams, Archuleta, Alamosa, Baca, Cheyenne, and Clear Creek counties).

Colorado Censuses & Substitutes Online

www.heritagequestonline.com
- 1870-1930 Colorado Federal Censuses.

www.ancestry.com
- 1870-1930 Colorado Federal Censuses
- 1885 Colorado State Census
- 1885-1940 U.S. Indian Census Schedules
- 1890 Veterans Schedules
- 1850-1880 Mortality Schedules

www.familysearch.org
- 1880 Federal Census – Every-name index linked to census page images at Ancestry.com

www.colorado.gov/dpa/doit/archives/1870/index.htm
- 1870 Colorado Territory Federal Census, an every-name index

www.rootsweb.com/~cogenweb/
- 1860 Nebraska Territory Federal Census, Colorado towns

www.ghostseekers.com/Cattle.htm
- Colorado Cattle Brand Records, 1885-1967

www.arealdomain.com/colorado1883.html
- 1883 Pensioners on the Roll, Colorado

www.colorado.gov/dpa/doit/archives/military/span_am_war/
- Colorado Volunteers in the Spanish American War (1898)

www.censusfinder.com/colorado.htm
- Links to county-by-county databases

UTAH

Timeline, 1776-1896

1776. Fathers Silvestre Velez de Escalante and Francisco Atanasio Dominguez search for a new route from Santa Fe to the missions in California. They are the first non-Indians to explore present Utah.

1819. A Spanish-American treaty sets the boundary between the Louisiana Purchase region and Spanish claims, which places present Utah entirely within New Spain.

1821. Mexico wins independence from Spain and reaffirms the Spanish-American treaty boundaries of 1819 which included all of Utah, now as Mexican territory.

1824. General William H. Ashley sends trappers to northern Utah and Jim Bridger discovers the Great Salt Lake.

1826. Jedediah Smith leads the first overland expedition to California via present northern Utah.

1832. Antoine Robidoux establishes a trading post in the Uintah region of present Utah.

1841. Capt. John Bartleson leads the first wagon train of settlers from Missouri to California. The route they followed included the northern Utah section of the California Trail.

1843. John C. Fremont and Kit Carson explore the basin of the Great Salt Lake.

1846. Near the beginning of their great migration from Council Bluffs, Iowa to the Salt Lake Valley, Brigham Young agrees to provide the U.S. Army with the "Mormon Battalion," with orders to march on San Diego and secure it for the United States. Wages for the Mormon soldiers are paid in advance in gold, and help finance the trip west. But perhaps more importantly, this act changes the Mormon plans to found an independent nation in the West. Their involvement in the Mexican-American war ties the Mormons to the U.S. thereafter.

1847. First parties of Mormon pioneers arrive in the Salt Lake Valley. It is the largest single migration group in American history. Over the next twenty years, as many as 50,000 would follow the Mormon Trail to Utah.

1848. Treaty of Guadalupe Hidalgo ends the war with Mexico, and present Utah is annexed to the United States.

1849. First Constitutional Convention in Salt Lake proposes the State of Deseret which would encompass the region from the Continental Divide to California between Oregon Territory and New Mexico Territory.

1850. In September, the U..S. Congress rejects Statehood for Deseret, but establishes **Utah Territory,** encompassing the same region as earlier proposed for Deseret. Also in 1850, the University of Deseret (later University of Utah) is chartered. The *Deseret News* starts in June.

1851. The 1850 Federal Census taken in Utah Territory. The territory was established in September of 1850, and the 1850 Federal Census for Utah Territory was taken with a census day of April 1, 1851. The population was 11,380. Hundreds of the original pioneers had already left Utah to establish Mormon communities in present Idaho, Nevada, Arizona, and California.

1852. LDS Church authorities publicly acknowledge the doctrine of plural marriage.

1853. LDS Church begins the construction of the Salt Lake Temple.

1854. A grasshopper plague endangers crops. Thousands of seagulls converge to feed on the grasshoppers, saving the harvest. The Mormons see it as an act of God, and the seagull remains a venerated symbol in Utah today – the California Seagull is the official state bird of Utah.

1856. The second Utah Statehood petition to Congress rejected. Handcarts are first used exclusively by the pioneers traveling to Utah. For the next four years, over 3,000 people traversed the Mormon Trail with only the means of human power to pull their possessions. A territorial census was taken in this year.

1857. Brigham Young is removed as governor by President James Buchanan who sends a 2,500-man military force to accompany the new governor, Alfred Cumming. to the territory, starting the "Utah War."

1860 Federal Census taken in Utah Territory. Population at 40,273. Also in early 1860, the Pony Express was extended from Salt Lake City to Sacramento.

1861. The final link of the first transcontinental telegraph line comes together near present Wendover, Utah. The telegraph essentially ends the need for the Pony Express, which ends after less than two years of operation.

1862. The third movement for Utah Statehood is rejected by Congress.

1869. Union Pacific and Central Pacific railroads meet on May 10 at Promontory Summit in Utah Territory. First non-Mormon church building in Utah (Church of the Good Samaritan) in Corinne is constructed.

1870 Federal Census taken in Utah Territory. Population at 86,336.

1871. Dedication of first Catholic Church in Utah (St. Mary Madeleine).

1872. Fourth Utah Statehood petition is rejected by Congress.

1873. Poland Act passed in Congress making it legal to prosecute Mormons for practicing polygamy by defining the practice as bigamy, already covered by law as a felony. As a result, the Mormons began making their marriage records secret with no civil recording. Without proof of marriage, the federal law was essential unenforceable.

1879. First telephone service established in Ogden.

1880 Federal Census taken in Utah Territory. Population at 143,963.

1882. The Edmunds Act passed by Congress making "unlawful cohabitation" illegal. Unlike earlier laws, The Edmunds Act removed the need for prosecutors to prove that actual marriages had occurred. More than 1,300 Utah men were imprisoned under the terms of this measure.

1887 – Sixth Statehood petition is rejected by Congress.

1890. LDS Church President Wilford Woodruff issues a Manifesto ending church-sanctioned polygamy. The 1890 Federal Census shows a growth in Utah Territory to 210,779 inhabitants.

1896. January 4th, Utah becomes the 45th state.

UTAH

Censuses & Substitutes, 1846-1930

Utah Territory authorized censuses in 1856 and 1895. The 1856 name lists survive and have been extracted and indexed. The Utah Bureau of Statistics reported to the first state legislative session that a "house-to-house canvas" was taken for Utah Territory in February and March 1895, but no name lists from this territorial census can be found.

The State Constitution of Utah, ratified soon after statehood in 1896, authorized state censuses to be taken every ten years, beginning in 1905, but no record of an actual state census has been found.

For the period 1914-1960, there are church censuses of members (head of households) of The Church of Jesus Christ of Latter-day Saints made public and filmed by the Genealogical Society of Utah that may act as substitutes.

The following censuses and substitute name lists are available for Utah:

■ **1830s to mid 1900s Card Index.** See ***Early Church Information File,*** microfilm copy of the *Early Church Information Card Index.* This is an alphabetical index of many members of the LDS Church, primarily from sources from 1830 to the mid-1900s. Sources include LDS church records, journals, biographies, cemetery records, immigration records and published books. Filmed by the Genealogical Society of Utah, 1991, 75 rolls, beginning with FHL film #1750655 (Aabbost, Ellen – Allen, Joseph W.). As a guide and finding tool, see also ***Early Church Information File: Resource Guide,*** prepared by the Family History Library, Salt Lake City, UT, 1993, 4 pages. FHL book 921.1 F21rg. Also on microfiche, FHL fiche #6105233.

■ ***We'll Find the Place: The Mormon Exodus, 1846-1848,*** by Richard E. Bennett, published by Deseret Book, Salt Lake City, UT, 1997, 428 pages. History of the Mormon pioneers from Nauvoo, Illinois to Salt Lake City, Utah. Includes a list of the original 1847 pioneers with birth and death dates and places. Includes index. FHL book 978 H2b.

■ **Index of the 1847 Pioneers,** photocopy of newspaper column originally published: Salt Lake City: Salt Lake Tribune, 1934. Consists of abstracts of biographical sketches arranged alphabetically, with date of publication in the newspaper series, *Day by day with the Utah pioneers, 1847,* by Andrew Jenson. FHL book 979.2 H2saa.

■ ***Mormon Pioneer Companies Crossing the plains (1847-1868): Guide to Sources in the Historical Department and Family History Library of The Church of Jesus Christ of Latter-day Saints,*** a typescript by Melvin L. Bashore and Linda L. Haslam, published by The Church of Jesus Christ of Latter-day Saints, Historical Department, 1988, 288 pages. From introduction: "This finding aid has been prepared to assist users who are seeking information about the experiences of a particular emigrant. The guide is arranged by year and, therein, by pioneer company." A bibliography of diaries, letters, articles, etc., which provide first-person accounts of the Mormon trek across the plains. Primarily includes materials found in the archives of the Historical Department of The Church of Jesus Christ of Latter-day Saints, as well as the Church's Family History Library. FHL book 289.3016 B291m. Also on microfiche, FHL fiche #6105191.

■ **1850-1886 Deeds, Salt Lake County, Utah,** microfilm of handwritten copies of originals in the Utah State Archives, Salt Lake City, Utah. Some records have indexes. Records include deeds, land certificates, transfers of city lots, and records of bounty land grants for military service. Filmed by Holton, Jacobsen, Roach, Salt Lake City, 1955-1983, 63 rolls, beginning with FHL film #929288 (Deeds, Vol. A-B, 1850-1862).

■ **1850 Utah Territory Federal Census, Population Schedules,** microfilm of original records at the National Archives, Washington, DC. The Utah Territory enumeration was conducted with a census day of April 1, 1851, revealing a population of 11,380 inhabitants. Filmed by the National Archives, 1964, 1 roll, FHL film #25540. See also ***First families of Utah as Taken From the 1850 census of Utah,*** a photocopy of the original census schedules, compiled and published by Annie Walker Burns; edited with an historical introduction by J. Emerson Miller, 1949, 115 pages. Includes index. FHL book 979.2 X2ba. Also on microfilm, FHL film #432616. See also ***Index to Utah 1851 [i.e., 1850] Census,*** typed by the Genealogical Society of Utah, 1950, 125 pages. FHL book 979.2 X22i. See also ***Utah 1850 Census Index,*** edited by Ronald Vern Jackson, et al, published by Accelerated Indexing Systems, Bountiful, UT, 1978, 53 pages. FHL book 979.2 X22u. See also ***1851 Census of Utah,*** transcribed by William Bowen, published 1972, 228 pages, a computer listing of all names in surname order. FHL book 979.2 X2b oversize. Also on microfilm, FHL film #924039.

■ ***California, New Mexico, Oregon, Texas, and Utah, 1850,*** a CD-ROM publication (Broderbund, Family Tree Maker Archives, 1999, 4 discs). Includes an index to and actual images of portions of the 1850 federal census. FHL CD-ROM No. 9, part 452. See also **1850 U.S. Census Index, Western States: CA, NM, OR, TX, UT;** extracted from the original U.S. Federal census schedules, a CD-ROM publication by Heritage Quest, North Salt Lake, UT, 2000. Includes 332,865 records searchable by surname, given name, age, sex, race, birth place, state of census, county, locality, and National Archives microfilm roll number. FHL CD-ROM No. 387.

■ ***Index to the 1850, 1860 & 1870 Censuses of Utah: Heads of Households,*** compiled by J. R. Kearl, Clayne L. Pope and Larry T. Wimmer, published by Genealogical Publishing Co., Inc., Baltimore, 1981, 402 pages. FHL book 979.2 X2k. Also on 5 microfiche, FHL fiche #6051336.

■ ***U.S. Census 1850, Davis County Utah,*** copied by George Olin Zabriskie and Dorothy Louise Robinson, published 1937. Lists name of individuals, occupation of head of family, age, sex, and state or county of birth from the 1850/51 census of Utah Territory. FHL book 979.227 X2p. Also on microfilm, FHL film #824060.

■ ***U. S. Census 1850, Iron County, Utah,*** copied by George Olin Zabriskie and Dorothy Louise Robinson, published 1937. 979.2 A1 No. 115.

■ ***Utah 1850 Mortality Schedule,*** edited by Ronald Vern Jackson, et al, published by Accelerated Indexing Systems, Bountiful, UT, 1980, 3 pages. FHL book 979.2 X2jm.

■ ***Utah Supplemental Census Schedules, 1850,*** microfilm of original records at the Utah Historical Society, Salt Lake City. Includes agricultural schedules, social statistics schedules; and mortality schedules for persons who died during the year ending June 1, 1850. Filmed by the Office of the Church Historian of the LDS Church, 1969, 1 roll, FHL film #1550328.

■ ***Tooele County, Utah, 1850 Census,*** copied from the original 1850 federal census records (taken in April 1851) by George Zabriskie, typescript donated to the Family History Library, 1945. FHL book 979.2 A1 No. 128. See also ***The 1851 Census Records of Tooele County, Utah,*** copied by

Sherman Lee Pompey, published by Historical and Genealogical Publishing Co., Independence, CA, 1965, 5 pages. Filmed by W.C. Cox, Tucson, AZ, 1974, FHL film #10000618, item 9.

■ ***Utah County, Utah, 1850 Census,*** copied from the original 1850 federal census (taken in April 1851) by George Zabriskie, FHL book 979.224 X2p. Also on microfiche, FHL fiche #6105059.

■ ***Sanpete County, Utah, 1851 Census,*** copied from the original 1850 Federal Census schedules (taken in April 1851) with an added index, by George Zabriskie, published 1945, FHL book 979.2 A1 No. 174.

■ ***Census, 1851, Great Salt Lake County, Utah,*** a photocopy of the original 1850 federal census schedules (taken in April 1851) with an added name index. Published by the Genealogical Society of Utah, 216 pages. FHL book 979.225 X2p. Also on microfilm, FHL film #1307594.

■ ***Census of Weber County, Excluding Green River Precinct: Provisional State of Deseret 1850,*** typescript prepared by the Historical Records Survey, Division of Women's and Professional Projects, Works Progress Administration. Includes index. FHL book 979.228 X2c.

■ **1853-1878 Salt Lake County Assessment Rolls,** microfilm of original records at the Salt Lake County Clerk's Office, filmed by the Genealogical Society of Utah, 1966, 7 rolls, as follows:

- Assessment rolls, 1853, 1858-1861, FHL film #485541.
- Assessment rolls, 1862-1866, FHL film #485542.
- Assessment rolls, 1867-1868, FHL film #485543.
- Assessment rolls, 1868-1869, FHL film #485544.
- Assessment rolls, 1870-1874, FHL film #485545.
- Assessment rolls, 1875-1876, FHL film #485546.
- Assessment rolls, 1877-1878, FHL film #485547.

■ ***1856 Utah Census Returns,*** microfilm of original records at the Historical Dept. of The Church of Jesus Christ of Latter-day Saints, Salt Lake City, Utah. Filmed by the Genealogical Society of Utah, 1981, 1 roll, FHL film #505913. See also ***1856 Utah Census Index: An Every-name Index,*** compiled by Bryan Lee Dilts, published by Index Publishing, Salt Lake City, 1983, 292 pages. FHL book 979.2 X22d. Also on microfiche, 3 microfiche, FHL fiche #6331392. See also ***Utah 1856 Territorial Census Index,*** edited by Ronald Vern Jackson, et al, published by Accelerated Indexing Systems, Bountiful, UT, 1983, (?? Pages). An every-name index. FHL book 979.2 X22u.

■ ***Handcarts to Zion: The Story of a Unique Western Migration 1856-1860, With Contemporary Journals, Accounts, Reports, and Rosters of Members of the Ten Handcart Companies,*** by LeRoy R. Hafen and Ann W. Hafen, published by Arthur H. Clark, Glendale, CA, 1960, 1976, 328 pages. Includes index. FHL book 973 W2hL. Also on microfilm, FHL film #1059487. Also on microfiche, FHL fiche #6031590.

■ **1860 Utah Federal Census, Population Schedules,** microfilm of original records at the National Archives, Washington, DC. Filmed by the National Archives, 1950, 1967. The 1860 census was filmed twice. The second filming (2nd) is listed first and is usually easier to read. However, since some of the records were faded or lost between the first and second filmings, search the first filming (1st) whenever the material on the second filming (2nd) is too light or missing. FHL has 3 rolls, as following:

- **1860 Utah:** (2nd) Salt Lake, Great Salt Lake, Tooele, Green River, Summit, Davis, Weber, and Box Elder Counties, FHL film #805313.
- **1860 Utah:** (2nd) Cache, Sanpete, Millard, Beaver, Iron, Juab, Utah, Washington, Shambip, Cedar, St. Mary's, Humbolt (Humboldt), and Carson, Davis, and Great Salt Lake and Slave Schedules, FHL film #805314.
- **1860 Utah:** (1st) Entire territory, FHL film #25541.

■ ***Utah 1860 Territorial Census Index,*** edited by Ronald Vern Jackson, et al, published by Accelerated Indexing Systems, Salt Lake City, UT, 1979, 576 pages. FHL book 979.2 X2j. See also ***Index to the 1850, 1860, 1870 Censuses of Utah: Heads of Households,*** shown earlier.

■ ***Utah Supplemental Census Schedules, 1860,*** microfilm of original records at the Utah Historical Society, Salt Lake City, UT. Includes mortality schedules for persons who died during the year ending June 1st, 1860. Also includes agricultural, industrial, and social statistics schedules. Filmed by the Office of the Church Historian, LDS Church, 1969, 1 roll, FHL film #1550328.

■ ***Utah 1860 Mortality Schedule,*** edited by Ronald Vern Jackson, et al, published by Accelerated Indexing Systems, 1980, 5 pages. FHL book 979.2 X2jm.

■ **1861-1865 Civil War Soldiers.** See ***Index to Compiled Service Records of Volunteer Union Soldiers Who Served in Organizations From the Territory of Utah,*** microfilm of original records at the National Archives, Washington, DC. Includes records from Captain Smith's Co., Utah Cavalry. Each index card gives name, rank, and unit in which the soldier served. Cross references are given for names that appear in record under different spellings. Filmed by the National Archives, Series M556, 1 roll. FHL film #1292645.

The above indexed names included in ***Index to Soldiers & Sailors of the Civil War,*** a searchable name index to 6.3 million Union and Confederate Civil War soldiers now available online at the National Park Service Web site. A search can be done by surname, first name, state, or unit. Utah Territory supplied 96 men to the war (all Union). To search for one go to the NPS Web site: **www.civilwar.nps.gov/cwss/.**

■ **1862 and 1867 Federal Direct Tax, Utah Territory.** See ***Assessment Book, Division No. 1, for the Territory of Utah 1867, 1862,*** microfilm of manuscripts at the Utah State Archives. Name lists of taxpayers and assessment details in alphabetical order. Filmed by the Genealogical Society of Utah, 1956, 1 roll, FHL film #25780.

■ **1870 Utah Federal Census, Population Schedules,** microfilm of original records at the National Archives, Washington, DC. Filmed by the National Archives, 1962, 1968. The 1870 census was filmed twice. The second filming (2nd) is listed first and is usually easier to read. However, since some of the records were faded or lost between the first and second filmings, search the first filming (1st) whenever the material on the second filming (2nd) is too light to read. FHL has 5 rolls, as following:

- **1870 Utah:** (2nd) Beaver, Box Elder, Cache, Davis, Iron, and Juab Counties, FHL film #553109.
- **1870 Utah:** (2nd) Kane, Millard, Morgan, Piute, Rich, Rio Virgin, and Salt Lake Counties, FHL film #553110.
- **1870 Utah:** (2nd) Sanpete, Sevier, Summit, Tooele, and Utah Counties, FHL #553111.
- **1870 Utah:** (2nd) Wasatch, Washington, and Weber Counties, FHL film #553112.
- **1870 Utah:** (1st) Beaver, Box Elder, Cache, Davis, Iron, Juab, Kane, Millard, Morgan, Piute, Rich, Rio Virgin, Salt Lake, Sanpete, Sevier, Summit, Tooele, Utah, Wasatch, Washington, and Weber Counties, FHL #25542.

■ ***Utah 1870 Census Index, A – Z,*** edited by Raeone Christensen Steuart, published by Heritage Quest, Bountiful, UT, 2000, 154 pages.

Includes name, age, sex, race, birthplace, county and locale of census, roll and page number. Arranged in alphabetical order by surname. FHL book 979.2 X22s. See also, ***Utah, 1870,*** (index) edited by Ronald Vern Jackson, et al, published by Accelerated Indexing Systems, North Salt Lake, UT, 1987, 273 pages. FHL book 979.2 X22u. See also ***Index to the 1850, 1860, 1870 Censuses of Utah: Heads of Households,*** shown earlier.

■ ***Non-population Census Schedules for Utah Territory and Vermont, 1870, Mortality (M1807),*** microfilm of copy at the National Archives, Washington, DC, introduction by Claire Prechtel-Kluskens. Includes 1870 mortality schedules for Utah and Vermont, giving information on persons who died during the year ending 1 June 1870. Some records may be hard to read. This is the best copy available. Filmed by the National Archives, 1994, 1 roll, FHL film #2155492.

■ **Mortality Schedules of Texas (1850, 1860, 1870, 1880); Mortality Schedules of Utah (1870),** microfilm of originals at the Texas State Library in Austin. Some pages wanting. Filmed by the Texas State Library, 1950, 8 rolls. 1870 Utah Mortality Schedules are on FHL film #1421046. Another copy of UT originals filmed by the Genealogical Society of Utah, 1971, 1 roll, FHL film #1550298. Another copy, FHL film #865236.

■ ***Utah 1870 Mortality Schedule,*** edited by Ronald Vern Jackson, published by Accelerated Indexing Systems, Bountiful, UT, 1980, 12 pages. FHL book 979.2 X2jm.

■ **Utah Supplemental Census Schedules, 1870,** microfilm of original manuscripts in the possession of the Utah Historical Society. Includes agricultural, industrial and social statistics schedules. Filmed by the Office of the Church Historian, LDS Church, 1969, 1 roll, FHL film #1550328.

■ **1880 Utah Territory Federal Census, Soundex and Population Schedules,** microfilm of original records at the National Archives, Washington, DC. Filmed by the National Archives, 12 rolls, beginning with FHL film #378011 (Soundex, A000 – C400); and FHL film #1255335 (Population schedules, Beaver, Box Elder, and Cache counties).

■ ***Utah 1880 Federal Census Index,*** edited by Ronald Vern Jackson, et al., published by Accelerated Indexing Systems, 1989, 380 pages. FHL book 979.2 X22u. See also ***Index to the 1880 Census of Utah,*** compiled by the BYU Research Center, Provo, UT, transcription filmed by the Genealogical Society of Utah, 1970, 7 rolls, as follows:

- Chinese and Indians; all others, A – B, FHL film #538587.
- C – Fe, FHL film #538588.
- Fi – I, FHL film #538589.
- J – Ma, FHL film #538590.
- Me – Q, FHL film #538591.
- R – S, FHL film #538592.
- T – Z, FHL film #538593.

■ **1880 Utah Mortality Schedules,** microfilm of original records at the Historian's Office of The Church of Jesus Christ of Latter-Day Saints. Lists persons who died during the year ending May 31, 1880. Also includes supplemental schedules for the defective, dependent, and delinquent classes and special manufacturing schedules. Filmed by Office by the Church Historian of L.D.S. Church, 1969, 1 roll, FHL film #1550325. See also, ***Utah 1880 Mortality Schedule,*** edited by Ronald Vern Jackson, published by Accelerated Indexing Systems, Bountiful, UT 1981, 31 pages. FHL book 979.2 X2jm.

■ **1880 Agriculture Section of the 10th Census for the State of Utah,** microfilm of manuscripts in the Church Historian's Office, Salt Lake City and National Archives, Washington, DC, filmed by the Genealogical Society of Utah, 1959, 2 rolls, FHL #205643 (all counties except Cache); and FHL film #1255336 (Cache County agricultural schedules filmed after the Cache County population schedules).

■ *1890 Utah Census Index: Special Schedule of the Eleventh Census (1890) Enumerating Union Veterans and of Union Veterans of the Civil War,* edited by Ronald Vern Jackson, published by Accelerated Indexing Systems, 1983, 15 pages. FHL book 979.2 X22jv.

■ **1883-1888 Salt Lake City Directories.** See ***The Utah Directory Containing the Name and Occupation of Every Resident of Salt Lake City, and a Complete Business Directory of Every City and Town in Utah, Together With a Compendium of General Information,*** microfilm of original published by J.C. Graham, Salt Lake City, 1883. Filmed by Utah State Archives and Records Service, 1975. 1 roll, FHL film #1004515. See also **1884** and **1885-1886 Directories**, FHL film #940049. See also ***Utah Gazetteer and Directory of Salt Lake, Ogden, Provo and Logan Cities for 1888, and a Complete Business Directory of the Territory,*** microfilm of original published by Lorenzo Stenhouse, 1988, FHL film #1004522. Another filming, FHL film #1670794.

■ **1890, 1915, 1935 Salt Lake County Assessment Rolls,** microfilm of typescript at the State Capitol Building, Salt Lake City, Utah. Includes 1915 index. Filmed by the Genealogical Society of Utah, 1966, 1969, assessment rolls beginning with FHL film #1654546 (1890); FHL film #497721 (1915); and FHL film #497720 (1935). There are indexes to the 1915 assessment rolls on 4 rolls, as follows:

- Index to 1915 Assessment rolls, A-E, FHL film #497717.
- Index to 1915 Assessment rolls, F-K, FHL film #497718.
- Index to 1915 Assessment rolls, L-Q, FHL film #497719.
- Index to 1915 Assessment rolls, R-Z, FHL film #497720.

■ ***Utah Death Index, 1898-1905,*** compiled by Professional Chapter of Utah Genealogical Association; edited by Judith W. Hansen, published by Utah Genealogical Association, 1995, 1998, 2 vols. Statewide registration of births and deaths began in September 1905, but most counties began in 1898 with a few earlier. Includes name, sex, age, death date, county page number and entry or registration number. Listed in alphabetical order by surname. Contents: vol. 1: All counties, excluding Salt Lake County; vol. 2: Salt Lake County. FHL book 979.2 V42u.

■ **1900 Utah Federal Census, Soundex and Population Schedules,** microfilm of original records at the National Archives, Washington, DC, filmed by the National Archives, 36 rolls, beginning with FHL film #1249012 (Soundex, B140 – B164); and FHL film #1241683 (Population schedules, Davis, Emery, Garfield, Grand, Iron, Juab, Kane, Millard, Morgan, Piute, and Rich Counties).

■ **1904-1951 Utah Death Certificates,** microfilm of original records at the Utah State Department of Health, Bureau of Vital Records & Statistics, Salt Lake City, UT. Arranged in chronological order by county of death. Some records may be filmed out of chronological order. Filmed by the Genealogical Society of Utah, 2001, 157 rolls, beginning with FHL film #2230661 (Death Certificates, 1904, Beaver County – Salt Lake County).

■ **Card Index to Marriage Records (Miscellaneous Marriage Index),** compiled from civil records by various wards and branches and organized by the Genealogical Society of The Church of Jesus Christ of Latter-day Saints. From intro: "The Marriage License Card Index (also referred to as the Miscellaneous Marriage Index) contains names of persons compiled from marriage license records in the following county court houses: 1. Utah (Box Elder, Millard, Morgan, Salt Lake, Sanpete, Sevier, Summit, Utah, Wayne and Weber) 2. Idaho (Franklin and Lemhi) 3. Wyoming (Lincoln)." Card index arranged alphabetically by the surnames of both bride and groom. Filmed by the Genealogical Society of Utah, 1972. 190 rolls, beginning with FHL film #820155 (A – Anderson).

■ **1910 Utah Federal Census, Population Schedules,** microfilm of original records at the National Archives, Washington, DC, filmed by the National Archives, 10 rolls, beginning with FHL film #1375615 (Population schedules, Beaver, Box Elder, and Cache Counties).

■ ***Utah 1910 Census Index,*** by Heritage Quest, North Salt Lake, UT, 2001, 750 pages. Arranged in alphabetical order by surname. FHL book 979.2 X22h. See also ***Arizona, Nevada, New Mexico and Utah 1910 U.S. Federal Census Index,*** CD-ROM publication by Heritage Quest, North Salt Lake, UT, 2001. FHL CD-ROM No. 1191.

■ **1914-1960 Church Census Records,** microfilm of original records in the LDS Church Historian's Office. Church census records include name lists arranged alphabetically by head of household for the years 1914, 1920, 1925, 1930, 1935, 1940, 1950, 1955, and 1960. Included with the 1914-1935 census are some delayed birth certificates which originated in the Church Historian's Office and a few Salt Lake Granite Stake genealogical survey cards. Filmed by the Genealogical Society of Utah, 1962, 651 rolls, beginning with FHL film #25708 (1914-1935: Aabo – Alex) See also ***LDS Church Census, 1930-1935, Peterson Miscellaneous,*** filmed by the Genealogical Society of Utah, 1966, 1 roll, FHL film #423837.

■ **1920 Utah Federal Census, Soundex and Population Schedules,** microfilm of original records at the National Archives, Washington, DC, filmed by the National Archives, 42 rolls, beginning with FHL film #1830770 (Soundex, A000-A126); and FHL film #1821861 (Population schedules, Beaver, Box Elder, and Cache Counties).

■ ***1920 Utah Census,*** a 3-disc CD-ROM publication containing all census sheet images from the population schedules, with an added index to the entire population. Compiled and published by the Utah Valley Regional Family History Center at Brigham Young University's Harold B. Lee Library; index by Deanne Roberts; Clinton Ashworth, coordinator. FHL CD-ROM No. 756, part 1-3).

■ ***Extracted Soundex Index, Utah, 1920 U.S. Census: From Microfilm 1830770 to 1830802,*** by Deanne Roberts, et al., published by Brigham University Library, Provo, UT, 2 vols., 2001. From intro: "Names in this index are extracted from card images on 33 Soundex microfilms for the Utah 1920 U.S. Census (LDS numbers 1830770-1830802). Generally only heads of households and occupants with different surnames are included." Contents: vol. 1. A123 - L200 (Evan); vol. 2: L200 (Mable) - Z612. Arranged in alphabetical order by soundex code, with some mixed codes. FHL book 979.2 X22r 1920 v. 1-2.

■ **1930 Utah Federal Census, Population Schedules,** microfilm of original records at the National Archives in Washington, DC. Filmed by the National Archives as microfilm publication T626, 12 rolls, beginning with FHL film #2342148 (Population schedules: Beaver, Box Elder, and Cache Counties).

■ **Index to Military Records of World War II, Veterans From Utah,** microfilm of original records at the Utah State Archives, Salt Lake City. An alphabetical index to veterans, with separate lists for army, navy, coast guard, marines, and maritime service veterans. Filmed by the Genealogical Society of Utah, 1966, 11 rolls, as follows:

- Army veterans, A – Comstock, FHL film #536228.
- Army veterans, Conant – Hjortsberg, FHL film #536229.
- Army veterans, Hoadley - Mortensen, FHL film #536230.
- Army veterans, Mortensen, E. – Shytles, FHL film #536231.
- Army veterans, Sibert – Zwillman, FHL film #536232.
- Navy veterans, Aagard – Gyll, FHL film #536233.
- Navy veterans, Haacke – Smyth, FHL film #536234.
- Navy veterans, Snarr – Zwaharn, FHL film #536235.
- Coast Guard veterans, A – Z, FHL film #536236.
- Marine veterans, A – Z, FHL film #536237.
- Maritime service veterans, A – Z, FHL film #536238.

Utah Censuses & Substitutes Online

www.heritagequestonline.com
Heads of Household name index linked to census page images:
- 1850-1930 Utah Federal Censuses.

www.ancestry.com
- 1850-1930 Federal Censuses
- 1890 Veterans Schedules
- 1910 Federal Census, Garfield County
- 1910 Federal Census, Iron County
- 1850-1880 Mortality Schedules

www.familysearch.org
- 1880 Federal Census – Every name index linked to census page images at Ancestry.com.

http://gen.gserver.com/genindex.html
- 1920 Utah Federal Census - Images

www.rootsweb.com/~utgenweb/
- 1850 Utah Federal Census – Images
- 1860 Utah Federal Census – Images.
- Index to Marriage and Death Notices in the *Deseret News Weekly* (1852-1888) Complete
- Index to Marriage and Death Notices unique to the *Deseret News* Semi-Weekly (1865-1900) Complete
- Utah State Death Certificates (1904-1951) – a catalog of films available at the Family History Library
- Burials Database
- Markers & Monuments Database

www.censusfinder.com/utah.htm
- Links to county-by-county databases

Wyoming

Timeline, 1742-1890

1742. The first non-Indian to visit the area of Wyoming is believed to be Francois Louis Verendrye, a French trapper from the Red River Settlement of the Dakota Country.

1807. John Colter, recent member of the Lewis and Clark expedition, now fur trapper, Mountain Man, and explorer, is the first to describe a place where "hot water shoots straight into the air, the earth bubbles as if it were boiling, and almost extinct geysers thunder as if possessed by angry spirits." He calls the area in his written reports, "Colter"s Hell." Most easterners believe he is either lying or exaggerating, and find it hard to believe such a place could really exist.

1811. The Wilson Price Hunt party, the first organized expedition through present Wyoming, crosses the state on the way to Astoria in the Oregon Country. His route across the Rocky Mountains, later known as South Pass, was to become the primary crossing point for thousands of covered wagons traveling the Oregon Trail.

1812. Robert Stuart and returning Astorians cross the Continental Divide in the vicinity of South Pass and build the first known cabin on the North Platte River at Bessemer Bend, a few miles southwest of present Casper, Wyoming.

1822. General William Ashley places an ad in a St. Louis newspaper to recruit able-bodied men for his new fur-trading enterprise. There is no shortage of willing young men. Ashley will not build a chain of forts to manage his fur trading operation. Instead, he sends his men out alone and makes arrangements to meet them all at a central place a year later. At the predetermined time, Ashley will load up his wagons with supplies and head off to meet his men.

1824. William Ashley's men rediscover South Pass. The Rocky Mountain fur trappers and traders, including Indians and mountain men, begin holding most of their annual meetings along the Green River.

1825. William Ashley's wagons are the first vehicles to penetrate into the west, blazing a wagon road for the Oregon Trail settlers who will follow twenty years later. When Ashley finally reaches his men each year, it is cause for celebration – a wild party they call "the rendezvous."

1832. Capt. B. L. E. Bonneville takes the first wagons through South Pass, then builds Ft. Bonneville (the Green River Rendezvous) near present Daniel, Wyoming.

1834. Ft. Laramie, a private trading post, is the first permanent settlement in Wyoming, established by William Sublette and Robert Campbell.

1836. Narcissa Whitman and Eliza Spalding are the first white women to pass over the Oregon Trail to the Far West.

1837. Rendezvous is attended by more than 2,000 trappers, traders and Indians. Styles have already begun to change and top money is not received for the furs.

1842. The great migration begins on the Oregon Trail. Also in this year, gold is discovered in the South Pass district, but the major gold rush will be delayed by the coming Civil War and will not start in earnest until the late 1860s.

1843. Ft. Bridger, second permanent settlement in Wyoming established by Jim Bridger and Louis Vasquez.

1846. The Mormon migration to Utah begins. In 1847, Mormon Ferry established on the North Platte River.

1849. U.S. Government purchases Ft. Laramie, turning it into a military post. Many of the great treaties with the Indians are concluded here over the next thirty years.

1850. Present Wyoming is now part of Utah and Oregon Territories west of the Continental Divide; and in "Unorganized Territory," east of the divide. In the 1850 federal census, the only population in present Wyoming was that of Fort Bridger, taken as the "Green River Precinct" of Weber County, Utah Territory. The Federal Census was taken in Utah Territory with a census day of April 1, 1851.

1852. Peak year for emigration on the Oregon Trail.

1853. Washington Territory created, taken from the area of Oregon Territory. The southwest corner of present Wyoming (west of the Continental Divide) was now part of Washington and Utah Territories; the area east of the divide was in "Unorganized Territory." Also in 1853, Ft. Supply, an agricultural settlement in present Wyoming was established as a re-supply station by the Mormons.

1854. Nebraska Territory established, extending from the Missouri River to the Continental Divide. The area of modern Wyoming is now within Nebraska Territory east of the Continental Divide; the area west of the divide within Washington and Utah Territories.

1860. Present Wyoming is in three U.S. Territories for the federal census taken in 1860, but population is recorded only at Fort Bridger, Green River County, Utah Territory; and Fort Laramie in Nebraska Territory. Also in 1860, the Pony Express was started, a mail route which followed the same path as the Oregon Trail through present Wyoming.

1861. Dakota Territory created by Congress. Present Wyoming east of the Continental Divide is now part of Dakota and Nebraska Territories; and Washington and Utah Territories west of the divide. Also in 1861, the first transcontinental telegraph was completed, and soon after, the Pony Express was discontinued.

1862. The Overland Stage Line changes its route from the Oregon Trail to the Overland Trail. From Denver, the Overland Trail went north to Ft. Collins via what is now Interstate 25, then from Ft. Collins into Wyoming to the Laramie River via what is now U.S. Highway 287; then west to Ft. Bridger along the same general route of today's Interstate 80. For Oregon or California bound travelers, the Wyoming leg of the Overland Trail was a much shorter connection than the South Pass route.

1863. Bozeman Trail established. The portion of the route from present Cheyenne, Wyoming to Billings, Montana follows the same general path as Interstate 25; and from Billings to Bozeman, Montana via what is now Interstate 90.

1866. Nelson Story drives the first herd of cattle through present Wyoming, going north to Montana, essentially along the route of the Bozeman Trail. (This cattle drive was the historical setting for Larry McMurtry's *Lonesome Dove*).

1867. The Union Pacific Railroad enters present Wyoming, still part of Dakota Territory. Railroad workers found the city of Cheyenne in this year; and Laramie County is created by the Dakota Legislature.

1868. Wyoming Territory created July 25, with the same boundaries as the present state. Cheyenne is named the territorial capital.

1869. Territorial census taken. Also in this year, John A. Campbell, first territorial governor, signed the Female Suffrage Bill giving women the right to vote. Wyoming was the first territory or state in the United States to do so.

1870. Federal census reveals a population of 9,118 in Wyoming Territory.

1872. Yellowstone National Park is created, the first national park in America. Most of the park is within Wyoming.

1880. Federal census reveals Wyoming's population at 20,789.

1889. The state constitution submitted to Congress for admission as a state includes an article that provides: "Elections shall be open, free and equal, and no power, civil or military, shall at any time interfere to prevent an untrammeled exercise of the right of suffrage," allowing Wyoming to become the first state to extend voting rights to women.

1890. Wyoming admitted into the Union as the 44th state on July 10th with Cheyenne as the state capital. The 1890 federal census reveals Wyoming's population at 62,555.

WYOMING

Censuses & Substitutes, 1850-1989

The first census which included inhabitants of the area of present Wyoming was the 1850 federal census: Fort Bridger was enumerated as the "Green River Precinct" of Weber County,

Utah Territory. The Federal Census was taken in Utah Territory with a census day of April 1, 1851.

The 1860 federal census included Fort Bridger, Green River County, Utah Territory; and Fort Laramie in Nebraska Territory.

Although an 1869 territorial census was taken in Wyoming Territory (which survives and is available on microfilm), the State of Wyoming has taken no state censuses.

The following censuses and substitute name lists are available for Wyoming. Included are compilations of biographies, histories, and guides to historical references:

■ **1850 Federal Census, Utah Territory,** microfilm of original records at the National Archives in Washington, DC. Wyoming people were enumerated as the "Green River Precinct" of Weber County, Utah Territory. Filmed by the National Archives, 1964. FHL has 1 roll, FHL film #25540.

■ **1860 Federal Census, Utah Territory,** microfilm of original records at the National Archives, Washington, DC. Two filmings by the National Archives, 1950, 1967. The Utah Territory census included Wyoming people enumerated in Green River County, Utah Territory, which can be found on FHL film #805301 (2nd filming) and #25541 (1st filming).

■ **1860 Federal Census, Nebraska Territory,** microfilm of original records at the National Archives, Washington, DC. Includes Fort Laramie, now Wyoming. The 1860 census was filmed twice. The second filming is listed first and is usually easier to read. However, since some of the records were faded or lost between the first and second filmings, search the first filming whenever the material on the second filming is too light or missing. Filmed by the National Archives, 1950, 1967. FHL has 2 rolls, as follows:

- Nebraska: (2nd filming) Entire territory, FHL film #803665.
- Nebraska: (1st filming) Entire territory, FHL film #14889.

■ See also ***Wyoming 1860 Territorial Census Index,*** edited by Ronald Vern Jackson, et al., published by Accelerated Indexing Systems, Bountiful, UT, 1984, 30 pages (front matter) 5 pages (names). Despite the title – Wyoming Territory was not created until 1867 – this index is for the residents of Fort Laramie, as part of the Nebraska Territory census. It does not include the Fort Bridger residents who were part of Utah Territory in 1860. FHL book 978.7 X22w.

■ See also ***1860 Census, Fort Laramie,*** name list in the *Colorado Genealogist,* Vol. 30 (Sep 1969) thru Vol. 31, No. 2 (Jun 1970), a periodical of the Colorado Genealogical Society, Denver, CO.

■ **1861-1865 Civil War Soldiers.** See ***Index to Compiled Service Records of Volunteer Union Soldiers Who Served in Organizations From the Territory of Dakota,*** microfilm of original records at the National Archives, Washington, DC. Includes soldiers who served from Wyoming areas, part of Dakota Territory until 1867. Filmed by the National Archives, 1 roll, Series M0536. FHL film #881616. See also ***Index to Compiled Service Records of Volunteer Union Soldiers Who Served in Organizations From the Territory of Nebraska,*** microfilm of original records at the National Archives, Washington, DC. Includes the soldiers from the part of Wyoming Territory taken from Dakota Territory in 1867. Filmed by the National Archives, Series M547, 1964, 2 rolls, as follows:

- Index, A-La, 1861-1865, FHL film #821905.
- Index, Le-Z, 1861-1865, FHL film #821906.

The above indexed names included in ***Index to Soldiers & Sailors of the Civil War,*** a searchable name index to 6.3 million Union and Confederate Civil War soldiers now available online at the National Park Service Web site. A search can be done by surname, first name, state, or unit. Dakota Territory supplied 269 men; and

Nebraska Territory supplied 5,275 men to the war (all Union). To search for one go to the NPS Web site: **www.civilwar.nps.gov/cwss/.**

■ **1869 Wyoming Territory Census,** microfilm of original records at the Wyoming State Archives and Historical Department, Cheyenne, WY. Filmed by the archives, 1 roll, FHL film #2261365.

■ ***The Historical Encyclopedia of Wyoming,*** edited by Thomas S. Chamblin, published by the Wyoming Historical Institute, Cheyenne, WY, 1970, 1,669 pages (2 vols.). Contains "representative citizens who have had an integral part in the growth and development of Wyoming and historical sketches of leading cities, counties and tabulated principal facts of interest regarding every city, town, county, and district of the state." 1,425 pages of biography. FHL book 978.7 D3h v.1-2.

■ ***Wyoming Biographies,*** by Lawrence M. Woods, published by High Plains Pub. Co., Worland, WY, 1991, 224 pages. Includes index. FHL book 978.7 D3w.

■ **1868-1991 Guides to Wyoming Archives.** See ***Wyoming Blue Book,*** edited by Virginia Cole Trenhold, Loren Jost, Jim Donahue, et al., published by the Wyoming State Archives and Historical Department, Cheyenne, WY, 1974, 1991, 5 vols. Reprint of *Wyoming Historical Blue Book* by Marie Erwin, who prepared the original 1,471-page book in 1943. In 1974 Virginia Cole Trenhold edited Erwin's work into 2 volumes and added vol. 3 as a supplement, bringing the blue book up to 1974. Loren Jost edited vol. 4 to bring the series up to 1990. Jim Donahue edited vol. 5, *Guide to the County Archives of Wyoming.* Each volume is indexed. Contents: Vol. 1: acquisition of land through territorial days; creation, organization, and government of the territory; history of territorial counties; territorial and federal officers; events leading to statehood; constitution; territorial data; bibliography of biographies; historical highlights to 1890; Vol. 2: statehood until 1943; constitution with amendments to 1943; organization of state government; federal government in Wyoming; history of counties; election statistic; bibliography of biographies; chronology 1890-1943; Vol. 3: government of Wyoming; branches of government and functions; constitutional amendments, natural resources, counties and municipalities, tourism, Wind River Reservation; chronology 1943-1974; Vol. 4: state government, Congressional representatives, education, economic and cultural resources, the counties, Wind River Indian Reservation, events from 1974-1990; Vol. 5, pt. 1 is the Guide to the County Archives of Wyoming; Vol. 5, pt. 2 is the Guide to the State Government and Municipal Archives of Wyoming. FHL book 978.7 N2b vol. 1-5.

■ **1870 Wyoming Federal Census: Population Schedules,** microfilm of original records at the National Archives, Washington, DC. The 1870 census was filmed twice. The second filming is listed first and is usually easier to read. However, since some of the records were faded or lost between the first and second filmings, search the first filming whenever the material on the second filming is too light to read. Filmed by the National Archives, 1962, 1968. FHL has 2 rolls, as follows:

- Wyoming: (2nd filming) Albany, Carbon, Laramie, Sweetwater, and Uintah Counties, FHL film #553247.
- Wyoming: (1st filming) Albany, Carbon, Laramie, Sweetwater, and Uintah Counties, FHL film #34519.

■ ***1870 Wyoming Territory Census,*** (believed to be) a photocopy of original manuscript, 142 pages. Copy at the Family History Library in Salt Lake City. FHL book 978.7 X2p.

■ ***1870 Wyoming Census Index, A-Z,*** edited by Raeone Christensen Steuart, published by

Heritage Quest, Bountiful, UT, 2000, 55 pages, an every-name index. FHL book 978.7 X22s.

■ **1870 Census, Fort Laramie, Wyoming Territory,** name list in the *Colorado Genealogist,* Vol. 24, No. 1 (Jan 1963) thru Vol. 24, No. 4 (Oct 1963), a periodical of the Colorado Genealogical Society, Denver, CO.

■ **1875 History and Directory.** See ***History and Directory of Laramie City, Wyoming Territory,*** by J. H. Triggs, facsimile reproduction of original published by the Daily Sentinel Print, Laramie, WY, 1875, 91 pages. Contains a brief history of Laramie City from its first settlement to the present time, together with sketches of the characteristics and resources of the surrounding country; including a minute description of a portion of the mining region of the Black Hills. Also a general and business directory of Laramie City (1875). FHL book 978.795/L1 H2t.

■ **1878 Directory.** See ***Wolfe's Mercantile Guide, Gazetteer, and Business Directory of Cities, Towns, Villages, Stations, and Government Forts, Located Upon the Lines of the Following Named Railroads: Union Pacific, Omaha & Northwestern, Sioux City & Pacific, Omaha & Republican Valley, Colorado Central, Utah Northern, Utah Central, Utah Western, Utah Southern, Bingham Canon [sic] & Camp Floyd, Wahsath [sic] & Jordan Valley, and American Fork Railroad and Towns in the Blackhills,*** compiled and published by J. M. Wolfe, published by the Omaha Republican Book and Job Printing House, 1878, 360 pages. FHL has microfilm of original located at the Utah State Archives and Records Service, filmed by the archives, 1974, 1 roll, FHL film #979411. Another filming, FHL film #1004514.

■ **1880 Wyoming Territory Federal Census: Soundex and Population Schedules,** microfilm of original records at the National Archives, Washington, DC. Filmed by the National Archives, ca 1944. FHL has 2 rolls, as follows:

- Soundex: A000 thru Institutions, FHL film #378158.
- Population schedules: Entire territory, FHL #1255454.

■ ***Wyoming 1880 Census Index,*** edited by Ronald Vern Jackson, et al., an every-name index published by Accelerated Indexing Systems, Bountiful, UT, 1980, 266 pages. FHL book 978.7 X22w.

■ ***Wyoming 1880 Mortality Schedule,*** edited by Ronald Vern Jackson, et al., published by Accelerated Indexing Systems, 1983, 31 pages (front matter), 3 pages (names). Includes deaths occurring prior to June 1, 1880. FHL book 978.7 X2.

■ **1885 Census, Fort Laramie, Wyoming,** name list in *Black Hills Nuggets,* Vol. 4, No. 4 (Nov 1971), a periodical of Rapid City Society of Genealogical Research, Rapid, City, SD.

■ ***1890 Wyoming Veterans Census Index,*** edited by Ronald Vern Jackson, published by Accelerated Indexing Systems, Salt Lake City, UT, 1983, 57 pages (front matter), 19 pages (names). FHL book 978.7 X22j.

■ **1896 Directory.** See ***Directory of Lander, Lander Valley and the Mines and Other Useful Information: 1896,*** microfilm of a reprint published by the Fremont Genealogical Society, Riverton, WY, 1990, 92 pages. Original published by Clipper Book and Job Print, Lander, WY, 1896. From Intro: "Please note the portion of this directory that is listed as the Lander Valley is all of the northwest portion of the state of Wyoming in 1896. This consisted of Dubois, Lost Cabin, Thermopolis, Meeteetse and Burlington areas, or everything north of Lander to the Montana state line. Also all of the settlements towards Casper,

Rawlins and Pinedale." Filmed by the Genealogical Society of Utah, 1990, 1 microfiche, FHL fiche #6075728.

■ **1900 Wyoming Federal Census, Soundex and Population Schedules,** microfilm of original records at the National Archives, Washington, DC, filmed by the National Archives, ca1944, FHL has 17 rolls, as follows:

- Soundex: A000 Amel thru B456, FHL #1249607.
- Soundex: B460 Archibald thru C300/346 Jos. H., FHL film #1249608.
- Soundex: C300/346 Lancey thru D252 William F., FHL film #1249609.
- Soundex: D260 Alfred thru F426 William F., FHL film #1249610.
- Soundex: F430 Albert thru G663 Valentine, FHL film #1249611.
- Soundex: H000 A. C. thru H626, FHL #1249612.
- Soundex: H630 Indian thru K450 William, FHL #1249613.
- Soundex: K460 A. thru L663 Sam, FHL #1249614.
- Soundex: M000 Indian thru M536 William H., FHL #1249615.
- Soundex: M540 Agnes thru O362, FHL #1249616.
- Soundex: O400 thru R126, FHL film #1249617.
- Soundex: R130 Indian thru S263, FHL film #1249618.
- Soundex: S300 Indian thru S600 William, FHL film #1249619.
- Soundex: S610 A. thru W142, FHL film #1249620.
- Soundex: W150 Adrian thru Z545, FHL film #1249621.
- Population schedules: Albany, Bighorn, Carbon, Converse, Crook, Fremont, and Johnson Co., FHL film #1241826.
- Population schedules: Laramie, Natrona, Sheridan, Sweetwater, Uinta, and Weston Co.; Yellowstone National Park and Fort Yellowstone, FHL film #1241827.

■ **1906, First Census, Riverton, Fremont County, Wyoming,** name list in the *Fremont County Nostalgia News,* Vol. 12, No. 2 (Apr 1992), a periodical of the Fremont County Genealogical Society, Riverton, WY.

■ **1908-1909 Directory.** See ***Business Directory of Cheyenne, Wyo.: Laramie, Wyo.; Rawlins, Wyo.; Rock Springs, Wyo.; Green River, Wyo.; Evanston, Wyo.; Ogden, Utah; Preston, Idaho; Pocatello, Idaho; Brigham City, Utah; Logan, Utah; 1908-1909,*** microfilm of original at Utah State Historical Society, Salt Lake City. Filmed by the Utah State Archives and Records Services, 1975, 1 roll, FHL film #1004510.

■ **1909 Gazetteer.** See ***Stockmen's Gazetteer [sic] of Wyoming, 1909,*** published by Given & Espy, Cheyenne, WY, 1909, 224 pages. Microfilmed by the State of Wyoming Microfilming Department, Cheyenne, WY, 1959. Contains cattle, sheep, and horse brands, arranged by type of brand and the Wyoming county, with the name of the person or company to which the brand belongs, and the town where they are located. FHL has 1 roll, FHL film #1759460.

■ **1910 Wyoming Federal Census: Population Schedules,** microfilm of original records at the National Archives, Washington, DC. No Soundex was created for this state. Filmed by the National Archives, Series T624, 3 rolls, (NARA rolls 1745-1747), cataloged at the FHL as follows:

- Population schedules: Albany, Fremont, Big Horn, Carbon, and Johnson Co., FHL #1375758.
- Population schedules: Converse, Crook, Sweetwater, and Laramie Co., FHL #1375759.
- Population schedules: Natrona, Park, Sheridan, Uinta, and Weston Co. and Yellowstone National Park, FHL #1375760.

■ ***1910 Wyoming Census Index: Heads of Households and Other Surnames in Households Index,*** compiled by Bryan Lee Dilts, published by Index Publishing, Salt Lake City, UT, 1985, 245 pages. Transcribed from National Archives microfilm no. T624, rolls 1745-1747. FHL book 978.7 X2d. See also ***Wyoming 1910,*** a name index edited by Ronald Vern Jackson, published by Accelerated Indexing Systems, North Salt Lake,

UT, 1986, 269 pages. FHL book 978.7 X22j. See also, ***Colorado, Montana and Wyoming 1910 U.S. Federal Census Index,*** a CD-ROM publication by Heritage Quest, Bountiful, UT, 2002. FHL CD-ROM No. 1164. Extracted from the original records of the National Archives Series T624, this U.S. federal census index contains over 555,000 entries for all counties and cities in Colorado, Montana, and Wyoming. Indexed names include heads-of-household and any person with a different surname than the head. (Available from Heritage Creations, see page 47).

■ **1911 Poll Tax & 1911 Dog Tax, Fremont County, Wyoming,** name list in *Fremont County Nostalgia News,* Vol. 10, No. 2 (Apr 1990), a periodical of the Fremont County Genealogical Society, Riverton, WY.

■ **1917-1918 World War I Selective Service System Draft Registration Cards, Wyoming,** microfilm of original records in the National Archives at East Point, Georgia. The draft cards are arranged alphabetically by county draft board, and then alphabetically by surname of the registrants. Filmed by the National Archives, series M1508. FHL has 14 rolls, as follows:

- Albany County, A – O, FHL film #1993029.
- Albany County, P – Z; Big Horn County, A – Z; Campbell County, A – R, FHL film #1993030.
- Campbell County, S - Z Carbon County, A – Z; Converse County, A – J, FHL film #1993071.
- Converse County, K – Z; Crook County, A – Z; Fremont County, A– Q, FHL film #1993072.
- Fremont County, R – Z; Goshen County, A – Z; Hot Spring County, A – Z, FHL film #2022239.
- Johnson County, A – Z; Laramie County, A – O, FHL film #2022240.
- Laramie County, P – Z; Lincoln County, A – V, FHL film #2022241.
- Lincoln County, W – Z Natrona County, A – Stock, Jay, FHL film #2022242.
- Natrona County, Stock, Jay – Young; Niobrara County, A – Z, FHL film #2022243.
- Park County, A – Z; Platte County, A – Z; Sheridan County, A – C, FHL film #2022320.
- Sheridan County, D – Z; Sweetwater County, A – G, FHL film #2022321.
- Sweetwater County, H – Z; Uinta County, A – Z, FHL film #2022322.
- Washakie County, A – Z; Weston County, A – Z, FHL film #2022323.
- Indians, Prisoners, Insane, In Hospitals, Late Registrants, FHL film #2022637.

■ **1917-1935 City Directories, Casper, Wyoming, and Surrounding Area,** microfilm of original records located in various libraries and societies, original records published for years as noted below by R.L. Polk & Company. Filmed by Research Publications, Woodbridge, CT, ca 1995, 2 rolls. FHL has the following:

- **1917-1918** Casper City and Natrona County directory, including towns of Alcova, Arminto, Badwater, Bishop, Bucknum, Cadoma, Ervay, Freeland, Miller, Oil City, Powder River, Salt Creek, Split Rock, Waltman and Wolton, FHL film #2310255, Item 1.
- **1920-1921** Casper City and Natrona County directory, including towns of Alcova, Arminto, Badwater, Bishop, Bucknum, Cadoma, Ervay, Freeland, Miller, Oil City, Powder River, Salt Creek, Split Rock, Waltman and Wolton, FHL film #2310255, Item 2.
- **1922** Casper City and Natrona County directory, including towns of Alcova, Arminto, Badwater, Bishop, Bucknum, Cadoma, Ervay, Freeland, Miller, Mills, Oil City, Powder River, Salt Creek, Split Rock, Waltman and Wolton, film #2310255, Item 3.
- **1924** Casper City and Natrona County directory, including towns of Alcova, Arminto, Badwater, Bucknum, Ervay, Evansville, Freeland, Lavoye, Miller, Mills, Powder River, Salt Creek, Split Rock, Teapot Station and Waltman, FHL film #2310255, Item 4.
- **1925** Casper City and Natrona County directory, including towns of Alcova, Arminto, Badwater, Bucknum, Edgerton, Ervay, Evansville, Freeland, Lavoye, Mammoth, Midwest, Miller, Mills, Powder River, Salt Creek, Split Rock, Teapot Station and Waltman, FHL film #2310256, Item 1.
- **1928** Casper City and Natrona County directory, including towns of Alcova, Arminto, Badwater, Bucknum, Edgerton, Ervay, Evansville, Freeland, Lavoye, Mammoth, Midwest, Miller, Mills,

Powder River, Salt Creek, Split Rock, Teapot Station and Waltman, FHL film #2310256, Item 2.
- **1934-1935** Casper, Wyoming city directory, including Natrona County, FHL film #2310256, Item 3.

■ **1920 Wyoming Federal Census: Soundex and Population Schedules,** microfilm of original records at the National Archives, Washington, DC. Best copy available (original census schedules destroyed after microfilming). Filmed by the National Archives, ca1944. FHL has 22 rolls, as follows:
- Soundex: A000 thru B366, FHL film #1831426.
- Soundex: B400 thru B650 Sylvia, FHL film #1831427.
- Soundex: B650 Thomas thru C566, FHL film #1831428.
- Soundex: C600 thru D546. FHL film #1831429.
- Soundex: D550 thru F636, FHL film #1831430.
- Soundex: F640 thru H163, FHL film #1831431.
- Soundex: H164 thru H620, FHL film #1831432.
- Soundex: H621 thru K366, FHL film # 1831433.
- Soundex: K400 thru L526, FHL film #1831434.
- Soundex: L530 thru M416, FHL film #1831435.
- Soundex: M420 thru N356, FHL film #1831436.
- Soundex: N400 thru P566, FHL film #1831437.
- Soundex: P600 thru R500, FHL film #1831438.
- Soundex: R510 thru S414, FHL film #1831439.
- Soundex: S415 thru T366, FHL film #1831440.
- Soundex: T400 thru W324, FHL film #1831441.
- Soundex: W325 thru Institutions, FHL film #1831442.
- Population schedules: Albany, Big Horn, Campbell, Carbon, and Crook Counties, FHL film #1822025.
- Population schedules: Converse, Goshen, Johnson, Fremont, Hot Springs, and Weston Counties, FHL film #1822026.
- Population schedules: Laramie, Lincoln, and Platte Counties, FHL film #1822027.
- Population schedules: Natrona, Niobrara, Washakie, Park, and Sweetwater Counties, FHL film #1822028.
- Population schedules: Sheridan, and Uinta Counties; and Yellowstone National Park, FHL film #1822029.

■ **1924-1989 Directories.** See ***Polk's Laramie (Albany County, Wyoming) City Directory: Including Albany County, Containing an Alphabetical Directory of Business Concerns and Private Citizens, a Directory of Householders, Occupants of Office Buildings and Other Business Places, Including a Complete Street and Avenue Guide, a Directory of Rural Routes...*** published by R. L. Polk and Company, Kansas City, MO. FHL has 1924-25, 1926-27, 1929-30, 1931-32 (fiche only), 1934-35, 1941, 1958, 1961, 1966, 1970, 1975, 1978, 1983, 1986, 1989. FHL book 978.795 E4pL. Also on 3 microfiche, FHL US/CAN Fiche #6047943.

■ **1930 Wyoming Federal Census: Population Schedules,** microfilm of original records, series T626. Best copy available (original census schedules destroyed after microfilming). Filmed by the National Archives, ca1944. FHL has 5 rolls, as follows:
- Population schedules: Albany, Big Horn, Campbell, Converse, and Crook Counties, FHL film #2342355.
- Population schedules: Carbon, Fremont, Goshen, Hot Springs, and Johnson Counties, FHL #2342356.
- Population schedules: Laramie, Lincoln, Platte, and Sublette Counties, FHL #2342357.
- Population schedules: Natrona, Niobrara, and Sheridan Counties, FHL #2342358.
- Population schedules: Park, Teton, Uinta, Weston, Sweetwater, and Washakie Counties; and Yellowstone National Park, FHL #2342359.

Wyoming Censuses & Substitutes Online

www.heritagequestonline.com Heads of Household name index linked to census page images:
- 1870-1930 Wyoming Federal Censuses.

www.ancestry.com Name indexes, linked to images:
- 1870-1930 Federal Censuses
- 1890 Veterans Schedules
- 1880 Mortality Schedules

www.familysearch.org
- 1880 Federal Census – Every name index linked to census page images at Ancestry.com

www.censusfinder.com/wyoming.htm

Statewide Census Records Online:
- 1860-1930 Federal Census at Ancestry
- 1880 Wyoming Territory Census, Partial (RootsWeb site)
- 1880 Federal Census – Images (at Ancestry)
- 1880 Federal Census Search at Family Search
- 1883 Civil War Pensioners – Statewide (RootsWeb site)

Wind River Indian Reservation Project (RootsWeb site)

Countywide Databases (Only those counties with databases are listed):

Albany County
- 1870 Federal Census Records Index.
- 1870 Federal Census Records
- 1880 Federal Census, partial
- 1883 Pensioners

Big Horn County
- 1900 Federal Census Records, partial
- 1901-1902 Business Directory
- 1904-1905 Business Directory

Campbell County
- Rozet Original Homesteaders List
- 1892-Present Mayors of Campbell County

Carbon County
- 1870 Federal Census Records Transcription
- 1883 Pensioners

Converse County
- 1900 Federal Census Records Transcription

Fremont County
- Homestead Index

Johnson County
- 1866-1868 Residents of Fort Phil Kearny (area presently in Johnson County)

Laramie County
- 1870 Federal Census Records and Census Index
- 1900 Federal Census Records, partial

Natrona County
- 1900 Federal Census Records, partial

Park County
- 1910 Federal Census Records, partial
- 1920 Federal Census Index (partial)
- 1930 Federal Census Index (partial)
- 1930 Federal Census Records Transcription (partial)

Sheridan County
- 1889 Jurors List
- 1894 City Directory
- 1895-1908 Naturalization Records Index
- 1896 Voters List
- 1959 Annual of Big Horn High School

Sweetwater County
- 1870 Federal Census Index
- 1870 Federal Census Records
- 1920 Federal Census Index
- 1920 Federal Census Records

Uinta County
- 1870 Federal Census Records

Weston County
- 1900 Federal Census Index (partial)
- 1900 Federal Census Records (partial)

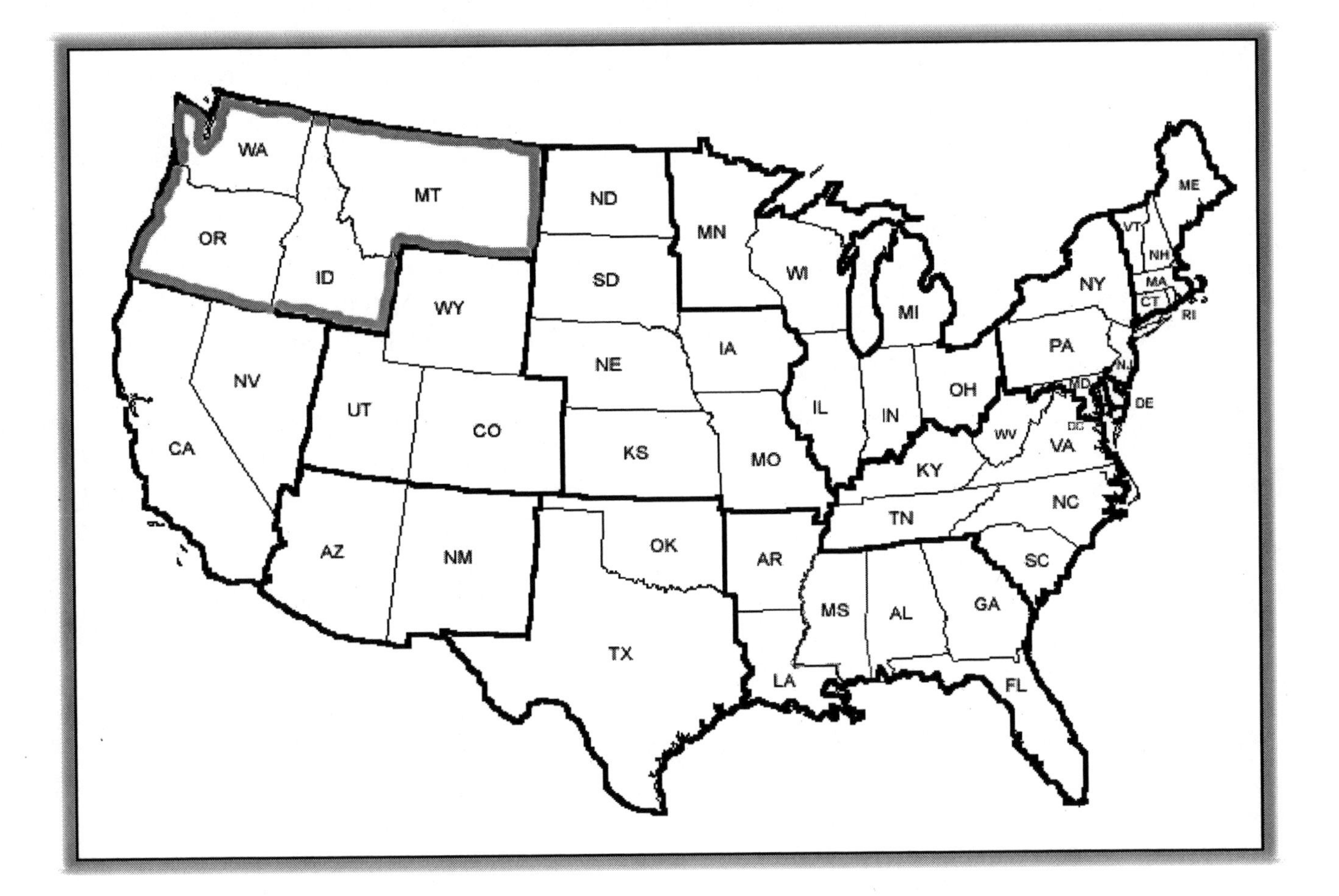

Chapter 5W – The Oregon Country

Oregon, Washington, Idaho, and Montana

The Oregon Country has a dramatic history, with discoveries and colonization of the area from competing groups, including the Spanish, Russians, British, and Americans. A timeline of historical events may be the best way to show the development of civilization, from the first discoveries to the time of statehood for each of the four states created out of the old Oregon Country.

A Timeline of Historical Events & Jurisdictions

1670. Hudson's Bay Company formed in London, with the intent of establishing trading posts in North America. They are granted the rights to exploit huge tracts of land by the British Crown, and become the dominate force in the settlement of British territory from the Great Lakes to the Pacific.

1725. Peter the Great of Russia commissions a Danish sea captain, Vitus Bering, to explore the Pacific Coast of North America. By the 1740s, the Russians had sighted and claimed Pacific coast areas ranging from the Bering Sea to as far south as San Francisco Bay. Although the Russians sent fishing and seal-hunting parties to Alaska and points further south, the first attempts at colonization did not begin until 1784.

1774. With mostly a Mexican crew, Juan Perez commands the first Spanish expedition to explore the Northwest Coast. His ship dropped anchor at a bay he named Rada de San Lorenzo de Nootka, known today as Nootka Sound, on the western shore of Vancouver Island. In return, he notes the entrance of what would be called the Strait of Juan de Fuca, but does not enter it. He also sights the Olympic Mountains of present Washington.

1775. En route to Nootka Sound, Spanish Capt. Bruno de Hezeta lands on the present Washington coast and claims the area for Spain. On his return south, he reports in his log the existence of fresh water emanating from what appears to be a very large river mouth, but does not explore it further. Based on the latitude-longitude noted in his ship's log, he was the first European to see the Columbia River at its mouth.

1778. British Capt. James Cook, fresh from Hawaii, explores and charts the Northwest Coast. He is intent on finding a "northwest passage" that would allow a ship to sail from the Pacific to Hudson Bay. En route, he looks for the mouth of a very large river in the area reported by the Spanish, but never finds it. Based on the latitude-longitude noted in his ship's log, he passed by the mouth of the Columbian River within a couple of miles. The river, it seems, was protected by numerous sand bars, spits, and shoals that hid its existence from passers-by for years.

1783. The United States Of America is recognized at the Treaty of Paris. From day one, the new government asserts a plan to inhabit the entire continent; with plans for explorations in the west, including the Pacific coast, by land or sea. George Washington once prepared a map of a future United States that extended from the Atlantic to the Pacific, with an extensive canal system as the main means of transportation.

1784. The first Russian settlement is established at Kodiak Island in present Alaska. Over the next 30 years, the Russians will establish trading posts in present southeast Alaska, British Columbia, and as far south as California.
– The North West Fur Company is formed in Montreal. It becomes a rival of the Hudson's Bay Company for dominance of the fur trade in North America. Although both companies were British-owned, the North West Fur Company is manned mostly by French-Canadians, who fought furiously for fur trading rights, attacking Hudson's Bay forts, burning their ships, etc., until the two companies were forced to end their differences by the British Crown, and merged into one company in 1821. The name North West Fur was dropped, but the Hudson's Bay Company continued. (In continuous business since 1670, the company is the largest retailer in Canada today, where its slogan is "Shop the Bay!").

1791. Spanish King Carlos IV, concerned that the Russians were colonizing in what should be Spanish territory, sends both Juan de Fuca and Juan Perez to explore and reinforce claims to the North Pacific region. After entering and naming the strait separating present Washington and Vancouver Island, British Columbia, Juan de Fuca and his party traveled inland as far east as present Saskatchewan.

1792. American Captain Robert Gray enters and names the Columbia River after his ship, the same ship he used to become the first American to circumnavigate the globe. Gray and party are in the area at the same time as British Capt. George Vancouver's party, who he meets with and reveals the location of the Columbia River. At first, Gray's news impresses Vancouver very little. He noted in his journal: "If any river should be found, it must be a very intricate one and inaccessible to vessels of our burden." But,

Vancouver then sent Lieutenant William Broughton to confirm the existence of the Columbia River. Broughton not only confirms it, he takes his ship well into the river, landing at a point 100 miles from the mouth on the Washington side, builds a temporary shelter, and names it Point Vancouver. Meanwhile, while Gray and Vancouver were chatting, a Spanish party landed at Neah Bay in present Washington. Capt. Vancouver went on to explore and name Puget Sound, naming many of the points visible from his ship after various friends and crew members, e.g., Vashon Island, Whidbey Island, Mount Baker, Bellingham Bay, Port Townsend, et al.

1799. Russia establishes the Russia-American Company at Sitka to manage fur-trading operations in present Alaska, British Columbia, and California. The Russian claims to North America now arbitrarily extend from the Bering Sea to San Francisco Bay.

1803. Captains William Clark and Meriwether Lewis lead the Corps of Discovery, the first transcontinental expedition of the lands west of the Missouri River. Their trek to the Pacific was mostly via river routes, beginning at St. Louis on the Mississippi, up the Missouri River to its source in Montana, then by foot across the Mountains, picking up Idaho's Clear River, to the Snake River of Idaho and Washington, and finally, the Columbia River all the way to its mouth at present Astoria, Oregon.

1805. Lewis and Clark explore the Washington side of the Columbia River, including Point Vancouver, the site of the future Fort Vancouver, but build their own Fort Clatsop on the Oregon side near the mouth of the Columbia River, where they spend the Winter of 1805-1806.

1807. British explorer and mapmaker David Thompson, former employee of the Hudson's Bay Company, now with the North West Fur Company, begins looking for routes from the Rocky Mountains to the Pacific Ocean. He established fur trading opportunities with any Indian Tribes he encountered, and charting detailed maps of the Columbia River. From 1807 to 1809, Thompson established the first trading post in present Montana at Kootenai Falls near Libby; the first in present Idaho (Kullyspell House), on Pend Oreille Lake; and the first trading post in present Washington, now Bonner's Ferry, on the Columbia River.

1807. Fur trader Manuel Lisa establishes Fort Raymond, a fur trading post in present day Montana, at the mouth of the Bighorn River.

1808. John Jacob Astor forms the American Fur Company to compete with the North West Fur Company of Canada in the northern Plains.

1809. By now, 25 colonies have been established by the Russia-American Company, strung along the northern Pacific coast as far south as California.

1810. John Jacob Astor forms the Pacific Fur Company to expand his trading empire to the Pacific coast.
– Fort Henry (1), first American fur post west of the Rocky Mountains is established near present St. Anthony, Idaho.

1811. (March). American fur traders build Fort Astoria near the mouth of the Columbia River as part of the Pacific Fur Company. Manned by two shiploads of men and supplies, it is the first permanent American settlement on the Pacific Coast.
– A Pacific Fur Company expedition travels overland to Oregon with the intent of arriving at Fort Astoria at the same time as Astor's ships. Called the "Astorians," they explore the Snake River Valley on their way to the Columbia River. Led by Astor's second-in-command, Wilson P. Hunt, the party discovers the Boise Valley.

– David Thompson completes his maps of the Columbia River from its source in present British Columbia to its mouth at present Astoria, Oregon. En route to the Columbia, he makes contact with the Astorians, and follows them down river to Fort Astoria. Thompson then sets up a rival fur trading post for the North West Fur Company next door to Fort Astoria.

1812. The Russian-American Company establishes Fort Ross at Bodega Bay just north of San Francisco Bay, mainly as a farming community to provide winter food for its northern outposts in present British Columbia and Alaska.

1813. After war is declared in 1812, British warships blockade Fort Astoria. The Astorians decide it is better to get out before shots are fired, and the entire Fort Astoria operation is sold to the British-owned North West Fur Company, who renamed it Fort George. The Astorians returned overland to St. Louis, and in doing so, became the first to cross South Pass, the route through the Rocky Mountains that would be followed by thousands of Oregon Trail travelers.

1818 Treaty of Joint Occupation. The United States and Great Britain agree to a joint occupation of the Oregon Country. The area is not defined precisely, but both parties accept the area in question as extending from the Continental Divide to the Pacific Ocean, and from about latitude 54° in present British Columbia, to the present Siskiyou Mountains (which lie on the modern boundary between Oregon and California). Though not stated in the treaty, it is clear that the intention is to see who can inhabit the area first. Although the British have well-established fur trading operations in the Oregon Country, the Americans have the advantage of being closer. With newly discovered overland routes from the Mississippi River to the Columbia River, they have the ability to supply new settlers into the region. In 1827 a provision was added to the treaty that allowed either party to invoke a conclusion of ownership, by giving 12 months notice to the other. Notice was not given until 1845, when President James K. Polk sought resolution, leading to a new treaty in 1846.
– Also in 1818, the Treaty of Ghent officially ends the War of 1812. Included in the treaty is a provision where Britain and the U.S. agree to the 49th parallel as the international boundary from the Lake of the Woods (now Minnesota) to the Continental Divide. This would have an impact later on the northern boundary of the Oregon Country.
– Invoking the Treaty of Ghent in 1818, John Jacob Astor uses the provisions for returning all occupied lands by the British back to the Americans, and gets the American government to allow his Pacific Fur Company to take possession of Fort Astoria again. Although the fort changed hands in ownership, the North West Fur Company continued to use it for their operations for several more years.

1819. The Adams-Onís Treaty sets the boundary between American and Spanish territory as the 42nd parallel, the current boundary between Oregon and California. The treaty also defines the boundaries between American Louisiana/Missouri Territory and Spanish Texas/New Mexico. In addition, Florida was added to the United States as a result of this treaty. Actually, the acquisition of Florida from Spain was the main impetus for the treaty at first. This landmark treaty is credited to the genius of John Quincy Adams, the U.S. Secretary of State at the time, who on his own came up with the concept of adding the western boundary agreements to the treaty. It is considered his crowning achievement, over any accomplishment before, during, or after his presidency.

1820. Czar Alexander closes Alaskan waters to foreign vessels and declares a fishing, whaling, and commercial monopoly from the Bering Straits to the 51st parallel for the Russia-American Company. Both Britain and the U.S. officially contest the move.

1821. Mexico wins independence from Spain. The southern boundary of the Oregon Country now touches the Mexican Province of California.
– Hudson's Bay Company and the North West Fur Company merge. The new Hudson's Bay Company now has a monopoly on fur trading operations in British North America.

1822. Rocky Mountain Fur Company formed by General William Ashley. He places an ad in a St. Louis newspaper to recruit able-bodied men for his new fur-trading enterprise. There is no shortage of willing young men. Ashley will not build a chain of forts to manage his fur trading operation. Instead, he sends his men out alone and makes arrangements to meet them all at a central place a year later. At the predetermined time, Ashley will load up his wagons with supplies and head off to meet his "mountain men." Ashley did establish one trading post east of the Rockies, Fort Henry (2), but it met with resistance from the local Indians who saw it as taking away their own trade for furs, and the operation struggled.

1823. The Monroe Doctrine issued. President James Monroe asserts the domain of the United States in the Americas and warns any foreign power to cease their interference to any Western Hemisphere areas supported and recognized by the United States. First proposed by Great Britain, that the United States issue a "hands-off" policy, the Monroe Doctrine was clearly a message to Russia, Spain, and Portugal, countries who were still meddling with colonies and former colonies in the Americas.

1824. The "Frontier Treaty" between the U.S. and Russia is signed. Russia cedes to the United States all lands below latitude 54 degrees 40 minutes. The Oregon Country boundaries of the 1818 Treaty of Joint Occupation are now official.

1825. The British-owned Hudson's Bay Company establishes Fort Vancouver as a center for their fur trading operations on the Pacific Coast. Fort Vancouver is located about 100 miles upriver from Fort Astoria, the center for the American-owned Pacific Fur Company. The Columbia River now becomes a highway to Canada, leading to routes for fur trappers that extend to the Great Lakes and beyond.
– David Thompson, now working for the reorganized Hudson's Bay Company, establishes a trading post, Fort Colville, on the Columbia River near present Kettle Falls, Washington. (Today, the site is underwater, part of Lake Roosevelt created by the Grand Coulee Dam).
– William Ashley's Rocky Mountain Fur Company wagons are the first vehicles to penetrate into the west, blazing a wagon road for the Oregon Trail settlers who will follow years later. When Ashley finally reaches his men each year, it is cause for celebration – a wild party they call "the rendezvous." In 1826, William Ashley retired a wealthy man, and began a life of politics. He sold his interest in the Rocky Mountain Fur Company to his employees.

1828. Fort Henry (2), first established by the Rocky Mountain Fur Company in 1822 at the mouth of the Yellowstone River (now Montana), is taken over by the American Fur Company and renamed Fort Union. It becomes the center for John Jacob Astor's fur trading business in the northern Plains. At its peak in the 1830s, American Fur Company forts in the region was sending to St. Louis an annual harvest of more than 25,000 beaver skins, 30,000 deer hides, and 55,000 buffalo hides. Between 1829 and 1867, Fort Union dominated the fur trade on the Upper Missouri River. But on the other side of the Rockies, fur brigades were replacing the need for trading forts by using independent Mountain Men as agents.

1830. Jedediah Smith and William Sublette, now partners in the successor to William Ashley's trading company, lead the first wagon train across the Rocky Mountains at South Pass and on to the Upper Wind River. The 500-mile journey through Indian country takes about six weeks, proving that even heavily loaded wagons and livestock – the prerequisites for settlement – can travel overland to the Pacific.

1834. Fort Hall established as a fur trading post on the Snake River in present Idaho by Nathaniel Jarvis Wyeth, a Boston entrepreneur. Wyeth soon gave up and sold the fort to the Hudson's Bay Company. Later it becomes the most important rest and re-supply point for all Oregon Trail wagon trains.

– Dr. Marcus Whitman and his wife Narcissa and also Rev. Henry H. Spalding and his wife Eliza set up a Methodist Mission at the junction of the Columbia and Snake Rivers. Narcissa and Eliza were the first white women to cross the mountains into the Oregon Country. Their travel route would become known as the Oregon Trail and used by thousands of future settlers.

– Rev. Henry H. Spalding establishes a mission near present Lapwai, Idaho, where he prints Idaho's first book, establishes Idaho's first school, develops Idaho's first irrigation system, and grows the state's first potatoes.

– Fort Boise established by the Hudson's Bay Company

1839. Fr. Pierre-Jean DeSmet arrives among the Flatheads in the Bitterroot Valley (now Montana). He and his staff would also set up a number of Jesuit missions in the present states of Washington and Idaho.

1841. The Western Emigration Society, a group of about 70 settlers bound for California and the Oregon Country set off on the Oregon Trail, beginning at Independence, Missouri. This was the first organized wagon train to head for California and Oregon. It is usually called the "Bartleson-Bidwell party" named for the two leaders. John Bartleson led about half of the group to Oregon's Willamette Valley. John Bidwell took the other half to California's Sacramento Valley, guiding the first wagon train across the California Trail through present Utah, Nevada, and California. Many descendants of Oregon Pioneers claim that when the Bartleson-Bidwell party reached a fork in the road in present southwest Wyoming, there was a sign-post, (← ***California*** | ***Oregon*** →), and those who could read went to Oregon.

– John Sutter buys Fort Ross north of San Francisco, ending Russia's thirty-year presence in California. Sutter dismantles the settlement and carries it to his newly established Fort Sutter at the junction of the Sacramento and American Rivers. In 1848, Sutter's mill was the site of the gold discovery that launched the gold rush to California.

– A group of Willamette Valley settlers meet to organize a provisional government under the protection of the United States. However, the Americans are outnumbered by French-Canadian trappers formerly employed by the North West Fur Company, and no action is taken.

1842. John C. Fremont leads an Army Topographical Corps Expedition to the Oregon Country. He witnesses an eruption of Mt. St. Helens. His maps of this expedition and one the following year are printed by the government and will be widely used by pioneers heading west.

1843. The Great Migration begins. A wagon train with over 120 wagons, a large herd of livestock, and nearly 1,000 pioneers head out on the Oregon Trail. They are led by Dr. Marcus Whitman, returning to his mission on the Snake River. Included in the party were three brothers, Lindsay, Jesse, and Charles Applegate and their extended families. As the party was rafting through the rapids on the Columbia River just outside The Dalles, one of their rafts capsized in the current and Lindsay's son Warren, age 9, Jesse's son Edward, also age 9, along with Alexander Mac (Uncle Mac, age 70) drowned. This tragedy made the brothers determined to save others similar grief and find a safer route to Oregon. Three years later, the Applegates were to blaze a southern wagon route into the Oregon Country.

– May 2nd, a group of 50 Americans and 52 Canadians meet in the Willamette Valley and take a vote to determine who should govern the Oregon Country. A vote of 52-50 favored keeping Oregon as American territory (two Canadians switched their votes). A group of nine was named to create a provisional government with Champoeg as its capital. A provisional government is established on July 5, 1843. The Provisional Territory of Oregon elects a governor, establishes courts, creates several counties, and functions with the consent of the local population until the U.S. Territory of Oregon is established by Congress in 1848.

1844-1846. In the 1844 presidential election, James K. Polk, Democrat, defeated Henry Clay, Whig, to become President of the United States. The two burning political issues of the day were the annexation of Texas and the acquisition of the Oregon Country. James K. Polk, as the "Manifest Destiny" candidate, was elected with campaign slogans of *Annex Texas!* and *Fifty-four forty or fight!* In 1845, Texas was annexed to the U.S. and war with Mexico began soon after. But in 1846, Polk settled for the 49th parallel as the northern boundary of the Oregon Country. At first, this looked like another one of those promises made that was never kept — but in fact, Polk was more concerned with keeping the Lower Columbia River in the United States than he was with extending the boundaries clear into present British Columbia. As it turns out, "Fifty-four forty or fight!" was a method of entering the bargaining table holding a strong starting point. The 1846 treaty negotiation team was led by James Buchanan, U.S. Secretary of State; while the British representative was Richard Pakenham, British Minister Plenipotentiary to the United States. Parlaying for the treaty began with the U.S. offering Polk's plan to extend the 49th parallel from the Continental Divide to the Columbia River, then NORTH to Latitude 54 degrees, 40 minutes, the same as his campaign slogan. But the British rejected that proposal and immediately countered with a proposal to extend the 49th parallel to the Columbia River, then SOUTH down the river to its mouth. The Americans said they would never give up the Columbia River, then countered with a proposal to extend the 49th parallel all the way to the Pacific Ocean. This is what Polk wanted all along. The British accepted the 49th Parallel with one exception. They did not want to lose Vancouver Island, and extending the 49th Parallel line would have dissected the island in half. A few days before the negotiations, the British had officially moved the British Columbia provincial capital from New Westminster on the mainland, to Victoria, at the southern tip of Vancouver Island. Fully prepared, they rolled out a new map showing the location of Victoria, and justification to run the line around Vancouver Island. The Americans went along with the modification and all of Vancouver Island became British territory. The treaty of 1846 brought the Oregon Country into the United States. And, in 1848, James K. Polk signed a bill that created Oregon Territory. Polk became the President who brought more territory into the United States than any other. During his administration, the Oregon County, Texas, and the Mexican Annexation were added to the U.S., and for the first time, America became a nation "from sea to shining sea."

1846. Barlow's Toll Road by-passes the Columbia River. The worst peril of the Oregon Trail was mainly that of the Columbia River, where treacherous falls near The Dalles had to be negotiated with rafts to carry people, cattle, and supplies. Portage around the falls was not any easier, since the area had high banks on either side of the falls. Either way, a whole industry was created in providing Oregon Trail travelers with rafts, wagons, and portage around The Dalles. High tolls were charged, regardless of the transportation method a traveler would choose. Samuel Barlow, recently arrived from Illinois, saw the situation and decided that if people were willing to pay such high tolls, maybe they would pay tolls over a new wagon road. Barlow constructed a road that skirted around Mt. Hood through the Cascade Mountains that by-passed the Columbia River. An earlier attempt at building such a road made it from The Dalles to the Tygh Valley, and Barlow continued the work from that point to Oregon City on the Willamette River. Barlow's Toll Road became the route of choice, because it avoided the perils of the Columbia. But it wasn't cheap. Barlow got $5.00 per wagon, plus 10 cents per person, and another 10 cents for every head of livestock; all for the privilege of passing over his road. In 1846, $5.00 was typically a weekly wage. The Barlow Family continued to operate and collect tolls from the road until 1916, when the State of Oregon purchased the Right of Way.

1846. Applegate Trail established. Jesse and Lindsay Applegate and about ten others headed down the Willamette Valley through what is now Corvallis and Eugene, continuing on to just south of Ashland, then turned east. From Lake Klamath, the party continued to what is now Lakeview, Oregon. Further east, they then crossed into present Nevada to a point where the present town of Humboldt is located, making a connection with the existing California Trail on the Humboldt River. At Fort Hall, the Applegates were able to convince a wagon train of about 100 wagons to change their plans and take the new route to Oregon. In August, the first wagon train to the Willamette Valley via the Applegate Trail made the trip. The trail became an alternative to the main Oregon Trail for many years, and contributed heavily to the first settlements in southern Oregon. In the 1860s, Jesse Applegate made his home near Ashland, Oregon, where he developed a toll road through a mountain pass of the Siskiyou Mountains into California. In 1872 he sold the toll road to Jesse Dollarhide. The Dollarhide Family operated and collected tolls on the road until 1916, when the Right of Way was purchased by the State of Oregon.

1847. Fort Benton is established on the Missouri River as a military and trading post. It soon becomes the "Head of Navigation" to the west, and the world's furthest inland port. Steamboats brought gold seekers, fur traders, settlers and supplies, making Fort Benton the "Birthplace of Montana." Of all the forts established on the Missouri and Yellowstone rivers, Fort Benton is the only one that continues as a town today. It is located in north central Montana, about 30 miles northeast of Great Falls.

1848. On February 2nd, the Treaty of Hidalgo Guadalupe is signed, ending the war with Mexico. As part of the treaty, the Mexican provinces of California and Nuevo Mexico are annexed to the U.S., which include the present states of California, Nevada, Arizona, New Mexico, Utah, and western Colorado.
– On August 14th, **Oregon Territory** is created by Congress. It encompasses the area between the 42nd and 49th parallels, from the Pacific to the Continental Divide. The first capital was Oregon City.

1849. Over 30,000 emigrants who join the gold rush come over the Oregon Trail into Idaho, and from there to the California Trail. The following year, it is estimated that as many as 55,000 made the trip Heavy traffic continues on the trail for many years. In 1849, a U.S. Military post, Cantonment Loring, is established near Fort Hall, now Idaho.

1850 Federal Census (June 1st). Census taken in Oregon Territory, which included the area of present Oregon, Washington, and Idaho; and Montana and Wyoming areas west of the Continental Divide. The population was revealed as 12,093 people. The population was limited in the present Washington area to a few residents of Clarke and Lewis counties, all south of Puget Sound and west of the Cascade Mountains. No population was recorded in the present Idaho, Montana, or Wyoming areas.
– Sept. 27th, Congress passes the Donation Land Claim Act. The forerunner of the 1862 Homestead Act, the Donation Land Claim Act is aimed entirely as an incentive to get settlers to move to Oregon Territory. From 1850 to 1862, land records for the areas that became Oregon and Washington provide detailed genealogical sources, revealing names, birthdates, birthplaces, marriage information, citizenship, and more.

1851. First settlers land at Alki Beach on Elliot Bay, the site of the present city of Seattle.

1852. The height of the Oregon Trail migrations. In this year, it is estimated that about 67,000 people traveled the Oregon Trail to Oregon and California.

1853. Washington Territory created. It encompasses the present area of Washington, but extends east to the Rocky Mountains, incorporating areas that today are in northern Idaho and western Montana. As a result, the original Oregon Territory is split in half. Oregon Territory now has lands on the same line as its present northern border stretching to the Continental Divide, and includes the southern half of present Idaho, and a portion of present western Montana and Wyoming.

1859. Oregon joins the Union as the 33rd state, a Free State with the same boundaries as present. The population of the new state was about 45,000 people. The eastern remnants of Oregon Territory, 1853-1859, were added to Washington Territory.
– The San Juan Islands of Washington Territory becomes the scene of a "pig war" between the United States and Britain and a dispute over the International Boundary. The 1846 treaty stated "...along the forty-ninth parallel of north latitude to the middle of the channel which separates the continent from Vancouver's Island, and thence southerly through the middle of the said channel, and of Fuca's Straits, to the Pacific Ocean." However, the described treaty line did not mention that a series of islands was on that trace, the San Juan Islands. The British believed the "middle of the channel" was Rosario Strait, east of the San Juans; while the Americans believed the main channel was Haro Strait, west of the Sam Juan Islands. As a result, both British and American farmers settled on several of the San Juan islands. A conflict began in 1859, when Lyman Cutlar, an American farmer, shot and killed a pig rooting in his garden. That pig was owned by an Irishman who was employed by the Hudson's Bay Company. The animosity grew into a face-off of some 500 U.S. Army soldiers and three British warships threatening each other. Calm prevailed, and the only casualty was an AWOL Irish pig. The dispute over the boundary was finally resolved in 1872, when both the U.S. and Britain agreed to have a third party arbiter settle the issue. The arbiter turned out to be Kaiser Wilhelm I, who ruled in favor of the Americans, giving them all of the San Juan Islands. The San Juan Islands settlers, both British and American, were enumerated in the 1870 federal census as part of Whatcom County, Washington Territory.

1860 Federal Census (June 1st). State of Oregon population at 52,465. Boundaries the same as today.
– Washington Territory population at 11,594. The area included present Washington and Idaho; and areas west of the Continental Divide

in present Montana and Wyoming. The only recorded population outside of the present Washington bounds was for the residents of the Bitterroot Valley and Ponderay Mountain areas of present Montana; and a few farmers in Idaho's Bear Lake area taken as part of Cache County, Utah Territory. (Idaho's first town was Franklin, a Cache Valley community founded by thirteen Mormon families three weeks after the 1860 Census Day of June 1, 1860. At the time, they thought they were in Utah).

– Present Montana east of the Continental Divide was part of Nebraska Territory, but for convenience the trading posts of Fort Union on the Missouri River and Fort Alexander on the Yellowstone River were enumerated in 1860 as part of Unorganized Dakota. Fort Benton and a couple of other outposts in Montana were missed.

1861. Dakota Territory is created, with boundaries that include all of Montana and Wyoming east of the Continental Divide; and the areas of present North Dakota and South Dakota.

1863. Idaho Territory is created, with boundaries that include all of present Idaho, and Montana and Wyoming areas west of the Continental Divide. The large area is short-lived, however, as much of Montana Territory is taken from the Idaho area a year later. When Wyoming Territory was created in 1867, Idaho Territory matched the present boundaries of the state. The first Idaho territorial capital was established at Lewiston, but a year later moved to Treasure Valley (now Boise).

1864. Montana Territory is formed, taken from parts of Idaho and Dakota Territories. From its beginning, Montana had the same boundaries as the present state. The first territorial capital of Montana was established at Bannack. The original area proposed for Montana Territory included what is now Idaho's northern panhandle, but Congress decided to keep that area as part of Idaho to offset the Mormon population in southern Idaho.

1867. Wyoming Territory created from parts of Idaho and Dakota Territories, with the same boundaries as the present state. As a result, Dakota Territory was reduced in size to the same area now covered by North Dakota and South Dakota.

1870 Federal Census (June 1st). State of Oregon population at 90,923. Washington Territory population at 23,955. Idaho Territory population at 14,999. Montana Territory population at 20,595.

1880 Federal Census (June 1st). State of Oregon population at 174,768. Washington Territory population at 75,116. Idaho Territory population at 32,610. Montana Territory population at 39,159.

1883. Northern Pacific Railroad completed to Tacoma, linking Washington Territory to the East.

1889 (Nov. 8th). **Montana** becomes the 41st state, with the state capital at Helena.

– Nov. 11th, **Washington** becomes the 42nd state, with the state capital at Olympia.

1890 Federal Census, June 1st – State of Oregon population at 317,704. Washington Territory population at 357,232. Idaho Territory population at 88,548. Montana Territory population at 142,924.

– July 3rd, **Idaho** becomes the 43rd state with the state capital at Boise.

1900 Federal Census (June 1st). Oregon population at 413,536. Washington population at 518,103. Idaho population at 161,772. Montana population at 243,329.

OREGON

Censuses & Substitutes, 1837-2000

Most of the original Oregon (non-federal) censuses are now located at the Oregon State Archives in Salem. They include the surviving censuses taken by the Provisional Government of Oregon, 1842-1843 and 1845-1846; those taken by Oregon Territory, 1849, 1853, 1854, 1855, 1856, 1857, 1858, and 1859; and Oregon State Censuses taken (but with only a handful of surviving counties) for 1855, 1865, 1875, 1885, 1895, and 1905. For more details, a list of these censuses and the counties included in each can be found at the State Archives Website at: **http://arcweb.sos.state.or.us/censuslist.html.** This site lists the state censuses by year and county, including hyperlinks to any which have been indexed in the new **Oregon Historical Records Index,** located at: **http://genealogy.state.or.us/.** Published territorial and state censuses, abstracts, extracts, indexes, and census substitutes are show in the chronological listing below:

■ **1837-1933 Oregon State Archives Combined Military Alphabetical Index,** microfilm of original computer-generated index at the Oregon State Archives in Salem, Oregon. This 12,000-page index was compiled by the State Archives staff and includes Oregon military and other names extracted from 1) Provisional and Territorial Government Documents, 1837-1859; 2) Supreme Court Case Files, 1855-1904; 3) Oregon Soldiers Home Patient Histories, 1894-1933; 4) State Treasurer Quarterly Reports of Estates, 1903-1913; and 5) Defense Council Personal Military Service Records, 1917-1918. Includes name, state archives number, and description of record. Arranged in alphabetical order by surname. Filmed by the Genealogical Society of Utah, 2000, 37 rolls, as follows:

- Aandahl (Architects) to Austin, Henry R., FHL film #2194727.
- Austin, J. to Beales, J., FHL film #2194728.
- Beall, L. D. to Bolton, Frank J., FHL film #2194729.
- Bolter to Brown, Furnander, FHL film #2194730.
- Brown, G. to Campbell, Ira L., FHL film #2194731.
- Campbell, J. to Clark, Israel, FHL film #2194732.
- Clark, J. to Cornwell, James N., FHL film #2194920.
- Cornwell, Raymond Lee to Davidson, Eugene C., FHL film #2194921.
- Davidson, Frank to Douellot, Augustus, FHL film #2194922.
- Dougherty, Asa Rolland to Esters, E. T., FHL film #2194923.
- Estes to Fount, Leroy H. B., FHL film #2194924.
- Fountain, Caleb to Gill, Mary, FHL film # 2194925.
- Gill, Rob't to Hackleman, Pauline, FHL film #2195100.
- Hackler, Marian to Hastie, John, FHL film #2195101.
- Hastings, A. to Hoback, H., FHL film #2195102.
- Hobart, Alvin Dewey to Hunting, Kenneth, FHL film #2195103.
- Huntington, A. H. to Jomon, James, FHL film #2195104.
- Jonalshan to Kisling (Kesling), James, FHL film #2195105.
- Kisor, Erb Lesley to Learne (Learn), M. M. , FHL film #2195252.
- Learned, Alva Lepas to Luther, William J., FHL film #2195253.
- Luthy, Christian to McKenty, Peter, FHL film #2195254.
- McKenzie to Martinson, S. , FHL film #2195255.
- Martle, Perry B. to Milne, J., FHL film #2195256.
- Milne, James to Mycoff, Peter, FHL film # 2195257.
- Myer, A. to Ordway, E. W., FHL film #2195258.
- Ordway, Julius to Petigrew, Thomas, FHL film #2195259.
- Petit, A. to Rainhart, G., FHL film #2195260.
- Rains, C. H. to Robertson, Charles A., FHL film #2195414.
- Robertson, E. E. to Scarboro, James Allen, FHL film #2195415.
- Scarborough, Frank to Simons, Daniel, FHL film #2195416.
- Simmons to Soyas, Gust, FHL film #2195417.
- Spady, Henry John to Stowers, Henry, FHL film #2195418.
- Strader, John to Thompson, Roy Marion, FHL film #2195419.

- Thompson, S. to Wacken, Herman, FHL film #2195420.
- Wacken, Rudolf Human to West, William S. , FHL film #2195421.
- Westacott & Co. to Wilson, Rose M., FHL film #2195422.
- Wilson, S. S. to Zwimpfer, Adolphe August, FHL film #2195571.

■ ***Oregon Memorial of Citizens of the U. S. and Miscellaneous Information: Census Records for 1843, Tax Rolls, Newspaper Clippings of Oregon Pioneers, Government Document on the Boundary Line Between the British and United States Territories in Northwestern America,*** microfilm of original ms. (1 v.), filmed by the Genealogical Society of Utah, 1966, 1 roll, FHL film #430055.

■ **Oregon Pioneers Card Index at the Multnomah County Library, Portland, Oregon.** (not the official title, but the library staff will know what you are talking about). Contains thousands of references to people of early Oregon from newspaper articles, books, and various public records. For more information, visit the library's genealogy webpage at: **www.multcolib.org/ref/gene.html#oregon.** Or, get a copy of ***Guide to Genealogical Material in the Multnomah County Library, Portland, Oregon,*** compiled by members of the Genealogical Forum of Portland, with the assistance and cooperation of the staff of Multnomah County Library, published 1967, 215 pages. FHL book 979.549 A3g. Also on microfilm, FHL film #1321456. See also, ***Oregon Biography Index,*** edited by Patricia Brandt and Nancy Guilford, published as Bibliographic Series No. 11, by Oregon State University, Corvallis, OR, 1976, 131 pages. Indexes subjects of biographical sketches from many histories of early Oregon. FHL book 979.5 D3b.

■ ***Territorial Papers of the United States for the Territory of Oregon, 1848-1859,*** microfilm of originals at the National Archives in Washington, D.C. Includes papers from the U.S. Senate, U.S. House of Representatives, U.S. Supreme Court, Department of Justice, Department of State, Bureau of Census, U.S. Post Office, Secretary of the Interior, Bureau of Indian Affairs, and the Department of the Treasury. Some pages wanting, faded, torn, etc. For complete explanation of information contained herein see beginning of each film for note. Filmed by National Archives, series M1049, 1977-1978, 12 rolls, as follows:

- Records of the 30th-35th Congress Senate and House, FHL film #1695681.
- Records of the 30th-35th Congress, House, FHL film #1695682.
- Records of the Supreme Court; Records of the United States Court of Claims General records of the Department of Justice, FHL film #1695683.
- General records of the Department of State, FHL film #1695684.
- Miscellaneous records of the Bureau of Accounts and other Departments, FHL film #1695685.
- Records of the Department of State, Records of the Bureau of the Census, Records of the Post Office Department, FHL film #1695686.
- Records of the Office of the Secretary of the Interior, FHL film #1695687.
- Records of the Bureau of Indian Affairs, FHL film #1695688.
- Records of the Department of the Treasury, FHL film #1695689.
- Records of the Department of the Treasury, FHL film #1695690.
- Records of the Department of the Treasury, FHL film #1695691.
- Records of the Department of the Treasury, FHL film #1695692.

■ ***1842-1859 Provisional and Territorial Census Records of Oregon,*** microfilm of original typescripts and manuscripts at the Oregon State Archives, Salem, OR. Includes alphabetical index of old and new counties at the beginning of the film. Filmed by the Oregon State Archives, 1970, 1 roll. FHL's copy is FHL film #899786. Names from this roll of film were indexed in ***Oregon Census Records 1841-1849,*** compiled by Ronald Vern Jackson, et al, published by Accelerated

Indexing Systems, North Salt Lake, UT, 1984, 79 pages. FHL book 979.5 X22o; and in ***Oregon Census Records, 1851-1859,*** compiled by Ronald Vern Jackson, et al., published by Accelerated Indexing Systems, North Salt Lake, UT, 1984, FHL book 979.5 X22o. The list of years and counties included are shown at the State Archives Website at: **http://arcweb.sos.state.or.us/censuslist.html.**

■ See also, ***History of the Willamette Valley: Being a Description of the Valley and Resources, With an Account of its Discovery and Settlement by White Men, and its Subsequent History; Together with Personal Reminiscences of its Early Pioneers,*** edited by Herbert O. Lang, published by Himes & Lang, Portland, OR, 1885, 902 pages. Includes "Census Returns of Oregon in 1845," for the five counties of the Willamette Valley; plus an extraction of the 1849 Territorial Census for 10 Oregon counties. FHL book 979.53 H2L. Also on microfilm, FHL film #1321001.

■ ***The Lockley Files: Voices of the Oregon Territory; Conversations With Bullwhackers, Muleskinners, Pioneers, Prospectors, '49ers, Indian Fighters, Trappers, Ex-barkeepers, Authors, Preachers, Poets and Near Poets, and All Sorts and Conditions of Men,*** by Fred Lockley; compiled and edited by Mike Helm, published by Rainy Day Press, Eugene, OR, 1981, 358 pages. FHL book 979.5 D2L. Fred Lockley (1871-1958), wrote a newspaper column for Portland's *Oregon Journal* for over 30 years. The main topics of his columns were interviews with Oregon Pioneers. His subjects represent the "Who's Who" of the history of Oregon. This book is an extraction of some of the more interesting subjects of his interviews. It should be noted that all of the names mentioned in Lockley's newspaper articles have been indexed and are part of the Oregon Pioneers Card Index at the Multnomah County Library.

■ **1842 Census of Willamette Valley,** in *Trackers,* Vol. 15, No. 1 (1975), a periodical of Mount Hood Genealogical Forum, Oregon City, Oregon.

■ **1843 Census of the Oregon Country,** in *Beaver Briefs,* Vol. 18, No. 3 (Jul 1986), a periodical of the Willamette Valley Genealogical Society, Salem, Oregon.

■ **Canadian Settlement in Willamette Valley,** in *Forebears,* Vol. 6, No. 3 (Aug 1991), a periodical of Clatsop County Genealogical Society, Astoria, Oregon.

■ ***1845 Census of the Territory South of the Columbia and West of the Cascade Mountains,*** abstracted by Julie Kidd, published by Oregon Territorial Press, Portland, OR, 1997, 27 pages. Includes Champoeg, Clackamas, Clatsop, Tualatin, and Yamhill Counties. Copy at the Oregon Historical Society Library, Portland, OR (REF 312 O66t 1845).

■ **1842-1880 Oregon Census Records,** original manuscripts, photostatic copies, and typescript transcriptions of original records, located at the Oregon Historical Society in Portland, Oregon. Census records include Photostat of original copy of Joseph Meek's 1845 Census of Oregon; and Elijah White's 1842 Oregon census; original handscript 1849 census of males over the age of 21; typescript of 1854 Benton County census; 1856 Washington County census; Jackson County census rolls (ca. 1854-1855, 1858); typescript copy of United States Census roll for Coos County (1860); partial typescript of 1880 United States Census for Wasco County; and a typescript report of 1850 census for Butte and Calaveras Counties in California. Oregon Historical Society Call Number: Mss 1.

■ **1845 Census, Clackamas County, Provisional Oregon Territory,** in *Trackers,* Vol. 12, No. 4 (Summer 1972), a periodical of Mount Hood

Genealogical Forum, Oregon City, Oregon. See also **Territorial Census, 1845, Clackamas County,** in *Oregon End of Trail Researchers,* (Salem, OR), Vol. 7, No. 2 (Fall 1976).

■ **1845-1846 Census of Twality County, Oregon, (now Washington County),** microfilm of original records at the Oregon State Archives in Salem, Oregon. Tualaly or Twallity County changed to Washington County in 1849. Filmed with the Washington County delinquent tax records. Filmed by the Genealogical Society of Utah, 2001, 1 roll, FHL film #2257683.

■ **1845-1859 Land Records of Oregon.** See ***Genealogical Material in Oregon Provisional Land Claims, Abstracted vols. I-VIII, 1845-1849,*** compiled by Lottie LeGett Gurley, published by Genealogical Forum of Portland, 1982, 300 pages. FHL book 979.5 R2gL; and see ***Index to Oregon Donation Land Claims,*** 2nd edition, 1987, compiled by members of the Genealogical Forum of Oregon, Portland, OR, 1987, 172 pages. FHL book 979.5 R2g. For an excellent history and explanation of the Lands Claims of the Oregon Provisional Government, and Oregon Donation Land Claims, visit the End of Oregon Trail Interpretive Center Website at:
www.endoftheoregontrail.org/road2oregon/sa28claims.html.

■ **1849 Census, Clackamas County, Provisional Oregon Territory,** in *Trackers,* Vol. 13, No. 1 (Winter 1973), a periodical of Mount Hood Genealogical Forum, Oregon City, Oregon.

■ **1849 Census of Foreigners, Linn County, Oregon Territory,** in *Oregon End of Trail Researchers* (Salem, OR), Vol. 7, No. 1 (Spring 1976).

■ **1850 Federal Census, Oregon Territory, Original Population Schedules,** microfilm of original records at the National Archives, Washington, DC. Filmed by the National Archives, series M0432, 1964, 1 roll, FHL film #20298. The 1850 federal census taken in Oregon Territory lists and names the entire population of 12,093 people. Taken in June 1850, the census was enumerated a few weeks before the implementation of the Donation Land Claim Act. In the 1850 "Value of Real Estate" column, a researcher can find the earliest land owners, and since the first officially recognized land grants began under the Provisional Territory of Oregon in 1845, the 1850 census may act as a pointer.

■ ***1850 Oregon Territorial Census,*** transcribed by Elsie Youngberg, published by End of Trail Researchers, Lebanon, OR, 1970, xxviii, 310 pages. FHL book 979.5 X2p. Also on microfilm, FHL #897219.

■ ***1850 Census of Oregon,*** compiled by William Bowen, microfilm of original manuscript at San Fernando Valley State College, Northridge, CA, 1972. p. 282-519. FHL book 979.5 X2pb (Large Q book). Also on microfilm, FHL film #908211.

■ ***Pioneer Families of the Oregon Territory, 1850,*** Pub. No. 3, Oregon State Library, Division of Archives, 64 pages. FHL book 979.5 X2o.

■ ***Oregon 1850 Territorial Census Index,*** edited by Ronald Vern Jackson, et al., published by Accelerated Indexing Systems, Bountiful, UT, 1978, 83 pages. FHL book 979.5 X2j.

■ ***Index to 1850 Census of Benton, Clark, Clatsop, Lewis, Linn, Marion, Polk, Washington and Yamhill counties in Oregon,*** compiled by Shirley Buirch, 377 page typescript filmed by the Genealogical Society of Utah, 1977, FHL film #982441.

■ ***1850 U.S. Census Index, Western States: CA, NM, OR, TX, UT; Extracted From the Original U.S. Federal Census Schedules,*** a CD-ROM publication by Heritage Quest, a division of Sierra Online, Inc., Bountiful, UT, 2000. FHL CD-ROM No. 387.

■ ***California, New Mexico, Oregon, Texas, and Utah, 1850,*** a CD-ROM publication by Broderbund (Family Tree Maker Family Archives No. 452), 1999. Includes an index to and actual images of portions of the 1850 federal census. FHL CD-ROM No. 9, part 453, 4 discs.

■ ***Oregon 1850 Mortality Schedule,*** edited by Ronald Vern Jackson, et al., published by Accelerated Indexing, Bountiful, UT, 1980, 10 pages. FHL book 979.5 X2jr.

■ ***Genealogical Notes on the Oregon Territory and State of Oregon, 1810-1910,*** by Sherman Lee Pompey, an unpublished manuscript. Includes some indexes. Contains miscellaneous genealogical notes compiled from census, marriage, territorial, military, and business directory records of Oregon Territory and State. Also includes information copied from the 1850, 1860, and 1870 census records of Oregon Territory and State, and an index to the 1865 state census. Filmed by the Genealogical Society of Utah, 1986, 1 roll, FHL film #1421678.

■ ***Linn County, Oregon Early 1850 Records,*** edited by Lois M. Boyce, published by Boyce-Wheeler Publishing, Portland, OR, 1983, 59 pages. Includes corrected 1850 Linn Co. census, lists of judges, clerks, recorders, sheriffs, etc., 1851 to 1853 assessment rolls. FHL book 979.535 X28L.

■ **1853 Census, Marion County, Oregon Territory,** in *Coos Genealogical Forum Bulletin,* Vol. 20, No. 2A (Spring 1985), a periodical of Coos Genealogical Forum, North Bend, Oregon.

■ ***Enumeration of the Inhabitants of Benton County, Oregon Territory, as Taken by Charles Wells, Assessor for the Year 1854,*** copied from the original by Mrs. James C. Moore, published 1947. Includes index. Includes name of the legal voter, number of males and number of females in house. FHL book 979.5 A1 No. 151. Also on microfilm, FHL film #1321058. See also **1854 Census, Benton County, Oregon Territory,** in *Genealogical Forum of Portland Bulletin,* Vol. 19, No. 3 (Nov 1969) through Vol. 19, No. 6 (Feb 1970).

■ **1854-1855, 1857 Clackamas County, Oregon Census Rolls,** microfilm of original records at the Oregon State Archives in Salem, Oregon. Includes names of individuals and age categories. No names are listed for 1854. Also includes undated census. Filmed by the Genealogical Society of Utah, 1999, 1 roll, FHL film #2168743. See also ***Census of Clackamas County, Oregon Territory and Territorial Road Petition,*** compiled by Eloise C. Mabee, published Mount Hood Genealogical Forum, Oregon City, OR, 1974, 28 pages. Includes the following years: 1845, 1849, 1856-1857, and road petition circulated in 1851 or 1852. Also lists sheriffs, 1841-1973. FHL book 979.5 A1 N. 21.

■ **1854-1900 Tax Lists, Election Records, and Censuses, Columbia County, Oregon,** microfilm of original records of the County Recorder and County Clerk, St. Helens, Columbia County, Oregon, now located at the Oregon State Archives. Includes tax lists, delinquent tax lists, delinquent road tax, list of taxable property for 1874, precinct register for 1900, poll books for 1884 and 1887, abstract of votes 1854-1888, tax assessments and county census. Film by the Genealogical Society of Utah, 2002, 10 rolls, beginning with FHL film #2293501 (Tax and election records, 1854-1900).

■ ***Pioneer People of Jackson County, Oregon: DLC Surveyor's Record, Census 1853, 1854, 1855, 1856, 1857, 1858, 1859, Hospital Outpatients, 1855-56, Militia Muster Rolls,*** compiled by Ruby Lacy and Lida Childers, published R. Lacy, Ashland, OR, 1990, 301 pages. FHL book 979.527 X28L.

■ ***1854 Lane County Agricultural Census,*** compiled by Wilma Stahl from an original book held at the Lane County Public Service Building, Surveyors and Road Department, published by the Oregon Genealogical Society, Eugene, OR, 1990, 95 pages, FHL book 979.531 X2s.

■ **1854, 1857-1858 Census Records, Tillamook County, Oregon Territory,** microfilm of original records at the Oregon State Archives in Salem, Oregon. Filmed by the Genealogical Society of Utah, 2001, 1 roll, FHL film #2313400.

■ **1855 Census, Coos County, Oregon Territory,** in *Coos Genealogical Forum Bulletin,* Vol. 21, No. 2 (Spring 1986), a periodical of Coos Genealogical Forum, North Bend, Oregon.

■ **1855, 1856, 1857 Census, Jackson County, Oregon Territory,** in *Rogue Digger,* Vol. 3, No. 2 (Summer 1968) through Vol. 5, No. 2 (Summer 1970), a periodical of Rouge Valley Genealogical Society, Phoenix, Oregon.

■ **1856 Census, Clackamas County, Oregon Territory,** in *Trackers,* Vol. 13, No. 3 (Summer 1973), a periodical of Mount Hood Genealogical Forum, Oregon City, Oregon.

■ **1856 Census, Columbia County, Oregon Territory,** microfilm of original records at the Oregon State Archives, Salem, OR. Arranged in alphabetical order by surname. Filmed by the Genealogical Society of Utah, 2002, 1 roll, FHL film #2293501.

■ **1856 Census, Curry County, Oregon Territory,** in *Coos Genealogical Forum Bulletin,* Vol. 24, No. 1 (Spring 1989), a periodical of Coos Genealogical Forum, North Bend, Oregon.

■ ***Copy of Census Roll for Polk County for the Year 1856,*** compiled and published by Adelina S. Dyal, Salem, OR, 1976, 27 pages. Cover title: "Oregon; Copy of Census Roll for Polk County for the year 1856: A Facsimile of Territorial Document No. 6912, Oregon State Archives, Salem, Oregon." Includes index. FHL book 979.5 A1 No. 37. Also on microfilm, FHL film #1036151.

■ **1857 Census, Clackamas County, Oregon Territory,** in *Trackers,* Vol. 14, No. 1 (1974), a periodical of Mount Hood Genealogical Forum, Oregon City, Oregon.

■ **1857 Census, Coos County, Oregon Territory,** in *Coos Genealogical Forum Bulletin,* Vol. 22, No. 2 (Spring 1987), a periodical of Coos Genealogical Forum, North Bend, Oregon.

■ **1857 Census, Curry County, Oregon Territory,** in *Coos Genealogical Forum Bulletin,* Vol. 26, No. 1 (Spring 1991), a periodical of Coos Genealogical Forum, North Bend, Oregon.

■ **1858 Enumeration of Inhabitants, Curry County, Oregon Territory,** in *Coos Genealogical Forum Bulletin,* Vol. 25, No. 1 (Spring 1990), a periodical of Coos Genealogical Forum, North Bend, Oregon.

■ ***Index to Soldiers & Sailors of the Civil War,*** a searchable name index to 6.3 million Union and Confederate Civil War soldiers now available online at the National Park Service Web site. A search can be done by surname, first name, state, or unit. Oregon supplied 2,754 men to the war (all Union). To search for one go to the NPS Web site: **www.civilwar.nps.gov/cwss/.**

■ ***Organization Index to Pension Files of Veterans Who Served Between 1861 and 1917,*** microfilm of original manuscripts for all states at the National Archives, Washington, DC. Filmed by the National Archives, series T0289, 1949, 765 rolls (16mm). Use the online index to civil war soldiers to locate an Oregon soldier/sailor, which will give the exact unit in which the person served. If the person applied for a pension, this series of records will give additional information about the person. This index groups the applicants according to the units in which they served. The cards are arranged alphabetically by state, thereunder by arm of service (infantry, cavalry, artillery), thereunder numerically by regiment, and there- under alphabetically by veteran's surname. Each card gives the soldier's name, rank, unit, and terms of service; names of relationships of any dependents; the application number; the certificate number; and the state from which the claim was filed. The index cards reproduced on this microfilm publication refer to pension applications of veterans who served in the U.S. Army between 1861 and 1917. The majority of the records pertain to Civil War veterans, but they also include veterans of the Spanish-American War, the Philippine Insurrection, Indian wars, and World War I. The index to Oregon pension records is contained on 1 roll, FHL film #1725944.

■ **1863-1935 City Directories, Portland, Oregon,** microfilm of originals published by various publishers. Filmed by Research Publications, Inc., Woodbridge, CT, 1980-1984. FHL has 34 rolls, with a complete run of directories, 1863-1935, beginning with FHL film #1377327 (1863 Portland Directory) through FHL film #1611935 (1935 Portland Directory).

■ **1865, 1870, 1875, and 1885 Agricultural and Property Assessment and Census for Umatilla County, Oregon,** microfilm of original records at the Oregon State Archives in Salem, Oregon. Includes name, number of acres, lots, and blocks, value of land, amount of state and county taxes, number of females and males and age groups, amount of bushels of various products, amount of various farm animals, amount of seafood, and remarks from the state 1865 and 1875 census. Filmed by the Genealogical Society of Utah, 2002, 2 rolls, FHL film #2319765 (Oregon state census 1865; 1870 Federal census; Oregon state census 1875 (p. 1-30); and FHL film #2319766 (Oregon state census 1875 (p. 31-end); Oregon state census 1885).

■ **1867-1873 Internal Revenue Assessment Lists, Oregon,** microfilm of originals in the National Archives Branch in Seattle, Washington. Some years missing. There are no volume numbers on books. Filmed by the Genealogical Society of Utah, 1989, 2 rolls, FHL film #1639854 (Assessment lists 1867-1870) and FHL film #1639855 (Assessment lists 1871-1873).

■ **1875 Oregon State Census, Lake County.** See ***Enumeration of the Inhabitants and Industrial Products of the County of Lake, State of Oregon for Year 1875,*** microfilm of original records at the Oregon State Archives in Salem, Oregon. Filmed by the Genealogical Society of Utah, 2001, 1 roll, FHL film #2260282. See also **1875 Census, Lake County, Oregon,** in *Oregon Genealogical Bulletin,* Vol. 34, No. 5 (Summer 1996), a periodical of Oregon Genealogical Society, Eugene, Oregon.

■ **1885 Oregon State Census, Linn County, Oregon,** microfilm of original records at the Oregon State Archives, Salem, Oregon. "Enumeration of the Inhabitants and Industrial Products of the County of Linn, State of Oregon, for the year 1885." Arranged in alphabetical order by first letter of surname. Filmed by the Genealogical Society of Utah, 1998, 1 roll, FHL film #2109932.

■ **1885 Oregon State Census, Umatilla County, Oregon,** in *Oregon End of Trail Researchers* (Salem, OR), Vol. 4, No. 4 (Winter 1973).

■ ***Oregon State 1890 Special Federal Census of Union Veterans and Their Widows: Eleventh Census of the United States,*** compiled by Jane A. Myers, published by Cottage Grove Genealogical Society, 1993, 460 pages. Extracted by county, enumeration district, and enumerator. Includes index of veterans and index of enumerators. FHL book 979.5 X28m. See also ***Oregon 1890 Census Index: Special Schedule of the Eleventh Census (1890) Enumerating Union Veterans and of Union veterans of the Civil War,*** compiled by Ronald Vern Jackson, et al., published by Accelerated Indexing Systems, North Salt Lake, UT, 1985, 87 pages. FHL book 979.5 X2j.

■ **1893 History.** See ***An illustrated History of the state of Oregon: Containing a History of Oregon From the Earliest Period of its Discovery to the Present Time, Together With Glimpses of its Auspicious Future; Illustrations and Full-page Portraits of Some of its Eminent Men and Biographical Mention of Many of its Pioneers and Prominent Citizens of Today,*** by Harvey K. Hines, published by Lewis Publishing Co., Chicago, 1893, 1,300 pages. FHL book 979.5 H2hh. Also on microfilm, FHL film #1000358. See also ***Abstract of Biographies Appearing in "An Illustrated History of the State of Oregon" [by Rev. H. K. Hines],*** compiled by Susan N. Bell, published by Willamette Valley Genealogical Society, Salem, OR, 1996, 138 pages. Includes index. Contains abstracts of biographies submitted by the individuals listed for publication in 1893. FHL book 979.5 D38b.

■ **1895 Oregon State Census, Linn County, Oregon,** microfilm of original records at the Oregon State Archives, Salem, Oregon. "Enumeration of the Inhabitants and Industrial Products of the County of Linn, State of Oregon, for the year 1895." Arranged in alphabetical order by first letter of surname. Filmed by the Genealogical Society of Utah, 1998, 1 roll, FHL film #2109932.

■ **1895 Oregon State Census, Marion County, Oregon,** see ***Oregon, Marion County, 1895 Census,*** abstracted by Jean Custer, et al., published by Willamette Valley Genealogical Society, Salem, Oregon, 1993, 2001, 2 vols. Contents: vol. 1. City of Salem, suburbs, Oregon state penitentiary, and Oregon state insane asylum; vol. 2. Ale, Aumsville, Aurora, Brooks, Butteville Champoeg, Chemawa, Detroit, Gates, Gervais, Hubbard, Jefferson, Macleay, Marion, Mehama, Mill City, Minto, Mt. Angel, Niagara, Rural, Scotts Mills, Shaw, Silverton, St. Paul, Stayton, Sublimity, Turner, and Woodburn. Includes alphabetical list by surname of name, place of birth, height, weight, complexion (light or dark), occupation, ailment, religion, voter status, sex and age. FHL book 979.537 X28c v. 1-2. See also **1895 Aumsville Census,** in *Beaver Briefs,* Vol. 17, No. 2 (Apr 1985), a periodical of Willamette Valley Genealogical Society, Salem, Oregon.

■ **1895 Oregon State Census, Morrow County, Oregon,** microfilm of records at Oregon State Archives, Salem, Oregon, 2 volumes. Includes names, gender, and age range, whether a voter, and agricultural census. Filmed by the Genealogical Society of Utah, 1995, 1 roll, FHL film #2027031.

■ **1895 Oregon State Census, Multnomah County, Oregon,** microfilm of records at Oregon State Archives, Salem, Oregon. Includes names of all persons in family with age, sex, color, profession, place of birth, and marital status, as well as a list of persons who died during the year. Filmed by the Genealogical Society of Utah, 1995, 3 rolls, as follows:

- 1895 state census, vol. 1-16 precincts (some missing) Vol. 3-4 precincts 25-30, FHL film #2026697.
- 1895 state census, vol. 4-6 precincts 31-46 Vol. 7 precincts 47-54 (some missing); Vol. 8 precincts 55-64 , FHL film #2026895.
- 1895 state census, Vol. 8 precincts 65-77, FHL film #2026896.

■ ***1900 Malheur County, Oregon Census,*** by Oregon Genealogical Society, Inc. and Louise Hill, published by Oregon Genealogical Society, Eugene, OR, 1998, 95 pages. Includes photocopy of the 1900 census for Malheur County, Oregon, and an index for that census. FHL book 979.597 X2o.

■ **1905 Oregon State Census, Linn County.** See ***Industrial Product Census of Linn County, Oregon, 1905,*** microfilm of original records at the Oregon State Archives in Salem, Oregon. Title at top of form: "Enumeration of the Industrial Products of Linn County, State of Oregon, for the Year 1905." Lists name, location, and agricultural products. Filmed by the Genealogical Society of Utah, 1998, 1 roll, FHL film #2109932. See also ***Linn Co., Oregon Census, 1905,*** extracted and indexed by Mrs. E.R. Browning, filmed by the Genealogical Society of Utah, 1975, 1 roll, FHL film #908958. See also **1905 Inhabitants, Linn County, Oregon,** in *Rogue Digger,* Vol. 25, No. 2 (Summer 1990), a periodical of Rogue Valley Genealogical Society, Phoenix, Oregon.

■ **1905 Oregon State Census, Marion County, Oregon.** See ***Oregon, Marion County, 1905 Census,*** an extract and index copied and compiled by Harriett Gaylord, published by Willamette Valley Genealogical Society, Salem, OR, 1998, 2 vols. Includes index. FHL has bound book 1 & 2 together. FHL book 979.537 X28g v. 1-2. The 1905 Marion County census names were originally published serially in the society's periodical, *Oregon End of Trail Researchers,* Vol. 2, No. 4 (Winter 1971) through Vol. 7, No. 2 (Fall 1976).

■ **1903-1970 Oregon Death Records Index,** microfilm of transcript of original at the Oregon State Archives, Salem, OR. Best copies available; originals destroyed. Each record includes name of deceased, spouse, county of death, date of death, certificate number, age. Filmed by the Oregon State Archives and Records Center, ca1975, FHL has 12 rolls, as follows:

- **1915-1924** Portland, A-Z, FHL film #1373869.
- **1903-1920** Statewide, A-L, FHL film #1373870.
- **1903-1920** Statewide, M-Z, FHL film #1373871.
- **1921-1930** Statewide, A-Z, FHL film #1373872.
- **1931-1941** Statewide, A-L, FHL film #1373873.
- **1931-1941** Statewide, M-Z, FHL film #1373874.
- **1942-1950** Statewide, A-Kl, FHL film #1373875.
- **1942-1950** Statewide, Km-Z, FHL film #1373876.
- **1951-1960** Statewide, A-K, FHL film #1373877.
- **1951-1960** Statewide, L-Z, FHL film #1373878.
- **1961-1965** Statewide, A-Z, FHL film #1373879.
- **1966-1970** Statewide, A-Z, FHL film #1373880.

■ ***Oregon Vital Records: Deaths, 1903-1998,*** a CD-ROM publication by Ancestry.com, Provo, UT, 2000. This is an index to statewide death records, taken from the microfilmed indexes prepared by the Oregon State Vital Statistics Office in Portland, Oregon. The state's microfilm series excludes the years 1981-1990, and it is not clear if this CD has those years or not. This same database is one of Ancestry's online searchable name lists. FHL CD-ROM No. 1228.

■ **1971-1980 and 1991-2000 Oregon Death Records Index,** microfiche of original records of the Oregon Board of Health, Division of Vital Statistics. Includes index of deaths from 1971-1980 created 07/01/96 and index of deaths from 1991-2000 created 06/21/01. (1981-1990 status unknown). Lists name of deceased, name of spouse, death county number, death date, certificate number, and birth date or year if known. Arranged in alphabetical order by surname of deceased. The county code number is given at the beginning of the series. FHL has 66 microfiches, as follows:

- **1971-1980** Oregon death index, (28 fiches), FHL fiche #6201552.
- **1991-2000** Oregon death indexes, (38 fiches), FHL Fiche #6201553.

■ **Oregon Statewide Delayed Filings of Births, 1842-1902,** microfilm of original records at the Oregon State Archives in Salem, Oregon. Arranged in chronological order by the year of birth (of the person filing a delayed birth record) and then alphabetical by county wherein the delayed birth was filed. (The place of birth could be anywhere, including out-of-state locations). Oregon is one of only a few states with statewide delayed birth records available to the public. These records are powerful genealogical sources. The delayed birth certificates were originally filed with the county circuit courts with copies going to the State Division of Vital Statistics. This series is the state's copy. (Another copy of the filing may be located at the county courthouse in which it was originally filed.). Most of these records were filed by individuals needing proof of birth prior to receiving Social Security benefits, which began in 1935. But there may be filings earlier than that (exact range of dates of filing not noted on the microfilm series). The first two rolls in the series contain an alpha index to the names of persons filing a delayed birth record, which includes the name, date of birth, and place of filing; allowing a researcher to find the roll of film containing the microfilmed image of the delayed birth record. The delayed birth record itself is more revealing than a standard birth certificate because it includes affidavits of relatives and acquaintances, and supporting documents such as Bible pages, identification papers, etc. The films are not in strict numerical order, but following the 2-roll index are 72 rolls of birth records, filmed by the Genealogical Society of Utah, 2001, 2003, beginning with FHL film #2363225 (State wide delayed birth index, Aamold, Walter – Hood, Helen Owsley) and FHL film #2363226 (State wide delayed birth index, Holzmeyer, Selma Elsie Johanna – Zysett, Lawrence Albert); followed by FHL film #2230783 (Delayed birth filings, 1842 - 1868, Deschutes County).

Oregon Censuses & Substitutes Online

www.heritagequestonline.com

Heads of Household name index linked to census page images:

- 1850-1930 Oregon Federal Censuses

www.ancestry.com

- 1841-1890 Oregon Census (AIS)
- 1850-1930 Oregon Federal Censuses
- 1890 Veterans Schedules
- 1850-1880 Mortality Schedules

www.familysearch.org

- 1880 Federal Census – Every-name index linked to census page images at Ancestry.com

www.censusfinder.com/oregon.htm

- 1842 Census Extraction of French Canadians
- 1845 Territorial Census of Oregon Territory
- 1850 Federal Census - Surname Index local database
- Oregon State Archives Database Search Engine
- Oregon Statewide Databases of Census & Genealogy Records

■ **Oregon Historical Records Index** of the Oregon State Archives. A search form can be used to search for evidence of a person in state and county records. (The database is an ongoing project, and has only a few counties represented. However, in the future, expect this database to be a primary starting point for Oregon research). Go to: **http://genealogy.state.or.us/.**

WASHINGTON

Censuses & Substitutes, 1847-1930

Washington Territory, created from Oregon Territory in 1853, had at least a dozen territory-wide censuses conducted every few years until 1889. There is excellent coverage for virtually all Washington Territory counties, some borrowed from Oregon Territory from as early as 1847-1851; and WT counties from 1856-1889.

After joining the Union as a state in 1889, Washington took at least one state-sponsored census, perhaps two – since censuses exist for a few counties dated 1892; and a few more dated 1894. But to cover the earliest possible censuses for the area of present Washington, a researcher needs to look at Oregon Territory first. For example, the 1850 federal census of Oregon Territory included **Lewis County** (west of the Cascade Mountains), and **Clarke County** (east of the mountains), covering all of the populated areas of what became Washington Territory. Between the time of the 1850 federal census and the creation of Washington Territory in 1853, the Oregon Territory legislature created six more counties in the area of present Washington. As a result, the area that became Washington Territory in 1853 began with eight counties inherited from Oregon Territory, all of which need to be reviewed for possible censuses. These eight and their Oregon creation dates and parent counties were as follows:

- **Clarke County,** 1844, as the original "Vancouver District" by the Provisional Oregon Government. The name Clarke came in 1849, the 'e' was dropped in the 1920s.
- **Lewis County,** 1845, an original county created by the Provisional Oregon Government.
- **Pacific County,** 1851, from Lewis.
- **Jefferson County,** 1852, from Lewis.
- **Thurston County,** 1852, from Lewis.
- **King County**, 1852, from Thurston.
- **Pierce County,** 1852, from Lewis.
- **Island County,** 1853, from Lewis.

All of the above Oregon counties were incorporated into the new Washington Territory as part of the organic act of 1853. The Oregon laws and county courts were to be continued until the new territory could form a legislature and make new ones. At its first legislative session in 1854, Washington Territory recognized the eight Oregon-born counties; then created eight more on is own:

- **Clallam County,** from Jefferson.
- **Cowlitz County,** from Lewis.
- **Chehalis County,** from Thurston. (Chehalis was renamed Grays Harbor County in 1915).
- **Sawamish County,** from Thurston. (Sawamish was renamed Mason in 1864).
- **Skamania County,** from Clarke.
- **Wahkiakum County,** from Lewis.
- **Walla Walla County,** from Clarke.
- **Whatcom County,** from Island.

The above sixteen counties represent the "original" counties of Washington Territory. The federal organic act creating Washington Territory in 1853 dictated that a census be taken "previous to the first election," but this was not a federal census, but a territorial census conducted in 1854 for the purpose of apportionment of the first elected territorial legislature. (Only a 1854 Pierce County census list appears to have survived).

A special note about Spokane County is necessary. Spokane County was created in 1858 from Walla Walla, and at the time of the 1860 federal census included most of Washington Territory from the Columbia River to the Continental Divide, including people living in the Bitterroot Valley of present Montana. For years, the main county guides show Spokane county as being created in 1858, *abolished* in 1864, then a new Spokane County recreated in 1879. The word *abolished* implies that the county ceased to exist and had no records generated after 1864. A better word and description of what happened would be that Spokane *merged* with Stevens. (The legislative act called it an *annexation* by Stevens). Spokane people thought it should be the other way around, that Stevens should merge into Spokane, and complained loudly about losing their name. But, the sentiment in the territorial legislature at the time was high to honor Washington's first territorial governor, Isaac I. Stephens, who had volunteered for service in the Union Army and was killed in action in Sept. 1862 at the Battle of Chantilly. Spokane County lost its name because of the emotions of the time.

Any researcher looking for records for old Spokane County needs to visit the Stevens County Courthouse in Colville, Washington – Spokane County (1) records are there for the period 1858-1863; continuing under the name Stevens County thereafter. Meanwhile, Spokane

County (2) records are located at the courthouse in Spokane, Washington, dating from its creation date of 1879.

Archival Census Records in Washington State

The state of Washington is a user-friendly place for family historians. The state has the most enlightened archival and document preservation program in the United States. Incorporating both public and private support, the state operates seven state-of-the-art archival facilities, the most modern facilities of any state. Moreover, the preservation and access to historical materials of interest to genealogists is given a high priority in Washington.

Since June 2004, the new Washington Digital Archives has embarked on a goal of digitizing and indexing every archival document ever produced in the territory and state of Washington. Included in the early phase of this mammoth project is the scanning and indexing of all of Washington's territorial and state censuses.

The Washington Secretary of State oversees the State Library, State Archives, and the new Digital Archives. The Secretary of State's Main Page gives access to all of these facilities. Go to: **www.secstate.wa.gov/**. The main State Archives is located in Olympia. WA. Materials maintained here are statewide in nature, documents created by various state institutions, statewide functions, past governors, and past legislatures. Visit the Genealogy webpage at the State Archives: **www.secstate.wa.gov/history/genealogy.aspx.**

In addition to the main State Archives, there are five regional archives, each holding original county records for a number of counties within their region of coverage. The various countywide archival records from Washington's 39 counties have been dispersed to the regional branches. Of primary interest to genealogists, Washington's surviving territorial and state censuses have all been microfilmed, and each of the regional archives has both the originals and microfilmed copies for the counties under their coverage area. Other original county records maintained at the regional archives may include birth, marriage, and death records; court records, including naturalizations, dockets, and civil, criminal, and probate case files; land records, including general indices to recordings, deeds, and patents; county council and county commissioner proceedings, county ordinances and resolutions; real and personal property tax records; school district and education district records, including school censuses; and many others.

The five regional branches of the state archives each have their own websites, where a researcher can review the types of original records available for the counties under their coverage:

Northwest Regional Branch, located next to the campus of Western Washington University in Bellingham, WA, this archives maintains original records from **Clallam, Island, Jefferson, San Juan, Skagit, Snohomish,** and **Whatcom** counties. Go to their Website at: **www.secstate.wa.gov/archives/archives_northwest.aspx.**

Southwest Regional Branch, located in Olympia, WA, this archives maintains original records from Clark, Cowlitz, Grays Harbor, Lewis, Mason, Pacific, Skamania, Thurston, and Wahkiakum counties. Go to: **www.secstate.wa.gov/archives/archives_southwest.aspx.**

Central Regional Branch, located next to the campus of Central Washington University in Ellensburg, WA, this archives maintains records from Benton, Chelan, Douglas, Franklin, Grant, Kittitas, Klickitat, Okanogan, and Yakima counties. Go to: **www.secstate.wa.gov/archives/archives_central.aspx.**

Eastern Regional Branch, located on the campus of Eastern Washington University in Cheney, WA, this archives maintains records from

Adams, Asotin, Columbia, Ferry, Garfield, Lincoln, Pend Oreille, Spokane, Stevens, Walla Walla, and Whitman counties. Go to their website at: **www.secstate.wa.gov/archives/archives_eastern.aspx.**

Puget Sound Regional Branch, located in Bellevue, WA, maintains records from King, Pierce, and Kitsap counties. An overview of their collections can be seen at their Website at: **www.secstate.wa.gov/archives/archives_puget.aspx.**

Washington State Digital Archives

Opened in 2004, the Washington State Digital Archives is the nation's first archives dedicated specifically to the preservation of electronic records from both State and Local agencies that have permanent legal, fiscal or historical value.

Located in Cheney, WA on the Eastern Washington University campus, the new facility was designed from the ground up to host this technically complex program. The web interface and database storehouse were custom designed specifically for the Digital Archives to hold the important electronic records found throughout the state, and to provide simple, straight-forward access to researchers.

A program to digitized the images of all of Washington's Territorial Censuses is well under way, and name indexes to the censuses as well as many other resources are being combined in one Digital Archives search system. In its first three years of operation, the Digital Archives indexed over 25 million names.

Of interest to genealogists, the other records being indexed include Marriage Records, Naturalization Records, Death Records, Birth Records, Military Records, Institution Records, Miscellaneous Historical Records, Physician Records, and Oaths of Office. To do a search in the Digital Archives databases, go to: **www.digitalarchives.wa.gov/.**

Washington Territorial & State Censuses on Microfilm

After the first territorial census of 1854, several more territorial censuses were authorized for the purpose of apportionment of the territorial legislature. Surviving census manuscripts exist for at least one county for the years 1856, 1857, 1858, 1859, 1861, 1871, 1879, 1881, 1883, 1885, 1887, and the last one in 1889, the same year in which Washington became a state. Those censuses taken in the 1880s are fairly complete for all of the counties in place during the territorial era.

All of these original territorial censuses were microfilmed as one 20-roll series by the Washington State Archives in 1987. Since then, a number of territorial censuses have been identified from various county repositories. A later series was filmed in 2003 on 35 rolls. Both the 1987 and 2003 series are identified below with the contents of each roll.

The first microfilm series includes the state census of 1892 for the few county name lists which have survived. In particular, the King County-Seattle and Pierce County-Tacoma name lists for 1892 are very complete. Representing the two most populated counties-cites of Washington, they provide researchers with a good substitute to the lost 1890 federal census.

■ **Microfilmed Territorial Censuses. (1987 Edition).** See ***Washington Territorial Census Rolls, 1857-1892,*** microfilm of originals from the Secretary of State's office, now housed at one of five regional branches of the Washington State Archives. This series is the only microfilm edition held by the Family History Library in Salt Lake City. In spite of the title, the date of the earliest territorial census in this series is for 1856 (King County).

This series includes 1860 federal censuses for Clallam, Clarke, Jefferson, Kitsap, Lewis,

Skamania, and Island counties. These unique records are county original copies of a federal census, either retained by the county or submitted along with the territorial censuses to the Secretary of State. (Another set went to Washington, DC). Comparing these local censuses with the federal 1860 versions confirms they are different – they often don't agree with the spellings of names, birthplaces, etc. Also, these county copies have the population schedules of the 1860 federal censuses followed by the agriculture and mortality schedules. (The microfilmed federal set separated these special schedules from the population schedules).

There are also 1880 censuses indicated for Jefferson, King (Seattle), and Mason counties. These appear to be identical to the federal copies sent to Washington, DC and originally filmed by the National Archives.

In many of the territorial census name lists, town names are incomplete or missing altogether, and one must search the entire county from start to finish to find a particular name. But, several name indexes have been published for various years and counties from this series. A separate list of the indexed counties/years is shown under the heading "Washington Territorial Census Indexes Online" below, followed by "Published Territorial Censuses & Indexes, by County."

Years in bold, e.g., **1857**, are unique to this series (not included in the 2003 filming). Organization of the microfilmed territorial censuses begins with:

FHL film #1841781:

- Adams: 1885, 1887, 1889.
- Asotin: 1885, 1887, and 1889.
- Chehalis: **1858**, 1871, 1885. (Chehalis was renamed Gray's Harbor County in 1915).
- Clallam: **1857**, **1860** (county original of federal Census), 1871, 1883, 1885, 1887.
- Clarke: **1857**, **1860** (county original of federal census), 1871, 1883, 1885, 1885 (repeated), 1887.
- Columbia: (Dayton only): 1883, 1885, 1887,**1889**.
- Cowlitz: 1871, 1883, 1885.

FHL film #1841782:

- Douglas: 1885, 1887.
- Franklin: 1885, 1887.
- Ferry: **1883.**
- Garfield: 1883.

FHL film #1841783:

- Garfield: **1885, 1887, 1889; 1898** (includes 1889), **1892, 1898** (different set than first one).
- Island: **1857; 1860** (county original of federal census), 1871, 1883, 1885, 1887.
- Jefferson: **1860** (county original of federal census), **1874, 1875, 1878, 1879, 1880** (federal?), **1881, 1883**, 1885, 1887, **1889, 1891.**

FHL film #1841784:

- King: **1856, 1857**, 1871, **1879;** and Seattle only: **1880, 1881**, 1883.

FHL film #1841785:

- King: 1885, 1887.

FHL film #1841786:

- King: **1891**.

FHL film #1841787:

- King: **1892**.

FHL film #1841788:

- King: **1892**.

FHL film #1841789:

- Kitsap: **1857** (as Slaughter County), **1860,** (county original of federal census), **1871,** 1885, 1887, 1889.
- Kittitas County: 1885, 1887, and 1889.

FHL film #1841790:

- Klickitat: 1871, 1883, 1885, 1889, 1892.
- Lewis: **1857, 1860** (county original of federal census) **1861**, 1871, 1883, 1885, and 1887.
- Pierce: 1857 (out of alpha sequence).
- Lincoln: 1885, 1887.

FHL film #1841791:

- Lincoln: 1887, 1889.
- Mason (nee Sawamish): 1857; 1860 assessment rolls, 1871, 1879, 1880, 1881, 1883, 1885, 1887, 1889, 1892.
- Pacific: 1883, 1885, 1887.

FHL film #1841792:

- Pierce: 1857, 1871, 1878, 1879, 1883, 1885, 1887.

FHL film #1841793:

- Pierce: 1889, 1892.

FHL film #1841794:
- Pierce: 1892.

FHL film #1841795:
- Pierce: 1892.
- San Juan: 1885, 1887, 1889.
- Skagit: 1885, and 1887.
- Skamania: **1860** (county original of federal census), 1871, 1885, 1887.
- Snohomish: 1871, 1883, 1885, 1887, 1889.
- Spokane: 1885, 1887.

FHL film #1841796:
- Stevens: 1871, 1878, 1885, 1887, 1892.
- Thurston: 1871, 1873, **1875**, 1877, 1878, 1879, 1880, 1881.

FHL film #1841797:
- Thurston: 1883, 1885, 1887, 1889, 1892.

FHL film #1841798:
- Wahkiakum: **1857**; 1885, 1887.
- Walla Walla: 1885, 1887, 1889, **1892**.
- Whatcom: **1871**, 1885; 1887, 1889.

FHL film #1841799:
- Whatcom: 1887, 1889.
- Whitman: 1883, 1885.

FHL film #1841800:
- Yakima: 1871, 1883, 1885, 1887.

■ **Microfilmed Territorial Censuses (2003 Edition) at the Washington State Library.** See *Washington Territorial County Census Microfilm,* microfilm of original territorial censuses now located at one of five regional branches of the Washington State Archives. Filmed by the Archives' Imaging and Preservation Services, for the Washington State Library, Office of the Secretary of State, 2003, 35 rolls, State Library call number: 929.3797-roll #. County years unique to this series (not included in the 1987 microfilming) are shown in bold e.g., **1885**. The county/census year on each roll is as follows:

WSL film #929.3797:
- Roll 1: Adams, 1885, 1887,1889.
- Roll 2: Asotin, 1885, 1887, 1889.
- Roll 3: Clallam, 1871, 1883, 1885.
- Roll 4: Clarke, 1871, 1883, 1885, 1887.
- Roll 5: Columbia, 1883, 1885, 1887,**1889**.
- Roll 6: Cowlitz, 1871, 1883, 1885, **1887**.
- Roll 7: Douglas, 1885, 1887.

Note: Ferry County not represented in this series.
- Roll 8: Franklin, 1885, 1887.
- Roll 9: Garfield, **1883**.
- Roll 10: Grays Harbor (nee Chehalis), 1871, 1885.
- Roll 11: Island, 1871, **1883**, 1885, 1887.
- Roll 12: Jefferson, **1871**, 1885, 1887.
- Roll 13: King, 1871, 1883, 1885, 1887.
- Roll 14: Kitsap, 1871, 1883, 1885, 1887, 1889.
- Roll 15: Kittitas, 1885, 1887, 1889.
- Roll 16: Klickitat, 1871, 1883, 1885, **1887**,1889, 1892.
- Roll 17: Lewis, 1871, 1883, 1885, 1887.
- Roll 18: Lincoln, 1885, 1887, **1889.**
- Roll 19: Mason (nee Sawamish), 1871, 1883, 1885, 1887, 1889, 1892.
- Roll 20: Pacific, 1883, 1885, 1887.
- Roll 21: Pierce, 1871, 1885, 1887, A-K; 1889.
- Roll 21A: Pierce, L-Y 1889, recapitulation 1889.
- Roll 22: San Juan, 1885, 1887, 1889.
- Roll 23: Skagit, 1885, 1887.
- Roll 24: Skamania, 1871, 1885, 1887; & Snohomish, 1871.
- Roll 25: Snohomish, 1883, 1885, 1887, 1889.
- Roll 26: Spokane, 1885, 1887.
- Roll 27: Stevens, 1871, 1878, 1885, 1887, 1892.
- Roll 28: Thurston, 1871, 1873, 1877, **1878, 1881**, 1883, 1885, 1887, 1889.
- Roll 29: Wahkiakum, 1885, 1887.
- Roll 30: Walla Walla, 1885, 1887, 1892.
- Roll 31: Whatcom, **1871**, **1885**, 1887, 1889.
- Roll 32: Whitman, 1883, 1885, **1887**.
- Roll 32A: Whitman, **1889**.
- Roll 33: Yakima, 1871, 1883, 1885, 1887.

Published Censuses & Indexes, by County

These books and published articles in periodicals are for the Washington territorial censuses, 1857-1889, listed by county. State censuses for 1892 are also listed (Pacific and Pierce counties only). Counties created after statehood are included, with a reference to parent counties where censuses may have included the progeny county.

■ **1851-1889 Territorial Censuses.** See *Transcribed and Printed Copies of Various*

Territorial Census Rolls, Done by Various Genealogical Organizations, copy at the Washington State Archives, Olympia, WA. Includes Adams County (1889), Asotin County (1889), Chehalis County (1885), Clarke County (1850, 1860, 1871), Columbia County (1889), Douglas County (1887), Franklin County (1885, 1887), Island County (1889), Lewis County (1851), Lincoln County (1889), Mason County (1889), San Juan County (1889), Snohomish County (1889), and Walla Walla County (1887). See State Archives Ref. No. AR3-A-25.

■ **Adams County, 1889.** See ***Census, Adams County, Washington Territory, 1889,*** transcribed and indexed by Dolores Dunn Ackerman, published by Stack Enterprises, Bellingham, WA, 1986, 1 vol., various paging. FHL book 979.734 X2c. Also on microfilm, FHL film #1697959.

■ **Asotin County, 1889.** See ***Census, Washington Territory, Asotin County, 1889,*** transcribed and indexed by Dolores Dunn Ackerman, published by Stack Enterprises, Bellingham, WA, 1986, 35 pages. FHL book 979.742 X2a. Also on microfilm, FHL film #1698010.

■ **Benton County** was created 1905 from Klickitat and Yakima. See **Yakima** for a publication including Benton areas for 1871, 1883, 1885, 1887.

■ **Chehalis County, 1885.** See ***Census, Chehalis (Grays Harbor) County, Washington Territory, 1885,*** transcribed and indexed by Dolores Dunn Ackerman, published by Stack Enterprises, Bellingham, WA, 1986. Includes index. Chehalis County was renamed Grays Harbor County in 1915. FHL book 979.795 X2c. Also on microfilm, FHL film #1698053.

■ **Chelan County** was created 1899 from Kittitas and Okanogan. See **Yakima** for a publication that included Chelan areas.

■ **1857 Census, Clallam County, Washington Territory,** name list published as "County Census, March 10, 1857," in *Clallam County Genealogical Society Bulletin,* Vol. 4, No. 2 (Jun 1984).

■ **Clallam County.** See ***Clallam County, Washington, 1889 Census,*** microfilm of originals at the Clallam County Genealogical Society Library in Port Angeles, Washington. Filmed by the Genealogical Society of Utah, 1994, 1 roll, FHL film #1940023. Extracted in ***Census of the Inhabitants in the County of Clallam, Territory of Washington, 1889: Washington State Centennial Project,*** compiled and published by the Clallam County Genealogical Society, Port Angeles, WA, ca1989, 118 pages. FHL book 979.799 X2c.

■ **Clark County** was created in 1844 as "Vancouver District" by the Oregon Provisional Government. The name **Clarke** was acquired in 1849, the "e" not dropped until the 1920s. See Online Censuses Indexes.

■ **Columbia County.** See ***1889 Columbia County, Wa. Territory Census,*** compiled and published by Ruby Simonson McNeill, Spokane, WA, c1980, 117 pages. Includes index. FHL book 979.746 X29mc. Also on 2 microfiche, FHL fiche #6051025.

■ **Cowlitz County, 1871, 1883, 1885, and 1887.** See ***Cowlitz County, Washington Territory, Auditor's Census With Surname Index,*** compiled and published by Lower Columbia Genealogical Society and Longview Public Library, Longview, WA, 1985. Includes territorial census years 1871, 1883, 1885, 1887. FHL book 979.788 X2c.

■ **Douglas County, 1887.** See ***Census, Douglas County, Washington Territory, 1887,*** transcribed by Dolores Dunn Ackerman, published by Stack

Enterprises, Bellingham, WA 1986. Includes index. FHL book 979.731 X2c. Also on microfilm, FHL film #1697961.

■ **Ferry County.** Created 1899 from Stevens County. See Online Censuses.

■ **Franklin County, 1885.** See ***Census, Franklin County, Washington Territory, 1885 and 1887,*** transcribed by Dolores Dunn Ackerman, published by Stack Enterprises, Bellingham, WA, 1986. Includes index. FHL book 979.733 X2c.

■ **1887, 1889, 1898, and 1902 Censuses, Garfield County, Washington Territory,** name lists published in *Washington Heritage* (Orting, WA), Vol. 3, No. 3 (Fall 1986).

■ **Grant County** was created in 1909, there were no territorial censuses under that name, but a ***"1885 Grant County Census,"*** was published in *Big Bend Register,* Vol. 19, No. 3 (Sep 1999), probably taken from the Douglas County census. *Big Bend Register* is a periodical of the Grant County Genealogical Society, Ephrata, WA.

■ **Grays Harbor** was created in 1854 as Chehalis County, renamed in 1907. See **Chehalis** and Online Indexes.

■ **1860 Federal Census, Island County, Washington Territory.** The county's original copy of the census has been scanned and made accessible online at the Secretary of State's **Historical Records Search** webpage.

■ **Island County, 1889.** See ***Island County, Washington Territory, 1889,*** transcribed and indexed by Dolores Dunn Ackerman, published by Stack Enterprises, Bellingham, WA, 1987, FHL book 979.775 X2c. Also on microfilm, FHL film #1697959.

■ **1860 Federal Census, Jefferson County, Washington Territory.** See ***Index to 1860 Washington Territory Census: With Mortality and Production of Agriculture Schedules,*** transcribed by members of the Jefferson County Genealogical Society, Port Townsend, WA, 1997, 13 pages. This was taken from the county's original copy of the 1860 federal census. FHL book 979.798 X2j. Also on microfiche. FHL fiche #6067412.

■ ***1871 Territorial Census, Jefferson County, Washington,*** extracted by members of the Jefferson County Genealogical Society, Port Townsend, WA, 1990. FHL book 979.798 X2j.

■ ***1875 Census of Jefferson County, Washington Territory: With Index,*** by the Jefferson County Genealogical Society, Port Townsend, WA, 1997, 46 pages. FHL book 979.798 X2j. Also on microfiche, FHL fiche #6067413.

■ ***1878 Census of Jefferson County, Washington Territory: With Index,*** by the Jefferson County Genealogical Society, Port Townsend, WA, 199?, 46 pages. FHL book 979.798 X2j. Also on microfiche, FHL fiche #6067415.

■ ***1879 Census of Jefferson County, Washington Territory: With Index,*** by the Jefferson County Genealogical Society, Port Townsend, WA, 1997, 37 pages. FHL book 979.798 X2j. Also on microfiche, FHL fiche #6067416.

■ ***1881 Census of Jefferson County, Washington County: With Index,*** by the Jefferson County Genealogical Society, Port Townsend, WA, 1997, 49 pages. FHL book 979.798 X2j. Also on microfiche, FHL fiche #6067417.

■ ***1885 Census of Jefferson County, Washington Territory: With Index,*** by the Jefferson County Genealogical Society, Port Townsend, WA, 1997. FHL book 979.798 X2j. Also on microfiche, FHL fiche #6067419.

■ ***1889 Territorial Census, Jefferson County, Washington,*** extracted and compiled by Illma Mund and Harlean Hamilton of the Jefferson County Genealogical Society, Port Townsend, WA, 1989, FHL book 979.798 X2t.

■ **1891 Census of Jefferson County, Washington Territory: With Index,** by the Jefferson County Genealogical Society, Port Townsend, WA, 75 pages. FHL book 979.798 X2j. Also on microfiche, FHL fiche #6067421.

■ **1857 and 1860 King County, Washington Territory.** See ***An Index to Early King County Pioneers: Includes Seattle,*** by M. C. Rhodes, published by the University of Washington, 1984, 76 pages. This index was compiled from the 1857 and 1860 census records. Includes photocopies of 1860 enumeration schedules for Seattle, King County. FHL book 979.777 X22r.

■ ***1879 Territorial Census for King County, Washington,*** transcribed and indexed by M.C. Rhodes. Published by the author, Seattle, WA, 1988, 110 pages. FHL book 979.777 X2r.

■ **1892 King County Census, Washington Territory,** see ***"Census, 1892, 100 Years Later,"*** an article in the *Seattle Genealogical Society Bulletin,* Vol. 41, No. 3 (Spring 1992).

■ **Kitsap County** was created as Slaughter County on January 16, 1857 from Jefferson and King counties. The name was changed to Kitsap July 13, 1857. See Online Indexes.

■ ***Kittitas County, 1885, 1887, 1889 Washington Territorial Censuses,*** abstracted and published by the Yakima Valley Genealogical Society, Yakima, WA, 1982, 295 pages. Includes surname index. FHL book 979.757 X28k. See **Yakima** County for Kittitas before 1885.

■ ***Klickitat County Territorial Census, 1871, 1883, 1885, 1887, 1889: Indexed,*** abstracted and compiled by Jack M. Lines, published by Yakima Valley Genealogical Society, Yakima, WA, 1983, 367 pages. FHL book 979.753 X2k.

■ ***1871 Lewis County, Washington Census,*** compiled by Darlene Stone and Linda Patton, published by Lewis County Genealogical Society, Chehalis, WA, 1979, 2001, 28 pages. FHL book 979.782 X2s.

■ ***1883 Lewis County, Washington Census,*** compiled by Darlene Stone and Linda Patton, published by Lewis County Genealogical Society, Chehalis, WA, 2001, 98 pages. FHL book 979.782 X2s.

■ **1889 Lincoln County.** See ***Census, Washington Territory, Lincoln County, 1889,*** transcribed and indexed by Dolores Dunn Ackerman, published by Stack Enterprises, Bellingham, WA 1987, 300 pages. FHL book 979.735 X2c. Also on microfiche, FHL fiche #6004530.

■ **1889 Mason County.** See ***Census, Mason County, Washington Territory, 1889,*** transcribed and indexed by Dolores Dunn Ackerman, published by Stack Enterprises, Bellingham, WA, 1986, FHL book 979.797 X2c. Also on microfilm, FHL film #1697959.

■ **1887 Pacific County.** See ***Census, Washington Territory, Pacific County, 1887,*** abstracted and compiled by Dolores Dunn Ackerman, published by Stack Enterprises, Bellingham, WA 1989, 60 pages. FHL book 979.792 X2c. Also on microfilm, FHL film #1425057.

■ **1892 Washington State Census, Pacific County,** name lists for various county locations, in *Sou'wester* (Pacific County Historical Society & Museum, South Bend, WA), beginning in Vol. 9, No. 2 (Summer 1974) intermittently through Vol. 16, No. 1 (Spring 1981).

■ **Pend Oreille County** was created in 1911 from Stevens County. There are no territorial or state censuses. As a substitute, see ***Directories of Stevens, Pend Oreille, and Ferry Counties, Washington,*** by R. L. Polk and Co., filmed by Primary Source Microfilm, Woodbridge, CT, ca1997, 1 roll, FHL film #2310409 (includes Pend Oreille County for 1909-1910; 1911-1912; and 1913-1914).

■ **1854 Territorial Census, Pierce County, Washington Territory,** see "Census, 1854," in *American Monthly Magazine,* Vo. 78, No. 6 (Jun 1944), a publication of the National DAR, Washington, DC. See also "Census, 1854," in *Researcher,* Vol. 1, No. 1 (Nov 1969) and Vol. 13, No. 3 (Mar 1982), a periodical of Tacoma-Pierce County Genealogical Society, Tacoma, WA.

■ **1878 and 1879 Pierce County.** See ***Pierce County, Washington Territory, Auditor's Census Extractions for 1878 and 1879,*** by the Tacoma-Pierce County Genealogical Society, Tacoma, WA, 1997, 103 pages. FHL book 979.778 X2p.

■ ***1889 Auditor's Census of Pierce County, Washington,*** by the Tacoma-Pierce County Genealogical Society, Tacoma, WA, 1987, 2 vols. Contents: vol. 1: A-L; vol. 2: M-Z. FHL book 979.778 X2a. v. 1-2.

■ **1892 Washington State Census, Pierce County, Washington,** name list published serially in *Researcher* (Tacoma-Pierce County Genealogical Society, Tacoma, WA), beginning with vol. 10, No. 2 (Nov 1978) through Vol. 13, No. 3 (Mar 1982).

■ **1887 San Juan County, Washington Territorial Census,** name list published in *Whatcom Genealogical Society Bulletin* (Bellingham, WA), Vol. 6, No. 2 (Dec 1975) and Vol. 6, No. 3 (Mar 1976).

■ **1889 San Juan County.** See ***Census, San Juan County, Washington Territory, 1889,*** compiled by Dolores Dunn Ackerman; indexed by Zelda Harlan Stout, published by Stack Enterprises, Bellingham, WA, 1986. FHL book 979.774 X2c.

■ ***1885 Census of Skagit County, Washington Territory,*** compiled and published by Whatcom Genealogical Society, Bellingham, WA, 1986, 60 pages. Includes index. See FHL book 979.772 X2s. Also on microfiche, FHL fiche #6100573. See also ***Skagit County, Washington 1885 Territorial Census,*** transcribed by Hazel Rasar, published by Skagit Valley Genealogical Society, Conway, WA, 2001, 52 pages. From title page: "The information contained herein has been transcribed from the original census books located at the Skagit County Courthouse, Mount Vernon, Washington." Names are listed in alphabetical order. FHL book 979.772 X2s.

■ **Sawamish County,** created in 1854, was renamed Mason County in 1864.

■ ***Skagit County, Washington 1887 Territorial Census,*** transcribed by Hazel Rasar and Diane Partington, published by Skagit Valley Genealogical Society, 2001, 69 pages. FHL book 979.772 X2s.

■ **1889 Skagit County.** See ***Census, Washington Territory, Skagit County, 1889,*** compiled by Dolores Dunn Ackerman, published by Stack Enterprises, Bellingham, WA, 1989, 153 pages. FHL book 979.772 X2c. Also on microfiche, FHL fiche #6002701. See also ***Skagit County, Washington, 1889: Census Taken Prior to Washington Territory Being Granted Statehood,*** compiled and published by Skagit Valley Genealogical Society, Conway, WA, 2001, FHL book 979.772 X2s.

■ ***Skagit County Washington 1892: First Washington State Census,*** transcribed by Mary Handstad, et al., published by Skagit Valley Genealogical Society, Conway, WA, 2001, 163 pages. FHL book 979.772 X2s.

■ ***Skamania County, Washington, Census records, 1860-1887,*** compiled by Daphne Hon Ramsay, published by Clark County Genealogical Society, Vancouver, WA, 1987, 101 pages. Include index. FHL book 979.784 X2r.

■ **1861 Washington Territorial Census, Snohomish County,** name list in *Washington Heritage,* Vol. 1, No. 4 (Fall 1983), a periodical of Heritage Quest, Orting, WA. See also "1861 Census, Snohomish County, and in Star, Vol. 5, No. 4 (Jan 1992), a periodical of Stillaguamish Valley Genealogical Society, Arlington, WA; and in *The Sounder,* Vol. 8, No. 4 (1994), a periodical of Sno-Isle Genealogical Society, Edmonds, WA.

■ **1862 Washington Territorial Census, Snohomish County,** name list in *The Sounder,* Vol. 5, No. 4 (1991) and Vol. 5, No. 3 (Fall 1987); and "1862 Snohomish City Census,", in Vol. 1, No. 3 (Fall 1987), a periodical of Sno-Isle Genealogical Society, Edmonds, WA.

■ **1883 Washington Territorial Census, Snohomish County,** published serially in *The Sounder,* Vol. 6, No. 1 (1992) through Vol. 7, No. 2 (1993), a periodical of Sno-Isle Genealogical Society, Edmonds, WA.

■ **1889 Snohomish County.** See ***Census, Snohomish County, Washington Territory, 1889,*** compiled by Dolores Dunn Ackerman; indexed by Zelda Harlan Stout, published by Stack Enterprises, Bellingham, WA, 1986. FHL book 979.771 X2c.

■ **1887 Census Index, Spokane County, Washington Territory,** in Eastern Washington Genealogical Society Bulletin (Spokane, WA), beginning with Vol. 38, No. 2 (Jun 2001).

■ **Stevens County** was created in 1863 from Walla Walla County. See Online Census Indexes.

■ ***1889 Census, Thurston County, Washington Territory,*** compiled and published by Olympia Genealogical Society, 1987, 57 pages. FHL book 979.779 X2c.

■ ***Wahkiakum County, Census: 1854-1892,*** compiled and indexed by Evelyn Morris Heurd for Lower Columbia Genealogical Society, Longview, WA, 1994, 227 pages. FHL book 979.791 X29h.

■ **1887 Walla Walla County.** See ***Census, Walla Walla County, Washington Territory, 1887,*** compiled by Dolores Dunn Ackerman; indexed by Zelda Harlan Stout, published by Stack Enterprises, Bellingham, WA, 1986, FHL book 979.748 X2c.

■ ***Whatcom County, Washington, 1871-1885-1887 Territorial Auditor's Census,*** compiled and published by Whatcom Genealogical Society, Bellingham, WA, ca1985, FHL book 979.773 X2w.

■ ***1889 Territorial Auditor's Census (Whatcom County, Washington Territory),*** compiled and published by Whatcom Genealogical Society, Bellingham, WA, ca1985, 126 pages. FHL book 979.773 X2wg.

■ ***Whitman County, Washington Territory, 1887 Military Census,*** compiled and published by Twin Rivers Genealogy Society, Lewiston, Idaho, 1997, 57 pages. FHL book 979.739 M2wh. Also on microfilm, FHL film #1750865.

■ ***Yakima County Territorial Census, 1871, 1883, 1885, 1887: Including Benton County (formed in 1905), Including 1871-1883 for Kittitas & Chelan counties, (Kittitas County formed in 1883, Chelan in 1899),*** abstracted and compiled by Jack M. Lines, published by Yakima Valley Genealogical Society, Yakima, WA, 1983, 199 pages. FHL book 979.755 X2y. Also on microfiche, FHL fiche #6088898.

Washington Censuses & Substitutes Online

www.heritagequestonline.com/ Heads of Household name index linked to census page images:

- 1860-1930 Federal Censuses.

www.ancestry.com Name indexes, linked to images:

- 1860-1930 Washington Federal Censuses
- 1890 Veterans Schedules
- 1860-1880 Mortality Schedules

www.familysearch.org

- 1880 Federal Census – every-name index linked to census page images (at Ancestry.com).

www.secstate.wa.gov/history/search.aspx
County indexes and/or images, territorial & state censuses:

- Adams: 1871, 1885, 1887, 1889, 1892, 1910.
- Asotin: 1885, 1887, 1889, 1910.
- Benton: 1910.
- Chelan: 1910.
- Chehalis/Grays Harbor: 1871, 1879, 1880, 1881, 1882, 1885, 1887, 1894, 1910.
- Clallam: 1857, 1860 (original county copy, federal Census), 1871, 1883, 1885, 1887, 1889.
- Clarke: 1871, 1883, 1885, 1887.
- Columbia: 1883, 1885, 1887, 1889 (partial), 1892.
- Cowlitz: 1871, 1883, 1885, 1887.
- Douglas: 1885, 1887, 1892.
- Franklin: 1885, 1887.
- Garfield: 1883, 1885, 1887, 1889, 1892, 1898.
- Island: 1860 (original county copy, federal census), 1871, 1883, 1885, 1887, 1889, 1892.
- Jefferson: 1860 (original county copy, federal census), 1871, 1874-1875, 1877, 1878,1885, 1891.
- King: 1857, 1871, 1883, 1887, 1892.
- Kitsap: 1857, 1871, 1883, 1885.
- Kittitas:1885, 1887.
- Klickitat: 1871, 1883, 1887.
- Lewis: 1847, 1851, 1857, 1871, 1883.
- Mason: 1857, 1871, 1879, 1880, 1881, 1885, 1887, 1889, 1892.
- Pacific:: 1883.
- Pierce: 1854, 1857, 1871, 1879.
- San Juan: 1887, 1889.
- Skagit: 1885, 1887, 1889.
- Skamania: 1871, 1885, 1887.
- Snohomish: 1871, 1883, 1887.
- Spokane: 1887.
- Stevens: 1871, 1878, 1885, 1887, 1889, 1892.
- Thurston: 1871, 1873, 1875, 1877, 1878. 1879, 1880, 1881,1885, 1887, 1889, 1892.
- Wahkiakum: 1857, 1871, 1885.
- Walla Walla: 1885, 1892 (Partial).
- Whatcom: 1871, 1885.
- Whitman: 1883, 1885, 1887.
- Yakima: 1871, 1883, 1885, 1887.

IDAHO

Censuses & Substitutes, 1863-1930

On March 4, 1863, President Lincoln signed into law an act creating Idaho Territory. The original area included all of present Idaho plus the parts of Montana and Wyoming west of the Continental Divide. Montana Territory was created in 1864; Wyoming Territory in 1867; reducing Idaho Territory to its present boundaries.

The first census report of Idaho Territory, dated September 1863, was produced to determine the population figures for its first election, leading to the apportionment of the first territorial legislature. Without names, the 1863 statistical census report gives only the number of voters, nonvoters, females, and children in each county and its subdivisions. However, a published ***1863 Idaho Territorial Voters Poll Lists*** exits, and can be used as a guide to the territorial census of 1863.

No subsequent censuses were taken during the territorial period, 1863-1890, and the state of Idaho has never taken a state census. Idaho population figures and apportionment from 1870 forward have been taken from the federal censuses.

Without census records other than the federal censuses, substitute name lists for Idaho need to be identified. The best place to do this is at the Website for the **Idaho State Historical Society Library & Archives.** One of the best state websites for genealogists in the country, a comprehensive list of microfilmed county records for every Idaho county has been posted.

The Genealogical Society of Utah (the microfilming arm of the Family History Library in Salt Lake City) has visited every Idaho county, filming virtually all county records of interest to family historians. In addition, the Idaho Historical Society has microfilmed records added to their collection since the FHL films were first made available. The microfilmed Idaho county records include vital records, probates, naturalizations, tax lists, deeds and deed indexes, civil court, criminal court, military lists, and more.

A review of censuses and substitutes available for Idaho follows:

■ ***Idaho Territorial Voters Poll Lists, 1863,*** transcribed, edited and indexed by Gene F. Williams, published by Williams Printing, Boise, ID, 1996, 52 pages. Includes index. Contains description of towns, voting districts, and a list by name of the voters for 1863, arranged in alphabetical order by surname. FHL book 979.6 N4w. Also on microfilm, FHL film #2055552.

■ **First Census Report, 1863,** statistics published in *Idaho Genealogical Society Quarterly,* Vol. 2, No. 1 (Mar 1959), a publication of the Idaho Genealogical Society, Boise, ID.

■ ***Territorial Vital Records: Births, Divorces, Guardianship, Marriages, Naturalization, Wills; 1800's thru 1906 Utah territory, AZ, CO, ID, NV, WY, Indian Terr.; LDS Branches, Wards; Deseret News Vital Recs.; J.P. Marriages; Meth. Marriages.*** CD-ROM publication by Genealogical CD Publishing, St. George, UT, ca1995, 1 disc, FHL CD-ROM No. 15.

■ **1865-1866, 1867-1874 Internal Revenue Assessment Lists For the Territory of Idaho,** microfilm of originals at the National Archives in Washington, DC and Central Plains regional branch, Kansas City, MO. Contains annual, monthly, and special tax lists. FHL has the following:

- Internal Revenue Assessment Lists for the Territory of Idaho, 1865-1866, FHL film #1578503. Another film copy, FHL film #1024432.
- Internal Revenue Assessment Lists for the Territory of Idaho, 1867- 1874, FHL film #1578504.

■ **1871-1881 Idaho Directories.** See ***McKenney's Pacific Coast Directory,*** or under the title, ***The Pacific Coast Directory: Giving Name, Business, and Address of business and professional men of California, Oregon, Washington, British Columbia, Alaska, Nevada, Utah, Idaho, Montana, Arizona, and New Mexico Together with Sketches of the Different Towns, Giving Location, Population, etc.,*** microfilm of original published by L.M. McKenney, San Francisco, 1871-1884. Filmed by the Genealogical Society of Utah, 1975, 1994, 5 rolls, as follows:

- 1871-1873, FHL film #1004513.
- 1878, FHL film #1004515.
- 1880-1881, FHL film #1004517.
- 1883-1884, FHL film #1697991.
- 1883-1884, FHL film #1004519.

■ **1880 Idaho Mortality Schedules,** photocopy of typescript, arranged by enumeration district. FHL book 979.6 X28m. Also on microfilm, FHL film #1321406.

■ **Idaho Death Certificates, 1911-1937; Index, 1911-1932,** microfilm of originals at the Department of Health and Welfare in Boise, Idaho (1988). Death certificates are arranged by filing order number, however, some certificates are out of order, or are missing. Some are filmed at the end of the film. Certificates are arranged somewhat chronologically. Includes index. Filmed by the Genealogical Society of Utah, 1988, 63 rolls, beginning with FHL film #1543485 (Index, Aakre, Ingeborg Saaveson – Bailan, Alex).

■ *[Idaho] Death Index For Years 1911 thru 1950.* CD-ROM publication by the Department of Health & Welfare, Bureau of Vital Records & Health Statistics, Boise, ID. Includes name of deceased, year and certificate number, city of death, date of death and birth. FHL CD-ROM No. 661.

■ **1930 Directory.** See *Idaho Gazetteer and Business Directory: And Buyers' Guide,* published by R. L. Polk & Co., Chicago, 1930. FHL book 979.E4p. Note: a more complete selection of directories can be found at the IHS website, noted below.

Online Resources at the IHS Library & Archives

The Idaho Historical Society Library and Archives has moved to a new building, named the **Idaho History Center.** To determine what records are available at the new Idaho History Center, and how to access them, the IHS Website is a starting point for genealogical research in Idaho. The IHS online program is aimed at indexing major collections and creating useful guides to finding manuscript records, rather than imaging the records online. Most of the records are still in archival manuscript form, and a researcher needs to identify and locate the records first, as in any other archives. In Idaho, a researcher has advantages not found in many other archives – good guides and indexes to the records of value to genealogists. The IHS participates in the national interlibrary loan program, and except for original archival manuscripts, all published materials and microfilm are available through interlibrary loan to another participating library/archives anywhere in the U.S.

Start your search by reviewing the **Library & Archives Collections** webpage at: **www.idahohistory.net/library_collections.html#.** From this page, you will be led to the following indexes and guides online:

■ **County Records on Microfilm,** For searching Idaho's microfilmed records, the Idaho Historical Society (IHS) has produced a source list of over 4,000 items of Idaho county records, all in one database. The list gives the IHS and/or FHL film number for every roll of film. This database was produced in *Microsoft Excel* format, which can be downloaded to a personal computer, printed, sorted, searched, etc. To access the **County Records on Microfilm Index** directly, go to: **www.idahohistory.net/IHS_County_Records.xls.**

■ **Idaho Biographical Index** (IBI). This is an index of persons named in state, county and community histories, regional periodicals, and selected newspaper articles from around the state and throughout its history. The index is downloadable into an *Excel* file containing over 33,000 entries.

■ **1870 and 1880 Agricultural, Industrial, Mortality and Other Special Census Schedules for Idaho.** This is a name list from the special schedules, downloadable as two Excel files, containing over 2,700 entries.

■ **Idaho Naturalization Records.** This is an *Excel* database which indexes names from naturalizations recorded at state and county courts in Idaho. The file contains over 3,500 entries.

■ **College/High School Yearbook Index.** The Archives & Library collection includes annuals, yearbooks, and reunion editions representing Junior and Senior High Schools, Colleges and Universities, and Private Schools, dating from the early 1900s to 1970s. This index is organized by town, name of yearbook, and years available.

■ **City, County, State, & Regional Directory Collection.** This a list of directories available for all of Idaho. Publishers vary and the publisher is not identified on this list. State directories and gazetteers, county directories, and special regional directories are shown in separate sections.

■ **Reconstructed 1890 Census for Idaho.** Using federal, state, and local government records; local newspapers, and materials published in nationally distributed genealogical publications; the IHS has attempted to identify as many persons residing in Idaho during the period, 1885-1894, as possible. ***Idaho, 1890*** is an ongoing project. At present, selected records from Ada, Alturas, Bear Lake, Boise, Cassia, Custer, Elmore, Idaho, Latah, Logan, Oneida, Owyhee, Shoshone and Washington counties have been indexed. Additional counties will be added in the near future. An alphabetical surname index for each county is contained in an *Excel* database that can be downloaded. For example, the Ada County database contains over 4,300 entries.

■ **Census Indexes Available at the IHS Archives & Library.** A list of published census indexes for all states and Canada.

■ **Idaho Cemeteries.** A list of published cemetery extracts for all Idaho counties held by the IHS Archives & Library.

■ **Guide to Adoption, Birth, Death, Divorce, and Marriage Information.** A guide to locating Idaho vital records.

■ **List of Newspaper Holdings.** This is an index to Idaho newspaper titles available at the IHS Library & Archives. The IHS is a lead agency for the United States Newspaper Program (USNP) to catalog and microfilm Idaho newspapers. To date, over 300,000 pages from 672 separate newspaper titles have been microfilmed. At this webpage, there is an alphabetical index in six parts, by city (A-B, C-G, H-K, L-M, N-R, S-Y), newspaper title, county, and dates of publication.

■ **Index to Mothers Pensions.** In 1913, the State of Idaho approved a program to provide a small monthly payment to mothers and orphans under certain circumstances. Originally maintained by each county, the records continue through the 1920s and are valuable genealogical sources.

■ **Index to Civil War Veterans of Idaho.** This is an online index in a downloadable *Excel* database with over 4,500 entries. Many veterans are listed more than once.

■ **Oral History Projects.** The Idaho Oral History Center collects the reminiscences of Idahoans who have lived through much of Idaho's history. Topics covered in the collection are as varied as frontier and pioneer life, the Civilian Conservation Corps, mining, the women's movement of the 1960s and 1970s, and various ethnic groups in the state. The oral history collection is held within the Idaho State Historical Society's Library and Archives. A list of oral history groups can be found at: **www.idahohistory.net/oralhistory_projects.html.**

Other Idaho Resources Online

■ **Western States Historical Marriage Record Index,** an online database created by the BYU-Idaho (formerly Ricks College) Arthur Porter Special Collections, in Rexburg, Idaho. Go to **http://abish.byui.edu/specialCollections/fhc/gbsearch.htm.** For nearly twenty years, this group has been extracting early marriage records from counties in the western part of the United States. Virtually all of the pre-1900 marriages are included in the index for Arizona, Idaho, Nevada, Utah. Many counties for those same states have been extracted into the 1930's and some, much later. Over 530,000 marriages from selected counties in California, western Colorado, Montana, Oregon, eastern

Washington, and Wyoming are included. In August 2006, this index was turned over to the Idaho Falls Regional Family History Center. Access to the index is still through BYU-Idaho's Special Collections & Family History website.

www.rootsweb.com/~idgenweb/
Idaho GenWeb Projects, part of the Idaho RootsWeb Links.
Quick Links:

- Idaho Web Links
- Western State Marriage Index
- Idaho Death Certificate Index
- Tombstone Project
- Digital Map Library – Idaho
- Idaho Military Records
- Mailing List – Idaho
- US GenWeb Archives – USA
- Idaho Statewide Message Board
- US GenWeb Archives – Idaho
- US GenWeb Census Project

www.heritagequestonline.com
Heads of Household name index linked to census page images:

- 1870-1930 Idaho Federal Censuses.

www.ancestry.com

- 1870-1930 Idaho Federal Censuses (AIS)
- 1890 Veterans Schedules
- 1860-1880 Mortality Schedules
- Social Security Death Index
- Obituary Collection
- Idaho Marriages, 1842-1996
- Idaho Death Index, 1911-51

www.familysearch.org

- 1880 Federal Census – every-name index linked to census page images at Ancestry.com.

MONTANA

Censuses & Substitutes, 1860-1993

As Montana Territory, 1864-1889, no territory-wide census was ever taken. Upon statehood in 1889, Montana's state constitution provided that an enumeration of the population be taken in the year 1895 and each succeeding tenth year. In 1893 the legislature established the Bureau of Agriculture, Labor, and Industry and directed the commissioner of the bureau to conduct a census. The next legislative assembly, however, failed to provide an appropriation for the work of the census and it was never carried out. Although authorized, no state censuses have been undertaken in Montana. Montana's federal censuses, 1860-1880, and statewide census substitutes are shown below:

■ ***1860 Census; Bitter Root Valley and Ponderay Mountains Area of Washington Territory, Now in the State of Montana,*** extracted & indexed by Margery H. Bell, Katherine Schaffer, Dennis Richards, no publication data noted. Includes index. The Bitterroot Valley extends through Ravalli and Missoula counties. From intro: "Includes an enumeration of the men attached to the American Boundary Commission 49 [degrees] North. These men, apparently surveying the northern boundary of the United States, could have been in Montana, Idaho, or Washington." FHL book 978.6 X2b. Also on microfiche, FHL fiche # 6049013. See also, ***Montana 1860 Territorial Census Index,*** by Accelerated Indexing Systems, Salt Lake City, UT, 1982, 6 pages. FHL book 978.6 X22m.

■ **1864-1872 Internal Revenue Assessments for the Territory of Montana,** microfilm of originals at the National Archives in Washington, DC. Includes annually, monthly and special lists of assessments for 1864-1872. Filmed by the National Archives, 1980 Series M0777, 1 roll, FHL film #1578505.

■ **1868-1869 and 1879-1880 Montana Histories and Directories.** See ***Montana (Territory) Directories,*** microfilm of originals published by various publishers, by Research Publications, Woodbridge, CT, 1980-1984, 1 roll, FHL film #1377090, including the following:

- 1868-1869 Historical Sketch and Essay on the Resources of Montana... by Herald Book and Job Printing Office,
- 1879-1880 Montana Territory History and Business Directory... by Fisk Brothers, Printers and Binders.

■ **1868-1929 Indexes to Naturalization Records of the Montana Territorial and Federal Courts,** microfilm of originals at the National Archives in Washington, DC and Central Plains Regional Branch, Kansas City, MO. Filmed by the National Archives, 1987, 1 roll, FHL film #1490886, including the following items:

- **Items 1-8:** Prefatory indexes to journals of proceedings: 1st district, 1878-1889; 2nd district, 1871-1880, 1888-1889; 3rd district, 1868-1888; 4th district, 1886-1887.
- **Items 9-10:** U.S. District Court (Helena): General index to naturalizations, 1891-1898; prefatory index to naturalizations, 1891-1893.
- **Items 11-17:** Butte U.S. District Court: General index to naturalizations, 1894-1906; prefatory indexes to declarations, 1892-1929; prefatory indexes to petitions, 1907-1927.
- **Items 18-25:** Great Falls U.S. District Court: General index to declarations, 1894-1902; general index to record of citizenship, 1894-1903; prefatory indexes to petition and record books.

■ **Early Settlers of Montana to 1929.** See ***First Families of Montana and Early Settlers,*** a project of the Montana State Genealogical Society to collect profiles of early pioneers, called the *First Families of Montana,* published by the society, 2000. The profiles were submitted by descendants. Al Stoner, project chairman. Includes lists of submitters. Contents: Part 1: To MT before 8 Nov 1889; and part 2: Early settlers of Montana 9 Nov 1889-31 Dec 1929. FHL book 978.6 D2s. Also on microfilm, FHL film #1440428.

■ **1870 Federal Census,** See ***Montana, 1870 Federal Census: Population Schedules,*** microfilm of original records at the National Archives, Washington, DC. The 1870 census was filmed twice. The second filming is listed first and is usually easier to read. However, since some of the records were faded or lost between the first and second filmings, search the first filming whenever the material on the second filming is too light to read. FHL has 2 rolls, as follows:

- **1870 Montana** (2nd filming): Beaverhead, Big Horn, Chouteau, Dawson, Deerlodge, Gallatin, Jefferson, Lewis and Clark, Madison, Meagher, and Missoula Counties, FHL film #552326.
- **1870 Montana** (1st filming): Beaverhead, Big Horn, Chouteau, Dawson, Deerlodge, Gallatin, Jefferson, Lewis and Clark, Madison, Meagher, and Missoula Counties, FHL film #14886.

■ ***Montana 1870 Territorial Census Index,*** edited by Ronald Vern Jackson, published by Accelerated Indexing Systems, 1979, 241 pages. FHL book 978.6 X22m. See also, ***Montana 1870 Census Index, A-Z,*** edited by Raeone Christensen Steuart, published by Heritage Quest, Bountiful, UT, 2000, 109 pages. FHL book 978.6 X22s.

■ ***Non–Population Census Schedules for Montana, 1870 and 1880 (M1806),*** microfilm of original records held by the Montana Historical

Society, Helena, MT. Includes non-population schedules for mortality, social statistics, products of agriculture, products of industry for 1870 and the schedules for mortality, defective, dependent, and delinquent classes, and products of industry for 1880. Arranged by schedule and then by county. Filmed by the National Archives, 1997, series M-1806, 1 roll. See FHL film #2155438.

■ **1870 and 1880 Mortality Schedules,** see ***Montana 1870 Mortality Schedule,*** edited by Ronald Vern Jackson, et al., published by Accelerated Indexing Systems, Bountiful, UT, 1981, 18 pages, FHL book 978.6 X2m; and ***Montana 1880 Mortality Schedule,*** edited by Ronald Vern Jackson, et al., published by Accelerated Indexing Systems, Bountiful, UT, 1981, 20 pages, FHL book 978.6 X2ms.

■ **1870-1957 Montana, Miscellaneous Records and Index,** microfilm of originals housed in the Treasure/Clerk Recorder, Lewis and Clark County, Helena, Montana. These miscellaneous records contain power of attorney, oaths, bonds, wills, rental of land and property, notary public assigned by the governor, mining claims, quit claims deed, loans, mortgages and etc. for the counties of Beaverhead and Lewis and Clark. Filmed by the Genealogical Society of Utah, 2002, 14 rolls, beginning with FHL film #2317890.

■ **1872-1900 Montana Stock Growers' Directory.** See ***VanDersal & Conner's Stockgrowers' Directory of Marks and Brands for the State of Montana, 1872 to 1900: Comprising an Alphabetical List of Names of all Live stock Companies and ... Also a Complete Classified Directory of Sheep and Wool Growers,*** originally published by VanDersal & Conner, Helena, MT, 1900; Reprinted by Review Printing Co., Glendive, MT, 1974,446 pages. Arranged by county and alphabetical by brand owner within the county. Includes brand index. FHL book 978.6 R2v.

■ ***Montana, 1880 Federal Census: Soundex and Population Schedules,*** microfilm of original records at the National Archives, Washington, DC. Filmed by the National Archives, 3 rolls, as follows:

- 1880 Soundex: A000 thru N666, FHL film #287767.
- 1880 Soundex: O100 thru Institutions, FHL film #287768.
- 1880 Population Schedules: Entire Territory, FHL film #1254742.

■ ***1880 Montana Territory Census Index,*** Dorothy Shammel, project chairman, Lewistown Genealogy Society, Lewistown, MT, 1987, 365 pages. From intro: "This index covers Montana Territory, which in 1880 consisted of eleven counties: Beaverhead, Chouteau, Custer, Dawson, Deer Lodge, Gallatin, Jefferson, Lewis & Clark, Madison, Meagher, and Missoula." FHL book 978.6 X2mt. See also ***Montana 1880 Census Index,*** edited by Ronald Vern Jackson, et al., published by Accelerated Indexing Systems, North Salt Lake, UT, 1984, FHL book 978.6 X2M. Copy 1: Contents: vol. 1. A-Lablano; vol. 2. Krunley-Z. Copy 2: vols. 1 & 2 bound together.

■ ***Montana 1880 Mortality Schedule,*** edited by Ronald Vern Jackson, et al., published by Accelerated Indexing Systems, Bountiful, UT, 1981, 20 pages. FHL book 978.6 X2ms.

■ **Election Registers, 1882-1915, Lewis and Clark County, Meadow Creek, Madison County, Chouteau County, and Richland County, Montana,** microfilm of originals located at the Montana Historical Society, Helena, MT. Filmed by the Genealogical Society of Utah, 2002, 1 roll, FHL film #2318557.

■ **1881-1928 Federal Land Records.** See ***General Land Office of the United States, Montana Territory, 1881-1928,*** microfilm of original records in State Treasurer, Clerk, Recorder Office in Helena Montana. These records include land

and mining records intermixed in Montana Territory. Filmed by the Genealogical Society of Utah, 2002, 4 rolls, beginning with FHL film #2317967 (Land Registrations Records, vol. 1, 1881-1901).

■ **1891-1929 Naturalization Records, U.S. District Courts of Montana,** see ***Declaration of Intent, 1891-1929; Petition for Naturalization, 1891- 1929; Citizenship Records, 1894-1906; Certificates, 1907-1927,*** microfilm of originals at the National Archives Branch, Seattle, WA. Includes general index with some volumes individually indexed. Filmed by the Genealogical Society of Utah, 1988, 3 rolls, as follows:

- District Court, Butte: Index to Declaration of intent, vol. 85, 1894-1902; Declaration of intent, vol. 86, 1894-1902; Petitions for naturalization, vol. 1-2, 1910-1923, FHL film #1492066.
- District Court, Butte: Petitions for naturalization, vol. 3-5, 1923-1929, FHL film #1492067.
- District Court, Butte: Index to citizenship, 1894-1903. District Court, Great Falls: Declaration of intent, 1924; Petitions for naturalization, 1926. District Court, Helena: Index to citizenship, 1894-1906; Citizenship records, 1894-1906; Index to naturalization, 1891-1906; Declaration of intent, 1891-1893; Records of citizenship, 1891-1898; Declaration of intent, 1896-1917. Certificate stubs, no. 21871-1541970, 1907-1927; Declaration of intent, 1917-1929, FHL film #1492068.

■ **1894 History.** See ***An Illustrated History of the State of Montana,*** by Joaquin Miller, original published by Lewis Publishing Co., 1894. Includes index. Reprint by Higginson Book Co., Salem, MA, 2000. FHL book 978.6 H2mj.

■ **1913 History.** See ***A History of Montana,*** by Helen Fitzgerald Sanders, published by Lewis Publishing Co., Chicago, IL, 1913, 3 vols. Includes index. FHL Library has volumes 2 and 3 in book form only. FHL book 978.6 D3s v.1-2. Also on microfilm (3 vols.) FHL film #1000174.

■ **1917-1918 Selective Service System Draft Registration Cards, Montana,** microfilm of original records at the Regional National Archives, East Point, Georgia. The draft cards are arranged alphabetically by state, then alphabetically by county or city, and then alphabetically by surname of registrants. Cards are in rough alphabetical order. Filmed by the National Archives, 1987, 37 rolls, beginning with FHL film #1684099. (Beaverhead County, A–Z; Big Horn County, A–Z; Blaine County, A–D).

■ **1921 History.** See ***Montana, its Story and Biography: A History of Aboriginal and Territorial Montana and Three Decades of Statehood,*** edited by Tom Stout, published by American Historical Society, Chicago, IL, 1921, 3 vols. (Biographies in Vol. 2 & 3). FHL book 978.6 H2s. Indexed in ***Every-Name Index to Stout's Montana: Its Story and Biography,*** by Hamilton Computer Service, Park City, UT, ca1985, 433 pages. Index includes names, birthdates, and birthplaces. FHL book 978.6 H2s index. Also on microfilm, FHL film #1320700.

■ **1930-1975 Newspaper Index.** See ***Date and Source Information For the Biography Files in the Montana Room at the Parmly Billings Library,*** compiled by the Yellowstone Genealogical Forum; editor Patricia K. Miller, microfilm of original card index (ca. 10,000 cards). Collection of cards indexing individuals who appeared in issues of several Montana newspapers between 1930 and 1975. Filmed by the Genealogical Society of Utah, 1994, 1 roll, FHL film #1307685.

■ **Cemetery Records of Montana,** copied by members of the LDS Church; typed by the Genealogical Society, Salt Lake City, Utah. Typescript. Contents: vol. 1. (1947) Granite County: Drummond, Valley Cemetery; Lake County: Arlee, Ronan, St. Ignatius; Missoula County: Missoula; Sanders County: Dixon -- vol. 2. (1959) Deer Lodge County: Anaconda, Lower Hill and New Hill Cemeteries, Warm Springs; Gallatin County: Willow Creek, Williams Family

Cemetery; Silver Bow County: Butte, Mount Moriah and Mountain View Cemeteries, Sunset Memorial Gardens; vol. 3. (1961) Gallatin County: Willow Creek; Silver Bow County: Butte, Mount Moriah and Mountain View Cemeteries. FHL book 978.6 V3c v. 1-3. Also on microfilm, FHL film #873694; and microfiche, FHL fiche #6051445. See also Montana Cemetery Records, prepared by the Lewistown Genealogy Society, Lewistown, MT, 1982. The index that precedes the cemetery records lists the cemeteries within each county of central Montana. The entries within each cemetery are alphabetically arranged. Filmed by the Genealogical Society of Utah, 1982, 1 roll, FHL film #1035938.

Montana County-wide Census Substitutes

Name lists for Montana that can act as census substitutes can be found at the county level, by using deed indexes, vital records, voter registrations, tax lists, or directories. Since the Family History Library has county records on microfilm for all Montana counties, a researcher should visit **www.familysearch.org** and do a search for these census substitutes. At the FHL opening page, click on Library / Family History Library Catalog / Place Search / "Montana" / (to get a list of topics) / View Related Places / (to see a list of Montana counties. Select any county to view a topic list specific to that county. (There may be "View Related Places" below the county level, where there are topics by town, cities, or districts within a particular county).

As an example, here are some of the records available for Beaverhead County:

■ **1906-1917 Dillon (Montana) City and Beaverhead County Directories,** microfilm of original records located in various libraries and societies. Records by various publishers, microfilm by Research Publications, Woodbridge, CT, ca1995, 1 roll, FHL film #2309340 (1906, 1907-1908, 1909-1910, 1912-1913, 1916-1917 Dillon City and Beaverhead County Directories).

■ **1909-1910 Directory.** See ***Dillon City and Beaverhead County Directory: Embracing a Complete Alphabetical List of Business Firms and Private Citizens,*** microfilm of original published by R. L. Polk, Helena, MT, 1909-1910, 235 pages. Filmed by the Genealogical Society of Utah, 1967, 1 roll, FHL film #528764.

■ **1870-1957 Montana Territory, Miscellaneous Records and Index,** microfilm of original records at the Treasurer/Clerk/Recorder Office, Lewis and Clark County, Helena, MT. These miscellaneous records contain power of attorney, oaths, bonds, wills, rental of land and property, notary public assigned by the governor, mining claims, quit claims deed, loans, mortgages and etc. for the counties of Beaverhead and Lewis and Clark. Filmed by the Genealogical Society of Utah, 2002, 14 rolls, beginning with FHL film #2317890 (Index to Miscellaneous Records, Vol. 1 (direct), 1870-1948).

■ ***Index of Obituaries from Dillon Tribune, April 1881 - December 2000; Dillon, Montana,*** compiled by Beaver Head Hunters, published by Beaver Head Hunters Genealogical Society, Dillon, MT, 2001, 92 pages. FHL book 978.669/D1 V42b. Also on microfiche, FHL fiche #6005381.

■ **Marriage records, 1856-1952; Index, 1856-1993,** microfilm of original records at the Beaverhead County Courthouse in Dillon, Montana. Filmed by the Genealogical Society of Utah, 1993, 6 rolls, beginning with FHL film #1905608 (Index to marriages 1876-1910 Index to marriages (men) 1887-1946 Index to marriages (women) 1887-1946).